The Startup Players Handbook

A Roadmap to Building SaaS and Software Companies

Charles Edge
Chip Pearson
Amy Larson Pearson

The Startup Players Handbook: A Roadmap to Building SaaS and Software Companies

Charles Edge
Minneapolis, MN, USA

Chip Pearson
St. Paul, MN, USA

Amy Larson Pearson
St. Paul, MN, USA

ISBN-13 (pbk): 978-1-4842-9317-1
https://doi.org/10.1007/978-1-4842-9315-7

ISBN-13 (electronic): 978-1-4842-9315-7

Managing Director, Apress Media LLC: Welmoed Spahr
Acquisitions Editor: Susan McDermott
Development Editor: James Markham
Coordinating Editor: Jessica Vakili

Distributed to the book trade worldwide by Springer Science+Business Media New York, 233 Spring Street, 6th Floor, New York, NY 10013. Phone 1-800-SPRINGER, fax (201) 348-4505, e-mail orders-ny@springer-sbm.com, or visit www.springeronline.com. Apress Media, LLC is a California LLC and the sole member (owner) is Springer Science + Business Media Finance Inc (SSBM Finance Inc). SSBM Finance Inc is a **Delaware** corporation.

For information on translations, please e-mail booktranslations@springernature.com; for reprint, paperback, or audio rights, please e-mail bookpermissions@springernature.com.

Apress titles may be purchased in bulk for academic, corporate, or promotional use. eBook versions and licenses are also available for most titles. For more information, reference our Print and eBook Bulk Sales web page at http://www.apress.com/bulk-sales.

Any source code or other supplementary material referenced by the author in this book is available to readers on the Github repository: https://github.com/Apress/The-Startup-Players-Handbook. For more detailed information, please visit http://www.apress.com/source-code.

Printed on acid-free paper

Table of Contents

About the Authors

Charles Edge is the CTO of bootstrappers.mn, the Founder of Secret Chest, and a former director at Jamf. He has 35 years of experience as a developer, administrator, network architect, product manager, entrepreneur, and CTO. He is the author of 20+ books on technology, business, and history, and more than 6,000 blog posts on technology. Charles also serves on the board of directors for a number of companies and nonprofits and frequently speaks at conferences including DefCon, Black Hat, LinuxWorld, the Apple Worldwide Developers Conference, and a number of Apple-focused conferences. Charles is also the author of krypted.com and a cofounder/host of the Mac Admins Podcast and the History of Computing podcast.

Chip Pearson began his entrepreneurial journey as the front man of the hardcore band Blind Approach. He later founded and sold an IT services company. He then became a cofounder and is a former CEO of Jamf Software. Chip and former partner Zach Halmstad grew Jamf to hundreds of employees from 2006 until Vista Software acquired the company in 2017. Jamf is now listed on Nasdaq (JAMF) and boasts half a billion in revenue. Chip now invests in early-stage companies through Bootstrappers.mn and sits on the board of several, where he has helped usher them to growth and, when appropriate, acquisitions.

Amy Larson Pearson attended Carleton College before embarking on a career helping companies in their go-to-market activities. She led a educational sales efforts at Jamf Software during some of the most formative years of the company. She is now the chief executioner at Bootstrappers.mn where she oversees many of the investments the organization makes and sits on the board of a number of companies and nonprofits. When Amy isn't doing the countless other things she is in charge of, she is the bass player for the classic garage rock band Beebe Gallini.

CHAPTER 1

The Mission

The gamemaster of life has prepared a new campaign, one that is as arduous a journey as any previously attempted. The party is woefully underpowered to make it through the gauntlet of encounters, each as much a riddle as it is melee—and each with real consequences.

During and after each encounter, we prepare for the next, without knowing what it will be. We conserve resources, and with each level we achieve, we realize there are more to go. At some point, we decide how the campaign will end—at least for us personally.

The adventure begins when we get this idea to evolve something. Evolution is innovation. The idea could take five minutes or a lifetime to form in our minds. But once formed, we simply cannot let it go. So we form an organization in support of the idea, create a product, and take it to market.

The product we create gets a little success. We use our network of friends and colleagues, and word spreads through word of mouth and our own self-promotion, maybe even experimenting with a few cheap ads here and there. We get a few customers. We think creating a company means freedom. But the idea is now a job, and we have less freedom than before.

We realize we can't do the job alone. We've bootstrapped thus far but need help. This is a turning point: do we go it alone, sell our fledgling company, risk our own financial freedom to hire cheaply, or take on outside angel funding and dilute equity and so sacrifice even more of our freedom?

C. Edge et al., *The Startup Players Handbook*,
https://doi.org/10.1007/978-1-4842-9315-7_1

As we grow, we realize scale is hard. When more people use our product, they reveal defects that were maybe always there or escaped due to how scale impacts quality. Our product gets more complex and less fun to work on as we add more features. The influx of customers inevitably brings an increase of customer feedback, some of which is not very personable or understanding. Bigger customers mean lower per-unit pricing due to volume, which drives down our ability to fix defects only bigger customers have or pulls precious development cycles from smaller customers. Our job can be a grind sometimes.

There are things that take us away from the deep industry knowledge that let us come up with the product in the first place. We bring on a sales team, build a marketing discipline, nurture content, train people to support our product, and so much more that customers see. And behind the scenes, we need to scale operations: accounting, legal, finance, sales, and technology. Scale isn't cheap; we have another decision to make.

The company has a lot of people who depend on the founders. One wrong move and a lot of families get hurt. Payroll is always a thing. Insurance, human resources, and taxes weren't what we set out to do with our lives. We keep a few months of cash around and grow smartly; the larger we get, the more cash we need to de-risk growth. But it's hard to grow fast enough to meet demand, keep demand increasing, and deal with cash flow. Do we give up even more control with a Series B like the angel investors are telling us to do, so we can scale better? That means diluting equity again, and more people seems to mean more problems. Or do we slow the growth? Or do we take one of the offers from those private equity firms that keep calling?

We introduce more products. We buy a couple of smaller companies—acqui-hires, really. Investors want us to keep the growth up, but to do so, we'll need to take on more funding. We know less and less about the people we serve, so we bring on product managers. We know less about the product itself, so we bring on engineers to make it better. Both are more diluted than we ever were, and it takes many people to do what we used to by ourselves. And they all scoff at our previous work.

The board of directors wants to put together a plan to take the company public. They didn't say the founder is the wrong person to lead the company any longer, but they did recommend we take a second look at a few people who would be great at it. And looking at the list of people, they aren't wrong! They've actually taken companies public before! But what does a founder do next? Maybe we should take the offer to buy us out from one of those adjacent companies. Or maybe we should... be on to the next adventure! Start a new campaign. Or help others with their campaigns! Or take a little time off and reconnect with loved ones who have, let's face it, forgotten what we look like!

This is the real world and not a game. However, the playbook for a startup is predictable enough that it can be laid out before us. And the game can go any way we want. We can step outside the defined parameters of a module, but we should understand where we're being led and know the risks of each potential path. The greatest campaign ever is the startup; choose your adventure wisely.

The Campaign

A campaign in most tabletop gaming platforms is a collection of games that follow a common storyline, usually with the same characters. Think of the lifecycle of a company founded to support a given innovation as a campaign.

The campaign that inspired many a game like *Dungeons and Dragons* is J. R. R. Tolkien's *The Lord of the Rings* series. In the trilogy, we follow a few characters, each inspiring different classes of characters in *Dungeons and Dragons*—and in so many modern computer games. None are as archetypal as Strider, the ranger. We begin the campaign with the ranger, exploring the wild lands, much as a founder (or founding team) explores different industries. Over time, though, Strider faces a choice: to set aside the wandering ways and take the rightful place as ruler of the lands (or, to extend the analogy, to turn into a paladin and put charisma over perception to become the chief executive) or to move on to the next adventure.

But Strider (a.k.a. Aragorn) doesn't do it all alone. Nor can any founder who sets out to change the world by bringing an innovation to the masses. A brave adventuring party is formed. Just as our companies grow, the party then consists of many a utility player, each with their own set of skills they bring to the table. As they explore the path to save the world, they encounter others with specialized skillsets. These are the basis of character classes in most modern role-playing games. Let's look at the analogous relationships with those we'll need in our startups:

- *Ranger*: The ranger has traits from a few different classes. They have limited spell casting abilities, fighting abilities, and some roguish characteristics. As mentioned, most founders wear many hats and spend a lot of time perceiving our industries and so begin the campaign as a ranger. As we grow, rangers become product teams or corporate development. The organizations that replace the individual continue to explore the wilds, looking for new opportunities to build new products and help more people.

- *Fighter*: Fighters are grinders. The most common types of grinders in a startup campaign are those who build the product (in a software company, these are software developers who likely do not think of themselves as fighters, but alas, they aren't writing the rule book) and those who sell the product (sales teams). The fighters often become the "tanks" of a party and rush into melee to fix products or sell products to customers. They are often the core of a party—yet need support from many others for successful outcomes.

- *Cleric*: The cleric is the healer. They keep the party healthy, bless their efforts, and protect them. Think of this as human resources and dedicated management positions that emerge in organizations. As we explore later, management and leadership are quite different— thus the paladin.

- *Paladin*: The paladin is often the leader of the party. These knightly characters have big armor, give inspiring speeches, and sometimes heal others. They are there to lead and inspire the party. The paladin is more devoted to the big picture than most in the party, which leads to something like a mission and values statement—which we'll cover in later sections.

- *Druid*: The druid speaks with animals and communes with nature. They are mystical and support those communities as much as they draw power from them. We all live in a community. Those who support the product, especially early in the life of an organization, are building a community, and even more, they become the primary window with which the community around us perceives the organization. They craft the full customer experience and so can be seen as our support teams.

- *Mage*: Nontechnical people often think of software developers as wizards. But in truth, anyone who reaches a high level of performance in their specialty is a wizard. The real magic in a company comes with operational excellence—which means the mages are the operations team. These are the people charged with efficiency, logistics (getting everyone where they're supposed to be when they're supposed to be there), and tranquility (keeping the organization humming along).

5

- *Monk*: We might initially outsource accounting, but as we bring it internally, we need people we can trust–and people who will always do what is right. In *Dungeons and Dragons*, the monk is the moral compass for many parties. But they're tricky. They're also a martial expert and will kick the crap out of anyone that doesn't pay their bills or turn their expense report in on time.

- *Bard*: We need people who can sing our praises and in doing so bring people to our way of thinking and into our circle. Marketers and evangelists are even more important in freemium types of SaaS offerings where an early sales team isn't in the plan.

- *Rogue*: Rogues nimbly find and remove the traps in dungeons. They can be played as thieves, but there isn't much room for those in a company. Looking forward to creating an End User License Agreement (EULA) that protects the party and developing contracts to find those traps is really where legal and then corporate compliance teams shine.

- *Illusionist*: As the party grows, we take on new specialties. Public relations (PR) is a discipline that often comes as an addition in larger adventuring parties and helps present the organization to the outside world in several ways. The most common is through interfacing with the media to project the adventuring party in a way that aligns with the mission and values. But the illusionist can also help protect the company when things go awry by casting a distraction or repositioning the way foes perceive the party.

The combinations of these classes are so much more valuable than each alone. So it is with organizations. A campaign with just bards would be no fun and likely wouldn't get far.

Each character gains experience as we go through encounters and games. With experience come new abilities. Most games use a leveling game mechanic to track these in a quantifiable fashion. As organizations grow, we institute leveling mechanics as well. It begins with an acknowledgment that someone did more, maybe going from engineer to architect. Sometimes, as the organization matures, we level within titles, such as software developer I and software developer II. As we mature to each stage as individuals, the party is capable of more and more feats of heroism.

This doesn't tell the whole story. The founder, like that lone ranger in the beginning of *The Lord of the Rings*, is out there doing what they do—they explore and learn the lore of the lands. As each class, or discipline, goes from being a part of a founder's job to the job of a whole department, the discipline has a level of its own. The individuals grow, but so too grows the maturity of the disciplines and number of individuals involved in each. In fact, there are plenty of coaches or consulting firms dedicated to helping level up each department, or discipline.

We can go a step further than most games do with leveling. Since the birth of venture capital with Georges Doriot following World War II, assembly lines of companies have emerged. We begin with an idea, bootstrap a product or prototype, get financial assistance to go to market from banks or angel investors, and move into a Series A of funding, then Series B, and then Series C through F. The campaign ends (and maybe a new one begins) as we get to an initial public offering (IPO), acquisition, or bankruptcy–almost as though the organization itself began at level 1 when we incorporated and ended at level 10 at the IPO.

As we get into each discipline, we will go through and identify common levels, or stages, that disciplines go through. We aren't prescriptive around company size or revenue amounts per level because every organization can grow differently. Think of this as leveling up with milestones.

For example, we once needed more than one person to do accounts receivable, calling customers to get payment for renewals, etc. These days that can be put on autopilot with a payment processing service like Stripe for some businesses but not for all. We also used to have to look up tax information so we could pay each state what they were due. That can now be done by automated tax compliance software like Avalara. We also used to... Get the picture?

Each business and the systems they use scale differently. Further, consumer-focused organizations lean heavier on marketing, and those who sell into enterprises typically lean more into direct sales (although both are required at most organizations once they reach a certain size). Some use distributors or have other routes to market. Therefore, we try to leave leveling as more a general mechanic, like milestone-based leveling up in *Dungeons and Dragons.*

We also equip our characters. Each typically has a weapon and armor or a robe and a wand, just as the company supplies computers and desks. As we level up, we also find new objects we can wield in different ways, much as we pay for software to automate various aspects of our jobs to make us more productive. Where appropriate, we'll mention some vendors who make magical items we can equip for various aspects of our company so we don't get overly dependent on having people perform tasks better suited for microservices (or even very small shell scripts).

Our paths are not certain. The gamemaster of life may have plans, but we can go our own way. We are operating in an open world game, not a railroad. However, before veering off the path set out for us, we should understand the traditions and norms and what others do and why. This allows us to be intentional about our activities and keep our eyes out for keen adventurers we'd like to conquer a dungeon or three with. Otherwise, we end up hiring or architecting reactively, and when that happens, who knows where the games will lead us!

What Kind of a Startup?

Our campaign is going to be a startup. Most startups are created in support of an innovation. The innovation helps people. Sometimes these are tools to support engineers or engineering teams. Other times, we're looking to help a company get more telemetry into the devices in the field or learn about where products are in a supply chain. Still other times, we're helping people connect to one another or buy or sell or find or even find peace.

In the software industry, these innovations usually fall into one of a few buckets, and this is important, as we'll call back to this list throughout the book:

- *Productivity*: The first few decades of the computing industry were all about improving productivity of first mathematicians, then scientists, and then other knowledge workers. Along came robotics, and new industries were created as computing became ubiquitous, and productivity gains took on all sorts of new shapes. It's important to consider the innovation a new company might support in this lens, because many a tool is focused on productivity. The best example of this might be how accounting was done before the 1970s: armies of human computers updated paper spreadsheets, using physical calculators to calculate each row as the column dictated. Then Dan Bricklin and Bob Frankston wrote VisiCalc, which was the first spreadsheet. Suddenly, a single person could get done what it previously took multiple people to accomplish.

- *Telemetry*: Once we moved a lot of processes and records into computers, we gained more and more insight into what data about each process or the metadata about people and processes meant. This is huge, because it

comes with connotations for so much more than just
productivity tools. Once computing became ubiquitous,
we saw more than how many widgets were delivered
to Pretendco and on what date and for what price.
Suddenly, we see the temperature in our homes, whether
there's a leak in the basement, how many people are at
our favorite mall, the price for a hotel if we get stuck at
the airport, or how active we were in a day and so how
many calories we need to consume. And these days,
we can go a step further (pun intended) and have that
information analyzed by various machine learning
algorithms to tell us the answer to almost any question
we can think to ask (many of the answers are still just the
number 42, but we get better and better every year).

- *Quality of life*: There are a lot of things we do on
  computers that have absolutely nothing to do with
  productivity. In fact, games are quite the opposite
  in most cases (for those still trying to convince
  themselves otherwise, embrace the game and stop
  kidding yourself). Quality of life goes beyond seeing
  the temperature in the home. We want to tell a smart
  speaker to make it more comfortable. Or we want
  instant access to every photo we've taken or every song
  ever recorded in the history of humankind.

Most innovations a campaign centers around will fit into one of these
categories. The mission of our organization is then to foster an innovation
around one or more of these. The mission is to bring the technology to the people
and so improve productivity or improve the telemetry to a given piece of data
not previously available or improve the quality of someone's life. Hopefully we're
able to do all three, because that's a mission for which we can easily recruit
others to join us. But enough of one of these is valuable in its own right.

Then the mission statement becomes simple. Okay, so not quite simple...

Define the Mission

A big idea just isn't enough. We have to build a party to go adventuring with us. That party is a company who needs a mission; otherwise, we just go meandering through the wilderness, unsure of what to do. To rally everyone around a common purpose, we need to distill our passion down into a simple-to-read statement about what we do, who we are, and why we do it. "The party must defeat Vecna or the known world will be destroyed" is a worthy and easy to understand mission. Writing a lot of text is easy. We have 400–500 pages to go through the grand campaign that is the life of a startup in this book. Writing a single, impactful sentence is hard.

Mission statements should be between one and three sentences. Nearly every startup ever founded should have a one-sentence mission statement. If it's two sentences, then we've likely overcomplicated what we're doing. We boiled our passion down into one powerful sentence long before Twitter began. We use it to be aspirational but honest about what this new organization is here to do. Remember: productivity, telemetry, and quality of life. We are improving one or more of those for humans. Once we have the what, the why is often self-explanatory.

We don't want to be overly aspirational or visionary—as that's what a vision statement is for (we'll get to that later). We want to ask a few questions and think about which are at the top of our priority list:

- Who are our customers?

- What do our customers value?

- What kind of image do we want the company to have?

- What problem is the company in business to solve? Do we have a purpose beyond that?

- Why do we want people to want to work here?
- What are the company goals?
- How do the products we make support those goals?
- How are we different from competitors?

Now that we've answered those, make a list and prioritize the items in the list. Try to connect them with a philosophical theme (think of that warrior monk in the party when doing so). What is under the hood of everything else? Take a Plato-esque stroll through an olive garden (not the restaurant) and consider the question: if most businesses fail, why start one? Pro-tip: It's about more than just the money. It's about the mission, and to recruit others to the cause, we need a good mission.

Write the Mission Statement

Once we understand and can articulate a little more about what we're here to do, let's try to put that mission into a single sentence called the mission statement. Before we try to write our own, let's look at a few from existing companies. For example, the mission statement should be inspiring. Take Tesla's:

"To accelerate the world's transition to sustainable energy."

It's succinct, and if we look at their website, ever since they integrated the panels from Solar City into the main Tesla site, we can see that it's about more than cars. If they weren't an Elon Musk company, that mission statement might seem overly inspirational. Take TED, the makers of TED Talks:

"Spread ideas."

Now, here's where ambition creeps into the picture with these mission statements. Once a brand name is a household name, we can have lofty statements like that. A startup is likely to more closely resemble the mission statement from LinkedIn, who was once a startup and still often acts like a startup (in a good way):

"To connect the world's professionals to make them more productive and successful."

Other than using the word "to" twice, we like this because the statement says they make professionals more productive and successful, and they do it by connecting people from around the world. Let's also look at Workday, a lesser-known brand but one almost universally known to people that have worked in large or growing enterprises (or our clerics in human resources):

"To put people at the center of enterprise software."

The makers of Workday were the CEO and former chief strategist of PeopleSoft. They created the company after Oracle did a hostile takeover in 2005. By 2012, they did an IPO for close to ten billion dollars. They are probably one of the simplest HR tools to use, and most workers would only see a fraction of what it can do. This is because they put the people first—which roughly translates to great UX and, when faced with a decision of code complexity vs. ease-of-use complexity, making the choice that helps people. Here, not only is the mission statement a flag in the ground that Workday is an enterprise software company—but it's an instruction to employees to put the user of a tool at the center of the decision making. It's part of the culture.

For our last example, we'll look at Patagonia because they pack a lot into a simple sentence:

"Build the best product, cause no unnecessary harm, use business to inspire and implement solutions to the environmental crisis."

If we pretend not to care about the lack of an Oxford comma in the Patagonia example, we can see that the organization puts product first, but only when not doing harm. And here we can use our imaginations: to the environment, to humans through predatory business, etc. And to go further and actually try to implement environmental solutions—which makes a reader think that maybe some of the Patagonia profits go to such ends. And indeed, 1% of Patagonia profits go to such endeavors.

The preceding examples are brands we all know and love. Let's go back to what our organization does, the innovation we will support. We make a thing, and we want to say why. If we're new, we need to keep it to a sentence. If we have space in the sentence, we can go further and say how (or inspirationally what) we might do if we're successful, like Patagonia did. But don't lose sight of which category our innovation falls into: we increase productivity, provide telemetry, increase quality of life, or do a combination of these.

Now let's just write the sentence. Or put it off until the chapter is over. First, it might help to think deeper about the big idea, which we'll cover in the next section.

The Big Idea

It happens differently for everyone. Maybe we're sitting in a peaceful orchard of olive trees, the way Thales and other seven sages of Greece came up with such strange concepts as democracy and geometry. Or maybe we're working a crappy job and realize that we can replicate the repetitive tasks we do and save companies millions of dollars. Or maybe we read something in a science fiction book and realized no one had bothered to build it yet.

Whatever the path led us to the idea, we likely need to build an organization to support the innovation that the big idea represents. An adventuring party is simple (we're there to beat the opponent). But in computing and companies, most of our big ideas are about increasing productivity. This goes all the way back to when the mainframes increased productivity for scientists and cryptographers, which helped in war (and then Cold War) efforts. But productivity increases impact real human lives by displacing jobs.

No industry is immune to the impacts of a displaced workforce due to automation. Whether it's various SaaS tools that help automate various tasks so each person can be more productive or whether it's having whole jobs get replaced by small scripts, we all have to be ready. This might be legal professionals who use software to look information up online rather than in books, people on construction sites who look at cameras rather than driving out to building locations, or even people in software companies who have chatbots replace support positions.

Someone has to write those tools. While there are people out there that just focus on code, that's its own skillset. Those developers need people with deep experience to get code written that actually helps real people so they don't just build random tools (left to our own devices, developers will often just focus on constantly paying down technical debt and not think much about new features). Most off-the-shelf software in an app store kind of world took 10–20 years of knowledge and a little automation to be useful–and then made it so that smaller companies with less mature practices in a given field could compete with larger, better-funded, and more mature teams.

We should each look to how we can get in front of designing the software to help people do more, get more telemetry, or improve the quality of life of our users. That's the best ways to keep from getting left behind and replaced with software. That requires a little understanding of how software works—but more importantly, to move into those product design roles, we need to think more deeply about what we do and why. In other words, we need to become rangers.

Other big ideas have to do with quality of life or telemetry. Many are the result of a combination of two technologies or changing regulatory environments. Whatever the idea, the company we found is likely there to support the innovation, which represents an evolution in our field or personal lives. And support of that big idea should easily be summed up into a mission statement, which we'll get to later in this chapter.

The Bad Idea

We're told early in life that no idea is a bad idea. Oh, wait. That's "no bad questions," not ideas. There's no gamemaster to tell us we're on the wrong path. So how do we know when our big idea is not a great idea as a company? Long term, if it loses money, then it might have been a bad idea. Or the execution was bad, but the idea was good? That happens too.

We all have those friends who are great at casting doubt on everything. Think of Eeyore. These types of friends have great uses, and this is one. While many stopped listening to their parents a long time ago, it's never too late to start listening to them again. See what Mom and Dad say as well. After all, if we have a good or service to offer to the market, we have the first parts of a business plan. And our parents likely have more business experience than us. And if they don't, they're wiser. Not to harp on this, but seriously, find a parent (or parental figure) to review a business plan.

Even if we've been in business for a few years, we need close business advisors. They are a key factor to the success of any institution (if a company lasts, it becomes an institution, maybe?). Beyond parents, it's time to look for other wise sages - mentors (more on these in Chapter 5), academics, and a board of directors once we've crossed a dozen employees (assuming we still plan on growing).

The board of directors comes with contacts. Contacts are the most important thing that you fledgling company can have in the beginning. It also comes with guidance that's worth more than an hourly rate. So pick others who have found success in parallel or adjacent industries without picking people who are going to compete. A board of directors can help navigate how to commercialize our offerings.

If we need advice, we can also pay a business consultant for services. They're more likely to sign a non-disclosure agreement (NDA) to help protect our intellectual property. The larger the endeavor, the more of these (and anyone else that will listen) we need to consult with. Finally,

another great aspect of investors is that if there isn't anyone willing to invest, we really need to think hard about whether the initiative is worth pursuing.

Commercialization Options for Intellectual Property

We've all had moments of inspiration. Sometimes those are about an evolution in technology not previously considered. Other times our evolution involves what we think is the next step in the journey of a horizontal or vertical application of technology along the path of technological determinism.

We want to see our idea taken to market and used to improve lives. We want to help as many people as we can to increase their productivity, providing deeper telemetry into anything we can, and we want to improve the quality of lives. That idea in our head spills out in the form of progress in our field, and there are countless tactical ways to implement the strategy. Some provide personal gain. Others benefit our organization. Others can lift an entire industry. And still others can change the world.

Only history is the arbiter of how successful the idea and implementation are. Some evolutions are deterministic and basically no-brainers. They were going to happen, whether it was us or someone else. Others are new ideas that only a deep understanding of an industry can bring. Some ideas can be implemented in a vacuum; others need broader support.

The modern options for commercializing our ideas began to crystalize in the post–World War II technology boom led by the military-university-industrial complex throughout Western powers. Here, we saw universities like MIT develop various aspects of computing, like core memory, modern CPU architectures, and, well, general-purpose computers. But that was part of the war effort when every scientist was doing their part. After the war, each university brought in law firms to try to figure out where they should get royalties. Driven by royalties or not, that intellectual property led to massive gains in productivity.

Today, there are more options to license, distribute, and/or commercialize our works than we can list (but we will list the primary ones). Philosophically, some believe all software should be free. Others choose to patent everything they create. Others choose to build coalitions between market leaders. We need each iteration between these as a society, as they fuel one another. Let's look at the main options and when each might be appropriate.

Open Source

Pivotal artificer George Graham perfected the concept of a cylinder escapement in clockworks to bring about the modern watch in the 1720s. In doing so, he changed navigation and timekeeping forever. If he had patented his (and Thomas Tompion's) escapement, the history of timekeeping might be completely different, and the dominoes that dropped and led to mechanical computing might never have fallen. Today, many developers post code to social coding sites like GitHub in much the same way, using a variety of licenses. Sometimes these are small scripts that might save others a couple of hours. Other times they're entire projects for complicated apps and services.

Not everyone is going to post something that changes the world, like Graham's designs did—but some projects have made technologies such as machine learning much more approachable. One thing certain is that the aggregate of open source software has certainly changed the world by hastening development of software in nearly every imaginable case.

The choice to open source, or effectively give work product away for free, is a choice. Doing so doesn't mean we aren't commercializing intellectual property in some way. Many earn higher salaries, earn money from those who license code, or maybe get stock grants, like Linus Torvalds did when companies commercializing his Linux went public (arguably this is extremely rare). Still, none of these are certain, and most open source solutions come from those who love what they do and feel passionate about it. Without open source tooling, web apps wouldn't be able to run in Tomcat, Rails, Go, Python, or PHP. It is the building block of nearly any SaaS or other enterprise software offering. Those paid tools can build on top of the open source tooling—but in many cases if they are distributed for on-premise installations with the open source tools, a license must be paid to a developer (or at minimum, a reference to the developer's ownership in the installation).

Copyright

We can go a step beyond open source and copyright our work. Not everyone wants to DIY their own game from the Old School Reference and Index Compilation (OSRIC) when they can play all the cool classes and settings in Wizard of the Coast's fifth edition of Dungeons and Dragons. Let's say we create a piece of software to sell or lease access to. We can copyright our code. This doesn't protect all of the ideas and innovations the code surfaces but does provide protection to the copyright holder against others using their code for commercialization purposes, if able to decompile or see unrendered source. Funny enough, this is actually what we're doing in a Free and Open Source Software (FOSS) license such as MIT or GPL, just with different nuances.

We often host our services on a Linux computer (or use one hosted by Amazon or Google); run a service like Apache, NGINX, or Tomcat on it to host a web app framework; and then bring add-ons (e.g., frameworks) into our web apps to make development faster, more secure, and more modern. We also write in a language like Go, Java, Ruby, or Python. These are all the products of the open source community. Yet there are (and often should be) copyrights and other protections on new and novel ways to put these Lego bricks together.

These practices date back to a case that dealt with a piano roll (to play music) in 1908 that then led to the Copyright Act of 1909 and then the

Copyright Act of 1976, both catching up to the next available ways we use technology to store information. We went from paper to drum storage for those player pianos to encoding data into bits on wax for records and then hard drives. The fact that source code uses a copyright, features might use a patent, and the design might use a design patent or a copyright only helps reduce how people go about protecting their intellectual property, but it is worth a call to a law firm who specializes in intellectual property protection to determine if such protections should be pursued.

Copyrighting software seems to be less and less of a thing over time, while open source becomes more and more a thing. One reason is that for most governments to issue a copyright, we have to pay them to effectively escrow source code. This is outdated in an era of continuous testing, continuous research, continuous DevOps, continuous DevSecOps, and the resultant sometimes nightly software release cadence.

Governments move slower than innovation. Much of the submission information from governments to copyright code discusses "the first 25 pages of code," and in an object-oriented programming world, it's likely we'll have potentially hundreds of paragraphed-sized microservices as separate bits of code rather than one big file. Or we're supposed to submit code on a CD-ROM. Thus, officially copyrighting software, while an important option to consider, is less feasible than it once was. This being said, the line between the entertainment industry (where copyright is crucial) and software can be incredibly thin. For example, there are works such as video games with rich audio and video materials that are easily copyrighted. We can copyright the words we use on a screen and not our code. To protect how we do something, a better option is typically to patent the idea.

Patents

Most technological progress combines two (or more) previous inventions or discoveries together that haven't been put together yet. Netflix didn't invent subscriptions or DVDs. But they did patent their subscription DVD service—putting a subscription model on top of movie rentals over the mail (yes, this was before they moved into a streaming service). In doing so Netflix upended the video rental market and became a household name. Their patent protected their new market for a time. That was their reward for years spent building and refining how they could deliver that service profitably.

One option any patent holder has is to license their patent. This is more common in cross-licensing arrangements like with microchip manufacturers and meant to foster innovation. Some organizations design; others manufacture. Hyper-specialization is arguably why civilization exists. Examples range from early mechanical calculators invented by Blaise Pascal (called a royal privilege when King Louis XIV granted his) to Jony Ive from Apple getting 1,628 patents ranging from the Apple Newton to the stand on an iMac to parts of the Apple Watch. His patents are often exclusively licensed to Apple. Here, inventors are granted a license to exclude others from making or using an invention in the same way, thus protecting their intellectual property.

Protected works are how society incentivizes research and development (R&D). We can see a sharp rise in innovation since the modern patent system began in Venice in 1450. This involves everything from stained glass in Renaissance England to chemical formulas that resulted in the plastics industry to computing. Patents can also be used as a security, further allowing inventors to profit off works. Nikola Tesla couldn't bring his electric inventions to the masses, so he licensed his patents to George Westinghouse, who later requested relief on the patents to make the Westinghouse Company more competitive. Creators have all kinds of options.

Do Nothing

We don't have to open source or patent our ideas or creations. Instead, we can just put them out to market in the hopes that a first mover advantage brands us as thought leaders and innovators, which helps win customers.

Most who choose not to do anything special with creations except maybe put them out there as a monthly service don't make this as a conscious decision. It's a valid decision, but often out of inaction rather than deliberation.

The choice to not open source, patent, or copyright often just happens because we build something and don't realize it's special. Every country has a period with which we can file a patent or provisional patent. If we don't do so, then others can copy our works. Again, this is fine, but each organization should make a conscious decision about it. A key question to ask ourselves is how we'll react when another organization copies us.

Once ideas and innovations are out there, there are still more options. As patents near expiration or when something wasn't protected and begins to gain mass appeal, we may choose to reduce the friction of consumers to use the innovation. That's when we look to create standards, more patents, or a combination of the two.

Standardization

Standards ensure a rapid proliferation of a technology in a manner that values interoperability. For example, we used electricity in experimental capacities for centuries, but the standardization once patents began to expire (and thus the formation of international standards boards) led to an explosion in the use of electricity for everything from lighting homes to food preparation and refrigeration.

We need interoperability when we are in a red ocean of competitors and an innovation is used by third parties who are dependent on us. Think of TCP/IP, DNS, HTML, and TLS. These are the building blocks of the modern Internet, and the standards are well defined, fought over, and ratified by the Internet Engineering Task Force (IETF). These allowed companies like MCI to commercialize leased lines to access networks, then web browsers, then digital commerce, and now the mobile revolution. Computers have communicated with one another since the early days of transistorized computing and throughout the era of teletypes and time sharing. But those splinter-nets were not world-changing like the Internet was, in large part due to the standards bodies created by the academics that did the original research.

Standardization is expensive. Qualcomm raised nearly half a billion to take CDMA to market and create the modern cellular infrastructure we now use. They sit on a $180+ billion market cap in large part due to their early work.

Most who read this won't require standardization. However, if the adventuring party is forging ahead with an innovation that sits on top of or requires cooperation from a large number of vendors to achieve commercial success, licensing patents might work against us, and we need to think of standards and developing a consortium to effectively own and promote those standards.

Consortiums

Sometimes your adventuring party needs to align with other parties to reach your common objectives - a wizard, a ranger, a rogue and a paladin can't take down the big bad alone. Consider how game-changing the ARM chip has been for ubiquitous computing. Apple, Samsung, and others license the ARM chipset architectures (which are protected via patents) and bolt their own patents on top of them. This allows for a base set of chips with refinements on top.

Because Apple and Samsung are members of the same consortium and license similar intellectual property, the number of transistors in an M1 is almost identical to a Samsung or a Qualcomm Snapdragon chip. But the Apple chip has a lot of extra attention to detail in places that make the Mac operating system run better by leveraging features they add to the SoC. Samsung puts extra effort into the ones used for Android. In other words, there's a consortium to either share large costs, like getting the size of a transistor down, or help spread a standard—yet vendors can still gain a competitive advantage. Others may gain that advantage by displacing previous methods (especially when those give another vendor a competitive advantage), reducing costs given supply chain standardization, etc. But the overarching ARM movement helped topple a near monopoly on CPUs for desktops held by Intel before, and massive innovation came as a result (both at Intel and those who use the ARM architecture).

Consortiums then represent yet another way to take an innovation to market. ARM itself is worth over $40 billion. One aspect of consortiums that can get hard is competitiveness. This may manifest itself in two researchers at universities who compete to have their ideas implemented in a standard. That competitiveness might also be derived from multiple companies who compete with one another.

As a consortium grows, so grows the potential impact. Therefore, working with competitors and inviting more competitors brings not only more legitimacy to the effort but also more ideas and support that can make the work infinitely more useful to consumers. Once a consortium grows to a given size, it will slow progress. But that slowed progress offers a greater diffusion of the ideas and thus further benefits to all members in aggregate. In other words, a number of adventuring parties can work together for a common good and each win in their own beachhead markets.

Blurred Lines

There are so many ways to take an innovation to market. The ones referenced so far are just the most common. One word of warning though: Before commercializing or distributing our creations for free, we should take care to acknowledge who actually owns the intellectual property. For example, if we created a tool while employed at a university under a grant provided by a corporation or governmental agency, there might be a dozen written agreements we need to comply with. If we were on staff at a company but didn't use any of their equipment during the development, we should be careful to have agreements reviewed before assuming we own that intellectual property.

There are plenty of areas where the lines between these get blurred. Consider this: The Eckert-Mauchly Computer Corporation received a patent for the ENIAC, which was developed at the University of Pennsylvania. That patent was overturned in part because every other computer company was paying them royalties—suffocating the entire computer industry at the time. Officially the reason was that the Atanasoff-Berry Computer out of Iowa State University was found to be "prior art" that the founding team knew about before they built the ENIAC. However, that device was never proven to be functional since the creators were called off to participate in the World War II effort prior to its completion. If the courts hadn't overturned the patent, we would likely be 20 years behind where we are today, just getting 3D graphics on game consoles in 2023.

Also keep in mind that patents have fixed terms, much like copyright. We don't get to keep an invention to ourselves forever. Most utility patents last 20 years, which in the world of technology is several lifetimes. 3D printers went from thousands of dollars to a couple of hundred almost overnight when the patent for fused deposition modeling (FDM) expired. That sparked a wave of new innovators. So hopefully each of our companies can make our innovation ubiquitous and stay ahead of the competition once our term expires! Continued innovation means new patents that then preserve our position as market leaders if our party is able to overcome the early obstacles and become heroes of the realm.

Let Creators Create

Creators need to create. It's just part of being creators. The laws and regulations we discussed in previous sections exist to help creators protect their creations. But we don't have to engage in all that. We can just build cool stuff. Only history can judge when we should have protected a creation. And maybe, like a Linus Torvalds or a George Graham, we don't worry about all that and forego intellectual property protections to change the world. Or maybe we need others to join us to bring an aspect of technology forward, so we choose to create a standard and possibly a consortium to support the standard. These are all practical and valid and on a case-by-case basis should meet with our own world view.

What we shouldn't do is try to stifle innovation. In his book *Managing Corporate Lifecycles*, Ichak Adizes tells us that's what organizations on the decline do. They become litigious rather than stay innovative. Protecting our intellectual property promotes innovation long term, but trying to box others out or overextending our interpretation of what belongs to us is a predictable indicator of a dysfunctional organization. And, as Kim Scott points out in her book *Radical Candor*, an innovative company is comprised of thousands of small innovations that make us operationally excellent. Therefore, making organizations excellent is about every person being open and honest and bringing their innovations to the table (at whatever level of the company they impact). We should then promote that great work so it spreads via whatever tactic makes sense.

Now that we've looked at the mission and how we plan to protect the mission, let's turn our eyes toward envisioning a world where our innovation has become prolific.

Translate the Mission into a Vision

A vision is a future state we see in the world and how we can help the world get there. A role-playing campaign might have a vision of "a world without tyranny." The party spends countless long nights forging ahead through countless perils to rid the realm of the evil something-or-other. They are aligned by the mission, and it is cohesive to the structure.

While that does sound lovely, it's probably not the mission most readers have. We want our coworker adventuring party to share our ideals insofar as they're appropriate to the mission. This means we need to explain them in a way that's easy to communicate.

The vision statement takes that vision and puts it into a succinct and impactful form. Let's take Microsoft's original vision statement:

"A computer on every desk and in every home."

That vision statement might have seemed lofty in the late 1970s and early 1980s, but today it seems antiquated. So vision statements can change over time as the world evolves around us and we unlock various achievements.

No matter how articulate we may be, writing a vision statement can be a challenge. Or for some, it comes instantaneously. It may be helpful to move on to values and then come back to constructing a vision statement. But think through the vision and how the innovation might help make the world just a little bit better, even if that does include an end to tyranny.

The Values That Help Achieve the Mission

Every organization has a certain set of values. In an old school adventuring party, we might talk about alignment when we are thinking about values. Values act like the DNA of the organization. New people immersed in the culture should share our values. The values then help guide the actions, so those we surround ourselves with then just instinctively know how to operate—because they share the same values.

These values are the philosophies and beliefs distilled down into a few core principles. Just because we don't list some doesn't mean that we don't practice them. For example, we don't see honesty a lot—yet we expect it of our team. Writing the values down helps with the motivation, morale, and security our growing teams feel. And they keep our adventuring party happy to tell others about how great things are. Values aren't just to promote retention, but employee advocacy is one of the best weapons for any organization to wield.

Let's distill some common values we see at various companies (feel free to borrow any listed here):

- *Integrity*: We want our teams to have strong morals and act honorably. They don't have to be lawful good, but it doesn't hurt. We might use words like *honor, morals,* or *truth*. But the word *integrity* goes a step further and can be applied to how we carry ourselves and work with customers.

- *Honesty*: We've seen this come in a few flavors including honesty to others, honesty to ourselves, and being honest even when we didn't have to be. Often listed as *trustworthy* or other synonyms that imply honesty as well.

- *Be kind*: Gentle founders often strive for affection toward customers, and their warmth often comes through in thoughtful user experience, generous technical support offerings, and patience.

- *Relentlessness*: This can mean a lot of things, so when paired with any of the others, it implies tenacity and sometimes resilience.

- *Self-improvement*: We all want our teams to get better. Each person improves, each discipline approves along with it, and the entire organization gets better. Sometimes listed as *education* or *learning* as well.

- *Practice candor*: We often see this in organizations that struggle with passive aggressiveness or where people can't provide effective coaching. It's great, but best when used proactively rather than reactively.

- *Fairness*: Implies no price gouging customers or lowballing employee salaries. Providing great benefits and a quality product for a fair price is a great way to do business. We also want our teams to treat each other fairly.

- *Accountability*: Indicates that we hold ourselves and those around us responsible for every aspect of delivering a great product. Often seen in traditional, top-down companies, but a great ideal for anyone (maybe more so in those with less rigid management structures).

- *Customer service*: These ideals embrace the customer experience as the sum of all interactions with a given organization. This can also be ideologically expanded as service within the organization - if you are an HR professional your customer is your coworker. The ideal of being service oriented should transcend the transactions with paying customers. Often associated with *support* but tends to indicate feedback loops regarding user experiences and how those feed our own development practices and priorities.

- *Selflessness*: Implies management puts employees above themselves, that employees put customer well-being above their own, and that inter-team squabbles aren't about self-gain. Selflessness is a wonderful ideal but terribly difficult to scale in political organizations.

- *Stay bold*: Often seen more in sales-oriented or aggressively growing organizations, some organizations actively encourage boldness, if not a step beyond.

- *Disrupt everything*: Rethinking everything doesn't mean irreverence, although it's often to scale a disruptive mindset without devolving into contempt.

Values are an interesting thing. Of the preceding values, would we ever want to tell the world we don't value our customers, honesty, or accountability? So how do we pick the ones that best apply to our mission? It comes down to behaviors.

The values we define are important above all others to drive behaviors in our organizations. These behaviors combined with the culture we create then drive the way people perform. And that performance against our mission can then be qualitatively and quantifiably analyzed. We'll expand on behaviors throughout this book, but in the meantime, let's take a step into the future and think about how we might analyze performance for the mission, vision, and values in a quantifiable fashion.

Validate the Mission with a Scorecard

How is our adventuring party doing? We might hand out experience points for each successful encounter in a game. What does success mean, though? In a company, it's really all about how the organization matures and develops against a clear and concise strategy. We'll get into strategy more later, but in the following sections, we align with the mission (and do so with the values we hold dear) to plot our course and use a scorecard to track our progress.

A scorecard is like a tune-up checklist at the mechanic and can be used to define the metrics that matter to us and keep us on track to achieve them. If we want to get to $120,000 in monthly recurring revenue (MRR), then we might want to think about whether we can add $30,000 per quarter—because if we put it all on the board in the 12th month, our adventuring party might starve when we can't recognize any money in the first 11 months of the year.

Key Performance Indicators and Frequency

Timely and relevant information is critical for leaders of any organization. Reports and performance indicators help improve our decision making, and charts that show the most important performance indicators help us evaluate our progress. Performance indicators also give governing bodies, like a board of directors, better oversight of our activities. This section examines general and specific goals, the purpose and pitfalls of reporting, and the considerations for the rhythm that gets critical information to relevant parties.

Goals

As organizations grow in size, complexity, and relevance on a domestic and international scale, we create plans that reflect how we believe our world will unfold in a particular year, quarter, month, and week. Over the years our plans necessarily get more sophisticated as leaders accept larger challenges to meet increased annual objectives.

Most successful organizations align goals around customer experience. We know that the pursuit of financial goals without taking care of our customers is an empty pursuit. We then seek metrics that reflect that foundational commitment: great customer experience. To gauge our overall success, there are three overarching goals to orient on, which, for the purpose of this section, we will call the cardinal goals. We'll define those as

- *Top-line revenue*: The number of recognized billings (in either bookings or accruals but not a mixture of the two) according to audited generally acceptable accounting principle (GAAP) rules. This answers the question whether an organization is seizing opportunities in the marketplace. We cover the accounting terms and practices in later chapters of the book.

- *Profitability*: What remains of top-line revenue once we factor in our expenses is known as *operating margin*. This holds us accountable for servicing our markets and customers in an efficient and profitable way.

- *Customer retention*: The number of customers who renew with us on an annual basis. There is no clearer indicator of success in the eyes of a customer than when customers continue to pay us for our products and services.

- A final cardinal goal is important to consider, and this speaks to another health indicator for the organization: Employee retention. We want our organization to be a place where people find purpose, community and prosperity. If we are retaining employees over time, it's a pretty good sign that we have built an organization that includes productive, motivated people inside and out.

Nearly every activity of an organization impacts these outcomes in one way or another. The results can then be used to guide variable compensation plans (e.g., bonuses or commissions) for employees and managers in the organization. They provide clear accountability based on the needs of the organization on a quarterly or annual basis. Leaders are then responsible for these numbers and have the duty to ensure departmental activities help positively affect these outcomes rather than building tools and programs to protect and enhance their individual positions.

Purpose

Iterative reporting on progress toward our goals helps us identify when the organization is under- or overperforming in pursuit of our objectives. This information is valuable to help accelerate or decelerate the pace of various initiatives and keep our focus on the required activities. In other words, if the fighters accelerate faster than the magic users, then we can step in and move a little effort from one to the other in order to speed up the development of a given discipline. We don't want anyone to slow down, but we do want to keep focus where it's needed.

Detailed reports then guide our tactics to achieve objectives. We allocate resources to teams so they can hit their objectives. This helps manage resources downstream as various organizations within a company grow. Lastly, reporting shapes our understanding of how reality has matched our plans and how we might modify our future plans to reflect our observed reality.

There are potential problems with reporting. In order to get the most out of the dissemination of information, it's important to examine some of the potential pitfalls in what we report. While this is not intended as an exhaustive study, the two major areas many organizations face are incomplete measurements and the historical nature of reporting.

Many areas of organizations can go well, despite these efforts not being reflected in the financial performance. For example:

- Efforts by development teams to quickly address new technical capabilities might be reflected in the number of attendees who listen to product announcements. This would have a long-term impact on new customers and financials, but it takes time for new leads to mature into paying customers. However, if leads fall out of the funnel quickly, then we might not be on the right track to help them solve their objectives.

- Efforts that bring in new, smaller customers where revenue isn't recognized or where the customers need to mature once they are obtained (e.g., free months of a service or freemium product that haven't crossed a threshold into billable customers). There is still value in smaller customers, but we might have to re-evaluate our business model if we get a lot of consumer customers and not that many enterprise customers.

- Large events and marketing plans that won't net new customers until later in the year (according to how long it takes for a customer to mature).

- Bringing on partners and resellers that haven't yet transacted.

These are just a few examples of the positive activities that can happen at an organization but where the efforts haven't yet impacted our financial performance. Reporting data only informs us of where we have been as an organization and not necessarily where we are going, even when plotted on a trendline. Yet we need to provide a scorecard to our organizations so leaders can make decisions based on the best possible data.

Reviewing the numbers is something that all of us can do. We also need that data to spur action, reallocate resources, or aid us in better planning. This is what is most relevant for leadership groups to discuss. Leaders should share successful innovations, seek advice from others, and ensure they have a common purpose and understanding of how the present can positively impact the future. The conversation about performance often begins with KPIs, or key performance indicators.

Key Performance Indicators (KPIs)

There are a lot of activities that roll up to the overall success of any organization. These efforts are decentralized into departmental efforts that each leader becomes accountable for.

These essential departmental contributions affect, or roll up to, the organization's cardinal goals. The KPIs relevant to growing teams then map to one or more of the cardinal goals. We'll show a model, but that model will be different for every organization, so should be tailored to what is reportable for anyone who implements a similar model.

The model will never be complete but should be narrowed down into a simple set of numbers, where leaders of each team agree on both the goal and the tactics. Senior leadership then focuses on changes to performance throughout the year. A good starting point for a growing software company might include any of the following KPIs, for the disciplines discussed earlier in the chapter:

Software development (fighters)

- Management of releases to commit dates based on the roadmap, including the approximate ship date of the next product

- Quality of release as measured by post-release bugs and an increase in calls to support teams

- Success of release in the marketplace (did we actually sell what we created?)

- Coverage of features and code that has been tested and documented

Product management (rangers)

- Rolling the product roadmap that aligns with the strategic plan and innovates our offerings to meet the changing marketplace

- Timely releases

- Unique visitors and page views

- Customer satisfaction score(s)

Human resources (clerics)

- Time to help vs. plan

- Voluntary turnover %

- Past due open jobs by department

- New candidates in the interview process

- New hires

Sales and marketing (bards)

- Closed sales as compared to the sales plan

- Sales close rates

- Total number of opportunities in the sales pipeline per sales stage

- Total dollar value of the current pipeline

- Current and following quarter sales forecast

- Reseller sales (by region)

- Cost to acquire a customer

- Cost to acquire a sales-qualified lead

- Cost to acquire a marketing-qualified lead

- Percentage of qualified leads per sales stage

- Non-software sales (revenues from services and training)

Customer service and support (a motley crew of fighters–some may be dual-classing as wizards)

- Retention (monthly or for on-premises, on-time renewal percentages)

- Customer growth vs. customer loss (in number of customers and dollars)

- Case volume, trend, and rates per staff

- Average time to respond (phone, email)

- Past due cases

We'll get into what the preceding aspects of a company are as we go through each discipline throughout the book. The specific items we track can change each year as the organization's needs shift and the organization matures. The preceding aspects are a grab bag of areas to choose from, but they should be departmental metrics that provide a scoreboard for different departments and roll up to a cardinal goal of an organization. We can then place each of those cardinal goals into a standard Four Box reporting template and define which parts of the organization need to receive reporting on those.

The Four Box

The Four Box is a standard reporting template that has—predictably—four boxes, each typically containing four attributes or scores. This allows for the cardinal financial objectives plus one that each of our organizations deems critical, often reflecting alignment with our own core mission and values.

The Four Box is just one way of visually aligning performance, and there are tons of other templates out there to use. The key is to decide on a set of attributes and then remain consistent in their application throughout the year. These numbers should be based on raw performance metrics and should not be overly synthetic. For example, if the metrics are algorithmically derived, then they can lead to missing key attributes that reflect a lack of performance in a critical area of the organization by masking that area by overperforming in a less important area.

Different levels of reporting are appropriate for different audiences at different intervals. If we accept the premise that the purpose of reporting is for leaders to help focus teams, allocate resources, and modify plans, the next step is how we address the reporting needs for our employees and the governing board of an organization. For simplicity's sake, let's break down our stakeholders as follows:

- The board of directors (B)
- Management team (M)
- The full organization (O)
- Departments (D)

So far we have identified two types of measurable activity: cardinal goals and KPIs. Where financial performance is a goal, these activities are measured in a budget and are reported as such. We report against the budget at several intervals through the year. One example of the frequency of reports (or intervals we gather than them) and target audiences or stakeholders would be as follows (with the letter for the corresponding target audience identified) going from the least to the most frequent reports:

- *Annually* (D, B, M, O): Performance should be shared and celebrated at an annual all-company meeting. This memorializes how the year went and often guides performance-based compensation when that is a factor in an organization.

- *Quarterly* (D, B, M): Now that we have collected all of the data on a routine basis, the numbers can easily roll up to quarterly activity (e.g., into the slides necessary for reporting to the board of directors on a quarterly basis). This also provides a bird's-eye view for downstream performance by senior leaders as organizations grow and those leaders can't maintain a connection with that level of performance.

- *Monthly* (D, B, M): Distribute KPIs to the management team for review. These should provide a snapshot of all activities across the organization in a simple but drillable fashion (e.g., a Four Box with hyperlinks to raw reporting data) and provide a basic understanding of each team's activities toward the common goals of the organization. These reports should allow for short-term iterative objectives and cross-team work.

- *Weekly* (D, M): Departmental KPIs at a minimum should be shared with staff to ensure common knowledge of their activities that are shared with the management team prior to biweekly meetings.

- *Daily* (D): This is the domain of leaders within their respective departments. Examples of daily reporting might be a daily Scrum team meeting (e.g., a standup), daily sales team meetings, a simple dashboard, or some other management framework that focuses teams and is done at the discretion of the team leader.

Note   With a little thought into how to do so, we should be able to have gauges or screens in tools like Salesforce that show us how we're tracking toward these on an ongoing basis, and it should take more than a few minutes to compile all the metrics when it's time to do so.

As we go beyond revenue outcomes (the cardinal goals) and turn our attention to KPIs, the details are a blend of reporting the progress made and the future activities that will improve that performance in the future. In other words, we move from just tracking how many gold pieces we have to tracking the leading indicators to how many gold pieces we will have. At each review we should not only cover the past but what we will do to improve the results in the future.

Conclusion

Our adventuring party has a mission. That mission is to take an innovation that makes people's lives better to market. We take on that mission because we have a vision of how the world can be a better place if our organization successfully brings the innovation to the masses.

We align to certain values that guide how we carry out our mission in pursuit of making our vision a reality. In the absence of values, organizations often create their own, and they don't always evolve in ways we like. We know the members likely to make up our party, and we have a rough idea of how to evaluate their performance.

We also understand how we can monetize our innovation and protect our intellectual property. As any organization matures, we find that what worked for us yesterday is insufficient for today. As we grow, we will hopefully all get to a point that we can't just sit around a table to communicate how our teams are doing. Therefore, a few simple, annual goals that get measured when the year is done are important. Drilling into the KPIs also keeps us on track as the year progresses and offers a defined cadence to not only review performance but also look to remediation or ways to outperform!

Our hope in providing this framework is that we can define a structure and some considerations to identify what is relevant and ensure we communicate critical information in a timely fashion as organizations evolve. This should create a common understanding of high-level and departmental goals and allow us all to better communicate with one another.

We want to help leaders adapt. We want to help our friends inform everyone from their board to their staff on an appropriate level of detail about the performance of the organization. We want to get the right information to the right teams at the right times. That helps each of us to not get flooded with information irrelevant to us while also being informed as to how we can maximize our impact and pivot where needed. This chapter shares some of our experiences in how to do that. The next chapter gets into broader company philosophy and helps translate that philosophy into strategy and then tactics.

CHAPTER 2

The Philosophy

Many a campaign begins with a mission, and if we like the characters we're using, we might choose to continue past the initial game. As we go through game after game, campaign after campaign, we still have a philosophy holding the party together.

Hopefully it doesn't seem like this is a chapter on philosophy (even though it's in the name), starting with the Greeks pondering the meaning of life and going through to Wittgenstein, Kierkegaard, and Kant. It's not. Instead, we look at the philosophy underlying a company. Founders with a solid background in philosophy are awesome, nonetheless.

There are several philosophies that dominate the startup world these days. The most substantial can be seen in memes like "move fast and break things" or "grow fast or die." It's important to make sure we are all on the same page philosophically before we bring in shareholders and employees to share in a journey to bring some innovation to market. That includes the mission as well as the philosophy the organization has when dealing with customers, employees, partners, shareholders, the society around us, and anyone else we might come in contact with as we go.

Let's take Apple's "Think Different" philosophy. Yes, it was more than an advertising campaign. The merits of the actual hardware that Apple uses can be argued until the end of the time, but it's an almost irrelevant argument. Going back to the original Mac, Apple has leveraged that single idea to revolutionize human interface design, first in their own brand of

© Charles Edge, Chip Pearson, Amy Larson Pearson 2023
C. Edge et al., *The Startup Players Handbook*,
https://doi.org/10.1007/978-1-4842-9315-7_2

BASIC, then establishing norms for the human interface design to mass-market the mouse, and then again in a multi-touch interface for the iPhone and beyond. It's not a hacker philosophy; it's one to mainstream things that might have previously only been available to hackers.

Note   It's also kinda easy to imagine Steve Jobs, Steve Wozniak, Randy Wigginton, and the other early employees sitting around a table playing games like in the *Dungeons and Dragons* scene from *E.T.*

The Google mantra to "Do No Evil" was a good philosophy. But these short phrases are emblems of a philosophy and not the full mantra. To get into what philosophy really means, let's start from the inside of the organization, with a philosophy on employees.

Customers, Organization, and Employees

We begin our journey alone. Customers see what we're doing and pay to take that journey with us. That gives us money to bring on staff to better support customers. And thus, an organization is formed. The organization takes on a life of its own—but we need to always keep in mind that an organization is comprised of humans.

Sure, there's technology. After all, this book is geared toward technology companies. We automate as much as we can and cut out waste as much as we can. But we need a philosophy around how the organization treats our customers and employees, which shapes how they in turn interact with the organization. Much of that is done through the lens of software automation in a modern company.

There's no single business philosophy. But there are a lot of elements that contribute to a philosophy. We'll work through the appropriate level of transparency, how we make decisions, how we create a great place to work, and how we shape that culture. Many startups forget about the humans because founders and executive teams get focused on fundraising or planning for the next stage of growth. We've never heard anyone say, "We wish we'd been less intentional with our activities" or "We wish we hadn't been clearer about what we want." And yet, we do hear the opposite.

Our teams trust us when they understand what rewards await them in exchange for what's expected of them. They are inspired when they can help customers and when they share in those rewards. They trust us when we do what we say we're going to do. And they trust us when we trust them by being transparent when it's appropriate to do so.

Transparency

A twist is fun in a dungeon crawl. Maybe the big bad isn't so bad after all, or the good king and queen who sent us on a mission turn out to be evil wizards in disguise. Startups should be fun for a whole other reason, namely, banding together with a party of adventurous souls to take some awesome innovation to market. Each of them needs to play their own way, though—and that requires transparency.

Transparency doesn't come naturally in a startup. We might think we need to shield employees from all the things that steal their attention from their job. Most countries consider it taboo to talk about finances (like salaries) among employees. We think the people we worked hard to recruit will be flight risks if they know how things are going. We don't think to post certain aspects about how the company is doing because we have so much going on. In short, we're taught to project an organization we want to be rather than the one we are.

Employees should have the autonomy to make their own decisions. Transparency takes work. But having an organization where people understand the inner workings of the business is worth it. How?

- Transparency makes our teams work harder. We spend a lot of time at work. Many will spend half of their waking hours at the office or at their job remotely. People have options when it comes to where they work and want to take pride in what they fill that time with. That means pride in what they personally bring to the company—but also pride in the company itself. When we help our teams understand how the company is doing, we help the individuals justify that pride. Or we make people try harder to close a sale, get profitable, write better code, or however they impact the bottom line.

- Taking the blinders off gives everyone the agency to innovate in their position. We often tell people who are new to a role to stop talking about the way they did things at their old company. We just want them to do things how we want them done. Turns out that when we hire people for their expertise, we then want them to leave what they know at the door. But what we need is to innovate how we do things with what they bring to the table once they understand how what they do impacts the rest of their new organization. Showing how the whole organism works provides that understanding and enables bigger, bolder ways of thinking—beyond where people came from and where we are. If we prove our thesis by building a successful company, our business model can be copied. But lots of new and innovative ways to run the company will be impossible to replicate.

- Sometimes we get it wrong. If founders got everything right, there would be no risk, and everyone would be a founder. The bigger an organization gets, the more collective brainpower we have. We need to take criticism and questions about the choices and assumptions we bring so the organization gets stronger—so solicit more constructive criticism where possible. The response can be to accept good ideas or to have a dialog about the best approach to something. We may refine and perfect our way of discussing and thinking about a topic, or we may end up infusing the organization with new ideas and embolden our teams to not only be more autonomous but also make the company better overall.

- Transparency keeps us honest with ourselves. The fear that we lose employees if they know how things are going is real. But if we can't inspire them, we might need to ask ourselves if the endeavor is worth pursuing. Founders need perseverance. But we also need to be mindful of the Gambler's Fallacy when the market is telling us something just isn't right.

- Transparency shows we trust our teams. Yes, they could leave and take our ideas and innovations to a competitor. Yes, they could tell others how we're doing when we might want to posture as a larger entity to close bigger deals. But we will do better when we trust our teams. Encouraging a culture of honesty inspires integrity in everything we do.

- Transparency frees us. Founders who internalize all
  the challenges of running the organization take on an
  unnecessary burden. We don't want to break down
  crying in every staff meeting, but we do want to connect
  with our teams. Sharing our performance gets the bad
  off our chests while making the good seem so much
  sweeter—and lets everyone in the organization share in
  the wins and the losses.

This is one of those places where we want to be like the lawful paladin
and true and just whenever possible. We want to be open with our teams.
But again, that takes time and effort. It's obviously worth the effort. There
are several ways we can stay vigilant when it comes to transparency:

- Share goals. We push ourselves to do better with
  goals. Our goals are milestones in the development of
  the startup. The more accurate we get with planning
  and attaining stretch goals, the more we can control
  our own destinies (personally and professionally).
  Everyone should know the goals for the organization,
  the goals for themselves, and how their personal
  goals connect back to the most important strategies.
  Set annual and quarterly goals and review them with
  everyone at meetings that everyone in the company
  attends.

- Show how we did at attaining our goals. Here, we want
  to break our quarterly and annual goals up into chunks,
  preferably every other week or monthly. If we did better
  than expected or missed any goals, then we want to
  solicit feedback on why. This not only makes us better
  at setting goals but also solicits fresh, new ideas that
  make us better.

- Provide a direct line between the goals, the level of attainment, and how that impacts the individuals on each team. This is simple in a two- or three-person company but gets more challenging as the organization scales. What features led to important sales? How did those sales impact the general ledger? How are we doing with customer service, and how does that impact renewals (or better, land-and-expand opportunities)? How does that impact potential share prices or profit sharing? Together, these stimulate and galvanize.

- Provide monthly financial reviews. This can be as simple as the burn rate against how many gold pieces we have (er, known as cash flow) but will likely expand to include sales, renewals, etc. When everyone understands all the hidden costs to operating a business (especially at scale), we're all a little less likely to judge others harshly—and maybe a little less entitled.

- Give the board deck to the employees at the last staff meeting before a board meeting. As founders who have empaneled a board of directors, we have likely diluted the equity of the organization in exchange for growing faster. The shareholders are then the boss of the boss. And our teams should see how we portray the performance of the organization to our bosses. As the organization scales, this is increasingly critical, although we will necessarily leave out any slides pertaining to an IPO or covering mergers and acquisitions.

- Make all data available to everyone (within what's acceptable based on societal norms and information legally required to remain private). This might include globally accessible calendars, documents, financials, spreadsheets, sales performance, wikis, etc. Don't put any barriers that aren't necessary. The exceptions are information pertaining to customer privacy, internal human resources systems, and banking codes, where a small slipup can mean big consequences.

We don't want to overdo meetings. We don't want to crush our teams with too much information. We don't want to provide information that could be harmful to careers or debilitating to the organization. But we do want to provide everyone the opportunity to know as much about the organization as they choose to know. We want our employees to know the work they do matters to the goals and outcomes of the company, and that the goals of the company are worthwhile. Knowing that they are critical to the success of a worthwhile project gives contributors purpose, which is an invaluable motivation to work hard and be creative.

This kind of integrity in a company scales. Trust and honesty inspire hard work. Transparency isn't a buzzwordy way to develop a company culture. It's real. Its vulnerable. It's practical. It's simple (although, again, does require effort). But most importantly, transparency gives everyone in our orbit the agency to make a conscious decision to join us in our mission. And they'll respect us for giving them the choice.

Decision Making

One aspect of role-playing games is to get in character. Think of this as our previous work when we defined our mission, vision, and values. We then make those clear to the organization and so inherently create clarity and expectations around how we make decisions as an organization. These help us make our philosophies clear and provide transparency for those to whom we need to delegate authority so that they can make decisions and the organization can scale beyond just one or two people. This also helps show who makes decisions and facilitates the transfer of that power. Many of us might not like that word. Power is exactly what is at play here, and we need to give that power to others as soon as we can trust them to wield it (and be prepared to pull it back should we lose that trust). Many choose to play games with power dynamics or use them in inappropriate ways, but this is another place we can just be transparent and so take the icky stuff around all that off the table.

Transparency around the philosophy of the company shows we've done the work to empower others to collaborate. Everyone should be allowed the power to provide feedback. This doesn't mean everyone can make decisions; otherwise, no decisions would end up being made (because committees suck at making decisions in startups). And yet intentional decision making requires different experiences and insights.

Startups move quickly. It's okay to make a bad decision. It's not okay to take too long to do so. A vacuum, or lack of a decision, leaves room for others to interpret the void to mean whatever they want it to mean. If we want to revisit a decision, we can always reverse course, provided we are collecting data and have a good reason to do so.

What becomes most important is that we define and outline how and why we make the decisions we make. Each level of an organization can run autonomously, within limits. Defining those limits provides a tiered approach to decision making. This happens per discipline, as each discipline levels up. For example, a hiring manager on any given team may make decisions around who we hire but solicit feedback from a team to inform a decision, thus acknowledging them as stakeholders. The hiring process may be dictated by a human resources professional (or team as we grow), who becomes an enabler in the process, and any potential dotted-line-reporting structures add more and more stakeholders. If every stakeholder had to be included in deciding who we hire, we'd only hire a person a year. Most startups need to grow faster than that.

Parts of the philosophy around decision making evolve over time. When we first meet someone, it's common to need to build trust. The trust is bilateral and increases with intentionality and with integrity. Intentionality comes in many flavors. When we communicate the why behind each decision and others communicate why they made decisions, we increase the level of mutual trust (and hopefully are educated).

Slowing down to be more intentional around how decisions are made saves time as we delegate more decisions downstream. Founders need to select great people to work with and empower them. A huge part of that is including others in how we make decisions—another is the people we surround ourselves with.

People

Name a part of an organization that works without people... Anything? Without people, there is no organization. There are no products, no customers. It turns out that role-playing games aren't very fun without people to play them with either. The same is true in business.

We went through many of the archetypes (or character classes) necessary to build a thriving organization in Chapter 1. Chapter 7 is all about the people and how they impact and grow an organization. People can be tricky. Some days we have unicorns flying across rainbows, and other days the mage shoots a fireball into the room with their own adventuring party, dealing 5d6 damage to everyone (the Wand of Wonder is a weird magic item). That's the way it is, and if we expect anything different, we're just kidding ourselves about running an organization that grows beyond a sole founder.

There are real and lasting impacts when we bring people into a company: how we onboard, how we set expectations, how clear we are about goals, and how we remediate the vacuum left when we neglected to do so. If we don't care for our people, we stifle growth.

Every organization should level up as we grow. The organization levels up by building, buying, or borrowing the right people. When we borrow people, we may level up temporarily. When we buy talent, we effectively spend our hard-won gold pieces to level up. But when we build talent, we grow along with the team and inspire a sense of loyalty, so long as we continue to provide opportunity for their growth and remain competitive with the total rewards we provide.

Remember that employee loyalty, as with the loyalty of characters in a good game, is earned over time, not given automatically. Our teams need to do what's best for them, their careers, and their families. If we forget to care for them, they will abandon us for better opportunities—sometimes at a competitor. Expecting people to show up and work hard in exchange for just a paycheck is not a holistic philosophy for managing humans. Instead, we need to think more deeply so we're able to better support situations that arise over the course of more and more humans joining us on our adventure.

Much as an adventuring party is the culmination of adventurers, the people *are* most organizations and so must be a core part of our philosophy. A lofty goal would be for people to be able to be unicorns dancing on rainbows and not burning cinders in need of reviving.

Win-Win-Win

We want everything we do to be a win-win-win situation. This isn't going out and winning business but instead creating a situation that results in a win for the customer, a win for the organization, and a win for our teams.

Not every situation will be a win-win-win. Teams may think they deserve more budget to grow their discipline than the organization is ready to spend. Customers may encounter a defect with a product that we aren't ready to fix. Employees may want us to increase pay bands beyond what our margins allow for. Leaders find equilibrium when we navigate these strings that pull us in different directions. It's about balance.

Things will almost always be out of balance somewhere. But just because one team wins doesn't mean another has to lose. Therefore, we should seek win-win-win scenarios to make each cohort we serve feel as whole as possible. We can't make everything we do high quality and free (and give out ponies and a ring of protection to each customer) just like we can't afford to give everyone on the team a 100%-per-month increase in pay. But we can operate within an appropriate level of profit margin and provide total rewards on par with others in our industry (above and beyond the pay band). We can also seek to make an acceptable margin to grow the coffers of the organization and pay dividends to investors (including ourselves) along the way.

Planning Matters

People often make excuses for why we can't spend the time planning for the future. Technology moves fast, so we can't know what will happen too far off in the future. Markets shift. People move on to new jobs. Pandemics happen. All that being said, we can't afford not to plan. It's better to adjust plans than not have one in the first place.

Our cleric wouldn't build a temple without a plan. A startup likely costs more to build and takes longer than a building. We can start with a blueprint and evolve that blueprint as we go. This is true for go-to-market teams just as much as it is for the products we sell to customers. Many in software development may say, "That's so waterfall," and a Kanban approach with stickies may appeal to our modern ADHD mindset in business—but when there is real money and people's incomes are on the line, having an idea of what we're working toward builds cohesion, creates clarity, and, when done in a collaborative way, tests our assumptions and ego.

The detail of the plan should be as granular as those who hold the purse strings require. Maybe we run down into a dungeon and hack away at kobolds. Or maybe we're seeking a sacred artifact on an island and if we manage to not kill any kobolds we get an extra reward, like procure a better ship. Knowing where we are headed, what we seek to accomplish, and why increases the likelihood of success.

Measure twice; cut once. Measure three times; cut once. Both are acceptable, and the level of measurement should be justified by the scale of the operation. If we seek investment, then we'll likely need more and more of a written plan to provide to those who fund our adventure. These come in the form of traditional business plans, roadmaps, Gantt charts, or whatever each investor needs to trust we've thought our chances of success through at an appropriate level and aren't just barging into a room full of dragons as first-level characters.

Communication Matters

Communication is one of the hardest things in any relationship. That's no different in our work relationships than it is in our personal relationships (or around a table with a bunch of other gamers). Communicate too much and the critical elements of what we're trying to communicate get lost. Communicate too little and people don't understand enough to grasp what we're saying.

The way leaders communicate establishes a culture, unintended or otherwise, at any organization. Most issues within an organization can be rooted to a breakdown in communication. Some of those are due to an overreliance on technology. Others are due to a lack of clarity. We covered communicating status for various aspects of an organization in the section "Key Performance Indicators" in Chapter 1. That included not only the what but also the who and when. There's also a how.

Each organization is different, and technology evolves rapidly, especially when it comes to collaboration. Here are some aspects to consider, keeping communication channels and expectations clear at the forefront of our minds. Each communication medium is useful in different scenarios. How and where are we communicating? Think through the following questions and expand the thoughts to include other areas unique to each situation:

- What tools do we use and when?

- Do we expect a response to a Slack message about an emergency at 2 AM, or should we pick up the phone and contact someone in an emergency situation?

- Do we need a call tree to react to emergencies?

- Who should be included in the approval chain when doing an update to an app or web app? How much diligence do we expect for each approval? Are there steps required by compliance frameworks to make sure all the appropriate parties have a paper trail?

Also consider how to communicate as a company, which includes the following:

- Think through the tone and tempo of communication. How long should we expect to go without someone responding, and how do we conduct ourselves?

- We don't need a service-level agreement, but we do have an expectation per communication medium, like whether we require an agenda for scheduling group meetings.

- Do we need to go through management for certain communications? As teams grow, we will certainly have leaders who don't want their subordinates communicating laterally or upstream with other teams.

- How do we communicate new initiatives vs. changes and reorganizations? Each type of communication might need to be handled more delicately—especially when there isn't a consensus, which happens less and less as we grow.

Also consider how we provide clarity and confirmation (we cover feedback loops throughout the book):

- How will we confirm that the messages and intentions are received and understood? Feedback loops might assume more than they should.

- Sending and receiving communication can be complicated, and messages are often missed or conflict with other messages during transmission. Just as we do when developing queues for messages in software, we then need to ensure there's a process and expectations for how we confirm messages were received and understood based on our intentions.

Founders should not only document how we communicate but also practice what we preach. Others see what we do and mimic our behaviors. We send mixed messages when we don't act the way we instruct others to act.

All this communication is to provide clarity to others around various aspects of how the organization runs. We can't have clarity without communication, and yet communication doesn't mean clarity. We'll move into developing clarity in our communications in the next section.

Clarity Matters

Clarity is critical if we want to grow a healthy company. Clarity stems from communication, but can't be had if we don't spend the time thinking through where we eventually want to be as an organization. What does the future state of the organization look like in two, five, or ten years? What do we look like after taking a Series A round of funding? This involves the humans, half-elves, and hobbits who join our growing enterprise, who dedicate their time to the cause, and who earn a say in how it evolves. It also involves how budget is allocated to each team, how customers perceive us, how customers interact with us, and so much more (that we'll go through in this book).

Clarity leads to intentionality. We can better articulate what we want from those who join our adventure. We also have to leave room to alter the plans and pivot as we grow. To grow we need an open mind and to remain pliable so we can achieve a new level of clarity that we can then articulate as we go. This doesn't mean we need to inform everyone when we change the percentage of the budget that goes toward marketing by 1% per year, but it does mean we want to understand what choices we make, think through them, understand the impact to others, and then reset the goals, and therefore expectations, on a routine basis.

It's best to start with a mission, vision, and values. We built those in Chapter 1 of the book, but it's worth reiterating. We then want to think through the strategies that help us accomplish the mission and do so in a way that the strategies and tactics that stem from them turn our vision into reality all while living the values we defined. Most organizations can't focus on more than four or five strategies per year without them becoming diluted. That doesn't mean as we grow that each leader might have their own strategies that link back up to our overall strategies—but that the overall organization is aligned to a core set of strategies as well.

Those strategies give our adventuring party a purpose. They inform why positions exist and how the work maps back to upstream strategies in support of the mission. We want every single person to have a sense of clarity about how their work supports the strategies of the company and how they impact the mission. That purpose can then be quantified into expectations, which we define as key performance indicators (or stretch goals or whatever buzzword is preferred). The key here is that we are clear with our teams and that they accept the role for what it is, agree that the goals are achievable, and inspire them to meet our expectations. We should also make sure they have a voice in setting the goals.

Clarity around roles, goals, and expectations is a common theme of this book. From the moment we interview to when people leave the organization, we want them to understand what makes for a successful member of the team. This, paired with total rewards (how much we pay them, stock options, insurance, etc.), keeps them engaged and on track. That doesn't mean we limit them. As we grow, others may have lanes or workstreams that mean going above and beyond their core job function interferes with the work done by others, but it's best to give freedom early and then applaud the efforts while gently defining lanes later.

Our organization evolves over time in other ways as well. Our clarity is most keen when it comes to short-term goals, but the more we can identify long-term goals, the more future-proof individual and team efforts are. That could manifest as simply as "We want a chatbot to be able to send these how-to articles eventually, so let's make knowledge base articles every time we have to help a human through a trouble ticket." That's different than "Close all tickets as quickly as possible" and helps harness the work being done now to contribute to projects that contribute to our long-term strategies.

We can't go back in time—or at least not yet. So the more people understand the strategies in place to reach our company's goals, the less productivity we lose and the better efficiencies we can create.

Each founder decides what their priorities are and how to clearly communicate them. We can't know every curveball coming our way. But we can build clarity, wiggle room, and compassion into our culture.

Culture Matters

Many organizations tout their culture as central to why people want to work there—and often why customers should pay them. Think about how many times we've heard or said these statements:

"Our culture makes us special."

"They are a great culture fit."

"Culture eats strategy for breakfast."

"Our culture is unique."

"Our culture is our secret weapon."

We often observe or make these statements with blind acceptance, strong bias, and minimal definition—yet we accept them as a foundation. We leverage culture as an evaluation tool to hire, promote, or terminate employees. The scary part is that most of us don't fully understand what we are discussing.

For example, "They are a great culture fit!"

- What does *culture fit* mean? Why?

- What does good fit vs. bad fit look like? Why?

- How do we define the word *fit*? Why?

- How does our culture impact customers/employees/ company? Why?

- What behaviors contribute to our culture? Why?

- What behaviors distract from our culture? Why?

- How do our values direct employee behaviors? Why?

- How does fitting our culture impact the performance of our company?

Unpacking and understanding the culture of our organization can be tricky work. The following sections help us clarify and articulate our culture and the behaviors that help it grow.

Culture: What Are the Behaviors?

Our behaviors are everything within an organization. Our behaviors shape company performance, customer experiences, and an organization's health. Everything comes down to behaviors—yet we often don't identify the behaviors we expect or need within our company.

Think about and document three behaviors we want to embrace that facilitate the culture we want within our organization. For this exercise, choose behaviors that reflect the values outlined in Chapter 1 and document the following:

What is the behavior?

Why does it matter?

How does it contribute to the company's performance? Why?

How does it build the company's culture? Why?

We set an expectation for employees when we define behaviors in this way. Employees know how we select, promote, coach, or potentially terminate employees and how we want the organization to evolve. To build unique cultures and performance, we need to ensure that everyone understands and experiences similar behaviors. Yet we want to leave room for each person to bring their whole self to the job.

Some think of famous ancillary benefits to startup life as part of the culture. Our culture reflects our behaviors, not the accumulation of things in an office. This truth will continue to expand as more organizations shift to remote and distributed teams where physical rituals become less normalized. Free soda, snacks, or table tennis are simply objects that represent the physical space where an organization might work. How employees engage with these items (or don't) becomes a better definition for an organization's culture, especially as more globally oriented organizations don't nexus in a traditional office setting in many startups.

Cultural Contribution vs. Cultural Fit

The objects don't define the culture, and nor does a homogenous workforce (at least not at scale). An adventuring party without a thief or cleric might not get far if they try to delve deep into a dungeon that's full of traps. Yet the paladin and thief come from different cultural backgrounds, and if the paladin had their way, there might not be a thief in the group. Meanwhile, most parties can do just fine without a paladin!

We find that cultural fit is often associated with social rituals and not the key behaviors (like those we defined earlier) that help grow organizations. We also find that cultural fit is more often associated with substantial bias levels in people who often feel comfortable with individuals like them or who share similar interests or hobbies. Yet we know we need a diverse set of skills and interests and so a diverse cadre of humans in an organization.

We often hear cultural fit described in terms that include happy hours or someone they might want to hang out with if they weren't at work. But culture should be about intellectual curiosity, the ability to research solutions, and proactive communication. These behaviors become critical to those who seek to build stronger teams and select talent on merit, who can contribute more positively to the company's performance and culture. The conversation then becomes more about cultural contribution.

If we find it hard to write down what cultural fit means, we often find it easier to document behaviors that promote the type of culture we want. It's then far easier to provide clarity around cultural contribution. We just need to slow down, provide time for reflection, and identify the right behaviors.

We also hear organizations talk about culture preservation. Let's dispel an illusion up front. The culture will not be the same at a three- or four-person company once there are 20 people. Instead, let's frame the conversation as cultural growth, stemming from the cultural contributions of a number of different people we bring into the organization.

If we manage to create a great and fun place to work, then it probably seems like we want to preserve that culture. We typically cause more damage the longer we try to do so. Established norms in smaller teams usually limit growth. The maintenance of the culture can reduce the innovative and developmental growth for later hires if not done with extreme care. We assume that great atmosphere we had early is the only way and so that's the organization's apex, the best we can do as a company. In all things, there is only progression or regression—maintenance is generally a comfortable status of regression. So the only way to maintain the culture is to stagnate. And without growth, it's difficult to keep a team together.

We don't have to abandon the behaviors that are foundational to the organization when we grow. To evaluate the behaviors that make the company fun and productive and then grow the culture to align with those values, consider the following questions:

- What behaviors got us to this point? Why?

- What behaviors will help us grow? Why?

- What behaviors will negatively impact our growth? Why?

Growing culture is not about abandoning what made us great but instead about intentionality, focus, and alignment. Armed with those, we can do anything.

Conclusion

The adventuring party survived its first game of a long campaign. The encounters helped shape and formulate who we are and who we want to be. Those are decisions we can make rather than situations we can haphazardly find ourselves in.

This chapter began with a look into how we can be proactive, or deliberate, with the philosophy of our organization. We then explained how we can be transparent with and create a win-win-win environment for our customers, employees, and the organization itself. We focused on communication, planning, and clarity. When done right, those contribute to a great culture at any organization.

Keep in mind that much of this is about our behaviors and our willingness to grow and evolve as an organization (and as individuals). The more we choose to define, articulate, share, and grow our culture, the more people we include in our organization's journey. That diversity of voices and experiences makes us stronger.

We like to put customers first. But every organization has a different journey and different philosophies. When we unpack what we mean by "culture," that is a behavior we put above all others. All of this then comes right back to the foundation that is the basic philosophy of an organization. If the organization is to thrive and the party is to survive the encounters ahead, we need a solid foundation. Now that we've looked at philosophy, let's move on to some tactics around founding a company, which we cover in Chapter 3.

CHAPTER 3

Found the Company

One of the hardest aspects to learn about any new game (and especially open-world games) is the game mechanics, especially when first-level characters often perish the first time something challenging comes along, as do first-level companies. Many hack and slash their way around a game without understanding what the game really is and how it's meant to be played. Some find their way to the end of the dungeon anyways—but many give up or perish in the process. Think of some of those mechanics, like creating character sheets for each of the party members or even a character sheet for the company itself, as founding the company.

Next is the actual tactical implementation required to create a corporation and take an innovation to market. The company creation is fairly boilerplate, although, when possible, it's best to hire an actual attorney to help with the process to make sure everything is filed properly. That will save time and expense later, when documentation is required to provide investors with a specific form like a K1 or to provide an acquirer with a barrage of the necessary documents if the company is sold or takes on institutional investors.

Before we get into some of the particulars around the type of corporation to form, let's first look at some of the aspects of doing both concurrently. This is important as many startups begin as a side hustle these days, so act as what is known as a pass-through corporation, or a Limited Liability Corporation (LLC) (if that).

© Charles Edge, Chip Pearson, Amy Larson Pearson 2023
C. Edge et al., *The Startup Players Handbook*,
https://doi.org/10.1007/978-1-4842-9315-7_3

Balance a Job and a Business

A common trope in a role-playing game is to have a powerful ally bestow magical items for the journey ahead. Another is for the adventuring party to play through lower-level quests to gain experience and gather the supplies and accoutrement necessary for the big boss at the end. This is like whether to take venture capital or bootstrap a company. Think of staying in a job while a project is developed as a little bit of both.

Companies who begin out of a personal savings or profits from work or products are often referred to as bootstrapped companies. Self-funded businesses don't need institutional banks or investors to provide capital because they don't usually have liabilities (or the money owed now or in the future) to provide the product they sell. Think of these as consulting services, software or sites that don't have a lot of hosting requirements, or those that grow slowly as founders are able to fulfill most orders. Examples some readers might know include Patagonia, GoPro, and GitHub (although the founders of GitHub already had successful exits so had the capital to fund their own operations).

There are a lot of ways to bootstrap a company. In the early days of building a product, this often means that we work a day job to fund a startup we're passionate about. We hedge our bets with the day job so we don't burn through our savings while we validate or finish a product. But when we do so, we serve two masters—or more, once friends, family, and other responsibilities are considered.

We can make a lot of extra income when we effectively work two jobs. Or we can afford to hire freelancers to help us with parts of a project we can't do ourselves. We need to be careful, though. If we choose to keep our day job while we run a startup, we can run afoul of logistical, health, ethical, and even legal issues. However, a bootstrapped business doesn't dilute equity, which is to say the founder owns the whole thing. That also means the founder has all the responsibility, which can be a huge drain. To help maintain that bootstrapped status for as long as possible, let's go through a few tips to help along the journey:

- **Document the vision.** We built something new for a reason. Put the inspiration on paper. Describe the "why" in ways others can understand. And test that with strangers to make sure it resonates. We are not on a simple journey. It will be hard. Stay conscious of why our innovation helps people keep the drive alive and keeps us from just spinning our wheels when trying to find the right project to give our attention to.

- **Prioritize.** Multiple obligations lead to the risk that we won't be any good at any of the things we work on. This might mean we alienate friends, put stress on familial relationships, or get fired from our day job. If we want to build a business, we will need to sacrifice something. But what? That's for each of us to decide, but if we make the sacrifice deliberately, we have control of our lives. Once we look for investment, most investors think the day job must go immediately so we can focus on the startup. But keep in mind this increases the risk, sometimes significantly.

- **Schedule time.** The shiny new thing can take over our lives if we let it. Once we have our priorities straight, it's time to dole out time–based on those priorities. The day job will likely occupy a large chunk of time. Family and friends would rather be put more on a schedule than just lose our attention entirely. And then there's the startup, the passion project. If we sandbox the time for the startup this way, we make sure not to let the rest of our life slip through our fingers unintentionally.

- **Stick with a Minimum Valuable Product (MVP).** What is the minimum amount of work to get something out in the market that satisfies the vision we documented earlier? It doesn't have to be feature complete. We also don't want to put a crappy product in the market that gives us a bad name. But we do want to ship as early as possible. That's a Minimum Valuable Product (not a Minimum Viable Product, because we want to keep value in the front of our minds). If we don't try to bite off too much, we can continually confirm that the vision resonates and that we're on the right path.

- **Make a plan.** Now that we know how much time we will spend on the startup, let's break the project down into parts. This doesn't have to be a comprehensive business plan, a complex Jira board, or some crazy Gantt chart. It can be but should at minimum include a general outline that allows us to pivot when needed and estimate how long the project will take (in hours and duration). In the future, those might become milestones on a project plan. But for now, they just keep us focused on the parts of the project that matter, namely, the Minimum Valuable Product, and provide insight into our velocity.

- **Get a good productivity tool.** There are a ton of list apps out there, like Trello. There are lots of other tools that help build a checklist of things to be done and even block out time on our calendars so we can stay focused on the right tasks at the right time. Pick a tool and stick with using a tool (even if the tool changes); it keeps us honest throughout this journey (and others).

- **Outsource.** If we keep a day job, chances are we make a good income and can hand off certain aspects of the new venture to someone else. No one will do as good a job as we would, since we're the founders—but that doesn't mean we don't try to get some help and some velocity here and there to speed things along. Access to good resources also opens up the viability they can become partners or employees once we get to that point.

- **Stay mindful of performance.** Even if we time-box our project and do everything right, our minds might just wander over the barrier and think about our project. Try to stay cognizant about the performance at work and the quality of the time spent with friends and family. Again, getting pulled in a lot of directions at once can be a challenge. But if we're passionate about the vision, hopefully putting that passion into the other priorities in our lives will be worth it.

- **Evaluate the viability.** The ability to leave a full-time job usually comes with money. The startup might need more and more of our time. But if that doesn't translate into revenue, consider how it might. Revisit the vision and how to monetize it. If the endeavor doesn't make money, it's a hobby until it does. Make sure we understand the return on our investment of time and money and what the horizon looks like to monetize that. It's fine to have hobbies, but it's also important to make an educated decision about what we're doing.

- **Talk to investors.** If we are to build a company, we'll eventually need more capital than the product brings in. When we bring in investors, it isn't always about raising money. We also want to validate the idea, align the business to be attractive for a capital infusion, and, one of the most important aspects, find mentors. Many investors have founded companies themselves and are empathetic to the cause.

Ultimately, it is always hard to start a company. It's potentially less stressful with a day job, but usually takes longer to get things off the ground. And another company might swoop in and build what we are working on, as few ideas are as unique as we tend to think.

If we continue with another job while we build our solution, some might question our commitment to the vision. But it can be worthwhile to keep the relationships at work, to have capital to bootstrap the company, and to keep our sanity if we might otherwise stress about money all the time. Good luck with all of it. You've got this!

What Type of Corporation to Create

We roamed the wilds of the land and found a need. That need became a passion. The passion now becomes a company. There are five main types of organizations that can be founded, from the legal or tax perspective. These aren't synonymous with levels, or stages, but can be as we get dozens or hundreds of people in an organization in order to face down the big boss at the end of a campaign.

Each type of corporation does come with positives and negatives, and there's really no perfect formula when we're first starting out, but there are some triggers that force us to switch to various types of businesses as a business evolves. The ones we'll cover in this section include the following:

- Sole proprietorship (DBA)

- LLC

- S Corporation

- C Corporation

- Nonprofit

Note   The types of companies are different in various counties, but most offer similar types of organizations. It's always best to work with a business or financial planner in a local county when incorporating. Further, some counties require a separate entity to be created when doing business locally, so consultants can help us understand the laws and requirements for our types of businesses as we grow geographically.

Again, these company types often aren't based on revenue or headcount. A solo entrepreneur might outgrow an LLC, while a C Corporation might exist for a decade with no income. In general, the longer we can remain structured as an LLC, the better, but there are a lot of good reasons to move past that as early as possible (and some bad ones).

A sole proprietorship is an organization that is, well, a person. This is a person who does business as (thus a DBA) the name of an organization. A DBA is fairly simple to create, and the owner doesn't have to file a tax return on behalf of the company. But there can only be one owner and one investor in the organization, and there's no liability protection. That means that the personal assets of the owner of the business can be pursued if the business goes into debt for more than the assets of the business can cover.

That liability protection is key, so in case we're concerned about legal issues (most people should be), it's usually best to just start as an LLC—especially given that the cost difference and tax implications between the two are fairly negligible.

The LLC

The next stage we normally see when we talk to newer startups is an LLC, or Limited Liability Corporation. Here, we increase the administrative upkeep and accounting burden of the business. This means we must file a separate tax return for the LLC and keep a separate ledger in support of that. But the business is no longer just us doing business as the owner. We get liability protection, and we have more options for how to file those taxes at the end of the year.

S Corporation

An S Corp is often used for smaller corporations. The benefit of an S Corp is that tax is only taken out on shareholders. There can be up to 100 shareholders but only one class of stock, and those shareholders must be US citizens and not foreign or institutional investors (which means a venture capital firm can't invest but individuals in the United States can). There's a bit of extra documentation required for annual filings, but the S Corp is common for organizations that don't foresee hyper-growth.

C Corporation

Most of us will end up with C Corporations eventually if all goes well. The C Corp will be necessary for international expansion or for organizations that plan to go public, as there's an unrestricted number of shareholders in a C Corp and they can be in foreign countries. There's a lot of liability protection, but the legal entity must be separate from the individual and so there's a lot of extra paperwork, which comes with cost to process and file.

That extra paperwork is also necessary because C Corps are subject to double taxation, which is to say they are taxed at the corporate level and shareholders are taxed. But it's part of the cost of doing business when going international, going public, or bringing in institutional investors like funds. And C Corporation profits are taxed at lower rates, to help soften the blow.

Nonprofit

Some organizations aren't meant to make money, but instead meant to raise money for a given cause. This might be in support of a movement, to build awareness, to establish a means for charitable giving, or to create a museum. The organization isn't required to pay income tax from the contributions and in fact makes those contributions tax deductible for the people donating. There are several requirements, like filing paperwork for a separate legal entity federally (e.g., a 501(c)3), and, rather than have an owner, they have a board of directors. Additionally, most will require corporate taxes be filed annually and paying fees to state and federal entities.

Overall, most startup organizations that seek investment will be an S Corp or a C Corp. This provides a structure where shares can be allocated to the investor. An organization can revoke an S election at any point and issue C Corporation shares. While this change can happen at any point, it must happen by the 15th day of the third month of the tax year to classify as a C Corp on corporate taxes.

The IRS will automatically require that a company moves to a C Corp when earnings, profits, and income exceed 25% of gross income for three years in a row. But by then any organization will likely have a business where the tax liabilities would have caused us to do that anyways. Additionally, once the election of an S is revoked, we likely can't move back to that type of corporation for five years.

These are things that we should bring in business advisors and tax specialists to deal with. This section isn't meant to be tax advice but more just a broad overview of the types of companies that startups often form.

The advisor can also expand on where the corporation is formed (e.g., many SaaS startups form in Delaware for a variety of reasons). But a savvy lawyer and business advisor will help navigate all those waters and more, so we should never jump into this stuff without a little help from them!

Keep Distractions at a Minimum

Distractions can destroy our productivity. But leading a startup means there's a constant barrage of things that need to be handled. There are a lot of distractions: a call with a lawyer, a potential investor who returns our call, a response to the latest Twitter post about our product, expenses so our team gets paid in a timely fashion, getting that last commit from the new developer we just hired who refuses to commit anything, figuring out how to run a refund in Stripe, and the list goes on and on.

When are we supposed to be productive when we're in that place where we're too small to hire people to deal with each of those but too big for them to go unattended? When we are under constant assault by all these things?

Here's the thing about answering those questions: it's not going to get better. When we get bigger, the problems that require our constant attention just shift elsewhere, and they amplify. So rather than try to eliminate them, we need to learn to schedule time for what's important and cope with the distractions.

This is no different than turning off notifications for certain friends on Facebook or deleting a game from our phone that constantly pops up an alert. Productivity killers come in a lot of forms.

So what are some good ways we can shift into a more proactive strategy for dealing with distractions now that we've accepted it's part of the startup life? Let's look at just a few of the ones we have found success with at Bootstrappers:

- **Set boundaries with coworkers.** We are allowed to tell people how we need to work and to update them when our styles evolve over time. And we need to if we're ever going to accomplish anything. We don't need to have unscheduled meetings, and we don't need to have extended impromptu pair programming sessions. But those will happen, and when we see patterns begin to emerge, we should move from random events at the whim of others into deliberate events on a schedule. That way we can be honest and accountable with ourselves about where our time is being spent.

- **Use the calendar.** Those scheduled events belong in a calendar. Every person on the team needs to know they can access us using that calendar. It's always a good idea to ask people to put an agenda in the event, to make sure we get everything covered and keep the meeting on track. The calendar can also be used for us to just block off some time to do routine tasks that otherwise might fall by the wayside. This includes writing blog posts, fundraising, or coding our expenses.

- **Have shorter meetings.** Once upon a time, we just booked an hour for meetings and then half an hour. Now it can be as short as 15 minutes, just to touch base on something. But there's no reason to only have shorter meetings. Sometimes it's good to have plenty of time to unpack more complicated topics. Sometimes we want to keep an hour on the books, and if the meeting wraps in 15 minutes, we get 45 minutes of time to focus on other tasks.

- **Batch process tasks.** For example, rather than log in to pay expense reports as they come up, do it on Fridays at 11. Just block off half an hour on the calendar and turn off notifications or alerts for that app or web app. This allows us to look out for repetitive tasks and put them in a block on the schedule. It also lets us more easily move that task to someone else. And if we finish early, maybe we can go get ice cream!

- **Change the device notifications.** This will allow us to concentrate better in general. A good way to think about this is to try and go a week looking at the notification settings for every single app we get a notification for. This forces a deliberate acceptance of those notifications rather than just continuing to roll with whatever the default settings were. And if we need to truly concentrate, we should give ourselves permission to just turn notifications off for a bit.

- **Retreat from the open floor plan.** The open floor plan is great. It gives us a feeling of togetherness and makes for a more intimate work environment. But it can be problematic as it also invites constant interruptions and distractions. We can reserve an office conference room for a few hours or head home to work from there when we need to get more into a flow state that can't be achieved by the constant distractions. This gives us time to really focus on getting the work that needs to be done completed in a timely fashion.

- **Rethink every phone app.** Do the social media apps make us happy or just cause stress? The games? We should be able to have fun and stay in touch with friends. There are distractions we create for ourselves that create joy in our lives, and we need to embrace those. But look out for when they step over that line and become stressful. And consider removing various apps from different devices, starting with the phone.

We just can't be productive if we surround ourselves with distractions. These are a start, but it's really about discipline. How well can we resist the temptation to jump in and save the day, to get embroiled in yet another political discussion on Facebook, to wage war about some esoteric technical minutiae on Twitter, to install the latest game all our friends are talking about, or to get validation by constantly solving every issue?

The earlier in the life of an organization that we can cut down on distractions, the easier it will be to do so. This means finding the balance between our own willpower and the needs of the organization. Moving distractions to proactive blocks of time allows us to actually enjoy the process of doing them and maybe even think of a better mousetrap for each. This has actually been the inspiration for many a second company!

Great Skills for Founders

There are several skills a founder will need. The traditional list might include verbs like *inspire, invigorate*, and *persevere*. Those are important for sure. Since football coaches have the market cornered on inspiration, we opt for a little more of a servant leadership approach.

Lead Through Service

An organization, almost by definition, has more than one person. A key goal for leaders in any organization is to keep people inspired. No matter what kind of organization, inspiration leads to higher retention and just a better place to work. There are plenty of ways we can inspire teams, and there are entire books on doing so. The traditional approaches involve identifying motivators, giving accolades, providing training, communicating more, doing what we say we're going to do, identifying a focus on the purpose, defining the mission, and dozens of other techniques. Inspiring our teams keeps people engaged, inspired, and active and creates a great sense of community that is infectious to our customers.

There are also demotivators. These negatively impact the team. There are obvious behaviors that just don't work, like when a boss yells at a subordinate. Strong emotional responses can make people feel unsafe in the office or like they can't be themselves. We also have to serve those on our team more than ourselves. Employees will feel like we don't value them if we tolerate poor behavior from others in order to avoid conflict. No amount of inspiration can overcome some negative behaviors. Some of this is easy to identify; other actions aren't. In general, put employees first and always try to see things from their perspective.

One demotivator is when we are possessive about our organization. We want to go from "I" or "my" when we describe a company or team to "we" or "our"—and that includes the activities of the organization or the organization's members. Think about it this way: try not to say "my staff" or "my team" but instead say "our team," because "our" is inclusive, whereas "my" is possessive. Saying "We work together" or "My colleague" versus "They work for me" or "My employee" models service, humility and respect for the other folks in the organization. We don't possess people that work at our organization, and we certainly don't possess our customers who are members of our larger community. Not everyone will get offended by this behavior. In fact, people in larger companies have likely not noticed it for years. But some will, and the larger the organization becomes, the more likely someone will be put off when we call them "ours."

Some may read this and think it's overly politically correct. Having gone through hyper-growth in companies as well as slow, continued growth, it's become apparent that we need to be as inclusive as we can be. The more people there are, the more these things matter, and the more every voice needs to be heard (even when it's harder to hear them through the noise). There's more value when those voices are heard. We also take on the success of others when we make the organization or team all about us, which it is not once we have others join the campaign. People want to be impactful and to be seen.

If we need to tell people the organization is ours, we should look inward at the insecurity that causes that behavior. We project a quiet, calm fortitude when we don't need to boast and when we are careful of how others feel. Ultimately, that wins the hearts and minds of the teams of people that choose to be with us—and they will want to help us get through some of the tough times bound to come our way when we truly share in their success.

The organization ultimately serves the customers, the staff, and the shareholders—and we serve the organization. Most functions in a company appear to be most productively executed when they are founder led. Founders sit in the chair of sales, marketing, engineering, etc. But just as the ranger never becomes a great druid, the functions can't reach their full potential. That often means each job takes longer to get a new type of result. Founders then have to shift our minds away from the expectations we have for how long each task takes in an organization as we no longer have telemetry into what the definition of done for a given task is. This comes up when we talk about when we were able to do all those jobs. We don't want to make the people who spend a third of their hours on this planet feel like their contributions are less than by doing a task that is their career.

Take Care of Ourselves

Everyone in an early-stage startup is constantly busy. We bounce between so many different roles, and that context switch means we can easily lose track of how much time we spend on the business. As we start to reopen offices and get back to normal (or find a new normal), there are a lot of new pressures we face. High turnover (e.g., during "the great resignation") further compounds the pressure.

We have what seems like thousands of things going on in life and work. We need to get sales and marketing nurtured. We must get that new feature committed. We have to raise money to keep the lights on. We need a better process to merge code. We have to... everything! On top of that, maybe the kids have to get picked up from school, we should visit our parents, or we should have dinner with friends after work. The list of responsibilities never seems to end.

We can easily forget to take care of ourselves. The signs appear differently for everyone. We get sick, perform poorly when fatigue sets in, or drop the ball for things we are normally great at. Sometimes we make ourselves busier because we did poorly at the things we took on. We can't always control the work-life balance in a startup. There are immutable pressures put on us by cofounders, investors, family, and friends. We must stay healthy, though. So what are some things we can do to stay well, both mentally and physically—and avoid that trap as we found our new company (think of this as character maintenance in a game)?

- **Rest.** It does no one any good if we get sick. That will happen if we go without sleep. Long-term fatigue can have devastating impacts on health, friendships, and family. Make sure to get plenty of sleep - get your long rest. Also don't brag about a lack of sleep—that sets an expectation that others will put themselves through the same unhealthy activities.

- **Track time.** There are courses, methodologies, books, apps, and systems to help people track time. We don't have to buy one, but that's always an option. We should pick something and stick to it. The lighter the data entry, the more likely we are to use it. A simple approach might be to create a Trello board or to use existing Outlook or Google calendars to block out time in our calendars for each task (even if they're tasks we do alone).

- **Exercise.** One of the easiest things to let go of is our exercise routine when we get busy. Maybe others see the time we spend at the gym as an indulgence, or maybe eight hours on a flight isn't conducive to a quick run. We can't let our bodies go without the exercise they need. Exercise gives us better self-esteem, makes us more resilient, and gives us time to let our brains relax.

- **Eat healthily.** Exercise is part of a healthy lifestyle. If we spend a lot of time in hotels or long days in the office, it's easy to get into bad eating habits. It's critical to eat well. We all need plenty of calories and a healthy mix of foods. Stay away from fast food and enjoy the art of cooking whenever possible.

- **Get help from others.** When we're spinning our wheels, we need to reach out to others for help. No one expects us to be perfect, so we can admit it when we aren't and accept help when we need it. Most actually trust us more when we're vulnerable from time to time. This might also include a coach or even a therapist to help us address some of the bigger issues that come up throughout the long and hard days.

- **Automate more.** If we have to touch a piece of paper or perform a manual task, we should search an app store to see if that task can be automated. If we have a bunch of apps that we have to manually move data between, look for whether or not we can automate that process as well. If we can't automate something, maybe we have our next startup idea.

- **Hire more people.** We can all get to a point where we just feel overworked all the time. If that goes on for too long, we need to bring in more humans. If we can't hire someone to help due to budgetary reasons, then we just have to try to do less because it will help no one if we burn ourselves and the people we have out.

- **Spend time with friends and hobbies.** It may seem silly to add more stuff to an overburdened calendar. We can't let the things we love slip too far. They often align well with career choices, and they give us joy, an important component in self-care. Maybe find a good DnD group.

- **Build a better mousetrap.** Is there waste in our schedule? Are there processes that, with a small tweak, would be more efficient? Can we remove steps without removing quality? Set a quarterly or monthly task to think about how we can do better at all the things.

- **Learn to say no.** Early on in our careers, we tend to say yes to way more things than we need to. As we progress and grow as people, there are a number of things that we no longer enjoy or benefit from. We still want to help our communities and stay involved in a lot of things, but ultimately, we must learn to say no here and there in order to maintain our own sanity.

If we're so busy that we can't take care of ourselves, we have to stop being so busy. Otherwise, we will burn out. We hope one or more of these tips help to spark an idea that saves time (or money) or maybe just makes a life just a teeny bit better, something every person deserves.

Be a Great Listener

A great listener is almost empathic. They can make anyone feel important and like they have something worth hearing. Everyone does have something we need to hear, and if we're talking to them, they deserve to be important until the conversation is over. We might not agree with everything they have to say, but they deserve a voice and if we give them our attention, they deserve our undivided attention.

Great listeners are rewarded for their time. Not only will people want to talk to us more, but we will understand them and their perspectives more deeply. And that knowledge and connection is invaluable as a human. Some things to keep in mind in order to be a more attentive listener include the following:

- **Understand intent.** This allows us to maintain a mental outline of the other person's message. It's okay to not have intent when we're with friends. But in meetings we should understand what the other person needs us to hear and understand (although we can leave room to expand the scope or unpack a specific item when needed).

- **Face the speaker.** This shows that we're listening and paying attention. We will hear better if we see the person actually move their lips, and it's a sign of respectful engagement in the conversation.

- **Lean in.** This could be literal, but also maintain an open posture. Think of having an open heart that's pointed at the speaker. When we lean in, maintain that open posture. The person we're talking to will thank us, as will our backs.

- **Make eye contact.** Don't let a desire to be intentional about the previous items distract from the speaker. Make sure to keep eye contact. Scan the room and make note of each other person, but always return the eyes to the speaker.

- **Don't touch the electronics.** This includes our smart watch, phone, and laptop. Not only is it a sign of respect but it also keeps us from missing an important point. This includes other distractions as well as electronics, but they're the ones that get in the way the most. If necessary, take notes on paper. We're big fans of old fashioned notebooks at the meeting table (and the gaming table).

- **Don't interrupt.** We don't need to propose solutions. We should listen and take in a full argument or topic before we respond. This helps with relationships, friends, and family as well. Instead, wait until the speaker has stopped for a few seconds (or as many as five) to interject. And when we do talk, we should start with questions to clarify any points.

- **Clarify.** Frame questions in a way that shows we listened. Use follow-up questions to make sure we understand what's being said and then expand on topics. Be deliberate and respectful when seeking clarity.

- **Paraphrase.** A great way to ask questions is to paraphrase the topic first. This shows we heard and understood what we were told and helps eliminate misunderstandings.

- **Pay attention to body language.** A lot goes unsaid. Nonverbal cues are important to notice with some people. Does the person talking slump when they talk about something specific? If so, it's best to dig into why. Do their eyes break contact when they talk about the future? Do they always have an itch when they talk financials? These are all things we can't notice if we don't face them and take note not only of the words they use but also of how they act.

- **Stay open-minded.** Don't be critical or judgmental. However, once an argument has been made, explain the position and, if need be, be firm with a result.

- **Words matter.** Listen to the speaker's words. Specific choices of what words to use can very much change the narrative.

- **Leave our own stories out.** We all have little stories, or parables, we like to tell. We can always add them later, but let's not take the conversation away from the speaker until it opens up to us.

- **Consider the speaker's perspective.** Think about how we might interpret something before saying it (and how the other party might). This type of compassion not only helps us become more intimate with the other party but also helps us better understand a message and leads to further enrichment in our own lives.

- **Care.** Again, we all have value. Our perspectives, our capabilities, and our intuitions matter. Understanding everything we can about someone else is one of the finest things we can do every day. And making them feel valued just makes our own lives better.

There are times we just can't help but pipe up or get distracted. These are sometimes involuntary reactions. It's just human nature. As we mature, hopefully we can have more rewarding and thoughtful interactions with friends, family, coworkers, customers, and partners. We deserve that, just as they do. What we learn from these types of interactions increases our understanding of so many subjects and on so many levels, even if it isn't something we're instantly drawn to.

Engage More People in Meetings

As technology founders, we often deal with famously introverted and brilliant people who have voices that we need to hear. However, many don't speak up very often. One technique to bring more people into conversations is to look for topics that they are experts on and ask them what they think specifically. Sometimes, we get a short response—and we can then ask for them to elaborate a little further. We might just get a treasure trove of information.

To get introverts (or anyone else) to contribute more in meetings, we want to make them more comfortable in the meeting. That might mean we look for things that interest them. Even introverts like discussing topics they're passionate about when we give them the floor in a kind way. We shouldn't ask people to speak because they haven't said much. Sometimes they don't have any thoughts, and it can kill the momentum of a great meeting. Instead, as leaders, we should keep our eyes and minds open and actively seek those diverse voices in the room.

As with a gamemaster, it's often on the meeting organizer to ensure everyone in a meeting gets an equal opportunity to speak. We can use timers and take notes of who's speaking, but the inorganic nature there leads to a meeting (or series of meetings) feeling inauthentic. We should try and keep a mental tally of who's been quiet. Do this by looking around the room at people's faces while others are talking. Whose body language shows they aren't listening to the speaker, but simply waiting for their turn to speak? Who has been silent so far but is leaning in, taking notes, or nodding along? That's where the golden insights are hidden!

Political Capital

Political capital is often thought of as a currency of incidence and trust that can be deployed or lost to achieve a given goal. We use political capital in various aspects of our lives. Let's focus on how we accumulate and deploy political capital internally at a startup. Many founders think once we hire people, they just do what we want. We sometimes get frustrated that the people we worked so hard to bring on end up with their own thoughts of how to do their jobs. Free will can be annoying that way. Our teams also need to be inspired here and there.

Many of us learned early in our careers that we could ride our horse in front of our troops and get them fired up any old time we want to. We think of this as the *Braveheart* method of getting what we need out of teams. Not everyone is a charismatic paladin, though. The first time we put on that makeup and bang our shield, we can usually get our team to do pretty much anything we want. We're sharing our passion with others. The second time, it becomes a little less effective on its own. The third, a little less than that. And so it goes, especially as we have more people to distribute little parts of our passion to.

Scalable Inspiration Is Perspiration

Inspiration is great, and we can use it to authentically drive performance. But it's often used alone when it needs to be coupled with something that benefits both the inspirer and those being inspired. This is not just quid pro quo. We drive behaviors when we let our teams know what we expect out of them and what, beyond a regular old paycheck, they can then expect from us in return. Paychecks are easy to come by for the skills most valued by startups. Inspiration and the passion derived from that inspiration are not.

To be authentic, we define our mission, values, and goals. We compensate our coworkers appropriately and do so in a clear manner. That kind of clarity allows us to find who share our ideals and sometimes our path to make the world a better place. It's the kind of political capital that lasts.

The people we surround ourselves with deserve the autonomy to make the choice to remain in our orbit. When we are clear with our teams, they trust us and can authentically believe in our mission. And that trust becomes a currency. If we choose to build more than we deploy, our culture is better. As we trust our teams more, we need to deploy political capital rather than issue orders. Just a few of the thousands of ways to build political capital in a startup include the following:

- Talk through issues and listen and respect the opinions of others.

- Promote the accomplishments of our team members over our own.

- Issue feedback, including the hard feedback, consistently and in a timely fashion.

- Win sales with customers.

- Get great PR for the organization.

These are great ways to run a role-playing game, and if they sound like good ways to run a company, that's because they are. Turns out that solid fundamentals are the best and most scalable ways to inspire our teams and get them to do what we suggest or need. Sometimes we even get better suggestions than our own. Notice that none of this directly benefits the founder. We could have said to go and get great PR for the founder rather than the company—but we didn't. In a smaller organization, political capital can be as much about inspiration as it is about wielding power. Let's make sure to inspire, and so motivate, and do as little to demotivate as possible.

How Political Capital Changes As We Grow

Political capital takes on another form as we grow: we have to influence other parts of our organization. There is certainly still a need for inspiration, but the larger any organization becomes, the more politics play a part, especially if we are successful. Founders are often insulated from this type of drama, but downstream the leaders we hire are not.

We want to foster a culture where the best idea wins; however, it's a fallacy to believe that any organization can avoid politics. When a leader or a team does a favor for another team, that then increases their political capital. This isn't to say we should do things we don't agree with just to win points from another party, nor should we want to see teams enforce some quid pro quo mandate. We still want to listen and talk through issues and lead by example to allow the best ideas to move forward whenever possible. But sometimes we have to realize we don't have all the answers and give space for others.

Political capital becomes what allows us to get stuff done. Some will treat this as a game. Heads are often buried in the sand as though it isn't necessary. But while it rarely appears as a value or part of a culture, there is always some form of political capital to be aware of. And the more it exists on the surface, the easier it is to understand.

Eventually political capital ends the tenure of many a great founder in a successful company, but it doesn't have to. It's on each of us to decide if we want to play that game. Part of the reward of success is the ability to control our own destiny and decide if we want to replace ourselves with a leader who can accept the political machinations of a growing company or if we want to continue on with that. Another part of success is the ability to decide where we want the company to be.

Office Space or the Internet?

Sometimes an adventuring party is based out of a specific place, like a keep or a city. Traditional companies lived in a physical location (or multiple physical locations according to how many employees there were). Many startups begin without a home base to return to in order to heal up—after all, rangers are typically fine sleeping out in the open. As we grow, many startups think they need an office or a home base. If we haven't had an office but we see that as a part of the next phase of development of the organization, let's just stop and think about it before we proceed. Let's also think a second time as well, because it's probably a larger step than most of us think we're about to take.

This conversation goes a little like many conversations we might have had with our parents while adolescents. Are we ready? Are we mature enough? Do we understand the consequences of our actions? Are we rushing into things?

If companies grow, an office will become necessary at some point. Offices are expensive, and people have to want to go there. If there's one thing our recent extended time at home has taught us, it's that some organizations can work from home just fine. In fact, many of our coworkers preferred working from home even before this moment.

There are certainly times we need an office. Here are some signs that mean it's time to think about office space:

- **We host customers at our facilities.** Anyone with a retail front or that has a lot of customers come in for meetings, trainings, sales demos, or interviews is going to need an office space. This is usually industry specific.

- **We have expensive equipment.** We need to get everyone access to research equipment and have the equipment insured properly, which might be difficult if we're storing it in our leaky basements.

- **We physically need to be together to be collaborative.**
  This isn't likely, but some teams can only really work
  together in person.

- **It's too disruptive at home.** If we can't set boundaries
  in a home, like when there are small children around,
  then that's understandable. If we just need to get out of
  the house, then we just need to get out of the house.

That's a pretty short list. And sometimes the needs can be satisfied at
a coworking space. Coworking spaces cover a lot of the needs a startup
has, and they're great places to make contacts as well. Most have a lot of
options for how often the space can be used, how much space, and how
dedicated the space we have is. But we should get an office space if the
costs of the coworking space outweigh the costs of rent and any tenant
improvements required to lease a dedicated location.

There are a number of reasons people want a space that are the wrong
reasons to enter a long-term lease too early. Let's go through some of the
common ones we hear and through some reasons to avoid the expense:

- *Image*: Office space doesn't make us any more
  legitimate. Making sound financial decisions makes us
  legitimate. Building great products makes us legitimate,
  not a snazzy new office.

- *Culture*: The company culture is not built in an office
  space but in the way we communicate and how we
  treat people. Effective leaders can steer a culture in a
  direction if they are thoughtful and deliberate toward
  a clear mission and a vision for the future and live the
  company values early. Use the savings on a lease to do
  team outings or introduce other perks.

- *Location doesn't matter*: It's important to remember that a home address, coworking space address, or postal box is an acceptable address to use up to a point. In cases where we do get space, the ease of access is far more important than if we are located in a coveted neighborhood. Also consider driving distance for the existing staff.

- *Tenant improvements*: Most offices don't come ready to move into. Build-outs can be expensive but don't need to be fancy. A coat of paint, some desks, chairs, tables for meetings, new gear for conferencing, phones, Internet connections, stocking food, coffee, and, of course, the ping-pong table all add up. They can easily put us in debt at a time when capital should be expended judiciously.

- *Taxes*: The office location could impact tax rates. Discuss that with a tax professional before factoring it into a decision.

- *Insurance*: The office will certainly impact insurance. Get a quote for that prior to signing any contracts and factor that into the financial impact as well.

- *Offices are more social*: It's easier to have a conversation with someone over Slack than to get up and walk to a coworker's desk. It's more efficient. If we're pair programming, it's easier to sit all day in a Zoom or Hangout while we work with someone and far more intimate.

- *Keeping a sales team together*: We don't need sellers in one room. Being on the phone all day can get loud. Calling customers with engineers trying to write code can be distracting. Having sellers hear everyone else can be disruptive.

- *Allow for flexible work arrangements*: We might think that our team won't show up on time if they're not coming to an office. We might assume that people in support need to check in for a shift and log on so we can see when they become an agent easily. There are a lot of scenarios that could work for teams if we think outside of what we've always done. Further, we should be more concerned about performance than hours for knowledge workers. If there's a performance problem, it's equally as likely that would happen at home or in a coworking space as it is in a physical office.

- *Valuations*: The company will not be more valuable based on the office space unless it's owned by the organization *and* it's considered an asset rather than a liability (or enough of the loan is satisfied so the office could be sold for more than the current debt). Contracts for rental spaces are a liability and may be considered a liability in a potential acquisition.

- *Equipment costs*: Centralized infrastructure is typically more expensive than SaaS solutions we might use for home users. For example, if we buy everyone a cheap printer, we're likely to spend less than if we purchase (or more likely lease) a big printer. And that same economy of scale is true for most things. Office equipment is typically harder to manage as well.

- *Long-term thinking*: An office will be required at some point, but it doesn't immediately make us a better long-term company. Instead, a plan that spans a year or three gives us additional capital to have more flexibility in our longer-term models.

- *People, not place*: Some might argue that talent requires space. However, the kind of talent we want requires vision and leadership, which should be more easily sourced if we aren't confined to a given physical space.

- *WFH is viable*: One thing a pandemic proved is that people can, in fact, work efficiently from home.

Some organizations need an office. If we need to physically be together, get inspired, and be social, then absolutely, get a standard coworking space (preferably without a long-term contract). If traditional office space is cheaper, fully loaded, than what we're spending on a coworking space, then it might be time to get an office. Just do so deliberately and with all the factors we've covered considered. It's more important to have a healthy startup than one with an office.

The Evolution of the Founder and CEO Roles
Accelerate with Intent

This chapter took us from the company as a side hustle to the company as a full-time job, and now it's time to move on to faster inorganic growth. In other words, we can bootstrap an organization for years—but when we take on additional capital to fund growth, we want to really understand why we're doing that (beyond a little extra money here and there).

The "why" should be just about money. Here's some math: if we sell a company we own half of for $100, then we walk away with $50—but if we sell that same company for $200 that we've further diluted our equity in and sold half of in order to accelerate growth, then we might still end up with $50. We've maybe spent an extra year of our life to do so, which comes at an opportunity cost for future investments (given the value of money over time) and endeavors. We've built something twice as valuable, but given that life is all about the journey, the process can be worth more than the cash we end up with (always take experience points over gold pieces).

Now let's say that we've instead evaluated exactly what we can do with that money and have a plan. Because we're more focused, we can sell the shares in the company for less, move faster, and ultimately end up with more cash from the transaction. This is why the investment community has stages of development for companies and different investors that bring different tools to the table get involved at each stage. We cover that more as the book goes through the journey, but for now, keep in mind that when we accelerate growth, we want to do so with intent.

The Cost to Grow Faster (Equity)

Our adventuring party starts out on a simple mission that turns out on a much grander quest. Until we have the larger vision, we might just be a "small business," but once we have the vision, we're a "startup"!

The party can get further, faster, if they buy equipment early. The equipment would be purchased on loan from a shop or from a wealthy financier in exchange for half the booty. A "small business" is a company in a traditional industry that uses conventional financing (or no financing) to get started. All "startups" begin life as a small business, but the way we think of startups today, they're looking to do something innovative, and since most innovations are deterministic, they're looking to accelerate growth before someone else goes to market with a similar idea. We leverage equity from outside investors who put money into the idea, and the perceived capabilities of the organization to execute on the idea, in exchange for a part of the company. By contrast, the traditional small business can often move slower but with a less dilutive means of capitalization.

On a larger scale, the stock market allows us to invest capital into an organization and receive quarterly dividends. We share in the success of the companies we choose to invest in. Prices increase during bull markets, or times when the market is doing well, and investors can grow wealth when they invest in growth stocks rather than those we seek to harvest dividends from. The investment community serves a much larger purpose in society than just wealth generation. At the heart of it, investment in companies funds innovative business models, technological advances, and people. We make the world better when it's done right.

Venture capital works similarly. The money funds innovation and helps get products to markets faster, helps innovative companies outgrow entrenched players in industries, and establishes market share. Startups are riskier to invest in than public markets or organizations like banks that provide traditional financing, so the rewards can be greater. This is one of the reasons that most venture capital firms invest in several companies in order to increase the odds they receive a return. For example, Y Combinator can boast early investments into Airbnb, DoorDash, Gusto, Reddit, Stripe, Dropbox, Instacart, Twitch, Coinbase, and Zapier. But it took investing in thousands of companies to get there.

Nearly every company who makes it to massive success, becomes a household name, and goes public will give up equity in exchange for the funds and know-how to accelerate growth. Not all, but many. Startups also often provide equity to board members who can help the cause in other ways, such as contacts, publicity, and business advice. That last part is important because most of us don't know how to scale sales, marketing, and finance teams. Those who do know often know their value and will only get involved for equity.

We do need to be careful whom we accept money from and how. As we take on "rounds" of equity, we start to give up varying degrees of control in a company. Others own a percentage and can exercise those rights in meaningful ways. Investors who aren't a great match for a startup can create a combative work experience, so make sure to get on the same page with what the investor wants out of the investment (other than to make ten times their investment tomorrow).

In a bull economy where interest rates are low, there are a lot of places to put investment money to work. Founders with a shipping product that's netting a positive return will find it easy to raise funds to accelerate growth. Those who have released products that haven't found a good fit in the market, or have incomplete products, may have to work harder, but there's still a good chance some investors will take a risk. Many begin with friends and family and then move on to the "angel" community and then venture capital beyond that. We cover raising money further in Chapter 17 because, in the beginning, we typically find that we prefer startups raise money from the most telling and least dilutive source around: customers who pay them for a product. Doing so proves the hypothesis that the innovation the founders are supporting with a company is valid. For that, we'll need a product and to improve our capabilities with product design and product management, which we cover in further detail in Chapter 4.

Conclusion

This chapter has focused on some of the philosophies and the mechanics behind how we start a new company. We looked at doing so while employed (as a side hustle) and some of the philosophies to keep in mind. We covered how many organizations grow. Keep in mind that every journey is different and every outcome can be different, like the same module from a *Dungeons and Dragons* game run with two different groups or two different dungeon masters.

When we started our first companies, the only background in sales and finance that we had were courses from college or selling candy bars at fundraisers. Once we had cash, we needed to account for it to fund the operations of a company. One of the biggest mistakes we made was to write our own accounting software to manage our AP and AR. That allowed us to bend accounting rules and not follow generally acceptable accounting principles (GAAPs). Luckily our accountant quickly forced us to migrate to a standard accounting system and then guided us through moving to an accrual-based accounting system. We then coded our receipts when we entered them and did a lot more that saved us time and heartache later.

A great business advisor is probably the single best thing a company can have to stay on track. That often begins when we have someone help us file those articles of corporation when founding the company. But if we choose the right advisor, they might be with us for the rest of our lives.

At this point in the book, we have a mission, we have values, and we have a company that's been established in support of an innovation (our adventuring party's quest). Now, it's time to sharpen our focus on the product we will take to market in order to achieve our mission.

CHAPTER 4

Product

The brave ranger sets out across the wilderness in search of a problem to solve. But great problems can't be solved alone, even by one so well versed in multiple disciplines. Maybe the ranger can write code but needs better coders around to help out. Maybe the ranger is solid at business and sales but needs others to help build products. Then now that it's identified, the problem must be solved. And so, the ranger assembles an adventuring party to amplify the good the ranger can accomplish.

A party, or team, makes adventuring and problem-solving much more fun. It's pretty boring to play a role-playing game by ourselves. Not only that, but being able to convince others to join our party validates the mission. As we move from a solo adventure to an adventuring party, the distribution of work naturally goes from one or two people doing everything to something very different. Now the founder has to plan and understand what the organization does and how best to package products in such a way that what we do helps people solve real problems.

Founders may perform this exploratory role until the organization hits 20, 50, or even 100 people. But whether it's the founder or someone brought in to be the next ranger, it's still a discipline that we can cultivate by learning from giants in the industry.

The fun part of creating companies for many is that exploratory research. Product management is a field that begins there and is the function in an organization that plans, organizes, and manages the products the organization makes at each stage of the product lifecycle.

© Charles Edge, Chip Pearson, Amy Larson Pearson 2023
C. Edge et al., *The Startup Players Handbook*,
https://doi.org/10.1007/978-1-4842-9315-7_4

The Evolution of Product Management in Startups

In an organization of one, it's pretty clear who's in charge of product management—the same person in charge of every single other job. As we round the corner to our third or fourth hire, our advisors often start talking about being more deliberate about the product lifecycle and roadmaps. This chapter lays out what product management is and the mechanics that go into building those roadmaps and so the products.

A roadmap was a rough plan to add some features to our product "soon" when we were a sole proprietor. With each new hire, it becomes a document that lays out what we will build and when. The level of detail in roadmaps varies across organizations and domains of expertise. They help us keep everyone productive and understand how each person's work is dependent on that of others. As we grow, the roadmap grows in complexity as well. Perhaps it starts as a simple list taped above our desk and then moves to a Trello (`www.trello.com`) board or a Miro (`https://miro.com`) board. That helps everyone on the team collaborate on the roadmap. But then it becomes more like a Gantt chart, invariably finding its way first into a tool like Airtable and then something larger like Jira, or maybe we even spring for a purpose-built road-mapping tool like Aha! (`www.aha.io`).

Now we're thinking about product management as a discipline. Founders often still have the responsibility for the product for the first few years. As the organization grows, we need to continually work at developing great product managers. That flow typically follows along a path similar to the following:

- *Level 1*: Plan out a tool or service. Here we are framing up the problem we want our solution to solve, how we want to go about developing the tool, and whom the tool is for. We don't want to be dogmatic, but we do want to start getting organized. This helps us get funding, plan what a release will look like, and take a deep look at what the gap is between where we are and where we want to be. That can often take shape in the form of a business plan. But keep in mind we're rangers; we aren't likely to build an army as a lone ranger.

- *Level 2*: We have a lot of feature requests coming in, but can't build everything at once. Now we need to break the work up into smaller chunks. This is where we talk to potential customers to decide what features we need to build and when. We want to make sure our market is clearly defined, our problems are well thought out, we understand what a marketing or customer acquisition strategy looks like, etc. In short, we want clear and concise requirements to develop and implement a roadmap and launch plan.

- *Level 3*: Once we have more developers, we want to work well with them. For many small teams (like a pair of cofounders), this might mean making sure we are in alignment on a technical stack, the developer is writing code that satisfies customer requirements, and we develop a cadence for checking in with potential customers to validate that what we are building looks and feels like something that solves a problem for them. This is also when we can start planning a pricing strategy, developing a marketing site based on the work we did earlier, and codifying a few user personas.

- *Level 4*: It's time to launch. To do that, we need pricing to validate product-market fit and have a documented roadmap that achieves our strategy. We also want to get tracking information into products that tells us what our customers are using and how (if appropriate). Much of the marketing and sales readiness can be found in those chapters, but product management can now move into won/lost calls, expanding use cases, supporting events, and product marketing for lead generation.

- *Level 5*: As the company acquires customers, our party grows to include people from other disciplines: support, sales, marketing, accounting, etc. Product management might still be up to a founder, but it's time to start thinking about which aspects we want to let a new ranger take on and which we want to keep. It might not be time to hire, but the presentations, demos, calls, program analysis, and roadmap maintenance will keep a founder from running the other parts of the company, which are equally as important. As we grow, some of these tasks can fall on others, and we need to look around the organization for others who might be a great product manager in training.

- *Level 6*: We should hire a dedicated product manager by the time we fill up a second Scrum team. Some founders might choose to hire someone to run the company and focus on product instead. Others bring in thought leaders in their industry as subject matter experts to drive the product forward. Others might hire people with strong backgrounds in product. Rarely will we find someone who can do all of these. Additionally, we don't want to overpromise what the position entails. Chances are that as we grow the product management discipline, the people we hire early will get new bosses and should know that up front.

- *Level 7*: Once we hit around 50–100 people on staff, it's time to think about a product position in senior leadership. We want to grow the product organization, not just a role—and we want them to be able to guide the product free of corporate politics. We are pumping out sales and marketing collateral, cleaning up both buyer and user personas, analyzing how our products are used, doing special events, and sitting on calls with large or strategic customers. Founders or CEOs can't do it all and need to find and build a team we can trust. Further, we need to speak the same language as those we hire, so we'll want everyone to be certified in a framework like the Pragmatic Marketing Product Management framework.

After level 7 our adventuring party resembles an army. Product management translates that vision into the tactics the army uses to win battles for customers. We might have teams in other organizations doing things like channel training/support or event management, presentations, webinars, etc. We now have technical debt, no matter how modern our product is. Here, product management often becomes more about task management in tools like Jira and less about developing ideas for bold new products. But it doesn't have to. Try and keep the team excited to change the world for as long as possible; complacency kills momentum.

But again, as we scale product management, there are some incredible resources at our disposal. Once upon a time, we would've said to head on over to the PMI website (www.pmi.org/certifications) and choose a certificate program. That's still a valid choice, but today there are many free solutions or programs out there such as those for product management on Coursera (www.coursera.org).

It's good to research what's in the various programs early, as that gives us knowledge to build our early processes in a way that they fit into a future rubric more seamlessly. But we all have tons of competing priorities early in the development of these programs. So let's skip all that for now and look at some lean project management tasks to embrace while growing and sitting in all the other chairs a founder has to sit in.

Analyze Market Conditions

How can we make the world a better place? "Analyzing market conditions" is a pretty fancy way of saying that we should understand what our customers might want out of our products, how many potential customers we might get for each of those features we build, and what's changing in the market. It all starts with a big idea, a problem we want to solve.

Think of a young ranger, just leaving their hometown, walking the wilderness in search of an adventure. They see something that needs to change. Maybe it's an orc attacking a farm or a farmer with crops that won't grow. They find a way to protect the village or make their new friends more productive. But did they solve a problem that's already been solved? Is the problem unique to that one person and therefore unprofitable to build a solution that helps others? We only know if we analyze the market we will be playing in.

This involves a number of activities, including but not limited to the following:

- Talk to as many people about the problem as can be found—especially those who own budgets and can pay for tools to solve the problem.

- Interview customers, potential customers, or others in similar roles to get feedback on efforts and new features of products.

- Identify potential competitors and keep an eye on what the competition is doing.

- Define product specifications for new features and products so developers know how to build them.

- Conduct won/lost calls with customers we win and those we don't win.

- Define personas or fictional characters that indicate segments of customers we build products for.

- Plan how we will address technical debt or areas where the product needs to be improved that aren't included in a feature.

- Develop and work on branding for products.

- Create a customer advisory board (CAB), which is a group of strategic customers whom we can get feedback from.

- Produce marketing assets to document new features and options, thereby further defining how we might solve (or are solving) a given market problem.

That last piece is often known as *product marketing* and is included in product management in some organizations or in a dedicated marketing department in others. The role of product marketing is to promote the product, often providing product information and updates to internal sellers, podcasts, social media outlets, and even prospects and customers.

Solve a Problem

The first goal of every company is to solve a problem. Rangers are excellent at finding problems. The narrower the problem set, the more we can focus on doing one thing and doing it really well, before we move on to the next adjacent problem to solve.

People have told us what we should be doing for a long time, and each has a different perspective. Product management means putting the ego aside and listening. Sometimes we hear the same things repeatedly. Sometimes we hear something once and think, "Hell yeah, I should be doing that." But much of finding new opportunities to build companies and expanding the reach of a company will come from a gut instinct. That instinct causes us to start a company that probably helps solve some problem we see in the world. Once we see opportunities and find a way to solve the problem, we then need to prove the hypothesis that we have come up with.

We need to do our best to validate that instinct. There's no way to know for sure whether something is a good idea, but we still need to try. There are clear indications and warning signs. Let's look at some:

- There is a huge gap in the market. Either no one is actually doing something, or those who are doing something are incompetent or miss the mark.

- Incumbents fail to deliver. Be careful not to fast follow (er, copy) too closely. We don't win wars by fighting an opponent's strategy. But sometimes we can see that a vendor has a good idea and that they're just not solving a problem in a way that makes sense.

- Nearly every customer, friend, or survey respondent (when doing market research) says that we should sell them a given product or service. If we hear something weekly, then we should take notice. We might not have to build a huge solution as we might be able to solve a problem quickly and easily, allowing us to rethink how an industry or category should work.

- Prices for a given category of products haven't changed (and the currency hasn't modernized) in 10–20 years. Those are ripe for disruption, if only regarding pricing (but usually in delivery and options in products as well).

- All companies in a given space have built feature on top of feature on top of feature until products are all really complicated and require a ton of customization and training. These spaces need down-market solutions.

- We recommend a given product or service a lot (and people buy it). If we say "but..." every time, analyze the costs and how to remove the "but...." and see if people are willing to use something different.

- We refer large amounts of business to someone and don't make enough (or any) of a markup or commission on it. Resellers are a great route to market for new companies, and if the commission isn't good, then others will be frustrated as well.

- An established product is constantly breaking. When customers get frustrated, they start looking for something new!

- We can prove the market is growing faster than the capacity of incumbents. If incumbents can meet market need, then think twice; if not, there might be opportunity for a new vendor to disrupt how a category is delivered.

Think through all of this and look for as many quantifiable ways to disprove an idea and each feature. The ways to prove something is a good idea will just come naturally. Once we've identified some initiatives and taken a step back to decide if they're a good idea, now ask again: What problem are we trying to solve? Take another step back and think about it even more critically. Why might we fail? What could go wrong? Let's look at that next.

Why Initiatives Fail

There is no greater momentum killer than a failed initiative (although complacency comes close). Backtracking can cloud all other lines of business, lead to employee turnover, and kill the growth rate if we aren't careful. Let's ask these questions before and after any successful or failed initiatives:

- How large is the total addressable market? Obviously, we need to identify the potential business and revenue impact from any new venture. We have to keep our blinders on for a bit and only look at a constrained set of customers that we can actually connect with meaningfully (we call these beachheads). We might find that the market is much larger than anyone thought. We might also find that there are a very small number of potential customers or that the market is saturated with other vendors and the needs of customers are being met (we call this a red ocean). This research also helps drive how we consider pricing beyond comparing the price with the current rates, so uncovers potential conflicts in what currency we think of when doing basic math.

106

- What will we need to accomplish to address the needs of the target market? We might have to hire new employees, create a small team that focuses on each potential new market, write apps or web interfaces, and much more. Understand the work required to prototype new features, products, or services, as well as to take the product to market and so sell products at scale. Once we understand the required investment, we can make the best decision whether or not to move forward.

- Are we able to sell the new service or product into different markets? Sellers might begin with one market but have to learn to sell into other markets because some demographics might be harder to reach than we think. We need to win at least a customer but might not have any leads beyond that. It's critical to find different go-to-market strategies and invest further resources when we find success in each route to those markets.

- Do we have buy-in from potential staff or investors? If we did the research previously and have solid arguments for either proceeding or stopping, then getting buy-in from others should be simple—if it's a good idea. Don't push too hard or let charisma get in the way of honest feedback. Instead, look for confirmation of market conditions that are perfect for a new organization to come in and disrupt existing vendors or create entirely new categories.

- What will the opportunity cost be? Do we have to go it alone? If we aren't getting buy-in even though we think we have a good business plan, we have to ask why. Is

this worth dipping into savings or personally backed
financing to fund a new adventure (and adventuring
party)? Take risks but only after using personal
networks and every ounce of logic and reason.

Additionally, make sure not to get blindsided by legal obligations.
These can keep us from building a product or entering a market. Most
notably these come up in employment agreements. Discuss any potential
conflicts with a former employer that might come up with an attorney
before proceeding. For example, if a founder has been a reseller for a
number of software vendors, then there's a chance that there's a contract
somewhere not to compete with them in the same industry they're in for a
certain number of years. Make sure to seek legal advice to avoid breaching
any contracts.

There are other reasons startups or initiatives at companies fail.
Sometimes we just don't have a good product fit with a given market or
never find a good message or offer that matches the market. Sometimes it's
just bad timing, or we went after enterprise customers without considering
how much runway SOC2 compliance would take. And sometimes we can't
lock in the right pricing, which we'll cover in the next section.

Pricing

Pricing is one of the easiest or hardest aspects of any startup. Let's unpack
that for a bit. We make a hypothesis that there's a need in a market that is
unfulfilled, and the guess is right. We sell a bunch. Life is good. That's easy.
Other times, we make a guess. The guess is high, and we don't manage
to gain traction selling products. We go out of business. Life is bad. Or we
don't charge enough to pay our bills but sell a lot of products only to find
out we can't ever get profitable. It would be the same for an adventuring
party trying to charge too much gold to chase off a kobold or not charging
enough to take out a dragon terrorizing a village.

Here's the thing about pricing: things are worth what people are willing to pay for them. We start with a guess and then need to validate that guess, preferably before we take a product to market.

There are a number of ways to price a good or service. One is based on a perceived value. Maybe we make a comparison with how much money a potential customer will save by purchasing something we have to sell. Maybe we randomly make up a number. Maybe we use comparisons with other vendors in the same or adjacent spaces. Products that are easier to use are perceived to do less and so often cost less. Products that appeal to smaller markets end up needing to cost more. Again, things are worth what people are willing to pay for them. But if we charge too little, successful go-to-market campaigns put us out of business, and if we charge too much, we end up alienating potential customers.

How much do we charge for our products? This is one of the hardest questions in all of software. We could write an entire book on the topic and still have every page be worthless. But we could also provide a bit of guidance based on the experiences of our own adventuring parties and those we've worked with in the past. We'll start with the absolute minimum we need to charge, based on margins.

Understand Margins

The simplest approach to pricing is to understand what it costs to deliver a good or service and then mark the cost up to an acceptable percentage. The revenue minus the cost is the margin, or put differently, the margin is how much money we make minus how much we spend.

Margins can easily be oversimplified. There's a prevailing wisdom that software is infinitely scalable. In other words if we hire two developers and pay $5,000 in hosting per month, then that's our cost. And yet as we grow, we have to create more features, and we need more support and more training. As our user base grows, we need more scalable infrastructure (even cloud infrastructure), which tends to be inexpensive until it becomes really, really expensive. Defects in software cost more to fix if they escape our testing environment, so we have to spend more and likely hire dedicated staff to more thoroughly test as we grow.

We might have to give up part of our income as well. We need more routes to market, so we give up 20–30% to a sales channel in order to incentivize others to sell our products. Our own sellers might need to be compensated on top of that so they don't compete with the channel. The amount we spend to negotiate larger contracts increases our cost to sell products, as does responding to requests to show it's compliant with various state or private regulations.

These are just some of the reasons a founder or two and some code can undercut large, entrenched organizations. But as we hire people, build teams, develop management structures, and go through all the other motions required to build and scale a company to support an innovative idea, we invariably raise our own costs to develop software—and not just by a little bit.

Meanwhile, if we're successful, we've potentially altered the pricing expectations for an entire market. Now if we need to raise prices, we can't because we're the low-cost alternative or because we undervalued the service we developed. It's easy to look at the pricing for entrenched incumbents in a market and assume we can do better; it's hard to follow through.

This is where a good business plan comes into the mix and where an advisor or mentor can help us work out a lot of the cost structures. Aggressive pricing actually makes more sense for some, because we make up a lower margin in volume and can develop a plan to build a "Pro" tier later. There is no magic bullet in pricing, but the adventuring party should ask around the village to figure out what they're willing to pay for our services.

Obviously real customers won't pay us in gold pieces. So let's look at how we think of pricing for various products in the form of what currency they will pay us in.

Define a Currency

Before any meaningful conversation about pricing can be had, we first need to understand currency. *Currency* is a term generally used to describe a system of money for a given country. Companies, like governments, establish a currency, usually based on the industry we are working in.

The total things we sell multiplied by the currency is our revenue, which should be above our costs described in the previous section. Once we understand our cost, we need to move downstream and figure out how much income each unit we bill generates in aggregate. Some of the ways we can bill customers include

- *Per item*: This is the original unit of commerce. Dating back past the ancient Romans, we as humans have been bartering and buying items for tens of thousands of years. When we go to the grocery store, we buy a dozen eggs or a pound of sausage. The currency of those who trade in those commodities makes up how much money they make per unit they sell. As various business models have emerged, we continue to innovate billing models.

- *Hours*: Most consulting firms start by selling hours. We might then move into a per-event model in the form of charging by the project; but our calculus used in bidding goes right back to trying to determine how long a project will take, add-in materials and related costs, and then margin. The net result is that our mental model still revolves around hours as a currency. This is common with pivoting into a managed service provider as well, where we ask how many hours we spent managing each device (on average). We still have conversations about hours, even though customers are thinking more about device-based pricing.

- *Per event*: Certain organizations have always billed based on an event. Businesses that clean homes, provide wedding services, and other event-driven packages often charge in this way. The currency is the event. This then translates to other types of events as well. This usually includes those same industries who have gone online, such as online conferences or webinar services. Many software startups who focus on back-end technology used similar models to help other companies build products faster. Think Stripe, Amazon Lambda, IFTTT, Avalara, and Zapier. Here, we pay per transaction—or a percentage of a transaction—every time we call their service.

- *Per device*: Software is installed on computers. In fact, that was once the most common way to distribute software: people went to brick-and-mortar stores and bought a box. The software evolved so the original media was no longer required. Most software companies that predate the advent of the SaaS business model still have this concept of per device. Over time, certain licenses allowed for installing software on "up to three" computers or through an app store, but the calculus used to derive pricing was still all about the number of devices. In meetings we talked about "devices" and how we wanted to grow those. This freed product and technical teams from talking about revenue and obfuscated that a bit. That mindset makes revenue the responsibility of sales teams to convert the number of devices into dollars.

- *Per impression*: This is more for display advertising but can work for other industries as well. Here, maybe we extend to per click or per transaction, but that is often considered as a percentage of impressions.

Note   The OEM (or Original Equipment Manufacturer) licensing model is also based on this per-device concept, but the license is usually not transferable from the equipment that a license came bundled with.

- *Per user*: People don't use one device any longer. That's why the number of companies where a user is the dominant currency has grown. This didn't begin with Google Apps or Salesforce, but their emergence and the subsequent validation of the SaaS model led to looking at revenue through the lens of users. Terms like *Average Revenue Per User*, or ARPU, began to arise, and the DNA of many an organization evolved to a user-centric worldview. These per-user licenses are typically sold as subscriptions, which accountants love as they can recognize the revenue more ratably (more on that later in the book), and any organization that began with a per-device currency typically still does the mental model to convert a user into a device, especially if there is also a per-device pricing model still in existence.

- *Freemium*: Many a per-user model realized the cost to provide a limited, free version of a product is negligible and allows for a simpler sales motion and streamlined marketing. To give customers a "trial" means a longer sales process in most cases, and freemium products require better useability in the onboarding experience (or when a customer signs up), which is more elegant programming, but ultimately costs less than more sellers. Services like Skype (now a part of Microsoft) gave certain features for free and charged for premium options. This has now become commonplace with a percentage of customers "converting" into higher tiers of services or adding more users. Because conversions tie into revenue goals, either paying customers or conversions become the currency.

- *In-app purchasing*: In addition to freemium, another currency that has emerged is the in-app purchase. We published an article called "The Immutable Laws of Game Mechanics in a Microtransaction-Based Economy" at www.bootstrappers.mn and since then watched many apps go from a per-user model to freemium and now to where each feature of the app is just another in-app purchase. Most investors want to see predictable monthly recurring revenue (MRR), and so we see many investors push that per-user model, which can leverage the in-app subscription options from the Google and Apple app stores. Those seem like in-app models but are usually freemium.

- *Bundles*: Bundles are usually an extension of one of the previous models. When a company expands their portfolio (the products and services they sell), they want to offer an incentive to buy multiple items. That usually comes in the form of tightly coupled integrations and a pricing discount. These bundles are then unpacked by our finance teams, and revenue is recognized to each, so we can track the profitability of products independently (and let that guide where we want to invest our resources). Here we might see multiple currencies obfuscated and products, subscriptions, and service hours bundled into one line item.

- *Credits*: Credits are one of the more challenging to teach sales teams. Here, rather than (or in addition to) bundles, we attempt to develop a baseline lowest common denominator and sell items on a credit system. Customers can buy credits and then apply them to different products in our portfolio. This can ease budgeting and allow our internal finance teams to accrue revenue to each product more easily; however, credits can put up a wall where customers have to understand our credit system in order to be able to do business with us—and they often become frustrated when credits expire because too many were purchased or when they have to buy additional credits. However, when done properly, credits allow customers to pick and choose products or bundles of items they'll actually use.

Every organization has a KPI, or key performance indicator, connected to revenue. The currency is usually used to set that KPI and establishes a common term that everyone in an organization can use to describe what the organization sees as its top goal. Many organizations have several metrics they look at to gauge performance over the years: things like employee retention, bugs fixed, features implemented, top-line revenue, EBITDA, and market share. But there is always a single KPI that validates that an organization is growing and is constant across time and products, which is defined by how many of the products were sold. How we speak about those products is our currency.

One form of innovation is to change the currency for an entire industry. For every company that does something truly unique, there's a potential innovation to the status quo of the currency for that industry. If there are no organizations in an industry that are trying to disrupt the monetization model, there will be. Before they became a streaming platform, Netflix changed the currency from per rental (or per event) to a monthly per-user subscription model, which they still use today. Before Google AdWords, the currency for online advertising was banner impressions.

The list of companies who streamline operations and layer on a different pricing model is endless. Every company should routinely look to innovate workflows and delivery but also look at the model being used. And we should think about whether another model (or a hybrid of models) might improve the experience of the customer, the go-to-market strategies, or profitability or any other aspect of a business. If we don't, it's guaranteed that someone will.

Finally, one of the hardest changes to manage in an organization is currency. Our meetings become infused with how to sell and help more users and gain more devices, more conversions, and more credits. We want to provide more value to customers, who need to understand our currency and any changes happening if we're to retain and grow those customers. But our own teams have to embrace those changes before that can happen. That's true in the beginning when we're just starting to develop a billing model, and it becomes even more true as we grow—especially as we establish a portfolio of products that sometimes have their own currencies.

Freemium

There have been products that were temporarily free about as long as there has been a software industry. We call this a *trial period*. The past decade or so has seen the proliferation of software and hosted services that are delivered over the Internet, allowing for new models to emerge. One of those is freemium, which usually comes in the form of an unlimited - but not fully featured - free trial.

Freemium is a model where a buyer gets a certain number of whatever the currency of the organization is (as defined in the previous section) for free. This may be accompanied by an unlimited number during a trial phase but is more often just two to twenty of something with no pricing, and then a nominal number of dollars per month per user, device, credit, etc.

As with trials, the freemium model reduces the friction in the buying process. Buyers should be able to create an account quickly and begin using the product. This means we want an excellent onboarding process, which is shorthand for creating an account and getting productive with a product. Given the rise in popularity of this model, customers have become familiar with buying freemium services - so much so that organizations that market products to consumer or prosumer users should have an explicit reason *not* to implement a freemium model if they don't. If that reason is that the onboarding process isn't good enough, fix the onboarding process.

Freemium models also work upmarket. Enterprise products often have more complicated requirements and thus are more complicated themselves. However, with user experience and user experience research, any product can be wrangled to work well for customers down-market using a freemium model. Having said this, software that needs to be recompiled or has extremely custom workflows is typically incompatible with this approach.

We'll get to marketing in a bit, but buyers have become accustomed to a call to action (CTA) (or a next task we lay out in our sales and marketing journey) that involves creating an account—a process that now just takes a couple of minutes with most sites. And the transactions are usually small, monthly amounts compared with the days when people bought perpetual licenses. This helps smooth revenue out on a timeline—revenue that can immediately be earned or accrued (which frees our capital up to be spent). Whether we're using a freemium model or a perpetual license model, the next step is to figure out how much it should cost.

Pricing and Return on Investment

Return on investment, or ROI, is a simple formula that takes the payout from an investment and subtracts the cost to show what the value of that investment was. When an organization sells a dozen apples for $6 that was purchased for $1, the ROI is $5. Pretty simple when discussing simple business models. But what about when we're working in the SaaS space to enable faster product cycles, increase uptime, or enhance decision making? How much is going to market faster worth?

The math starts to get a bit more synthetic if we aren't careful. And yet, we want to show customers what kind of return they're getting for the investment they make in our product! We can do this in several ways, covered in the following sections.

Cost Savings

ROI is short for the return on investment, or how much a customer makes or saves from purchasing a product. The simplest way to show ROI is to show how money was saved. Many tools on the market today are single purposed, yet it can be challenging to calculate the ROI.

Let's say we have a product management tool that, when we survey real customers, shows our customers spend an average of two or fewer sprints (or a fixed period of software development) per year to get the same amount of work done. If they know a sprint costs $75,000, then we saved them $150,000, and if they spent $15,000 with our organization, then there was a 10:1 ROI just from reduced development costs.

This is a standard time-saving model that can be applied to calculate ROI. We could also try to layer in work done on products that fail to reach a product-market fit, time lost in context switching, or (and this is one of the hardest) the value of better decision making or beating competitors to market by shipping features faster. However, the more variables, the less obvious the ROI model, which causes the savvier business leaders to call the model into question.

Revenue

Solutions that increase revenues can easily be analyzed as well. Let's say we buy an ad for $1,000 that produces $10,000 in sales. That's a ten times return. Do that all day every day, add in a little word of mouth, and no sales team will be enough to handle all the inbound orders potential customers will want to make.

There are a few challenges with that model. The first is attribution. Did the customer first encounter us at a trade show and we used a multi-touch attribution model—if so, the ad that produced the conversion only receives $4,000 worth of ROI? Or are there weights to factor in as well? Another challenge when showing an increase in sales is that each organization might look at what a "sale" is differently. Average contract value, cost to acquire a customer, retention, and many other factors come in. However, sticking with that top-line revenue number makes for simple math, and simple is easy to communicate.

There are a few ways to obtain data used to calculate ROI. We can survey existing or potential customers. This might also uncover factors or options we hadn't yet considered. We can also look at trade information like statistics that are publicly available. One of the best ways to get started is to just go sit with some customers and ask them to show you how they do something. And bring a stopwatch.

Margins

Some tools can impact revenue *and* save costs. For example, the ad described earlier might convert through a web form, thus bypassing sellers with commission structures. Here, we speed up the sales process and save on paying out commissions. Or taking the order online might allow for fulfillment to bypass other processes (e.g., demos, compliance paperwork, etc.) or resellers, saving commission and the cost to run those other processes. When we look at the ROI as it relates to margins, we're trying to isolate cost savings and streamline an approach that can have knock-on effects down the line.

Let's look at an example of leveraging automation to streamline product delivery. Let's say we built a portal to book services for a yoga studio. We take 5% of the services' revenues. The buyers no longer need to have a team booking services and can provide immediate feedback to customers, resulting in 10% less lost bookings. The net result might be a 20% increase in sales by guiding new customers through our portal, savings of $53,000 per year in labor, and an additional 10% conversion rate. Then we might want to layer in other variables like ease of advertising, more walk-ins, etc. We can end up with so many variables that numbers get inflated, so again we have to be careful not to build too many formulas and keep the numbers simple.

Reach

Reach usually refers to how many people see an ad or some piece of content. Free services (or at least free to end users) can be a bit different. This is more of a social networking, marketing, or blogging statistic and often ad- or data-supported. Here, we look at the reach of users multiplied by the new usage they bring and the value the organization derives (usually how many people buy a product based on the increased reach the content has). Once we understand that full financial impact, we can subtract the development cost for an ROI.

An example might be a guerrilla marketing tactic that drives 10,000 users to our site. The ad impressions for those 10,000 people might be worth $50,000 and the cost to implement $5,000—thus a 10:1 ROI.

The value to the business we mentioned is often referred to in LTV, or lifetime value, and also requires quantifying conversions, renewals, or subscriptions. Increasing the value or percentage of any of those has an ongoing financial impact that can be layered into an ROI model.

Telemetry and Agility

Telemetry is the ability to see information or trends so we can better analyze our situation and make better decisions. Move business processes into a database and we can see where each order or task is, check how long a task took, and allow customers to see the status. Move inventory into a database and customers can see what our supply is and buy more quickly. The impact of such telemetry into business processes, inventory, tasks, or whatever makes a given line of business special can be revolutionary. When orchestrated properly, we suddenly have insight into where everything is at any given moment.

Our understanding through that instant telemetry leads to more agile and accurate decision making. We can reduce the risk of decisions, get products to market faster, find new ways to save costs, grow revenues by making data-driven decisions, increase margins by finding inefficiencies, develop better models, and the list goes on. That makes us more agile as an organization.

Knowledge is power. Just understanding more about our organizations then becomes one of the best ways to get more from what we spend on software. And yet, this also becomes one of the hardest places to calculate ROI because there are so many different outcomes. The only real way to get at this information reliably is to survey or interview an appropriate sample size of customers.

Surveys

The real power of truly great SaaS offerings is a blended ROI across the board. Layer on the power of platforms, the fact that the SaaS world is becoming more and more a series of interconnected object-oriented endpoints, and we have robust capabilities for only a few dollars a month in many cases.

This is also where we start to potentially get eye rolls when we over-synthesize our numbers. Yet better decisions through increased telemetry are what drive the modern economy. Organizations understand this, or they don't. For those who don't, sometimes we have to meet them where they are at in order to show them the path forward.

One of the easiest ways to prove the impact a tool can have is to simply ask those who use our solution how it benefits them. This blend of qualitative and quantitative research often means surveys. A simple Google Form, SurveyMonkey, or another tool helps affirm what we think we know about our software and helps us make our solutions more meaningful for those who rely on us and prove to potential customers how we can transform their bottom line.

Most surveys should be simple. We can always go back and ask customers more questions once we start to understand our own impact. We don't want to be overly prescriptive, but we want something meaningful to bring to potential customers. For example, if we're specifically looking to put ROI in our marketing, we might present customers with questions that get at cost savings or revenue multipliers.

Case Studies

Sometimes it helps to dig a little deeper into the quantitative analysis of some statistics surrounding cost savings. Other times we want to put a name and face to those in order to make them more relatable. Our personas (which we'll get to later in the book) are a great place to start the conversation about which customers are great candidates for a case study. Then, along with any survey results, we can look for a customer who's willing to go on record as a customer and write a case study about their experiences with the product.

Case studies should identify a problem or opportunity for improvement. That means understanding where a customer is, where we can get them, and the gap between those two points—as well as how our tool helps close that gap. The case study (especially for smaller companies) is more than the data. It's a story that comes with characters (who often resemble our personas). We should spend time explaining the issues and concepts and why they matter to the customers in the story and then dig into a little data. But the customer needs to agree to share that data, so be up front with the intent and make sure the customer is willing and allowed by their employer to do so.

Note   For those new to writing case studies, there are tons of templates online to help get started. Just do a quick search for case study templates and select one that best fits the target audience!

There are about as many ways to calculate ROI as there are products. And there are tons of ways to show the findings to potential customers. As with many things in software, simplicity is the best path. The closer we can get to an ROI metric that is easy to understand and can be displayed on a website (e.g., an ROI calculator at myawesomedomain.com/roi), the better we'll be able to distribute, share, and convert based on our efforts.

To repeat, don't overthink or complicate the algorithm used to derive an ROI number. If a potential customer finds that the numbers don't work, then it'll be difficult to win their trust again in the future!

Competitive Analysis

Every organization has competition. We might go into an industry where there are well-entrenched vendors. When market conditions or legislation evolves, we might find a new paradigm that results in a gold rush of companies to establish themselves as a market leader. Even if the product is blue sky and completely unique, there's competition for budget, and it's usually only a matter of time before a product in an adjacent industry moves slightly into our lane. Other times we might not be competitors but might compete for budget dollars.

We have a thesis. We have values and a mission. So do our competitors. We don't want to copy our competitors—but we should be aware of them and make sure to include their moves in our plans. Most companies have licensing agreements that restrict the use of their products from competitors, so here are some ways to track developments. Even if they don't, we should probably keep out of their products.

Still, competitors might help us uncover insights and ideas that help entire industries. Here are some ways to keep an eye on competitors, without crossing that boundary of logging into their products:

- *Google images*: Customers often post screens from inside competitor products. We have our own design language and heavily researched UX workflows, but how competitors visualize complex themes can help us better understand problem spaces we help address. Sometimes we even find product documentation posted in public places.

- *Websites*: The pages on a competitor's website tell us what markets they're going after, how they're going after them, and sometimes the names of customers they're winning. This can also surface case studies, publicly available webinars, etc. When visiting a website, use ToR or some other tool that helps us stay anonymous as many of us use retargeting or have snippets of code that feed information back into a CRM, and while we're not doing anything wrong by viewing publicly available content, it's best to have our browsing habits kept private.

- *View the page source*: The page source tells us a lot about how competitors see the world. Pay attention to headers and any areas where there are words or phrases that aren't displayed on the screen.

- *Google*: It's easy to search for terms in our industry and see who else is buying ads or getting organic search results. Don't click the ads or engage in anti-competitive behavior, but be aware of them.

- *Keyword analyzers*: Keywords are out there for anyone to see. It's part of the money machine that is Google. We can use tools like Google's Auction Insights (https://support.google.com/google-ads/answer/2579754?hl=en), similarweb.com, Semrush, Ahrefs, KeywordSpy, Ubersuggest, QuickSprout, Siteliner, SpyFu, SE Ranking, and iSpionage to see what competitors for keywords (which aren't always the same as competitors in our space) are doing to drive traffic and how. Note: There are a few in here because they can come and go.

- *Sales calls*: Any time a competitor comes up on a sales call, that should be logged into our CRM, and we should have reports that tell us how frequently they come up (and report on how often we win or lose deals to them).

- *Battlecards*: These are short (typically a page) cheat sheets that sellers can use to understand how to position products when competitors come up. These should include talking points we see as making our product more valuable, but we should also train sellers never to use them to bad-mouth a competitor. We can simply speak to our strengths without drawing the correlation to the weaknesses of a competitor.

- *Crayon.co*: As we scale, it's hard to consistently train teams what not to do. Crayon is a SaaS company that does many of the preceding ways for us. They aggregate information, generate battlecards, surface insights from competitive analysis, and help us do so safely. Also check out Klue or ask.suzy.com, and search for any other products that have come out since we wrote this section to see if there are new alternatives. Outsourcing this allows us to instruct our own teams not to creep on the competition and might just provide better insights than we can get on our own.

We have a strategy and shouldn't over-index on what the competition is doing. But no strategy is complete in isolation. We should have an ethical boundary and never cross it, so monitor the competition within reason. This is a great impetus to revisit and work from our company's alignment and values. It's best to keep competitive analysis to a small team within the organization and let our teams know that when competitors come up, they simply say things like how happy we are that competitors are doing well as it helps validate the market.

Again, no strategy is complete in isolation—but we should also not obsess about what competitors are doing. After all, we have our own company to run and don't need too many distractions!

The Value

Now that we've looked at margins, competitors, and currency, we should know a range of what we can charge for a given product. Pricing is like throwing darts. All the research makes the bullseye bigger for us, but we can still get it wrong.

The next thing we like to do is pick a price and play through how we came to that price with a potential customer. We don't want to be defensive, but we do want to validate that our price makes sense and that we're looking at the world the same way they are. There are a lot of ways to take that conversation, but one of the best is to focus on what value the product brings.

The value conversation often begins with the currency we defined. We'll add the concept that most software exists to do one of the following:

- Increase efficiency. This might be the efficiency of a human performing an action and so automating repetitive actions. This also might be trapping for errors so we don't have to redo work done or putting something on autopilot like our thermostat in a home automation workflow and thus saving money by increasing the energy efficiency of a home. Often the value-based pricing here is based on how much time or money is saved. The optimal point is when we can go beyond savings and start discussing things like improving the time to market for a product, which can have an incalculable value.

- Provide telemetry. These products provide insight into how an organization or personal life is doing based on data and help us aggregate and improve our understanding of things. Apps might show us the balance of all of our financial accounts or the fan speed on our computers or the progress of a package being delivered, to name a few. We can then enrich that data with other data, like seeing the package on a map. These simple examples have much further-reaching impacts when we can suddenly manage global supply chains using a fraction of the effort than was required just 20 years ago.

- Enhance safety and provide peace of mind. This is often an important combination of the first two. A security system in our home is often about telemetry into what is going on around the home physically and automating alerts. Antivirus software is about telemetry to a file or persistent threat on a device and alerting or taking automated action when discovered. Here, the value is peace of mind. The market comparisons usually begin with brick-and-mortar or real-world equivalents, and so it's no surprise that early antivirus tooling came with pricing similar to what a subscription to a security service for a home cost at the time.

- Improve the quality of life of users. This might be scene control in a home automation setup, including automated shades so we don't have to get up to go open or close the shades ourselves. There's not a ton of productivity gain, but many love it (and can then spend saved time watching Netflix or working). Or software and services can put us in touch with friends on a social network (although some might argue those reduce rather than improve the quality of life). This also includes making things more accessible for those with an injury or disability.

Think of these as being akin to the six simple machines in engineering. Each simple machine passes energy to the next, amplifying the impact into a complex machine. A wheel and axle on a fishing pole drives a pulley that uses the pole as a lever. Suddenly with a very small action, a fly is able to be cast an incredible distance. Automatically combining telemetry into something a potential customer needs to track like how much is in a bank account with an action to improve efficiency like alerting when a transaction occurs or coding an expense based on a machine learning algorithm has a value that can then be sold: we save people two days a week. Layer in fraud detection and an alert when an account dips below a defined threshold, and now there's peace of mind, making the tool worth a multiple higher than if it was only saving time.

The peace of mind concept can be applied to a large organization or to the actual impact we have on the well-being of those who use our products, and as each of the aspects we compared to those six simple machines combines with the next, the impact and thus value increase with each—unless we make the product too complicated to use or fail to achieve an actual market fit. No matter how we price a product (even if it's free), if it doesn't do what people need, no one will use it.

Market and Market Fit

We have a product (or an idea for a product) that does some stuff. We have a market we think the product will appeal to. We have a price and can explain the value the product brings to the table. But markets are fickle, and we often think they want something (maybe because they told us) that they then prove not to.

The term *market* goes back to the Latin *mercari*, and it's easy to imagine early marketers yelling to the crowds to buy grapes, olives, or iron rations to make a long journey in a role-playing game. Those are simple market fits: people like grapes. If we price the grapes correctly and describe them in ways that Bacchus would swoon over, people will buy the grapes, and if they like the taste, the merchant has proven a product market fit and will return to sell more grapes.

Then came the industrial revolution and the desire to put everything on an assembly line. Just one problem. If we put a product that no one likes on that assembly line, then no one will buy it. Product designers, whether for textiles, automobiles, Brillo pads, or software, then test prototypes in the market before we develop an automation to create a product. No need to build the assembly line if we don't know the product will sell. This is one reason the software industry is irreverent toward "waterfall" approaches where we build a big plan and then proceed, in favor of more "Agile" approaches (more on Agile later).

This is because software gets more complex in a few ways. When we build features, sometimes we get various aspects "for free" or find existing code or a framework or API (Application Programming Interface). These help us do more faster. Or we realize we can get 90% of what's desired with 5% of the time but that other 10% will take years. Or the product designers or managers have wildly underestimated the time to develop a feature. Or there's technical debt in an area of the product that keeps us from building something quickly. We need to prototype, test, and research before we build things In doing so, we build what people want, we understand what is required, and can pivot when needed.

Product-market fit then is when we develop a product that the market wants. Product-market fit is found a lot of different ways. One might be to build a product and put it in the market. This works sometimes. Another might be to develop a wireframe using tools like Sketch, Adobe XD, Figma, UXPin, InVision Freehand, Justinmind, Mockplus, or even traditional graphic design tools like Photoshop or InDesign. There are also Miro boards and other options.

Some of the tools we use to prototype require specific skillsets, or we have to learn as much as it would take to build something as it would take to learn how to build the product in a programming language like Swift,

Go, or even Java. However, the ability to mock up a tool and show a high-fidelity (or functioning) mockup to real humans before we build all the logic or back-end services allows us to test the market for feature sets that make a product compelling and validate a price point, which is crucial to developing a business model. Mockups allow us to punt building all the logic to a later stage of the software development process.

We recommend checking out all the tools we mentioned previously and thinking about the following attributes of each when deciding to use one:

- *We like the tool*: This is important. Some tools are built in ways not everyone will like or find intuitive. We are all different and come with our own ways we like to work, so it's important to pick something we like (and we can always move to another tool later).

- *Fidelity*: As our understanding of the mockup tools matures, we want to be able to make them more high-fidelity, which is UX speak for making them as responsive as they would be in the app or web app we build.

- *UI kits*: We want to be able to build our own UI component libraries (or libraries for various languages that can easily be imported into projects) and maybe import those from other designers. This saves a lot of time and helps create realistic mockups fast.

- *Export options*: More high-fidelity mockup tooling can export code. This might be CSS or even a basic app. Usually these have plenty of cruft, and sometimes it's not useable, but it's great to have the option.

- *Feedback*: We want people on our teams or potential customers or even actual customers to give us feedback for the mockups we build. Some of the tools have built-in collaboration options.

We can then build a mockup and go to the local coffee shop and give out gift cards (or wherever potential customers might be) to get feedback on what we build before we write a single line of code. This is part of a field of study called UX research. Additionally, there are services like UserTesting and UserZoom where we can scale this up and put our product in front of dozens if not hundreds of people to test. While UX research as a field is often brought to later-stage companies, it is important to understand the basics and bring the development of the discipline in earlier as it can help reduce development time even in smaller projects by helping us avoid building features customers don't want or building them in ways that don't resonate with users. We'll go deeper into aspects of UX research later in the chapter.

Surveys and other tools also help us validate prices. There are a few different ways to measure product fit. But as with writing a book or designing an awesome role-playing adventure, we want to keep the motivations and needs of our potential customers in mind. One way to do so is to build archetypes of those users, and so we'll begin our quest for product-market fit with personas.

Personas

A persona is an archetype of a group of users whose characteristics represent those of a larger group of users. Consider the physically weak mage of the party who avoids taking hits during battle or the lawful paladin who cannot break a vow or avoid combat. Characteristics like these can translate to how we document and think about customers and potential customers. Rather than templates for character sheets, we make personas.

Characteristics we put in those personas can include jobs, attitudes, backgrounds, behavior patterns, skills, goals, and even details like where they typically work.

We often begin a persona with a template with information about who a persona is and fill in that template based on users we think of as typical of those that use a given product or service. We might even include real quotes from those people. When possible it's also best to survey customers (or potential customers) to see where our qualitative analysis of the people we serve matches with a quantitative analysis.

The persona is an important aspect of creating, designing, marketing, and selling. In fact, in some organizations, each of those functions might use a different persona tailored to their needs. Next, let's create one that can be used for multiple use cases, a common step in a small team.

Parts of a Persona

Personas can be as simple as an index card or as complex as a full-on dossier of a user. Therefore, they can have a lot of components. We'll start with some basic insights into motivations. Here, it's important to define why the user might want to use our product. This guides conversations and helps define patterns, choose design patterns, and define whether they would buy a product that solves a given problem (and if they would). Let's start with some basic questions that define the persona in the context of our product:

- **Who is the user?** Feel free to include the average age, where they live, and what they do. For example, if our software targets advertising buyers from agencies, this might be "advertising buyer at a large agency."

- **What is their goal?** Here, we look at what their larger goals are, what task or job they need to accomplish, and how our product fits into their lives. The more

133

succinctly we define the problem they are trying to solve, the better. For example, our ad buyer might be looking to "show customer ROI from ad purchases."

- **What keeps them from that goal?** This is where we look at the solution our product provides and how it makes their lives better. Don't forget software usually exists to make people more productive, increase their quality of life, and/or provide more telemetry into areas where people can gain insights from the wealth of information about their jobs (or with machine learning where we can provide insight on their behalf). For example, to continue with the ad buyer, they "hate spending hours per day entering ad responses and clicks into Excel."

If we can answer these questions, we can more effectively build products that help real people accomplish goals they define, rather than the ones we assume they have based on a limited sample size. In the preceding example, we might be able to develop a solution that pulls in data from multiple sources to help our ad buyer accomplish what once took hours per day in seconds. Now we just need to figure out what might keep them from buying the product once we've managed to save them so much time (and frustration), so they have more time to think about how to better leverage those ad dollars! To help us get there, we can develop a quick survey to send to ad buyers. Here are some example questions for this kind of buyer:

- What is your job title?

- How big is your company?

- How do you describe your job?

- On average, how much time do you spend every day on data entry?

- What tools do you use to help with the process today?

- What other tasks do you do with that data once you have it?

- What other tasks do you struggle with?

- What do you enjoy doing when you're not at work?

- How can we make our product better?

Notice that most of this information is qualitative in nature. Some quantitative demographic data helps us develop good products, but one of the most dangerous things we do with data is tell ourselves what we want to hear. What we're looking for in all of this is key insights that help us build better products, not insights that back up our views. That means looking for patterns in the feedback we're getting and where our vision or assessments match or diverge.

At this point, we've laid out the three most basic aspects of a persona and a few questions we can ask to gain more insight, validate our theories, and look for trends in pain points. We also know from plenty of online tools about what each position description makes on average and about how much time we can save them (if we're building productivity tooling), and so we can start to think about pricing. Value isn't just about saving time, so see the section on pricing for more aspects to consider. But in general, we have a good starting place to see trends and build a persona (or preferably three).

We'll base our first persona on a template found online (`https://krypted.com/uncategorized/simple-persona-template/`) and use it to take a few of the insights we gleaned and create a composite user out of them. Here's what we came up with so far:

User Persona

Jill Doe

About

Jill is an advertising executive that works for one of the largest advertising agencies in the US. She moved to San Francisco to take the job and lives in an apartment with two of her sorority sisters. She went to school for graphic design and hopes to get into selling art some day so moved to San Francisco, but hasn't found much time to work on her art. She thinks she might apply for her manager's job when she goes to work for a customer next month but isn't sure yet.

"I am obsessed with getting my customers the best ad buys"

Age	29
Title	Advertising Buyer
Location	San Francisco
Education	BA, University of Texas

Stylish   Analytical

Compassionate   Energetic

Favorite Tools

Google Analytics

Goals
- Spend more time
- Take the
- Do a bit of

Needs
- Spend more time
- Take the
- Do a bit of

Pain Points
- Constantly re-learning tools like Google Analytics as they change the features
- Spend hours every day manually pasting information between tools
- Cannot bring in others to help/collaborate on live documents

Personality

Introvert	Extrovert
Analytical	Creative
Busy	Open Schedule
Chaotic	Organized
Independent	Team Oriented

The personas help explain the people who use our products to new hires and help us build features that resonate with Jill or for the inevitable persona of (we hope) Jill as the boss. As we develop these, there are a few important things to keep in mind:

- Start small. There are tons of great persona templates out there (ones that put ours to shame). But start with a small amount of information and work more in later. After all, there's no shortage of other things to do! Keep in mind, unless a single sheet is meant for different teams with different goals (e.g., sales persona, marketing persona, etc.), then each should be one page or less, with plenty of white space.

- Base the persona on a real person. This allows us to use much more information about the people we're working with and appeal to them. The names can (and probably should) change, as can the photos.

- Don't over-index on a real human. The Pareto Principle is important here; we want to represent 80% of our users in a given cohort. We once created a persona called Josh, based on a real person named Josh. Every time we had a question about Josh, we'd go ask the real Josh. Later, we surveyed real users to confirm what Josh told us. Start with a real person and tweak it as we understand users better.

- Personas are more than demographics. One mistake made by a lot of people is to put a lot of quantifiable information about the customers we serve in personas. We should be looking to quantifiably measure how we help. But personas are deeper and more personal, thus the name.

- Don't make assumptions. We have to avoid our own bias. To do so, be open, listen, and ask simple and open-ended questions to real users. If we don't do this, we risk making mistakes when we had the chance to avoid them and, worse, doubling down on what we think we know. We must keep an open mind and look for insights, not just what we want to hear.

Ultimately, the personas we start with will likely end up in the garbage. As we hire people with "user experience" in their title, they'll likely scoff at our early examples. But it's important to start with these early in the life of a company. The preceding template could be filled out in less than ten minutes, and as three seems to be a great starting point for personas, making three over a nice glass of wine is a great way to spend a little time letting those creative juices flow.

Now that we understand personas, let's move into more UX research with keeping them, and other things we assume we know on the behalf of our users, up to date by continually updating them.

Continuous Discovery

Once upon a time, we tried to figure out what products and features we should develop on an annual basis. We set a strategy and went forward, coding like a machine for the year. In fact, we developed management rubrics to facilitate doing so. But after Marty Cagan wrote a blog post on Continuous Discovery in 2012, many product and UX teams started to think about a better model, if they weren't already.

This new continuous discovery model is about constantly looking for ways to improve products based on what customers actually need and using that to feed the product development process. This is the crux of continuous discovery. Many were experimenting, but now they had a label. And companies of all sizes can make use of the growing body of research on continuous discovery.

Organizations that embraced this philosophy reduced the time to market for products, reduced the cost of bringing those products to market, reduced the overall cyclomatic complexity of code, and avoided burning valuable development cycles with features customers didn't want or need. They often delighted users and created advocates, if not straight-up fans, while doing so.

Most of the organizations that embrace continuous discovery have larger product teams. But it's even more critical for startups, even when most startups don't know it exists (or don't realize they're doing it when they already are). Whether doing these processes or not, here are a few tips to get organizations on the right path to decide where development efforts are best placed:

- Identify where research (or discovery) can make a difference. This looks different for every organization, but a good place to start is to understand what teams are currently working on and how they plan that work. Root out the places where decisions are made with limited information. This is an opportunity to improve product decisions and develop plans grounded in what customers want or need to achieve.

- Place links to raw research findings in the task tracking system. Products like Jira (or maybe Trello in the early days) help align teams around what to design and build. Every startup should use a tool like this from day one, if only so future developers understand why we made early design decisions (the developers we hire to replace us are likely to be incredibly judgmental after spending years paying down the technical debt we left for them, but they have jobs based on our early work, so such is the cycle). It's simple to paste a link in Jira so teams who do the work can easily reference relevant findings. The easier we make information accessible, the more people will consume our data. So start with the processes and schedules used to plan development efforts and put information there in a timely manner that is consistent and helpful.

- Ask why. If it isn't clear why a decision was made or why a team is working on this and not that, ask why. These are likely opportunities where customer discovery could help people make better decisions or establish clearer priorities. The more teams can be held accountable to a strong rationale for their work, the more demand there will be for research.

- Include research in product delivery processes. Growing teams constantly redefine processes and shift the responsibilities and ownership over various parts of those processes. When this happens, it is an opportunity to help teams understand the value of continuous discovery and where research can make a difference.

- Use their words. Each industry has its own words. User research and product management are no different. Pay attention to the words that customers, other developers, product managers, marketing teams, and leaders use. Bring in vocabulary from support teams, the people on the front line who deliver training, and customers. It's easier to empathize when we can speak the same language, and that helps us be kinder when we teach our language to others. And remember, the term *continuous discovery* was derived from CI/CD (continuous integration and continuous delivery), so as we grow, UX teams may just find allies in those teams given the philosophical link.

- Design sprints. If the organization does design sprints, make sure that the people doing discovery work are included. Design sprints are a great opportunity for people with experience in customer discovery to help others develop skills and get comfortable with the discovery process themselves. Startups with a lot of developers benefit when there is an experienced designer or researcher around, if only for a couple of days, to help prototype a new product or idea with the least amount of work possible.

- Invite everyone in the organization to participate in research studies. When they see the research process and contribute as notetakers, they have more trust in and demand for research. Sellers and marketers can also benefit when they better understand how and why we build various options in products.

- Look for ways to impact the organization outside of just the product. Most research teams are responsible for a growing amount of discovery on their own product(s). However, apply the fundamentals of research to internal projects. This is a great way to socialize the value of research beyond the founder doing research, the dedicated researcher, or even a research team as we grow.

- Keep research materials and insights in a research repository. There is a lot of power in a centralized repository of notes that everyone has access to. This provides more knowledge about customers and their motivators—especially when development teams need to scale up fast and focus on tools for development rather than customers (all organizations go through this). It is equally important to give broad access to everyone in the company; great insights come from so many places within an organization. The more insights in the repository, the more likely others will find information that's impactful for them. This can begin as a collection of documents in Confluence or a tool like Airtable.

Every organization is different, so the mileage may vary. Be undaunted.

When existing insights from research aren't considered in the decision-making process, it can be a hard pill to swallow. Growing organizations have had to make judgement calls, and it can take time for people to embrace research done to make more well-informed, defensible decisions on strategy, direction, or features. Find opportunities for wins and grow the continuous discovery practice to have a greater and greater impact.

Build a Plan

We sure did do a lot of deep thinking and research about what to build so far. Or if we had a product, we extensively investigated what to add to the product in the preceding sections. Now for the easy part: the plan (and it's only easy because we did all this hard mental modeling and work already).

The project plan for a software startup often refers to a roadmap. When we first start out, the roadmap can be a simple Gantt chart, a Kanban board, or whatever else we want that's light and easy. It will get more complicated over time but keep it simple for as long as possible. We'll focus on using a third-party product because that gets us to fit into a paradigm laid out by the product managers at the product management software company.

Software tools provide us with access to decades of experience out of the box. This is just as true for product management tools as it is for tax software. Like a budding Picasso, once we've mastered using a third-party tool, we can go our own way if we still find it too simplistic, cumbersome, or restrictive. But chances are we'll benefit greatly from the experience of the developers and designers of these tools and the access we get to their insights through the lens of their tools.

As we grow, the product management discipline needs to level up to keep developers on task, avoid repeat or overlapping work, make sure tasks are appropriately prioritized, make sure items are delivered in an order that makes sense, and in general keep the voice of the customer (and needs) at the top of everyone's minds. When a product organization grows and we end up with an entire team dedicated to product management, the career professionals might look on the work of a founder as somewhat pedestrian. This is true for each discipline we hand off as we grow.

Even so, the future product organization and the current development organization benefit greatly from the roadmap we build. The roadmap and status of tasks (or groupings of tasks) should also be included in our board decks. However, it is usually best to avoid showing roadmaps to potential customers as it can cause customers to wait for that one feature and then the next and then the next.

In addition to a document with tasks, also document strategies. Earlier in the book we defined a mission. What are the strategies that get us to the next step to achieve our mission? This can be four to five items, and each can be a year's worth of a workstream. As founders we may sit in all the chairs in the beginning, but as we grow, some of the strategies may be handled by others. Therefore, it is important to connect the tasks with the strategies they support. And not all have to be technical. For example, if a product sells through value-added resellers (VARs), then we might have a strategy to expand the sales channel. A more technical example might be to "enrich customer data with machine learning to make our users more productive."

The Roadmap

Each strategy (and/or theme) should then be linked to one or more epics. Epics function to organize tasks and create dependencies and task groups (or a hierarchy) for developers. These are larger pieces of work that get split into several smaller tasks we call *user stories*. A given epic likely covers multiple sprints (increments of work) or teams. From the epic we then split the work up into small, logical blocks and add a customer story to each so that as we grow, developers understand why they're building what they're building.

The logical blocks, customer stories, and epics can then be tracked as a roadmap. The main solutions to look at for roadmaps include the following (and this list changes every now and then):

- Aha! (`www.aha.io`) is one of the most commonly used tools out there. Usually begins at $59/user per month but has a startup special worth checking out. This is the most mature tool that's specifically built with product management in mind, especially when it comes to the ability to integrate with other tools in a stack such as Jira, Teams, Slack, GitHub, Salesforce, and Zapier (from Zapier it can connect to most anything).

- Craft.io (`https://craft.io`) starts at $39/user per month and is built for larger teams. It also has a healthy set of similar integrations with other organizations. The guru features can help budding product management organizations future-proof some of their work if the discipline will be created in the near-term future.

- Productboard (`www.productboard.com/`) begins at $20/maker per month for a slimmed-down experience, but the price jumps as additional users come on. It doesn't have to be complicated to get started as the tool is pretty approachable.

- ProductPlan (`www.productplan.com/pricing/`) starts at $39/editor per month. As with Productboard, it's free for users who just view.

- Canny (`https://canny.io`) begins with customer feedback and analysis, which flows to a roadmap. A bit more of a workflow than some of the other tools but that might be perfect for some teams who get stuck when there are too many options to choose from.

- Monday.com, Infinity, ClickUp, Asana, Wrike, Zoho, and Airtable all have templates that are specifically built for roadmaps and other product management tasks.

The specific tech selected isn't all that important. Test everything and choose something that looks good but forces the team to document the components of a roadmap. Then it's just a matter of a cultural shift to get everyone to update the software while doing the work. From there we can track our progress in the form of reports that can be automated like burndown charts.

As mentioned, we want to clearly define our strategies and how those connect to the specific tasks performed. We can also build an ethos around how our strategies tie back into our overarching values defined earlier.

Product Management as a Discipline

Ultimately, founders make great product managers until we don't. Over time, if we are successful, the product management function becomes a central hub of any technology startup. It's where great ideas go to get refined and better and come to life or die a horrible death. There will come a time when we build features that go unused, when customer acquisition slows, when developers frequently complain about technical debt, when the look and feel of the product seems dated, and when customers don't think we listen. This is when it's time to bring in dedicated product management.

The first hire is important. We want someone who knows our target market. This might be a stakeholder or champion from a strategic customer. But we need to make sure that it's not just an evangelist but someone who has an eye on structured improvement, preferably someone with a background in both the subject matter and project or product management.

Some organizations elect to bring in a seasoned product manager. For this, consider someone with previous experience in product management at a similar type of company. Appendix 4 lays out ways the gaming industry has shifted over time. This is not exactly the mission, vision, or values—but instead laws that govern how we should monetize those types of businesses. For each product we have, consider the laws we want to implement around not just monetization, but privacy, go-to-market activities, and how we want products to look, feel, and evolve.

* The founders need to work closely with the person we hire to do this job (even beyond codifying laws about how we act based on our values). We shouldn't micro-manage our product team or make them feel like they aren't empowered. Instead, we should lean on them for experience and do everything we can to keep the new dynamics from getting political. There will always be a push and pull between the product manager who is constantly pushing for customer-facing improvements to the product and the technologists who deliver on those improvements. Add in the customers who need new features, and the job quickly becomes difficult. One simply cannot make everyone happy all the time. The more data-driven the next rounds of efforts, the easier the job becomes, and the easier it becomes to scale.

Build a Portfolio

At some point, people in our adventuring party might look to play other types of games, especially if more and more people join the party and we have a diverse set of backgrounds and constituents where the intersectionality of experiences happens to overlap with adjacent markets where we can monetize new products.

Do one thing and do it well. That's one of the best pieces of advice any startup gets. But there comes a time when we need to grow beyond that one thing. That might be ten years or six months into the life of a company. It may come as we saturate a given market or when we take a Series B investment. It can be pulled forward when we see an opportunistic way to expand use of our tools—but should always be done in the context of impact to core products. Perhaps the main campaign the party plays becomes a bit diluted, but we get to play with a lot of other characters now!

There are many motivations to move beyond one product and into a portfolio of two to dozens of products. Let's look at a few:

- A customer engages (and pays) us to create another product.

- We identify a market opportunity and a new way to delight users in that market.

- A company from an adjacent market develops a competitive offering so we move into their space as well.

- We see a company with complementary offerings we can acquire or merge with to provide additional value to customers.

- We see ways to leverage our technology to enhance other industries.

There are about as many other reasons as there are portfolios, but those are some of the most common. Before we start on any of them, we should be deliberate about what we're doing and identify whether there are better, more attractive opportunities that we haven't explored yet. We'll start this process by defining adjacencies. We should do this even if we think we have a new product we want to focus on, just to make sure we're spending our gold pieces on the best areas of the business.

An *adjacency* is a place that shares a border with us. When we're thinking about products, that could mean a shared market, a common buyer, feature overlap in products, or other similarities. The key is often with buyers and value. Do we have a similar value proposition? Can we provide more value with two products that can integrate? Are both products sold to the same buyer or persona? A great exercise is to just write down every idea for a new product and then categorize them based on which are similar and then rate them based on attractiveness, which is likely based on complexity to build, ease of routes to market, risk, or whatever else works for a given industry.

Once we have a set of adjacencies, let's think about whether we want to build, buy, or partner. Here we want to see if there are partners who we can have a symbiotic relationship with first. If someone is building a great offering, treats their customers well, and can align sales teams, then we can get most of the benefits of another product by integrating with them and move on to the next item on our list.

Once we identify the optimal adjacency, build a project plan. Sometimes it's best to start with a wireframe and reverse engineer development required to achieve a set of goals from there. Other times, it's best to start with a business plan and go-to-market strategies and then define which parts of a tool we might build when and how each unlocks a market potential. Either way, our efforts here will be familiar, as they're the same as developing a roadmap and doing all the other tasks that got us here in the first place—just with more experience this time!

New products are risky, no matter how much deliberation is involved. Some of the risks to be aware of include the following:

- Taking our attention away from our core mission and product

- Alienating the team

- Underestimating the cost (development, go-to-market, compliance, etc.)

- Overestimating the market potential

- Miscalculating the need for a new product in the market

- Regulatory restrictions or changes

- Different selling motions and cycles than expected

- Existing products not integrating well with new products

- Too much scope creep

Consider these when planning and add extra attention where needed. Run the project plan by existing employees and ask if they see any of the preceding risks as a showstopper. This especially helps when we don't want to alienate a team to get ahead of some risks to the plan. Also, keep in mind that the adventuring party joined up for a mission and we may be going in a whole new direction that doesn't work for some members but can still be right for the organization as a whole. A paladin who joins an adventuring party to kill a dragon doesn't have to stick around when the party does jobs for the thieves' guild in town!

Now that we've analyzed the market, built a plan, and verified it wouldn't be better to just partner with another company, it's time to develop a product and, if we are large enough, build an organization to support the new product. Always plan on a future state with specific teams for given tasks (e.g., DevOps, product marketing, etc.), but for now, consider a team like a strike force and get the team assembled to carry out a mission. Remember that any tasks can be outsourced, or even look to buy another company if adequately capitalized to do so. Historically, there are even cases of entrepreneurs who join forces to build a suite of products, in lieu of enough dry powder to make acquisitions.

As with most things, proceed with intention, and do so collaboratively to help reduce some of the risk, especially when it comes to our team. We should check in regularly on the progress, monitor the burn rate (how fast we go through capital), and fail fast or make big changes, if it gets out of control or looks dire.

When to Pull the Plug

This was initially a section as part of expanding into a portfolio, but it's true for our core products as well, especially when they're new. New products don't always work out like we want. There's no concrete rule that says when to end an initiative. Many startups have gone on to succeed after a founder funded the adventure on their own personal credit cards or lines of credit (e.g., the founding team of Instagram made cereal boxes when they couldn't get funding). So the simple rule of thumb is we should pull the plug when we lose faith in the project.

One way to do this is to plan every business assuming it will fail. This is why we say "fail fast" so often. Before we do anything, plan on what failure looks like and how to reallocate resources if one (or more) of those failure conditions is met.

Think about when the party ventures down into the Underdark, encounters a beholder, and gets slammed with a death ray. In a role-playing game, it might be easier to know when to retreat than in some areas of a business, so look for the following:

- The cost doesn't justify the expenditure. The economic incentive to run a business is to make money. Entrepreneurs necessarily oversimplify the industries we enter. That helps us ship a product. As we build a product, we might realize that the calculus we were using doesn't back up a planned cost or number of customers.

- The team isn't excited, inspired, or even showing up to work anymore. Heck, maybe some abandon the project or company. These are red flags, and we need to pay a lot of attention to morale and culture as it evolves.

- The customers aren't interested. This is huge. If there's no one to buy something, we can't sell it. We want to get at this with research, especially UX research, early.

- Strategies change. Maybe our core product was going one way, and now it's going another. Maybe the company sees what we're doing, and we all decide that once we unpack what's required and get started, we should take a different strategy. Any of these can cause problems.

- Politics get in the way. People in a company or a potential customer can railroad a project if they don't see how it benefits them. Look out for those and try to incentivize them, even in a small way, to get them to help the adventuring party succeed. For example, a software development or DevOps manager can be brought in to interview those parts of teams since they will eventually report through them.

- The unexpected happens. Maybe a big company with an established brand enters the market at the last minute. Or we get a market shift or have huge problems that need to be resolved elsewhere in a business. Some of these could probably have been considered in hindsight but not proactively given the information at hand when decisions were initially made.

One reason organizations like Y Combinator love a founding team with at least one technologist is that even if no funding ever comes in, the product can continue. So pulling the plug can take on a lot of different forms. Startups often say they pivoted into a new industry. That can be just one way of saying, "Our vision evolved, so we pulled the plug on the old thing." If our new idea is too adjacent to reuse parts of our old vision, we may choose to start over.

We also have to remember to take care of the people that joined us for a given journey. The employees need to be considered as do the customers. Help customers move to competing tools, or at a minimum, provide them with good data exports that another tool can import, when exiting a given initiative.

Conclusion

We put this chapter early in the book for a reason. The product function at an organization is crucial. Product management creates a roadmap and breaks the roadmap up into digestible parts for other teams. Without product management, we risk running amuck, building things we think people want but aren't sure—or just building technology to improve our existing technology (also known as paying down technical debt) without thinking to build features that customers might buy.

If we are overly controlling with the plan, those involved might not have the level of autonomy to feel like they own their part of the outcome. Yet every campaign is more fun when the adventuring party has a purpose and can strive toward a common goal, even in an open-world setting. Product management can mean a lot of things to a lot of organizations. The key is to strategically drive the development, launch, and continual improvement of products. The function usually begins with a founder: a ranger out in the wilderness who uncovers a purpose to build a party around.

As the organization levels up, the founder must deal with finances, human resources, development, and everything else required to build a sustainable company and thus long-term support of an innovation. So the deep knowledge of the domain our products operate in becomes the responsibility of someone else, then a team, and then a team with other disciplines inside the team, like launch management and UX research, competitive intelligence, data analysis, Scrum masters, and product owners who keep growing teams on track.

Product management can contain a wide range of responsibilities, but at the core is that roadmap, the plan to accomplish what's on it, and the ability to communicate the plan and the vision. Let's get stuff that's the most valuable for our customers into the roadmap and then get the things in the roadmap done. Let's not allow our technical debt to get too out of control in the process. That frees us to delight our customers when we surface valuable features. After all, when we spend too much time looking up rules in books, the game gets less interesting to play. It becomes too mechanical.

We want founders to keep the value they bring to customers at the core of every decision made. That's why product management is so early in the book. Now that we've gone through how to create a company, swarm around an idea, and plan a product, let's look at how to keep everyone aligned and inspired, moving on to the paladin's leadership foundations in Chapter 5.

CHAPTER 5

Leadership

Leaders motivate people toward a common goal. Leadership can get confused with management, which is about aligning people in the execution of a common goal. They are similar and often overlap. But leaders win people to the cause, motivate them, and keep them motivated. Think of the paladin, who rushes into battle after delivering an inspirational speech (which gives the rest of an adventuring party a bonus to dice rolls). That's inspiration, a key aspect of leadership. But so is setting up a strategy or organization that is, in itself, inspirational with or without the leader.

Many become successful leaders but aren't sure how or why. Sometimes their success is just a short burst of motivation engendered from a high amount of charisma. But an adventuring party needs sustained motivation to stay together and make it to the end of a quest. In the words of The Hold Steady's Craig Finn "It's one thing to start with a positive jam and it's another thing to see it all through." That means leaders need to think about the future, make sure the party is cared for, look within themselves to prepare the next generation of leaders, and improve their own abilities.

What works for some leaders won't work for all. It's common to provide recommendations based on the success we've found. But seeing the success in others and how they achieved it is integral to unlocking more and more success. It helps almost every leader when we truly believe in the mission. This allows us to constantly strive toward the vision and to live the values. That is where long-term leadership comes from.

© Charles Edge, Chip Pearson, Amy Larson Pearson 2023
C. Edge et al., *The Startup Players Handbook*,
https://doi.org/10.1007/978-1-4842-9315-7_5

Success is a great motivator as well, thus a good strategy. These aspects get us through the good times and the hard times. As we go through what leadership means, keep in mind that these are spectrums. Leadership comes in many styles, as we'll cover in the next section. Every founder should be able to take what works and know that the parts that don't work for them are still valid in others.

Note   Leadership development doesn't follow a standard flow in the development of organizations. Therefore, we won't be providing a leveling guide for this chapter.

Leadership Styles Through Television

Much of the conversation around leadership can be a bit meta, but it's important to observe great leadership out in the real world. We're going to look at some of the most common leadership styles in the following sections: authoritarian, democratic, laissez-faire, inspirational, narcissistic, paternalistic/maternalistic, and servant.

These words might not mean much when we're first getting started. Maybe we've been motivating people our whole lives and don't have the words to describe or codify how we do it. But when we see the words paired with those we've seen in the real world, they can become powerful examples that make what we do to motivate others easier to understand. When we are open to naming our feelings and actions, the places we can find authentic examples that help us improve our own leadership capabilities abound.

Many won't think of, say, Walter White of *Breaking Bad* as a great leader—but the various styles of leadership great characters like him represent are valuable lessons for many an entrepreneur. Not only do their flaws mirror our own (although hopefully readers don't share his profession), but they provide depth to the character, just as our flaws give us depth. Let's look at the seven most common leadership styles, along with some great television personalities we can learn from:

- A **servant** leader puts the needs of team members ahead of their own. They typically develop teams to perform at their maximum potential and share power throughout their organizations. Mandy Patinkin's characters in *Homeland*, *Criminal Minds*, and *Chicago Hope* are a great example of a servant leader. Servant leaders are always looking out for the best interest of the team, even if it means Patinkin ends up somewhere getting tortured. Omar Little of *The Wire* is a Robin Hood stereotype, which is usually a servant leader—if not a tad bit narcissistic for depth. Little serves the community and himself concurrently because, let's face it, most leaders do that to some degree. And of course, Aragorn son of Arathorn is an archetypal servant leader mixed with a heavy dose of inspiration.

- **Democratic** leaders foster collaboration through getting buy-in from teams. This is a common leadership style for startups and many a technology company. Here, we develop mutual respect (not that there isn't any with other styles of leadership) and work together to develop the best outcomes. Some examples of democratic leaders from television include Peggy Olson from *Mad Men*, Selina Meyer from *Veep*, and Richard Hendricks from *Silicon Valley*. And of course, most politicians we see on television from democratic countries have democratic leadership styles as well (by virtue)! We do have to be careful *not* to avoid conflict—and yet if we require unanimous buy-in, little is likely to get done.

- **Inspirational** leaders often take on some characteristics from other styles of leadership but rely on motivation for results. Inspirational leaders thrive in startups, on new teams, and in environments where charisma increases results and gets products to market faster. Joe MacMillan from *Halt and Catch Fire* pushes teams to produce more, faster. Khaleesi Daenerys Targaryen from *Game of Thrones* builds armies out of inspiration (and the fear of dragon breath). Or Ted Lasso from, er, Apple's *Ted Lasso*. Of course who can forget Aragorn's inspirational speech before the Black Gate "This day we fight!" Just remember that many who think they're being inspirational forget the inspiration part and just end up being laissez-faire.

- **Laissez-faire** leaders are one of the most common in early-stage technology startups, often just because we don't have time to dedicate to leadership as a discipline—or don't think we need to focus on it. After all, as each chapter in this book shows, there are a lot of moving parts to stay on top of. Laissez-faire leaders trade autonomy and the latitude to do what needs to get done for trust. Some don't even realize we're in a position of leadership yet. We can be hands-off if we build a great team, capable of focus and self-direction. It's fine if we say we're "staying out of the way," but are just too busy, provided we recognize that. One thing to be careful of: Over time, it's not scalable to let great people self-direct. No matter how good the people we hire, we eventually run into problems. That's why some leaders are best at certain sizes of companies. John Snow in *Game of Thrones* is this kind of manager, as is Captain Kirk of the original *Star Trek*.

- **Maternalistic or paternalistic** leaders often act more as a parental figure than a boss. This often manifests itself in showing concern for team members in exchange for loyalty or leaning on mentoring as a means to inspire. These leaders are excellent direct supervisors on production lines and sales teams— anywhere that efficiency is more important than creativity—like the field hospital from the old TV show *M*A*S*H*, led by the great Col. Sherman T. Potter. Other examples are actual parents and grandparents, such as Phil Dunphy from *Modern Family*, Violet Crawley from *Downton Abbey*, and Diane Lockhart from *The Good Wife*.

- **Authoritarian** leaders are the opposite of laissez-faire. They communicate tasks in a downward fashion through clear and direct lines of reporting. This isn't always the best in a startup but tends to work well as we grow into an environment where tasks need to be managed more closely. If the word *compliance* enters our needs or when people can get hurt by falling out of the lanes of their jobs, then it's likely a better match. We see this in the military or with police, but not as much in creative and knowledge work environments. We don't see much innovation come out of teams run by authoritarian leaders. Yet they are everywhere on television. Red, the head prison chef in *Orange Is the New Black*, rules her kitchen with an iron fist. Commander Adama from *Battlestar*

Galactica is another great example, as well as Wanda (the Scarlet Witch) from *WandaVision* and Bishop from *Mayans M.C.*

- Most of the leaders who are antagonist characters on television are **narcissistic** leaders. These leaders attempt to squeeze every last ounce of utilization from their teams and do so to benefit themselves rather than the organization (often taking personal credit for everything as well). Ramsey Bolton from *Game of Thrones* became the most hated character for his narcissistic (and usually sadistic) ways. Gavin Belson, the billionaire CEO from the show *Silicon Valley*, is also very unpopular on the show—and, as with most narcissistic leaders on comedy shows, is the butt of many a joke. Other examples: Negan from *The Walking Dead*, Claire and Frank Underwood in *House of Cards*, Wednesday from *American Gods*, Harvey Specter from *Suits,* and Fiona Goode from *American Horror Story*. And the list goes on. Not exactly uncommon in real life as well.

There are other types of leadership as well: Olivia Pope from *Scandal* is a great example of a super-team leader. They build teams with exceptional and complimentary skills. Of course, every superhero team could fit into this one. And then Captain Picard from *Star Trek: The Next Generation* is one of the best transactional leaders. He strictly enforces rules and punishes offenders when need be.

Continual Improvement of the Leadership Skill

Now that we've discussed some leadership styles, we can talk about some specific leadership challenges for startups throughout the rest of this chapter. As we develop, we can focus on the style that works best for us or add additional elements from other styles because, let's face it, sometimes the ranger is a more effective leader than the paladin. We defined the vision in a previous chapter and will set systems for goals and rewards and motivations when we get into Chapter 7. All of this can be a bit much for first-time leaders who have a great idea but not a lot of history in leadership.

Luckily, there is a lot of traditional content now available for free to help us on this journey. There are countless books on the topic. There are online courses (we'll list a few in Appendix 1) and in-person courses at local universities. We can also see great leadership live and in action around us all the time if our eyes are open. Maybe the shift lead at the coffee shop is providing encouragement to the cashier, or maybe we see someone who reports to us providing gentle but firm feedback.

Mentors provide great feedback. Few, if any, should be in a position of leadership without a mentor with whom to discuss challenges. Board members are a great resource for mentorship, but can get too close to the company to stay neutral on given topics. If there's no one in the community who seems like a good match, do a search on the Web for mentor matching services.

There are so many places to learn how to be a better leader. But there's no substitute for doing the work to get better. Some need to focus on tactics, while others might need a good therapist to dig into why they're being avoidant or anxious. Think about that while going through the rest of this chapter.

Learn to Agree Even When We Disagree

One aspect of leadership that's important is consensus building. Let's not confuse getting to the point of a unanimous vote with the idea of a consensus. Sometimes a leader needs to learn to find a common place where we can agree with and among our teams but to make the hard decisions.

When different people have different opinions, it's easy to let that stop the work we're doing dead in its tracks. That might be how to build a feature, where to build a button, how to go to market, where to advertise, or even just who should deliver coffee to the office. Working with others isn't always easy. And disagreements happen. We want to give space for them to work themselves out but also don't want to be avoidant in our behaviors. Let's look at a few techniques to use when these happen.

People often disagree because they don't hear one another. This can be the easiest to overcome. Getting to a consensus then involves getting people to listen and feel heard. Here, we make sure to bring everyone into a conversation and try to guide different stakeholders to hear or even repeat what the other is saying. We also want them to sit on it and think more deeply.

Even when heard, we have different values, experiences, needs, and goals. This means we might not understand what we hear in the way intended. Here, we have to identify what causes people to misunderstand the position others take and bridge that gap. This can be done by unpacking our different backgrounds and can be incredibly rewarding as we learn more from diverse points of view than sitting in an echo chamber of others who just agree with us.

The hardest thing to overcome in a disagreement is when it's not just based on communication. Personalities, politics, power struggles, past history, and a host of other factors can get in the way of a consensus. This might become untenable in smaller organizations, as we only have a handful of people on the team and anything that gets in the way of productivity is more impactful. There are a few techniques that can help, which include the following:

- Bring in an outside opinion. This might vary with different issues. Business issues could involve bringing in a board member with experience in the domain. Technical issues might involve hiring a consultant, or we may call that one friend who happens to be an expert in the domain. A bevy of outside opinions can cloud the answer but can also bring clarity and diverse opinions without the baggage of personality or politics.

- Take a break. Maybe discuss the issues privately with the stakeholders or just give them space to work things out. Not everything can work itself out immediately.

- Discuss the strengths and weaknesses of different opinions. Here, we can build a criteria list and score the attributes of each item on the list, use sticky notes to rank things, and have fun with it. Fun happens to diffuse personality clashes in many cases.

- Lay out alternative views. This allows us to find an alternative solution. Sometimes the best solution is neither point of view but instead a new and innovative approach that's in the middle. Again, there's a reason we want a diversity of opinions and people in our organization. There's a wealth of information on business sites for "merging alternatives," so feel free to continue reading about different techniques as there are entire books dedicated to the topic!

Sometimes we won't be able to find consensus. If a leader wants to get an important workstream back on track, though, we need to step in. Think of this as a finite resource—we don't want to take sides, pick favorites, or disturb the natural order too much, or others will assume we just want to surround ourselves with people who just agree with us, or they'll think we still want to control everything. We can't allow disagreement to stifle innovation, so if our coworkers can't settle disputes themselves, it's time to be more proactive.

Accept Evolution, Not Revolution

For those in newer fields, the scale of growth in a given profession can feel like a revolution. We've gone from a world where organizations mostly get by without a discipline to that discipline driving us toward a better world.

That world is increasingly about trying hard to listen and develop empathy for the people we serve. We're still looking for productivity gains and often want to streamline and standardize processes, but also need to allow for custom workflows.

Revolutions don't happen overnight. They take years, arguably even decades, to develop—and the more substantial the gains from new ways of thinking, the longer they can take, to the point where it ends up being evolutions in thinking that are revolutionary over time. It turns out that shifting mentalities is hard, especially for those stuck in a cycle of reacting to a torrent of customer requests by shipping updates as fast as they can. And yet shifting mentalities is what "disruption" is.

Revolution Through Evolutions

We know that evolutions in how we work throughout the business and product lifecycles can break cycles of reactivity. It helps to understand the deeper "why" behind all the changes. Unfortunately, we still face many challenges to convince our colleagues of the benefits of evolutionary changes and get budget to fuel innovative approaches toward new directions. And then just as we convince everyone what we're doing is necessary, the demand for our not-so-new-anymore disciplines grows, and we struggle to find talent and secure budget. We are forced to do more with less.

Because of this pressure, we can easily get caught in the trap where we always feel behind and are unable to catch up. Don't get overwhelmed with what can feel like a lot of operational debt! Keep in mind we don't have to do everything at once.

A big piece necessary to scale the use of automation and central repositories of information about what we do is that a lot of organizations wrestle with an inability to make good use of existing assets. They're stored all over the place and in a variety of formats. There's no one place to search and to find out what's been done.

Centralize All the Things!

This impulse to do everything at once is reasonable. We see the problem, and we want to fix it. However, when the solution takes on the form of a large initiative that requires significant organizational change, we increase the risk of failure. People resist change, our champions get "reorganized," and the whole thing gets delayed and delayed and delayed. We've seen this across tons of new and innovative approaches across hundreds of industries.

Instead of this type of revolutionary approach, think of continuous evolution. Consider identifying a particularly valuable area of the field or data and centralizing that work first. Show the value of an incremental change to gain more resources for the next wave of effort. A great benefit of organizing a smaller, more focused area is that it can help us quickly establish a place for future assets to go to be better organized from the start.

Evolution over revolution is a key takeaway for investors as well. Look at how long it takes for industries to shift into a revolutionary approach vs. how long to make a small step, get some gains, and then increase the value with the next step (often with costs that correlate to productivity gains or insights and so the potential to grow within existing customers). This also lets us get to market with products faster (e.g., an MVP).

To simplify the thought even further, pick one thing and do it well. This might mean allowing a single member of a team to use a tool with a freemium account and nurturing them into a paying customer. As more people can do more, they can convert when the cost makes sense and grow into "enterprise" customers when that makes sense.

Those enterprise features often mean we need to support a given discipline at scale. Enterprise customers need a lot of infrastructure features, though. They often need secure access through single sign-on (SSO). Or compliance. Or tiered account types not previously supported. Or professional services to help teams successfully evolve their practices over time. Larger organizations are unique snowflakes and have unique needs. But it's a great problem to have when we get there!

Tools that grow with organizations allow customers to plan for the future more reliably. Customers and tools that grow with organizations give everyone permission to think incrementally. Find a pace of adoption that works for the target customers, their teams, and the rest of the organization. Get some early wins and build on that impact. We like to see revolutionary new ways of thinking. But put a plan together to get to a utopian future state incrementally and become self-sustaining along the way.

Mentorship

We can learn from people who have gone through what we're going through. We level up in a role-playing game when we spend time with a mentor in a given character class (or that's the way it was written in the 1970s). In real life, mentorship can be a simple comment on an airplane, a lunch, a series of calls that span a few months, or a life-long relationship where we learn from one another. We might also pay a coach to mentor us or recruit a board member to gain access to a wealth of knowledge they often bring to the table.

Mentorship is a symbiotic relationship. Each party gets something out of the relationship. Because a lot of things we do are about motivators, let's look at what each person gets from such a relationship: The person seeking mentorship receives hard-won knowledge handed down from a mentor about a small slice of what we do for a living or about an entire industry. This helps with the journey ahead. The mentor gets to think more deeply on an aspect of their own journey, maybe come to terms with the parts they didn't do well, and maybe share the parts they did do well in a form of euphoric recall.

Many really enjoy mentorship and sharing experiences, given that it can be quite rewarding. Learning from one another is an important aspect of mentorship. But another aspect is networking. Both parties can provide valuable contacts to the other. Each party might be in a place to help the other in the future as well, especially in the startup world where investors are always looking for places to deploy capital and startups are always looking to network with people or organizations that can help fuel growth with capital infusions.

But mentorship, helping one another, is at least in part altruistic. Both parties need to be willing to accept insights from the other and act on them. While we aren't responsible for what triggers strong emotions in others, we can be gentle in how we hand out feedback.

Being a Mentor

Founding a company means wearing a lot of hats. One hat that we're likely to wear for the life of the company (or at least our involvement) is mentoring. Mentorship is not career or life coaching, but can be a little of both. We often pay for coaching, but mentoring comes with a different set of expectations and results.

Mentorship comes in many forms. As founders, we can put the types of mentorship provided in three primary categories:

- *Skills mentorship*: This is how to be better at the specific tasks a position requires. This might be insights into how to more successfully implement a given framework in code, rejection handling tips on sales calls, or asking whether we can help with anything else on a support call. These are skills, and while the technical skills are easier to train, the soft skills require more finesse and a deeper understanding of what people are going through.

- *Role mentorship*: Beyond skills, we want to mentor people on how to better handle their roles in the organization. Here, we can ask questions that lead to a deeper understanding of how a role contributes to the organization, how to improve the role, and how to improve interactions between a given role and others.

- *Career mentorship*: We also want to prepare for growth. This means not only growing the organization but also preparing the next generation of leaders (whether technical or managerial) in the organization. Here we seek to understand the motivators and gaps between where someone is and where they want to be.

We can also help with work-life balance. But notice that we're not helping people with their personal relationships or finances. For personal relationships, there's therapy, and for finances, there are apps, financial planners, and accountants. Instead, we help our coworkers navigate how to accomplish all the things they need to get done and to improve professionally. We can do more as friends, but there are boundaries, and we all have permission to define them proactively or when crossed.

It's easy to define boundaries when we actually can't help our coworkers. As founders, supervisors, managers, directors, or friends, we don't have to provide mentorship. Maybe we just hired someone in a role we know nothing about and simply can't offer effective and impactful guidance to grow one or all three of the preceding mentorship categories. Here, we can use our network to find others who can help them. Maybe there's someone on the board of directors who can offer a contact. Asking a mentor how to find mentors for others is a great way to spend time receiving mentorship—and for the record, if we're not being mentored ourselves, it's going to be difficult to see our good and bad mentorship techniques.

The time we spend mentoring is about others. Now that we've explored areas and types of mentorship, let's look at some specific things we can do during our time with those we mentor. Here are a few aspects to consider when we provide mentorship:

- Ask questions. This is the most important thing we can do. Open the floor for those we mentor to get what they need out of the relationship. Open-ended questions are best in the beginning, unless we need to get a specific point across, in which case a closed-ended question followed by a "why" is a simple tactic to allow others the agency to find their own answers (with a little guidance). We don't need to have a set path for our questions, but we can.

- Listen thoughtfully. As others tell us of their challenges and goals and ask for feedback, it's easy to provide flippant responses. This isn't about hearing ourselves talk; it's about providing quality feedback.

- Share feedback. Our feedback is why people come to us as mentors. Questions and active listening are to get to a deeper understanding of what others need.

That feedback can come in the form of ideas for further exploration and growth opportunities, but we have to keep in mind that our experiences may be different, so we can share them but also need to leave room for what others are going through.

- Provide examples. Stories are a great way to reflect on what we've been through and allow others the benefit when our experiences are concentric. This can be a trap as many mentors go straight into storytelling without first really listening and providing direct feedback. We can't expect others to make connections unless we've provided the points to connect.

- Offer to make introductions. We might not be able to assist with something, but an introduction to someone who has been through a similar situation or a vendor who can assist with a need is a great way to help others. For example, let's say someone needs to build a community and we know a passionate community organizer—we can make an introduction rather than dwell on an area we aren't really experienced at.

- Set and reflect on goals. A final aspect of mentorship is to be honest about our goals, motivators for the goals, and progress toward them. This isn't always necessary and could overlap with guidance our teams receive from front-line managers. So it's always good to understand these and to keep the rest of the conversation aligned to the goals when possible.

Don't get frustrated at slow progress but do hold people accountable. We're here to offer encouragement. Keep in mind that we all grow at different paces. We must be patient with others on a different path, as they may have areas of personal growth or family challenges they're dealing with outside of work. We want to help people progress and set goals, but life can be complicated, so we need to give room for that. And hopefully at some point, our mentorship will be less effective because people have outgrown what we have to offer. At that point, it's time to set our ego aside and help them find a new mentor who can help with their next set of challenges.

If we manage to scale the organization, over time we will have less time to mentor those outside our senior management team. When we feel like there needs to be more mentorship in an organization, it's time to get a bit more formal and create a program for our brave adventuring party to get help where they need it.

Creating Mentorship Programs

Mentorship programs are really easy and really hard to start. It's fairly easy to tell a company or community that there's a mentorship program and recruit members or define rules, like a person responsible for matching people who want mentorship with available mentors.

Most mentorship programs fizzle out over time. The sponsor of the program moves to a new position, or the organization doesn't get a quantifiable value from the program, and the program dies out. But we hope there's a lasting impact, while not quantifiable, in how the guidance provided grew various people in the organization.

Don't have time to think about or do anything with mentorship programs? That's probably not a good sign, but there are alternatives to building these ourselves. Check out torch.ai or chronus.com, or work with a local academic institution (like an MBA program) to get more community engagement.

Finding a Mentor

The last aspect is where to find mentors. This might be a board member who's also a mentor, a site dedicated to mentorship, or others around growing organizations. Mentors are people who have had success in a given career path or who have navigated the dynamics of similar organizations to get things done.

Mentors can be found in a number of places. Consider the following:

- *Technical or management leaders in our organization*: Here we can work with people in positions to provide feedback about the organization and what it takes to succeed, not only in a role but in our careers at the organization. This might be a founder in an early-stage startup, and as we scale to 100 people or a given revenue metric for an industry, that might shift downstream.

- *Similar roles in other organizations*: We want to avoid competitors. They don't need to know what we're going through. It's a shame, but true. Instead, we can look for similar titles in adjacent organizations. If we're a new sales engineer, we might find a sales engineering manager at another organization to talk through what the role entails routinely. There are lots of roles that are similar between organizations like software developer, accounts receivable, etc. Domain experts might be best matched with people who have successfully navigated either remaining domain experts at a high-growth organization or pivoting into a different career path, such as product management, which often becomes more diluted when those with product experience rather than domain expertise join the organization.

- *Similar types of organizations*: This doesn't mean competitors but instead other organizations on similar trajectories, for example, another recently funded, hyper-growth startup. It helps to have mentors who faced similar challenges at a stage beyond where we are to understand how to navigate that journey in a way that befits the organization and serves our own individual needs (without putting our needs over those of the company). One tactic here is to find other companies that just got funded and research people in similar roles at those organizations. Most companies in each series of funding are similar, despite the domain expertise and mission. Company building is its own assembly line that way. There are nuances with B2C or true enterprise or companies who are down-market from an enterprise player (or upmarket from a true consumer play)—but the similarities and shared experiences are more than many think.

- *Academia*: Business schools and other research organizations have a wealth of advice to hand down. Many in technology startups might be suspicious of academics (which goes back to the 1970s personal computer revolution when a guy like Jef Raskin pretended he didn't have a PhD when interviewing at Apple and then came up with the idea for the original Macintosh to prove his value). However, there are plenty of professors or postdocs just looking for hot new startups to drop some wisdom on!

- *Career coaches*: Finally, we can hire a career coach. Coaches come with all sorts of backgrounds, and some veer more into life coaching. It's important to find someone we can talk through our issues with, and coaches are a great resource for the right scenarios.

We need to be candid with mentors and with ourselves about what we want out of the relationship. We might not really know yet—and that's fine. To maximize the impact of the relationship for both parties, we should be as forthcoming as possible. Maybe we have a single meeting, or maybe we meet for years—they're all valid and hopefully remain mutually rewarding for all parties.

As a company moves to each stage of growth with each series of investments or revenue milestones, we have to take off a hat or three—so the best mentor can probably be the one who can help us decide which of those hats we'll keep wearing and navigate the next stage. Over time, founders and those we add to the adventuring party that is our company will hopefully learn to be deliberate about which hats we keep and which we remove.

Conclusion

Great leaders are not born but forged like a great magical weapon. They are molded by success and failures, but tempered by the ability to look inward and accept, learn, and move on from each. We focused on mentors so much because they are far more helpful than a few paragraphs of text that get applied universally when they shouldn't. There is no substitute for deep thought and introspection, especially for leaders.

Leaders inspire those who join our cause. As leaders, we need to align people to a common mission. Leadership can mean different things to different people, as we showed with the most common leadership styles. But each is a spectrum, and we can borrow bits and pieces from others that authentically work for us.

Let's dispel a common misconception. Leadership is not the same thing as charisma. In fact, a high charisma score can let us become manipulators and not leaders. Leaders show others how much we care for the mission and for those around us and find ways to inspire others. That could be an impassioned speech. But it could also be inspirational language in our commits on GitHub, a great blog post, or a decision that puts the well-being of the party above our own.

The big, grand gestures are great. But it's the small things we do as we live our everyday lives that really inspire others in a lasting way. Modeling and living the values based behaviors we want to see in our organization is critical - we can't expect our colleagues to take our values seriously and operate independently within these guidelines if we can't show them what that looks like. Now that we've looked at the basics of leadership, let's help each member of our party have the best character sheet ever and move on to more of the performance management of an organization in Chapter 6.

CHAPTER 6

Management

A curious aspect of growing companies is that as we add more people, we find our teams are not as effective per capita as they once were. Sometimes it feels like a growing adventuring party is all focused on the same opponent in a round, even though the foe has been vanquished. This is because people need coordination. The previous chapter focused on leadership as a source of inspiration for an organization, but leadership becomes less effective over time when execution falls short. That often happens because we aren't intentional with how we coordinate our efforts.

Operational excellence comes from managing all the things that need to happen in a given day, week, month, quarter, year, and so on. Without management, our teams clash, and decisions get made in vacuums or by committee (and so not at all). Management layers might ultimately consist of a supervisor, a manager, a director, a vice president, executives, and chief executives (although hopefully most startups won't need six layers of management). Each of these can also end up with a senior or junior in front of the title, denoting sometimes political and sometimes logistical differences.

The stages where a company adds additional management hierarchies are different based on the maturity of each industry and the maturity of each founder. It's not uncommon to bring people on with lofty titles only to hire others to manage people that we previously called directors or vice presidents, just so we could get them on the team. Some early employees

© Charles Edge, Chip Pearson, Amy Larson Pearson 2023
C. Edge et al., *The Startup Players Handbook*,
https://doi.org/10.1007/978-1-4842-9315-7_6

are only willing to take the risk to join a newer adventuring party provided they get those titles. This is all part of the nature of startups, and most new organizations aren't immune. However, being the president of the pillow fort is not impressive - titles need substantive functions to be meaningful.

Make no mistake though. Despite the arbitrary titles, management is necessary. In those early stages, the founders likely do the people management, task management, individual contributions, set strategy, and all the other aspects required to run an organization. We therefore need to understand early on how to be effective managers and, at later stages, how to direct the managers. In the previous chapter, we looked at leadership, but that's not interchangeable with management in our vernacular.

Leveling Up Our Management Game

The earliest stages of a company likely don't need much of a management infrastructure. The founders take that responsibility. As we grow, we can't focus on helping the team become better contributors to our mission, so we need to bring on managers to provide that guidance and help level up the staff we hire.

A seasoned manager can handle between four and eight direct reports, according to multiple factors. The direct reports are people that, in a chart that shows how a company is organized, report directly to a given manager. Factors that impact how many reports a manager can handle include other responsibilities (e.g., doing things rather than just managing people that do things), experience as a manager, company politics, maturity of the staff, and how much guidance each employee requires.

To put this in perspective, let's lay out an example of an early-stage company. Let's say we have two founders. One founder is a bit more outgoing and takes on the role of the CEO. The other is much more familiar with coding and takes on the role of the CTO. Together, they hire two software developers, someone in marketing, and someone in sales. The natural progression is that the two developers report to the CTO and sales and marketing report to the CEO. The CEO and CTO are now managers of the two people they've hired, but we haven't yet brought on anyone dedicated to management.

Now, let's go a step further and say that we now have four people in sales, five software developers, and a bookkeeper. The CTO can't get any code written because they're constantly managing merge conflicts, showing the newer developers where to find some weird piece of code, and offering guidance or resolving personality clashes around naming conventions, API styles, priorities, etc. The CEO is constantly helping the sellers and answering questions about discounts and no longer has the pulse of the finances and board decks prepared on time. And it's time to hire someone to support customers, so where does that fall?

This is around the time that dedicated managers need to either be promoted internally or brought in from the outside. Because management is necessary at later stages of growth, we'll start our leveling guide a little later than we do in some of the other chapters and gloss over the earliest stages. Let's look at some basic guidance around developing the discipline:

- *Level 1*: We bring on our first employee, who reports to the founders. The founders provide guidance for the tasks the employee is hired to do. According to whom we bring in, the company might just seem like a group of friends where one is vaguely the leader. But we should be looking for the natural leaders to groom for leadership and/or management positions later.

- *Level 2*: We bring on a few more employees, and rather than the founders sharing responsibility for the tasks being performed, the teams are split per the example laid out earlier in this section. This is a bit more like a larger, unwieldy friend group who happens to share space or a domain name. Here, we hit a place where there are certain people that just don't fit in at morning standups anymore. But it's good to have everyone together routinely for as long as we can.

- *Level 3*: Once we get to around eight to ten employees, we're no longer able to provide the necessary guidance to keep employees happy and productive, so it's time to bring on a manager. By now we've probably proven a product-market fit and have a little investment or cushion in the bank. We'll naturally look to the largest team to bring someone in to manage; however, given that each team likely isn't all that big, the person we hire may share some duties that will be assigned to an individual contributor (like selling rather than just managing a sales team or handling some aspect of coding or technology rather than just managing a development team). We should avoid hiring "supervisors" where they share the management and individual contributor burdens but don't have salary control and instead just embrace getting bigger and preparing for scale when revenues justify bigger teams.

- *Level 4*: The team keeps growing, and now we need a second or third manager. Our onboarding documentation likely needs to scale to offer a track for managers and a track for individual contributors. Further, we likely also need to have meetings specific to managers. And we need to plan when each manager hires or delegates tasks they do that fall outside of management.

- *Level 5*: Managers who manage managers are called directors. But we call them directors because we need them to do more than just manage managers. We need them to offer direction so the founders can continue to focus on top-level issues, like close big sales, work with the board, maintain cash flow, deal with investors, and provide vision for the company and product. Here, we need to let go of the budget for these teams and make the directors budget holders. Provided they understand the vision, we can let them decide the best strategy for their team to help us accomplish the vision.

- *Level 6*: Modern software companies likely use Agile, Scrum, Kanban, or some other framework for splitting up task management and human management. Here, we see managers managing careers, product managers managing what goes into products, and Scrum masters/coaches handling process. And yet we get less done per capita. The alternative is to have everyone stepping all over each other's work.

- *Level 7*: The moment we hire another officer or a vice president, we're clearly headed for another level. If we haven't already gotten a Series B, then we're likely on our way, and it's time to let the executives we hire for our executive team take over managing most managers and directors. We should let their specialties and past records guide the emergent disciplines we see working well for our organization.

Beyond level 7, we must stay diligent to sniff out waste, partisanship, and poor performance of managers. We need to evaluate key performance scores for each team and read the surveys we'll discuss in Chapter 7. Our adventuring party has turned into an army, and the officers who manage the army heavily impact morale and so our success at winning every battle we fight.

Managing Managers

It is hard to make the transition from a small adventuring party to an army (we have a whole chapter about scaling). A well-trained management team makes scale easier and more deliberate. They help us not get caught interviewing for weeks and stay out of day-to-day disputes, career guidance, and other time-consuming tasks that are necessary to keep our teams happy and productive.

Many founders fall into two camps: those who undermine managers or those who depend on managers. The first is when we still assign tasks directly to the people who now report to managers. This can work out at smaller scales, but the longer we have a manager around, the more they need us to trust them to be effective. That trust is earned, but often begins with just making sure we hire someone we have trust in from the outset. From there, we want to actively develop managers, which we cover in the next couple of sections.

Hiring Managers

We recruit managers the same way that we recruit developers or sellers. We post position descriptions to job boards or look in our circle of business associates. Then we evaluate who to hire out of a pool of potentially suitable candidates or repost. Maybe we even have someone with great management skills in our organization, network or extended network.

The manager is there to boost productivity and morale of the team. These become the primary ways we evaluate a potential manager. We can also use those two simple aspects of the job to track performance. We'll cover morale further in Chapter 7, but for now, we will oversimplify the role of a manager and say their purpose is to align the tasks an employee does with the mission of the company—particularly, how the team they manage contributes to the overall strategies implemented to achieve that mission.

This means we can focus on these aspects of management when interviewing. We can ask how candidates improved morale at past organizations, how they take direction and break down strategies into tasks, and how they dealt with drama in the past. There are tons of resources out there for great questions to ask, but keep focused on the primary job in front of the manager when interviewing.

One trap we see with early managers is when they sit in multiple chairs. Because many founders haven't managed, they gloss over the management and instead focus on the individual contributor aspects of a job. We need them to do all of the necessary tasks at both stages, but if we are to grow, we want to focus on their ability to manage and/or lead (we'll get into the differences between the two later in the chapter).

Many characters in a party can begin as dual-classed, which means they have multiple jobs (like being both a thief and a fighter), but over time, the character naturally gravitates toward one class and may stop developing the second altogether. This is likely to happen when we hire managers who maybe still write code and manage humans. The upside is that they are often better able to lead when they've sat in the chair. The downside is that the development in each area suffers over time. We must add experience points to each. Still, it's natural in an organization to start out this way. Just be mindful that when one skillset needs more focus, it's time to either decide for the manager what one thing they should focus on or let the manager decide if they've earned the right to choose.

One place we can find a great manager is often within the company. Company morale is always improved when we hire a manager from within—unless, of course, the manager does a bad job. Then it's hard to retain them if we demote them and bring in a manager from the outside. To keep that from happening, pay extra attention to how potential managers embrace the mission, vision, and values the organization has centered around.

Once we've hired our first manager, it's time to turn our attention to onboarding.

Training Managers

Managers manage people. Therefore, the most important aspect to start a new manager off right is to be deliberate about how we introduce them to the people they'll work with. If a team of sellers or engineers has reported directly to a founder, it can be a culture shock to suddenly have someone who sits between them and a founder. However, system shocks are a part of growing a company, and we're usually best positioned if we tell the team how their lives will get better under the new organizational chart.

We should also arm the new manager with information about the team proactively. Before the person we hired begins their tenure, we can anonymously survey the team to see how things are going. There are a number of tools like Culture Amp, Qualtrics, and Lattice that have a mature set of questions, but at a minimum, find questions others have used and use a free survey tool. This further provides a before-and-after snapshot of how the manager is doing once we hit a month or so with them on the team. Every new manager should appreciate seeing an unfiltered survey of what the team thinks they need to be better, and we can provide that to the new hire on their first day, which should also make them feel like they're part of a really proactive organization.

To effectively onboard a manager in a new team, let them ease into it. They can sit in standups for a week while getting all the HR paperwork set up, configuring computers, and getting access to the tools used. They can watch how founders interact with the team. They can get a debrief about the particulars and motivators of each person they'll manage. They should probably avoid much change in those first few weeks and instead just learn why things are done the way they're done. Factor culture shock into the onboarding process when possible. Additionally, be clear about roles, responsibilities, and expectations.

The first two weeks are also a good time to set boundaries. What should a founder do if a member of the team reaches out to them? How are requests for time off handled? Who moderates conflicts? We can choose how much of this to codify or communicate to the team while erring on the side of transparency. It's better to have disagreements or discomforts come up earlier rather than later as they get amplified over time. By the end of the second week, we likely want to be at the point where we're able to transfer the team to the manager in the HR system.

The third week is when a founder can listen in on standups, team meetings, and one-on-ones—but not actively contribute. This is the point where founders can start to let go of the day-to-day aspects of managing and focus on leadership. We want to promote the successes of the team but also the manager and be supportive whenever possible and appropriate. Any disagreements between a founder and the manager should be handled away from the team. By now we've seen the manager in action and hopefully become more capable of trusting them.

The fourth week is when habits can set in. Before we let that happen, we need to return to the reasons we bring on someone to help us manage teams: to improve morale and productivity. We likely had an idea as to key performance indicators (KPIs) we wanted to give a manager. Maybe we want more features to get shipped, more code, less cyclomatic complex code, higher quota attainment, more leads, higher engagement with leads, etc. We want to revisit assumptions we made when we hired managers and validate or augment them where appropriate. At this point, we want the manager to come back to us and tell us what worked, what didn't, and where we can confirm or alter our expectations.

Beyond the fourth week, most startups will see the first couple of managers able to be at the helm of their own little adventuring party that contributes to the campaign in a predictable fashion. We'll delve further into onboarding and how to work with individual contributors in the following chapter, which is a task that over time will be done more and more by the managers we hire, supported by human resources teams.

Once we've onboarded a couple of managers, we can develop more official onboarding materials. We can ask managers we hired what worked and what didn't. Using that information, we can tweak our process so we get new managers onboarded more effectively over time. Notice we said "more effectively" and not "more quickly." Putting in a minimum of a month of effort into new managers should be a long-term expectation. We just hope to improve the results with each iteration.

Morale and productivity are key aspects of the manager position. Those can be looked at as managing humans and managing tasks, respectively. We'll transition into the differences in the next section (and go much further into thoughts and philosophies of people management in Chapter 7).

People Management vs. Task Management

Let's take a look at two types of management: task management and people management. Both are necessary. We'll cover task management first, as there is a large body of existing knowledge for this, especially for software startups. And no conversation about task management in software startups is complete without discussing the methodologies.

Great products require great people with great coordination to execute against a great idea. That's a lot of greats. The industrial revolution allowed us to put objects, like cars, on an assembly line and mass-produce them. The same is necessary to keep quality code shipping. Assembly lines have people who design products, people who design the process to manufacture products, and then mass assembly in the form of the assembly line (okay, so this is an oversimplification, but stick with us here). Software development is similar. We create a tool, and then as the code grows, multiple people work on different parts of the tool. This might be microservices developed by disparate teams, APIs, or different modules or jar files.

Historical Perspectives on Work Management

We covered product management in a previous chapter, which is how we determine what goes into a product and write descriptions of how it should be implemented, when, and why. The organization of work for development teams comes in several variants, including Agile, Scrum, Kanban, Scrumban, Extreme Programming, Lean Software Development, and tons of others. Some of these are almost polar opposites, and we still hear people talk about what Agile is and poke fun of people doing things an old way, calling it waterfall. That's because the methodologies don't fit every possible scenario.

Rulebooks for role-playing games are similar. They help but can't possibly cover everything, just as nothing was ever really waterfall development, given that we learn on the fly, find reusable bits, or hit a dead end. The point here is that Agile is, well, weaponized to back up what a person wants someone to do or how they want a team to be run. And it isn't always done from an informed point of view. Therefore, treat Agile like an anti-methodology. Think of it more like a classification.

Agile is the biggest but certainly not the only methodology. We could also use Extreme Programming, Scrum, Kanban, Feature-Driven Development, Adaptive Software Development, Rapid Application Development (RAD), and Lean Software Development. These came out to bring shape around a very similar idea. But over the course of 10–20 years, each has been developed in isolation.

Many harken back to "Adaptive Software Development," which always adapts what we're doing based on speculation of how long something will take, collaboration on that observation, and what we learn when we sit down to actually build a product. This is still the spirit of most methodologies since the era of the space race. Waterfall worked well if you were building a computer to land people on the moon.

The rapid proliferation of the Internet and computers led to the emergence of Rapid Application Development, where we let interface requirements determine how we build. Then Kent Beck built a methodology called Extreme Programming—or XP for short—in 1996, and that was the next hotness. XP released software in shorter development cycles so that software developers, like police officers on patrol work in pairs, could review and test code without writing each feature until it was required. The idea of unit testing and rapid releasing really came out of the fact that the explosion of the Internet in the 1990s meant people had to ship fast, and this was also during the rise of mainstream object-oriented programming languages.

The nice thing about XP was that we could show a nice graph where we planned, managed, designed, coded, and tested software. The rules of Extreme Programming included things like "Code the unit test first" and "A standup meeting starts each day." Extreme Programming is one of these methodologies. Scrum is probably the one most used today. But the rest, as well as the Crystal family of methodologies, are now classified as Agile software development methodologies. So Extreme Programming is like a parent to the others.

Is Agile just a classification, then? By 2001, Kent Beck met with Ward Cunningham who built WikiWikiWeb, the first wiki; Dave Thomas, a programmer who has since written 11 books; and Jeff Sutherland and Ken Schwaber, who designed Scrum. Jim Highsmith, who developed that Adaptive Software Development methodology, and many others were at the time trying to align an organizational methodology that allowed software developers to stop acting like people that built bridges or large buildings. Most had day jobs, but they were like-minded and decided to meet at a quaint resort in Snowbird, Utah.

They decided to start with something simple: a statement of values. Instead of bickering or digging into specific details, they were all able to agree that software development should not be managed in the same fashion as engineering projects are run. So they gave us the Manifesto for Agile Software Development. The Manifesto reads:

We are uncovering better ways of developing software by doing it and helping others do it. Through this work we have come to value:

- *Individuals and interactions over processes and tools*

- *Working software over comprehensive documentation*

- *Customer collaboration over contract negotiation*

- *Responding to change over following a plan*

That is, while there is value in the items on the right, we value the items on the left more.

But additionally, the principles dig into and expand upon some of that adjacently. The principles behind the Agile Manifesto:

- *Our highest priority is to satisfy the customer through early and continuous delivery of valuable software.*

- *Welcome changing requirements, even late in development. Agile processes harness change for the customer's competitive advantage.*

- *Deliver working software frequently, from a couple of weeks to a couple of months, with a preference to the shorter timescale.*

- *Business people and developers must work together daily throughout the project.*

- *Build projects around motivated individuals. Give them the environment and support they need, and trust them to get the job done.*

- *The most efficient and effective method of conveying information to and within a development team is face-to-face conversation.*

- *Working software is the primary measure of progress.*

- *Agile processes promote sustainable development. The sponsors, developers, and users should be able to maintain a constant pace indefinitely.*

- *Continuous attention to technical excellence and good design enhances agility.*

- *Simplicity—the art of maximizing the amount of work not done—is essential.*

- *The best architectures, requirements, and designs emerge from self-organizing teams.*

- *At regular intervals, the team reflects on how to become more effective, then tunes and adjusts its behavior accordingly.*

Many of the phrases here are easily weaponized, for example, "satisfy the customer." Who's the customer? The product manager? The end user? The person in an enterprise who actually buys the software? The person in that IT department that made the decision to buy the software? In the Scrum methodology, the customer is not known. The product owner is their representative.

Canned methodologies don't work for everyone. For example, let's take "continuous delivery." People frequently just lump CI in there with CD. Or use a buzzword like continuous design, continuous improvement, continuous deployment, or continuous gaming (yes, we made up that last one). We could spend hours going through each of these and identifying where methodologies aren't specific enough for specific use cases. Or, again, we could revel in their lack of specificity by pointing us into the direction of a methodology where these words get much more specific meanings.

Ironically, there are accounting or legal teams at very large companies that have Scrum masters or engineering teams for big projects with a project manager and a Scrum master and even a team of judges that use Agile methodologies. So broad methodologies can be used for specific environments they weren't designed to serve. But some adjustments might be required. Now we'll look at one of the more common methodologies involved in breaking up that work to be done so we can have multiple teams doing the work.

We can see in the preceding section that putting software on an assembly line has been all about the Scrum methodology for a long time. This isn't good or bad; it's just a framework. Scrum is really about task management, not about people management. So it doesn't absolve us from developing raw management and leadership skills. In fact, many large software development organizations have people managers and leaders who are different from the people helping to manage the tasks (product managers and product owners) and the people who manage the process (Scrum masters). Any time a framework matures, we end up with derivatives or other means of management. This is where Kanban comes into software development.

Kanban

Toyota has made great cars for a long time. Part of making cars is ensuring the quality of automobiles as they come off the assembly line. Any defect can have massive consequences, not only for the finances of a company but also for the lives of drivers. This is one reason Taiichi Ohno and Eiji Toyoda developed the Toyota Production System in the years following World War II. The goal was to improve on the assembly line concept that Henry Ford introduced but to go a step further and design a system that is flexible, allows appropriate levels of production, and eliminates waste.

191

The whole concept actually started in American supermarkets where shoppers took a specific number of items off a shelf and paid for them and then they got restocked. There were less processed and frozen foods at the time, so most people didn't buy too much and stores didn't order too much—so it was less wasteful than it might be today. While less wasteful, products did disappear and expire more quickly.

The same philosophy could be applied to just-in-time manufacturing. By buying just what they needed when they needed it, Toyota kept their inventory low. They could have less wasteful processes and buy parts as needed (think of the value of money over time at a mass scale). This would go on to be one component of Lean manufacturing and the basis for applying a Lean methodology to software development.

Kanban involves visualizing work so developers and other stakeholders can see the process and the progress. Each developer pulls work they can perform based on capacity, and if things get wrapped up early, they might go get some more. Often, the simpler the visual, the better—and bonus time, it's compatible with Scrum, especially in an era of continuous everything.

Continuous testing is when we execute our automated tasks in our software delivery pipeline. This allows us to get feedback as we go. From there, the software industry started making everything continuous. From DevOps to security testing to user experience to user experience research, hosted (or SaaS) services work well in this paradigm as we make less changes but make them more frequently. That wouldn't have worked as well when we were building client-server architectures where the client and the server needed to run the same version, nor with early monolithic object-oriented architectures; however, as we evolve into more of a microserviced mindset, we can build a contract for what a given service, endpoint, or presentation of these requires and provides (inputs and outputs, respectively), and we can take a sticky note off a board, make some minor tweaks, and introduce less breaking changes. Change comes quickly and we have to react continually.

At a minimum, it's a good idea to experiment with Kanban in most software startups. Even if it's just as a solopreneur, getting into a mindset of just-in-time software development helps us begin developing just the right amount of process rigor. Just don't overly prescribe to ceremonies and the baggage that comes with out-of-the-box task/work management frameworks nor their underlying philosophies.

There is a chance that the next newfangled management system will be out before this book. In that case, we can always work with teams to do the latest and greatest in our routine one-on-ones.

One-on-Ones

Every manager should meet with team members on a routine schedule. There are a lot of names for these meetings. The one we'll use is a one-on-one, as we're meeting with each member of the team individually. These allow us to check in on team members, see if they're happy, let them know what they're doing well, and challenge them to be better where needed.

Each company has a different definition of what should happen in these routine meetings. Early in the life of a company, we're wearing so many hats we often forget to have routine meetings and show that we care about people. Later, when companies are mature, we often dilute meetings with checklists and make the meetings less about human interaction and culture, so they become more about the formality of hitting a button in a database to show meetings happened.

One-on-ones should be valuable to both the employee and the employer. The employer has a certain level of performance that is expected. People not meeting that performance need to know in a clear and concise fashion. Those who meet and exceed the expected performance should know as well. And our teams should get feedback not only on the current job but on how they're tracking toward the next job as well.

The frequency and duration of one-on-ones is based on the needs of a given organization. For those new to routine check-ins with staff, begin with a half-hour to one-hour meeting that occurs every other week and increase or decrease how often meetings occur and the duration based on how much time is needed for each team member. Remember these are about the team members, but also about making sure the organization is getting what we need from the team and finding ways to help everyone excel in their role.

There are a few main points to cover in our routine meetings. Consider the following:

- Ask how things are going. Make sure to be personable, even when there's an agenda. Make sure to understand a little something about each person's personal life without coming across as being contrived in the process. Authenticity is important as we won't pick up on some of the most important things we need to if we don't actually care about people.

- Inquire laterally. Are there any issues with other team members? Are there places where we can help facilitate cross-team alignment?

- Communicate any changes in the organization that are impactful to the individual (staffing, alignment, budgets, new customers, etc.).

- Review any areas of exceptional achievement or areas that need to be addressed (it's best to bookend problem areas with achievements when possible).

- Ask how the role can be made better. This is a great way to give teams the ability to innovate their position or explain any areas of concern.

- Review steps toward an Individualized Learning Plan.

We don't have to cover each of these in every meeting, but it's helpful to have a cheat sheet of items to cover and show action. If a problem area is identified by the employee, identify what was done and potential timelines to resolve issues at the next meeting. This helps set an expectation that they'll do the same when there are issues they need to resolve or deliverables requested. Then each meeting starts with old business or items left over from the previous meeting.

Notice that up to this point, we haven't delved into task management. Many developers will use Scrum or Kanban for the process of task management, and so careers and humans get managed separately from the necessary work to be done. But these meetings are also an okay time to review tasks and update project plans. Just make sure to put in the time to address the well-being of each person as well.

Good news and adulations give managers and employees a great feeling. Delivering areas of improvement is harder but much more valuable for everyone involved. Don't back away from this, but instead be direct and concise. Problems don't go away on their own usually. Our teams need and want coaching—it's what improves their careers.

It's often easy to overlook one-on-ones when employees are busy with customers in the field, when we have to ship a feature, or when there are too many sales calls. Don't. Keep the routine check-ins, even if we need to move them around. It can be tempting to do so, but don't put them after hours, either. We've made the commitment to hire someone and guide their career, and while we can certainly grab coffee or drinks after hours, we must show a continued commitment by doing business during business hours and by continuing to care about the well-being of those who joined us on the adventure to bring our innovation to market.

How We Know When Management Is Broken

Management is about improving teams. This means the satisfaction of the team, the impact the team has on the metrics they are responsible for, and each area of contribution. We only know that our teams are dissatisfied if we ask. Not only should we be asking in one-on-ones, but we should also be asking on a routine basis using anonymous surveys.

We can survey customers with tools like Culture Amp (see cultureamp. com). Here, we leverage decades of experience from people who study culture and employee satisfaction and use that to help us manage teams better. Don't be defensive with results or feedback. Instead, always look for ways to be better and help the teams get better.

A major aspect to consider about HR and management is that they are there to protect and benefit the company. One way we do this (which we've been working through in this chapter) is to improve the individuals that join us in our adventure. But we also need real impact from teams. The primary way we see that is for managers to show steady productivity gains, thus making the organization more scalable long term.

Therefore, a few red flags to look for (especially as a management layer grows in an organization) include

- *The culture*: Do people know, share, and practice the values of the company?

- *Employee engagement*: Are teams aligned with our mission? Here, we can work to take a pulse of the organization and plan actions to increase engagement.

- *Performance*: Do teams get more effective in a quantifiable manner? Provided we have a good strategy and good tactics, the previous items should lead to great performance. We want to track that on a scorecard and show it to our teammates.

Early in the life of a company, when everyone is connected to a founder and fired up, it's easy to have a great culture, high engagement, and so great performance, whether from long hours or from effective planning. Now that we've looked at reasons to tracking these, let's move into how to read what is going on and help everyone improve.

Improving Our Teams (and Engagement)

Employee engagement eventually dips, no matter how good a manager a team reports to. But as managers, we can make the workplace more appealing in a number of ways. We can invest in initiatives such as employee training and development, so investing in the team. We can do so on a budget or earlier in our lifecycle that might be bit more ad hoc.

An employee might ask for more training and get the green light. But then something funny often happens: nothing. Giving our teams approval for training doesn't necessarily mean that they'll do it unless we follow up methodically and sometimes even micromanage the process. Why does this happen, and what does it show about how employers and employees alike can do a better job to make sure team development happens? There are as many reasons as there are teams, but there are six main buckets they tend to fall into:

- **The employee doesn't know what kind of training they want or need.** We can address this by asking for three or four ideas or work with them to create an individual learning plan. Here, we collaborate on an overarching objective for the training so our teams feel included. Collaboration gives diverse ideas; they could bring up areas neither party would have considered on their own, for example, public speaking skills, management, becoming a subject matter expert with products, or something else entirely.

197

- **The employee's goals don't match team goals.**
  It's a mistake to lay out a training program without
  considering what an employee wants out of it. We
  should always ask about goals and not assume.

- **The employee knows what they want but feels
  pressed for time.** Earmark a specific amount of time
  per week for training and then be sure to firewall that
  time so that employees aren't pulled away to work on
  other tasks.

- **There's no budget.** Not all training costs $5,000–
  $10,000 per employee per week. We can get custom
  courses (even with vendor-led certification courses)
  that cost a fraction of that if there are enough
  participants. There are also podcasts, books, online
  courses, and other free resources on the Internet.

- **Employees don't like the teaching methods.** Some
  people can't learn in a classroom. Others can't do self-
  paced training. Others need exercise or goal-oriented
  learning objectives. Be flexible to allow employees to
  learn in the ways they need to learn, not just in the ways
  we think they want to learn.

- **They simply don't want training.** Maybe they have a
  new family or a sick parent or just don't see training as
  a priority. If teams don't make time for training, make
  sure they feel comfortable. Make sure they have enough
  time and make sure it can happen during typical work
  hours. They'll thank you for making that investment
  into them.

Not everyone is driven in their professional career. We want our teams to have more drive to improve themselves and so the team. But it's our responsibility as an employer, and hopefully friend, to keep employee skills up of date and make sure our coworkers are happy and have plenty of opportunity for growth. Part of this is to help employees understand the resources available to them and why it's important to take advantage of those resources. But sometimes it means going a step further to understand a lack of personal drive. If the reason is that people prioritize the company over their own needs, they deserve even more attention to get more training.

Individualized Learning Plans

Role-playing games use character sheets to keep track of where a character is at. These include attributes like dexterity and strength, hit points, skills, spells, and languages. It would be inappropriate to put age and a constitution score on our character sheets at work, but we can instead track how our teams are doing and keep a leveling guide for them on hand, based not on a rulebook but what they actually want.

Everyone is in a different place in their careers. We can't make our teams want more than they want. But we can codify how staff spends training time and budget on an individual level. This can be done in the form of an Individualized Learning Plan. These plans lay out priorities for training, as well as tactics to achieve those priorities.

The plans evolve over time, but here is a sampling of what they should contain:

- *Three areas to improve on*: This is the most important aspect: what does each employee want to learn? They are individualized to each person, and then the rest of the plan tracks how to get there. For some environments, three might be too many, but we should rarely go higher. Three offers flexibility and just enough variety so when people tire of one domain of knowledge (or, better, finish an area), they can move on to another. It's preferable when the areas are connected in some way (e.g., all in the same domain of expertise).

- *Quarterly goals toward mastery in each area*: These should be SMART (or Specific, Measurable, Attainable, Realistic, and Timely) goals. To explain that

  - **S**pecific might mean that someone writes a script or microservice that performs a specific task (or completes a task, customer story, or epic in that direction). Or less technical might be a seller has a specific number as a sales quota.

  - **M**easurable might mean that we expect a blog post or presentation for team members who want to put themselves out there or an external certification on an area of knowledge they're learning about.

  - **A**ttainable means that the employee can get a goal accomplished (and that we're not saying, "Refactor ten years of code by Friday or ten times a quota").

  - **R**ealistic should mean that it's possible to accomplish the goal with the amount of work time available and that the goal is relevant to the rest of a job.

  - **T**imely means that the goal can be completed in the time allocated.

- *Keep a journal of professional development activities*: Professional means that this isn't about hobbies but about work (although we're all happiest when our work seems like a hobby). The key word here is *development*.

What is each person doing or learning that makes them better (and so more valuable not only internally but on the open market)? Hopefully learning activities align with company goals, but they don't have to. An often-underappreciated aspect of great leadership is sometimes helping our team members outgrow the organization.

- *What position do you see yourself in next?* It's great when people are honest and say they want our job. But not everyone really wants that once they understand what the field of jobs are in front of them and really unpack what each job entails. Many want to go deeper and deeper into various aspects of the technology. Some want to follow big paychecks and move into bigger sales. Others will honestly tell us they want to start their own companies. The question is to validate that the training aligns the motivators of each team member with goals.

- *Are we on track toward the next position?* This is a great early warning sign that people are tracking ahead, or behind, of their own schedule or that they will outgrow their current role (a goal of all this). Remember that these shift as external motivators change.

- *Peer coach feedback*: Once we get big enough, peer coaching allows team members to help one another. This allows us to spend more time reviewing feedback while we get telemetry into how team members deal with limited forms of leadership (and how leaders handle such decentralization).

- *Active research projects*: These should be projects that are part of SMART goals from earlier in the chapter. The best engineers often have the most fun in this section as it provides a real-world application, sometimes also giving benefits to the products we build or future ideas for products.

- *What progress has been made since the last meeting?* Think of this as version control. "What's changed" is much easier to read than every single line of code—especially when teams grow to the point that there are 20–30 learning plans to keep track of. We're after finding out if progress was made and if the motivators changed.

Over time, the learning plan documents grow, but the meaning of what's inside them doesn't. This is true with all processes as they mature and then get old and need to be reconsidered from the beginning. Stale is bad. In general, the more doctrine we introduce, the less people take away from their one-on-one and other meetings that are really meant to be all about them. In other words, we try to put management on an assembly line. Technology should help managers do more, not dumb down what we're there to deliver.

We should start over from time to time. Keep training plans short. If there's too much information on a character sheet, it gets too hard to figure out what a successful dice roll is very quickly! Only put enough detail into them to explain how targets were hit or missed. And keep in mind that if targets are missed, then some small area of the plan you didn't care about is invariably to be blamed! And so the documents and process will start to grow again. It's the cycle of life. Or our coworkers have more going on in life and can't focus on career improvement for a time (but may soon). Keep in mind, unlike a role-playing game, when we're not sitting in front of that character sheet, their life continues on. Keep them inspired, though—that takes leadership.

Management vs. Leadership

We often see leadership and management used interchangeably, but it's important to keep in mind that they are not the same. In fact, while some traits overlap in what it takes to be a great leader and a great manager, they are often quite different. The biggest difference is probably that between the two, leaders have others who follow them and managers have people who simply work for them (and often for a limited time). Managing and leading mean inspiring and consistently delivering results for the humans and the company concurrently.

As companies grow, there are paths for leaders and managers. But for small businesses and startups, owners who want to be successful need to be a strong manager and a solid leader in order to get their team on board while working toward their vision of success. Remember leadership is all about getting people to comprehend and believe in a particular vision set by the company or the organization to work on achieving goals. Management, on the other hand, is more about administration and day-to-day activities. Both are critical to the success of any organization.

Management and leadership don't have to exist in the same person but do need to go hand in hand. Sure, they aren't the same—but they are necessarily linked and are complementary to one other. Efforts made to separate the two might cause serious problems in the future. For an organization to be successful, it needs proper management who can organize, plan, and even coordinate the staff all while leveraging leadership to motivate and inspire. This allows our team to perform to the best of their ability.

Let's look at all the traits that can make up a strong leader and a strong manager, starting with leaders:

- *Vision*: Leaders must know where we are and where we want to go and energize the team in charting a path to get there.

- *Integrity and honesty*: Both are very crucial for the team to believe in us and buy into the journey we are on together.

- *Communication*: Communication keeps the team informed about the people involved, where we are on our journey, and where we are going.

- *Inspiration*: Remember that inspiring and motivating and stimulating the team is critical for them to understand their role properly—especially as their role impacts the bigger picture.

- *Challenging ability*: Leaders should never be afraid to challenge the status quo, especially allowing the team to contribute to our own understanding. We should have the ability to think out of the box while doing things differently between teams.

The Venn diagram of characteristics and traits that usually signal a strong manager can overlap with that of a strong leader, but consider the following as more important for managers:

- *Ability to direct*: A strong manager must have the ability to direct day-to-day work efforts, review all the needed sources, and anticipate all the needs of their team all throughout the way.

- *Focused on people*: A good manager should always look after the needs of their people, listen to them, and involve them in daily activities.

- *Proper execution of a vision*: A manager must have a tactical path to implement a strategic vision and should always break it down for the team to have a proper roadmap they can follow.

- *Management flow or process*: An able manager should establish work rules, standards, processes, and other operating procedures so our teams are clear about what they can expect and what we expect from them.

It's great when those in charge can inspire, lead, be organized enough to get all the tasks done that are required, delegate effectively, develop systems and processes to report on the status of every part of an organization, and put up with the changing whim of an organization seeking product-market fit. We might find a couple people like that, but it doesn't scale. Not everyone we hire can, or should, be both a good manager and leader. To manage a successful startup, a founder needs some mixture of both, along with other skills that aid in the mission.

Each new hire is then an opportunity to have a team greater than the parts, which we can do by hiring people that aren't just carbon copy clones of us. Founders with skills that lie squarely in the management circle of our Venn diagram should look for someone who has those complimentary leadership qualities to add to a company—or leaders hire strong managers. This helps us develop one of the biggest competitive advantages of all time: operation excellence paired with inspiration.

Conclusion

The previous chapter covered leadership. That's important to inspire. But to sustain inspirations, those we surround ourselves with need to trust that we're going to do great things and not just talk about doing them. This chapter gets into more tactical aspects of maintaining the company. That could be on a technical or organizational level.

Different people lead and manage differently. Knowing how we can be better is important, but also knowing how we prefer to do these things is critical to our own happiness as well. Without great leadership, we lack inspiration. Without great management, we don't get anything done, or people are off working on whatever they want to work on—or teams duplicate efforts, and we end up stepping on toes.

Ultimately though, leadership and management are about humans. The next chapter covers how to keep those humans at the center as we scale. Here, we're veering toward human resources, but given that most startups should outsource human resources, we'll focus much more on hiring, retention, and keeping our teams focused on exceptional outcomes rather than the mechanical bits that should be paid for as a monthly service.

CHAPTER 7

Humans

Our adventuring party starts small, and it's easy to understand the role of each member of the party. A great role-playing game considers the motivations and backstory of everyone in the party. A company is no different. We want those employees to be able to bring their whole backstory and look for the interpersonal issues that can arise.

When the first employee or three are hired, it probably seems easy to manage them. *Let's go make money and do this thing!* That's an easy message. We can see what they do on a day-to-day basis and help them get better. We can look for how they embody the company vision and work with them closely. The more we grow and bring in diverse thoughts, perspectives, and people, the more assumptions are made, and the more our message needs to mature. Or did that need to start with our first hire and by the time we hit four or ten we're far behind in developing our humans? We all know the answer to that, whether we want to admit it or not.

Humans know where the weird spots are in the code. Humans learn who our customers are and how to support or sell to them. Humans are the lifeblood of any organization. When humans leave, we lose the institutional knowledge in their heads. So good recruiting and retention is key to the success of every organization. That begins even before the first hire when done correctly. Let's consider the roles to hire, the goals for each, and the expectations for them.

© Charles Edge, Chip Pearson, Amy Larson Pearson 2023
C. Edge et al., *The Startup Players Handbook*,
https://doi.org/10.1007/978-1-4842-9315-7_7

The Adventuring Party: Unique Skills, Perspectives, and Abilities

The adventuring party starts small: often just a ranger. More people mean the organization gains new abilities, and those allow the company to do more. New perspectives allow the organization and the founders to know more about the world and the disciplines required for a successful campaign. Some companies can grow by hiring a lot of people exactly like the founders, but that wouldn't create the functions that support a scalable company. This is called diversity.

Many of those hired as an organization grows are experts at things a founder just spent a few hours a week or month on. Founders don't always fully understand what these new players do, especially when there are teams who do things founders never even knew were things to be done. And yet until an organization reaches over 100 people, the founder or CEO might assume they could still sit in any chair and do any job. Don't let early successes during early stages mislead.

Let's look at the evolution of the human resources team—the humans—in an organization:

- *Level 1*: The founders are out in the wild and realize that it's time to hire the first person on staff. Be clear about what each role entails and what the expectations are. Make sure the organization is set up to pay the person legally in the country, state, and municipality they are in.

- *Level 2*: It's time to expand to another few people. The company will likely need to outsource the human resources function until there are about 20–25 people and needs to develop an onboarding process so behaviors are set early and people are prepared for their tasks.

- *Level 3*: Focus on talent foundations. Review the total rewards (things like salary bands, stock options, paid time off, flexible work schedules, and benefits) to be competitive in the market and understand what adding other markets does to policies. Do so in accordance with local laws and norms and be able to grow into a larger outsourced human resources provider.

- *Level 4*: The bigger the organization gets, the more likely the company will outgrow the local market. Understand what a pipeline of talent looks like (much like a pipeline for sales prospects) and be prepared if that goes outside a single geography. Being bigger also makes the company a more attractive target for legal actions, so develop a plan to continually review contracts and policies to keep from getting sued (and in general to stay competitive and not screw people over).

- *Level 5*: Create a formal approach to evaluate performance. Focus on not leaving anyone on the team behind while the company grows. Understand the goals of each member of the party: what the next moves in their careers are and how founders can help them achieve those goals (preferably at the organization but also a plan for when they're ready to move on and how to help them at the next stage of their career development).

- *Level 6*: It's time to hire people in human resources position if that hasn't been done already. Leave much of the mechanical aspects outsourced (e.g., payroll, taxes, benefits, etc.) as long as possible. Companies are likely to need recruiters and a manager or director for the human resources team to oversee all the bits and pieces. Remember, humans are the most important aspect of any organization. Nothing gets done without them. Someone needs to look out for them while also protecting the organization, often from itself.

- *Level 7*: Most organizations like to think they've been developing leaders and managers throughout the earlier stages of development. But as a company scales and starts to talk about scale as a discipline, laser focus on leadership development and build formalized programs that result in ladders per role while retaining the mission, vision, and values of the organization as it evolves into something new. Also be prepared for pushback against that evolution because change can be hard.

Beyond level 7, the human resources function likely has an executive leading the charge. Nothing that can be put into a book on startups will equal what they bring to the table. Before making key decisions regarding humans, consult these executives. After all, the organization by then is full of people that know far more about their domain of expertise than founders ever want to know. Look at annual survey results, chat with individual contributors, work with leaders, and try to do right by the customers, the team, and the investors. They all have their own functions that the founders likely no longer fully understand. Such is the life of turning an adventuring party into a full-on campaign.

How an organization effectively manages people to do something when those people know more about what it is they do than the founders is a challenge. Leaders learn to get out of their way and stay in their own lane. Define their role, enlist them to validate the role, and set clear and reasonable goals that highlight the organization's expectations.

Roles, Goals, and Expectations

A common theme throughout this book is to be clear about roles, goals, and expectations (see the discussions on key performance indicators for an organization in Chapter 1 and clarity in Chapter 2). This includes how the adventuring party itself develops, what party members do, how they go about conducting themselves, the goals they agree to when hired, how those goals shift over time, and any expectations of individual contributions, team contributions, and the organization overall. A good party is made up of a cleric, a thief, a fighter (or other tank), a ranger, a mage, or other utility players. The expectation of the cleric is they will heal and bless the party. Maybe they turn undead or do other tasks, but like a good human resources team, they keep the party healthy.

Clarity is a central theme of this book, as is intentionality. Clarity is central to growing the people that join the party, from a first-level magic user to an arch-mage capable of throwing chain lightning to take out an entire army of trolls. Founders can't do every task that's needed in every discipline of the organization on their own, but we can build something amazing and take it to a mass market by surrounding ourselves with great allies who understand the part they're playing in the campaign—and how their role can shift over time.

All of this is important because founders should want to build an amazing place to work—a place that is successful and shares its success.

Build a Different Place to Work

Each player gains good experiences and bad experiences during each adventure they embark upon. They take the good and bad on to the next adventure or campaign. It's important to remember that not everyone is identical or wants the same things from the game. What works for one person might not work for everyone or might work differently given the culture being built.

Founders can learn a lot from those that join the campaign. Each of their experiences then helps shape a new adventuring party capable of more than a founder could have accomplished on their own. Giving each person a voice, allowing them to bring their whole self to work, hearing the wisdom they provide, combining all of those magical elements—that's where we go from a run-of-the-mill game to an epic journey.

Who do we surround ourselves with? How do we treat them? How do we want them to treat us and one another? A company is a collection of humans, and the kind of organization we build is then an amalgamation of all those humans. In a previous chapter, we covered philosophy—from transparency to a mission to values—and that philosophy must be held by our people. Let's look at how we find those people and give them the best possible start in our organization.

Buy, Borrow, or Build Talent

Nothing impacts organizational performance and culture like the people selected to become a part of the company. Ensuring we get the right talent for the right opportunity is one of the most challenging and essential responsibilities founders own, especially early on. To help select the right talent, understand what the role entails. Leverage different perspectives to balance the short- and long-term realities of the organization, customers, and employees. To balance selecting the right skills against the right organizational needs, decide whether to buy, borrow, or build talent (often on a per-discipline basis and re-evaluated annually):

- *Buy*: Should we hire this talent as part of this organization?

- *Borrow*: Should we partner with contractors to complete this work?

- *Build*: Should we build or train the talent we need over time?

The right talent strategy should balance the needs, capabilities, and capital of the organization. The following sections cover each of these strategies to explore their intentions, benefits, and challenges.

Buy Talent

Most adventuring parties employ a henchman here and there. Sometimes they become a permanent and often indispensable part of the organization. When a company "buys" talent, they usually pay someone with all the skills at a higher wage than if bringing someone in to train into a role. They usually need these people to be able to hit the ground running. Companies look at the required skills or experiences for the position with the understanding that salary and benefits expectations will be market dependent. Roles can be as a part-time or full-time (W2) employee of the organization. In this capacity, the human in the role participates in organizational benefits, technologies, services, and growth opportunities.

The current market demand for skills, experiences, and available talent pool helps determine the market rate for this role, adjusted based on geography. This is amplified with more tenured professionals. For example, when we look at software engineering as a segment, there are more jobs available than talent. As expected based on supply and demand, salary and benefits expectations are high for in-demand talent.

Buying talent makes sense when the organization believes that the investment in this role supports the longer-term vision and goals of the organization, employees, and customers. The process of hiring talent should also identify and select specific experiences, skills, and abilities required to help the organization grow.

Expected Compensation

Figuring out where to start new employees can be tricky. Consult with an internal or external HR professional. These individuals can help develop position/job descriptions and develop cash compensation ranges based on the role, market/labor realities, and geography. Salary fluctuates across different locations (Minneapolis vs. San Francisco), so prepare for varied expectations.

Alternatively, there are many salary benchmark services that can help founders get started, for example, Payscale (`www.payscale.com/`). Developing pay ranges is as much an art as science, but Payscale does a good job building solid compensation foundations. None of these services are perfect, but they can be a great starting point. Be prepared to pay a bit of money for HR or compensation services. These fees tend to be fractional when compared with the salary we will be spending. Let's look at some pros to outsourcing talent acquisition:

- Good hires impact short- and long-term performance and culture.

- *Talent mobility*: Good talent should help grow different parts of the organization through different roles over time.

- Potential infusion of industry or role experience can accelerate the perspectives, maturity, and growth of the organization.

- New employees are able to be instantly productive.

A few cons to be aware of include the following:

- Market conditions and available talent pool drive compensation rates and expectations.

- Poor hires can negatively impact the culture and performance of our organization, and performance management takes time, resources, and energy.

- While cash compensation gets the most attention, traditional benefits (health care, 401k, etc.) can be large expenses, costing the organization 15–20% (as an estimate) of the employee's salary.

The younger the startup, the more likely friends or people founders knew in school will be hired. As the company scales, however, that becomes less a part of the hiring calculus because the organization needs to scale faster—especially if there's a round of funding to grow the adventuring party faster (and thus an expectation to grow revenues faster). Another means to scale quickly is to borrow talent from other organizations.

Borrow Talent

When an organization decides to borrow talent, those parts of the workforce are contracted through an individual or organization to outsource the work. Borrowing talent generally allows organizations the ability to access specific skills, expertise, and experiences. When borrowing talent (using 1099 or outsourced services contracts), expect to pay a premium for the projects provided and hours worked (especially when outsourced to larger firms with more layers of management).

Borrowing talent allows the company to scale skills up or down quickly within the organization based on demand. Provided that most of the work is project or time based, it also becomes easier to extend, limit, or eliminate contracts as needed. Borrowing talent makes the most sense when work is limited, time based, well defined, established, and understood. Temporary staffing augmentation, specific marketing projects, and new market/product exploration tend to be great opportunities for borrowing talent. Also consider some pros to outsourcing:

- Fast access to skilled and experienced practitioners.

- Contracts are generally project- or time-specific, allowing for more dynamic adjustments in the relationship.

- No benefits or incurred internal services costs.

Be careful not to borrow talent and then treat contractors like employees. Fundera put together a great resource to help businesses understand the contractual and behavioral differences and expectations between a W2 and a 1099 contractor available at www.fundera.com/blog/1099-vs-w2-employee to provide further guidance. Some of the other potential drawbacks of working with outsourced talent can include the following:

- Project and hourly premiums tend to be higher costs.

- The organization has limited controls over the contracted relationship and expectations.

- Leveraging an external relationship is still work and will require time, attention, and intentional focus.

- The knowledge that talent gains leaves when the contract is over (often called "brain drain").

More information can be found at www.nerdwallet.com/article/small-business/contract-vs-full-time-workers. But remember, always work with internal or external HR partners to understand the needs and expectations of any contracted role. Another great way to source increasingly complicated talent requirements is to build earlier-career staff into those roles, which we'll look at in the next section.

Build Talent

When we build talent, we make a mindful selection of individuals based on their potential, not necessarily their current skillset. Like buying talent, we intend to hire a part- or full-time employee (W2) to the organization. The difference is committing to helping this individual grow into their role within the company. This is often the choice many organizations make, without a strong understanding of what is required to accomplish this task. If your talent strategy is "They will figure it out," please don't build talent; instead, buy your talent. Growing talent requires long-term perspectives and the ability to invest our time, effort, energy, and capital into emerging talent.

Building talent makes sense when our internal expertise and systems help onboard, mentor, and grow new talent. Building talent works well when there is a directed career path (entry-level support to support supervisor to product manager and so on) for employees to grow within. Apprenticeships can be alternative ways to build talent. This approach usually establishes a tight 1:1 relationship that allows for high levels of engagement, coaching, mentorship, and knowledge transfer.

Understanding how to grow talent starts by understanding how adults learn. The 70/20/10 approach provides a framework to understand how adults best learn and grow. This includes

- *70%–experience*: Most people tend to learn the most through our experiences and opportunities. When given the chance to leverage and expand new skills in action, most tend to see high levels of growth and development in talent.

- *20%–coaching and community*: Peer and manager feedback is fundamental to developing new skills. When there's a network to supply feedback and direction, it helps employees leverage the experiences

(70%) provided. The feedback and coaching should be provided frequently and from multiple sources (managers, coaches, peers, and partners).

- *10%–classic training and courses*: Without some fundamental training, courses, or conferences, the coaching and experiences we provide tend to fall short. Virtual courses and resources are more diverse and accessible than ever before. Employee growth often involves training courses, and while this is an important part of the process, it is less impactful than most hope.

Building talent can also be incredibly rewarding to mentors. It's gratifying to know we are helping others, and watching people achieve professional wins and milestones can be both exciting and humbling. Other pros to growing our talent base include the following:

- Develop deeper, more personal relationships that support higher engagement and tenure levels.

- Develop the specific skills, abilities, and approaches necessary in the organization.

- The ability to expand opportunities and access to more people.

- Built talent is often more loyal to the organization.

There are drawbacks as well. Some of the reasons organizations choose not to go this route include the following:

- Significant time and effort are needed up front to get employees started on the right path.

- Longer-term planning is needed to ensure proper systems are defined to grow employees effectively.

- Programs may require several months of operations before desired outputs are realized.

Combining courses, coaching, and intentional experiences builds an environment where growth can be optimized. Organizations that embrace building talent must be intentional and create the optimal conditions for growth. Growing talent is challenging work that, when done right, can completely change the health of an organization, the growth of the employees who join in the mission, and the success of customers. The buy, borrow, or build talent strategy helps solve short- and long-term needs. Remember, the supply chain for a software company is the people. Before hiring, take the time to slow down and evaluate the best talent strategy that aligns with the type of customers and how quickly the organization has to scale.

Clarity: Goals, Roles, and Behaviors

The adventuring party rushes into battle. The cleric blesses the party. The ranger pulls out their bow and shoots an arrow. The paladin charges in to pummel the monster. The mage fires off a lightning bolt. The thief hides in the shadows. Everyone has a role. But as the party grows and each member levels up, the roles and even the goals of each player become less clear. A lack of clarity contributes to some of the most challenging, stressful, and sometimes dangerous moments experienced in business (and life). From not understanding the expectations or goals at work to driving a wagon of supplies down a mountain pass in near-whiteout conditions, clarity matters.

Reduced clarity naturally creates a human response or behavior. People tend to move with more caution, restraint, and fear in that vacuum. Clarity provides intentional, directed, and appropriately placed behaviors. In times of change, uncertainty, growth, or maintenance, clarity helps organizations and individuals make better decisions. Clarity drives behaviors and actions that move organizations forward, but not just forward in random directions. Instead, everyone is aligned toward common goals.

The next few sections outline a few simple steps to help organizations increase clarity around direction, expectations, purpose, roles, and key behaviors. More clarity improves the likelihood everyone performs better and helps establish authentic cultures!

Start with Organizational Goals

Organizational goals help make sure everyone understands where the organization is focused and the impacts each person will make. To define these, consider the top three goals the organization is trying to accomplish. Document why the goals matter. Write down who needs to know the goals and how they will be communicated. Also consider the impact to the customers, the company, and the employees at the company.

The goals we document early in the life of the company won't be 100% perfect. They should be clear enough that anyone can understand how to orient teams and individuals within the organization to work toward the objectives. Once there's clarity on the organization, focus on departments and teams. Ensure teams and individuals have clarity of purpose and objectives.

Once everyone understands where the organization is headed, ensure that departments, teams, and people are aware, aligned, and empowered. Document why each team exists and why they matter. Record goals for teams (or departments) and why those matter, even if the team is just one person at the time. The way a team operates is also important. Define how they should make decisions, communicate, collaborate, and execute. Consider meetings, rituals, workflows, tools, and resources as well. Finally, give room for the team to grow and evolve over time.

The following goals ladder up to the organizational goals. Each role on a team should feed up to the team goals as well. For these, go from thinking about teams to the impact each individual has on the team. Define the top three primary responsibilities and goals for this role, why those matter, and any additional or secondary responsibilities and goals for this role. Further, document why any secondary responsibilities are such. For example, a software QA engineer in a smaller company might also handle some support cases until a larger support organization is built. These goals and responsibilities should then be prioritized in a realistic manner. Consider that QA engineer who gets too many cases to do any QA work per day. If an expectation is set that they will prevent escape defects while they're handling support, then they're being set up for failure.

At this point, if the work is done to define the roles within the company and how their goals and expectations feed up to the objectives in support of the mission, the hiring team (often just the founders in the beginning) should be on the path to increase clarity, expectations, and orientation for future sub-organizations, departments, teams, and individuals. The next aspect to focus on, and possibly the most important, is the behaviors to set for the entire organization so it embodies the vision and values. This impacts the organization's output and culture.

Confirm the Key Behaviors That Matter Most

Increasing clarity, roles, goals, and priorities won't matter if they are not met and driven by key behaviors. Simply put, the manifestation of the organization's performance, values, and culture simply comes down to behaviors. Leaders' and employees' behaviors drive the organization's performance and culture. It isn't the beer fridge, cool furniture, or foosball table—it's how people behave that truly determines the performance and culture of a company.

Values are the bedrock for how groups of people behave as an organization. As realities shift, the values should serve as a foundation for direction, orientation, and expectations in both calm and chaotic moments. Those values were covered earlier in the book, but now it's time to look deeper and think about the behaviors they drive and why those matter. Consider short- or long-term key behaviors that best support the organization's growth and performance. Document why they matter and the most important behavior leaders should lead with. Then think about why that most important behavior matters. This does as much to set the alignment (lawful good vs. chaotic neutral) of the organization.

The most important part of this exercise is simply to be deliberate about how people should act and what leaders of those people should expect out of themselves and one another. Taking a few minutes, hours, or even days to slow down to increase clarity makes all the difference when leading organizations through uncertain or critical moments. These points of reflection and contemplations will increase the clarity and purpose of any organization and may help leaders understand a little bit more about their own ethos.

Talent Foundations: Art and Science

It is time, energy, and capital intensive to define, find, select, onboard, and grow talent. Often, an organization's most substantial expense will be acquiring, paying, retaining, and replacing talent. Especially when there aren't a lot of users, a software company's largest cost center is often its people.

The talent we select as part of an organization makes a direct impact on our performance and culture. When we get it right, amazing things happen to an organization. When we get it wrong, it can set us back months, quarters, or years or even create an existential crisis. Recruiting is as much a science as it is an art. In the following, we have outlined several elements to consider before, during, and after we hire an employee.

Virtual and In-Person

As workforces continue to diverge geographically (a process hastened by pandemics), virtual teams have become more of a norm than an outlier. These ideas and approaches work for both virtual and in-person experiences. We'll dive deeper into better practices for virtual recruiting tactics and onboarding a little later. Before looking for the right humans to join our organization, provide clarity on our purpose and the orientation of the organization. Ask the following:

- Why do we exist as a company?

- Where are we headed as an organization?

- What are our goals this year?

- What are our values?

- Who do we help? Why?

- Why us?

Much of this was done earlier in the book, but double-check that it's still accurate. The more clearly the purpose of the organization and the role of each human is defined, the greater the chances the right talent is sourced, onboarded more fluidly, and given an increased chance for employee success, growth, and retention. We recommend every position require a role clarity checklist and marking this as a milestone in the onboarding process (covered later in the chapter). Here we're looking to ask the following at regular intervals (and see movement into a more mature understanding of the role as we go):

- Do we understand the goals of this role?

- Have we defined a salary range for this position?

- Do we understand the required skills and experiences
  we must have and would like to have for this role?

- Have we confirmed the budget?

Once we've considered and documented the role, we have one more step before we start recruiting. We must understand federal, state, and local compliance when it comes to hiring and staffing employees. Beyond compliance, it's a good idea to have key documents created and ready before we hire an employee. This is another milestone, which should include the following (at a minimum):

- Required insurances

- Company handbook and policies

- Government, state, and local reporting

- Agreements, which include a non-disclosure
  agreement, an agreement protecting intellectual
  property, and an employment agreement

Note   We recommend most organizations identify an internal or external certified HR professional to help understand regulations, compliance, and best practices. Don't know where to start? Check out Best HR Outsourcing Services for Small Businesses in 2020.

Total Rewards and Motivations

The size and status of the organization impacts the types of benefits that can be offered in a cost-effective manner. Each company is unique, and one size of programs will not fit all. Most importantly, go beyond thinking about money and build a philosophy around total rewards across three buckets: compensation, benefits, and experiences.

Here are a few ways to think about the various rewards we might provide to prospective and existing employees, with a number of attributes for each bucket:

- Compensation
    - Guaranteed pay, including a base salary and any guaranteed bonuses
    - Individual performance rewards, including any incentives such as sales commission
    - Routine discretionary bonuses and spot bonuses
- Benefits
    - Health, dental, and vision benefits
    - Life and disability benefits
    - Retirement planning and 401k options
    - Pre-tax accounts, such as a health savings account
    - Time off and parental leave
    - Flexibility
    - Other benefits, such as bus passes, parking, etc.
- Experiences
    - Organization mission, vision, and values
    - Engaging work
    - Employee growth and development opportunities
    - Culture and relationships with other team members
    - Perks and the work environment itself

Clarifying our philosophy across these three areas helps define what we can offer current and prospective employees. This brings us to our next hiring milestone for a documented set of total rewards and the motivations they map to. The first two buckets are fairly straightforward. Next, let's get into the candidate experience we want to provide during the recruitment process. Remember that when you are hiring, your candidates are your customers.

Recruiting Workflow and Candidate Experience

Software is eating the world. This has created a bottleneck in the supply chain for talent (although the occasional layoff at large companies might free up some resources). Recruiting is harder than ever before, so we must be more mindful than in previous eras when doing so. Before we start recruiting, consider the candidate experience we want to create for the talented individuals we select or reject. Here are some potential areas of focus:

- *Communication*: How will communication work throughout the entire workflow?

- *Clear milestones*: What are the key milestones, and how will we keep candidates informed throughout the entire experience?

- *Interview expectations*: How will the interview be conducted (Zoom, Google Hangouts, etc.), and what should prep for the conversation look like?

Now that we've defined several expectations we can set and how we want to recruit, we can get into the actual workflow. Defining our recruiting workflow clarifies both internal and external expectations and timing. This helps clarify the expectation and focus for each phase of the recruiting process. Consider this as a typical flow. We post a job, we get some resumes, and then we do two video screenings and an interview. Provided the candidate is hired, we then move into onboarding and long-term career development. These add up when we have five, ten, or twenty candidates we might be talking to at each step of the process. Let's look at what we want to accomplish at each step:

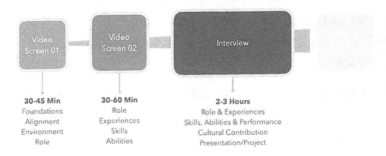

In the preceding scenario, three significant phases/milestones are part of our workflow. We established two candidate video screens focused on intentional topics and a final long-form interview (which can be delivered virtually or in-person) with deeper discussions and a review of a presentation or project.

Define Recruiting Roles, Goals, and Expectations

Once the process has been established and communicated, take time to understand the part of the founders in moving candidates along the defined path. Here think about the roles, goals, and expectations. To help understand what the company is looking for, document the following (e.g., on a Confluence page):

- *Roles*: What is the job?

- *Goals*: What does success look like?

- *Expectations*: How do I behave? What tasks do I need to accomplish? Why?

- *Recruiter*: Responsible for partnering with a hiring manager to define, create, and drive a recruiting workflow that sources and identifies the right talent.

- *Hiring manager*: Responsible for defining and aligning the goals and needs of the role while partnering with the recruiter to screen, interview, and select the right talent.

The goal is to build a workflow that identifies and selects the key behaviors, talents, and motivations that will grow the right performance and culture within the organization and to do so equitably. Sometimes it's important to slow down in order to go really fast. If we have the opportunity (or can create it), this serves as a valuable area to spend a few additional cycles clarifying, aligning, and preparing to share. Sharing the process and clearly stating the expectations makes the organization and founders look like we know what we're doing and instills a sense of confidence in those who are interviewing and their potential coworkers.

In the next section, we'll work through developing a pipeline of great talent, moving talent through that workflow, qualifying talent, and great behaviors to exhibit during the interviews.

Planning, Preparation, and Talent Attraction

It's now time to shift our focus toward identifying, attracting, qualifying, and selecting uniquely talented humans. This experience is where all our considerations, perspectives, and ideas are put to the test.

Talent selection is one of the most challenging, critical, and defining decisions we make as leaders. The culture and performance of our organizations depend on our talent choices. The goal of this section is to help slow down to increase clarity, focus, and alignment surrounding the recruiting practices and workflows. When we understand what we are looking for and why that matters, we are more likely to select the right perspectives, abilities, and talent to grow our organization.

Planning and Prep

Focus on known approaches to create a fairer and equal experience. How we build equity into the recruiting experience is determined by the decisions we make, the barriers we eliminate or sustain, and what we value as an organization. We should question everything.

The approaches we take focus on clarity to increase alignment and accountability. The more requirements we establish for candidates, the narrower our talent pool becomes. It's important to consider that we may exclude talent or communities when we increase barriers to employment. We need to question all the established barriers (experiences, skills, degrees, etc.) that we "require" and to make sure they are necessary and not just habitually (or systemically) set. For example, we want our doctors to have medical degrees; we may not care if our salesperson has a degree. Instead, identify if they listen, are responsive, and offer a real solution to customer problems.

Recruiting and selecting for these types of behaviors instead of requiring degrees tends to expand our potential talent pool. To change the dynamics of our talent pool, we can consider if we should buy, borrow, or build our talent, as discussed earlier.

Bias Is Real

Bias is real, and before conducting an interview, get in tune with unconscious and conscious biases. There are lots of resources, coaches, and organizations committed to helping us better understand and evolve beyond our own biases. We will walk through technical solutions for increasing clarity in our recruiting workflow, but mitigating our biases is up to us.

Note   For more on noticing our own implicit bias, check out Harvard's Project Implicit at `https://implicit.harvard.edu/implicit/takeatest.html`.

Another tool to help with bias (and generally be better at hiring) is a recruiting scorecard. These simple documents help align hiring managers, centralize feedback, and combat biases. The more information the hiring manager can provide, the smoother the process and the more the recruiter can help. Before implementing, ensure the scorecard helps collect and assess the behaviors and experiences fundamental for a candidate to succeed in the role.

For more on scorecards, check out the Harvard Business Review article available at `https://hbr.org/2016/02/a-scorecard-for-making-better-hiring-decisions`.

As covered in the introduction of this book, we can't cover diversity enough. The more time spent looking inside, the more insight we have. The more we learn, the better humans we are and the more aware of how our actions impact others. Being able to hire others is a place of privilege, and that deserves attention of itself.

Confirm What We Value, What We Have, and What We Need

Slowing down to go fast allows a few moments to reflect on what is needed (and will be needed) in an organization beyond skills and experience. Here are a few additional perspectives to reflect on before actively selecting talent:

- Will this person make the organization more well rounded, or will they just copy and paste more of the same assets?

- How can this person's approach help get to better discussions and decisions?

- How can this person add to the total value (composition) of our team?

- What skills and experiences am I missing on my team that this person has?

- What has this person learned from their experiences?

- How does this candidate already live our values?

How these six topics are approached and discussed will show up in the decisions made when creating candidate attraction and recruiting workflows. The next section breaks down the core elements of the recruiting process to help explore, define, and create systems to attract and grow amazing talent.

Talent Attraction

The logistical and technical elements of recruiting mean we focus first on attracting talent to the organization. There are several foundations to establish as a part of this process, which include the following for most organizations:

- Job/position description

- Behaviors

- Talent branding vs. company branding

- Pipeline development and management

- Posting jobs
- Candidate sourcing: passive or active

This process begins with the position description.

Job/Position Description

Without an intentional and specific position/job description, the likelihood of finding and selecting the right talent decreases significantly. A majority of recruiting processes start by Googling the position title, making a few minor "cultural" tweaks, and posting the job. When borrowing another organization's job/position description, there's an assumption that their role expectations and behaviors are the same as what our organization needs. This is one reason that most job/position descriptions are generic, ripe with buzzwords, and poor reflections of the actual work performed within the job.

To build an effective position description, start by confirming role clarity. Check out the section "Clarity: Goals, Roles, and Behaviors" to work through some proven tactics for enhancing role clarity and expectations. Once role clarity has been established, transition this into a working position or job description.

Always consult an HR team or practitioners when building a position/ job description. Our company type and location may require certain considerations (FLSA job classification, Affirmative Action Plan, Equal Employment Opportunity, etc.). An HR practitioner will walk through the final steps in converting this clarity into a great position/job description. Once we have a thoughtful position/job description, we have a map for success. For some additional assistance, check out How to Develop a Job Description (SHRM).

A great position/job description helps us build an intentional recruiting process that focuses on the work, behaviors, and experiences needed to excel in the role. Ignoring this foundational work is one of the most dangerous shortcuts leaders make. In our roles as leaders, we must do this work and do it right.

Behaviors (They Matter More Than Most Think)

Building a great position/job description is the first opportunity to help us begin to think about key behaviors when it comes to identifying and selecting talent. Behaviors are everything in organizations—there is nothing that can impact, destroy, or grow the culture and performance like behaviors. At their cores, culture and performance are byproducts of our behaviors.

Identifying key behaviors within a recruiting process increases the likelihood any company will find the right people that exhibit the right behaviors. Let's make sure there's clarity about the role and that there's a good position description; get the position description approved by a human resources professional, and identify the key behaviors and outcomes desired—and why they matter.

Talent Branding vs. Company Branding

Most organizations have a firm grasp on company branding—that is, how to identify and communicate the value (products, services, support, etc.) provided to current or prospective customers. When it comes to talent branding, many organizations are just waking up to the importance of this concept. Talent branding focuses on connecting and sharing the opportunities and experiences that are an authentic part of working for your organization.

Each organization provides its own unique experiences and opportunities, and talent branding helps us share an authentic story with prospective employees. Idealized misrepresentations of the experiences we provide and the company we pretend to be can attract the wrong talent and negatively impact retention. Get an authentic grip on the opportunities and experiences that can be provided, and then share them with individuals who resonate with what can be delivered.

The opportunities and experiences available at the organization identify and communicate the types of behaviors and talents that thrive within our company. The following questions can help guide how to brand the organization to potential talent:

- What problem is the organization solving and why?

- Who does the organization help and why?

- What is it like to work at the organization?

- How do people at the organization behave as humans?

- What is it like to grow with, at, and within the organization?

- What are the benefits provided?

- What are we most proud of as an organization?

- How do the values translate into talent branding?

- Does inclusion, diversity, and equal access to opportunity matter to the organization? If so, what actions actively promote those?

Now that much of the work to prepare is done, much of the remainder will be a lot of cut, copy, and paste! Let's continue to where many a reader might have thought we'd be by now: posting jobs. And trust us, the work put in so far will make the next part go by quickly!

Pipeline Development and Management

By increasing the clarity of the position description, authentic experiences, and opportunities, there's a solid foundation for recruiting. Now it is time to attract talent to the open position.

Try to include as many qualified candidates as possible when posting jobs. Think about where all the candidates that aren't known to the organization might exist and how to share the opportunity with them. It's easy to jump right to those that are known. It's harder, but often more rewarding, to encourage everyone to think about what isn't known and so how to increase the perspectives or experiences within the organization. An adventuring party of just barbarians isn't as effective as one that's well rounded.

Start with tools that work coast to coast, and then focus on industry groups, community organizations, and finally personal networks that can help expand the candidate pipeline. These include tools like LinkedIn, Indeed, AngelList, ZipRecruiter, and traditional job boards, but extend to postings in specific industries and communities and, of course, the personal network of existing team members.

Active or Passive Candidate Sourcing

Posting jobs is a passive tactic. Recruiters post the job and wait for candidates to apply to the opportunity. Depending on the market conditions, this tactic might be all that is needed, but to find the biggest pool of candidates, actively source and entice candidates to the opportunity.

LinkedIn Recruiter Lite is an effective tool for active sourcing, organizing, and managing communications with prospective candidates. Other tools/websites will also work, but LinkedIn was built with this purpose in mind. When sourcing talent, continually go back to the job/position description to ensure the hunt is on for the right talent, experiences, and abilities. Also look at previous resumes as our views on a position, need, or team might have evolved and a candidate that wasn't originally thought to be a match might now be perfect.

Qualification, Flow, and Talent Selection

Take the time to clarify the job description and focus the talent pipeline to make selecting talent an easier process. This section will help work through how to best qualify, manage, and select talent that is best for the role and organization. Next, let's focus on how to guide, assess, partner, and select candidates for open positions. This begins with a focus on how to qualify and move talent through the recruiting workflows.

A strong alignment between hiring managers and recruiters is important when moving qualified candidates to initial screening conversations. This arms recruiters with the information they need to bring in more qualified candidates and reduces the amount of time hiring managers need to spend in interviews. Alignment also sets the rules of engagement for how candidates are selected (or not) to participate in our interview process.

Done correctly, companies develop a clear and known set of expectations to determine if a candidate is qualified or disqualified. These expectations also help focus on the requirements of the job and reduce any conscious or unconscious biases. Established correctly, the recruiting workflow clarifies the phases, questions, qualifications, and expectations for the process and people.

Phases

The process to qualify candidates can be broken up into phases. From selecting or rejecting resumes to initial candidate screens and final interviews, each of these components represents a phase or part of the recruiting process.

For each phase, answer the following questions:

- What is the purpose of this phase? Why?
- What is assessed and needed in this phase? Why?
- What questions are asked in this phase? Why?
- What are the desired responses? Why?
- Who is responsible for moving candidates through the phases? Why?

A few of the more common phases in the recruiting process include the following:

- *Resume selection*: Resumes that come in are reviewed and selected for screening by the recruiter or hiring manager.

- *Initial screening*: Phone or video conversation to qualify the alignment between the company, the role, and the candidate's desires, expectations, and abilities.

- *Hiring manager screening* (or interview): Phone or video conversation to qualify the alignment more deeply between the role and the candidate's desires, expectations, and abilities.

- *Team interview*: Generally, it consists of one or multiple rounds of final interviews with key members of the interviewing/selection team, focused on specific experiences and abilities that are foundational to the role. This phase generally includes an ability assessment, evaluation, and/or presentation.

Reviewing Resumes

Once the job is posted, it's time to start reviewing resumes. A single job posting may pull in anywhere from five to a hundred or more resumes. Keep in mind what qualifications and experiences are required in a candidate—and what isn't. At one point, we would get 100 resumes for every posting. Many can easily be overlooked. For example, an entry-level desktop support job likely doesn't warrant getting a visa for someone from another country, so that resume can quickly be disregarded.

Let's look at some red flags to help filter through resumes:

- *Infected files*: A file with a virus, in *our* industry, is a showstopper.

- *Listing outdated skills and technology*: Yes, someone may have spent ten years as a COBOL programmer, but the last two were with Swift. Focus on the skills needed and how recently they were applied.

- *Multiple grammatical errors and typos*: If a candidate can't spell-check a resume, they probably won't spell-check their emails or pay attention when their grammar gets flagged. This lack of attention to detail may extend to other areas of their work.

- *Lack of brevity*: A 30-page play-by-play of every time a candidate called a support desk to get a problem fixed is a huge red flag. The ability to communicate succinctly (whether in the written form, on a call, or in person) is one of the more underrated job skills to look for when hiring.

- *Inappropriate email address*: It's amazing that Google would actually authorize some email addresses we've seen. The bad judgment from a candidate in not creating a sanitized account could be concerning.

- *Missing cover sheet*: We can often learn more about a candidate from the cover sheet than from the resume. If a cover sheet isn't included, that's telling in its own way.

Each organization has their own criteria, and most will be better than ours. But this should help get anyone started. Be patient; there are a lot of great people looking for work! Go through all resumes in batches, in and out of busy seasons. The best potential employees will get hired quickly, so quick action is required to snag them. Put in the time and effort to keep the ball rolling through the hiring process.

Candidate Evaluation

Be clear and intentional with conversations when interviewing with candidates. To provide a fair and consistent process, each candidate should be asked the same set of qualifying questions. These questions should be defined ahead of time and ideal responses documented. This doesn't mean not to ask follow-up questions; absolutely qualify or dig deeper into responses. But have a consistent set of questions to use as a starting point in order to provide each candidate with an equal opportunity to respond to questions pertinent to the role/opportunity.

Look for win-win-win scenarios. This means to check each of these boxes:

- *Win 1*: This is a great opportunity that is aligned with what the candidate wants.

- *Win 2*: This individual is a great contributor to the performance and culture of the organization.

- *Win 3*: Aligning the talent, opportunity, and company strongly supports the customer.

If all three are in alignment, more qualified talent will be hired. They will also contribute more to the growth of the organization and the success of customers. To help through this process, let's look at an example of the screening, phases, and final interviews.

Example: Screening, Phases, and Final Interviews

Depending on workflows, there might be several screening processes (e.g., one per department) or a single screening process. Each organization is unique, and the workflows need to support operations, intentions, and needs. When phases are intentional, defined, and aligned, there's a greater chance at identifying and selecting the right talent.

In the following example, each phase of the process has a different focus:

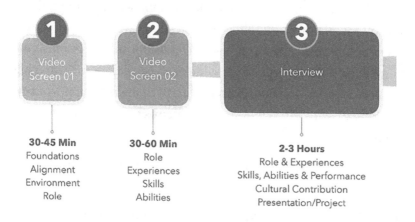

Each phase then has a purpose:

- *Phase 1–Alignment with the environment and role*:
  Focus on foundations of the role and what the
  candidate looks for in a job and organization. The goal
  is to ensure there is a balanced alignment between the

organization, opportunity, and candidate. When strong alignment is identified, the candidate is moved to the next phase for deeper analysis and evaluation.

- *Phase 2–Experiences, skills, and abilities*: Here, look at the primary responsibilities of the role (per the job/position description) and focus on questions that relate to the expectations of the role.

- *Phase 3–Team interview and project presentation*: The final interview is usually a team-based interview experience. When interviewing as a team, it is again critical that each individual understands their roles, goals, and expectations.

Structures vary, but should be intentional with the questions asked and the desired responses and clarify the roles, goals, and expectations for candidates who participate in the interview phase. It's great to have candidates come prepared with a presentation or a report, project, or repository if that more closely aligns with the responsibilities of the job. These projects should be able to be completed within two to three hours over seven days to ensure everyone has a fair opportunity—but the projects should provide insights into the style and quality of work they can reliably produce now. This informs those who hire about how much work will be involved to get candidates where they need to be.

Talent Selection

It's critical to take a deep breath and slow down (before we go fast) when we arrive at the moment of selection. To do so, stay hyper-intentional with conversations and be mindful of preferences. All the work done thus far has led to this decisive moment, and the people hired will shape the culture and output of the team.

As humans, it's in our nature to compare candidates directly against other candidates. Instead, first compare each candidate against the job/position description we have created. This involves asking the same questions independently, including the following:

- Where will they thrive? Why?

- Where will they struggle? Why?

- How will they best grow and develop? Why?

- Are they willing to grow and develop? Why?

- Can they do the job? What leads us to that conclusion?

At this point, how candidates align with the work is more important than how well they'll work with each other, while still considering whether a candidate can perform in a startup environment. When comparing candidates it's easy to lose sight of the role and work that must be completed and expand the scope of the position in ways that haven't been more deeply considered. Another aspect of comparing candidates that's overanalyzed is cultural fit.

Cultural Contribution

Culture is a byproduct of behaviors. What are the behaviors that make up our organization? Where does this candidate live out these behaviors? Most hiring managers are looking for cultural fit. But that should be recalibrated to cultural *contribution* and not *fit*.

Cultural contribution is an alignment in the behaviors needed and the people who live and embody those behaviors. An individual's actions should contribute to the growth of the company. Cultural fit tends to sound more like "I like this person" or "I would want to have a beer with this individual." That's all good, but how does having a beer contribute to the culture and performance of our organization? For those in recovery, that seems like a very unfair assessment of their ability to contribute meaningfully to the culture.

Cultural fit is equated with cultural comfort. People are naturally drawn to those who look like us, talk like us, have similar experiences to our own, and so remind us of ourselves. The question to think about is whether two of the same people would be better to have than someone that balances and compliments the party on a grand adventure.

Cultural fit is a slippery slope and potentially riddled with bias. Remember to focus on the behaviors that contribute to the culture, not the comfort they provide us. In moving toward cultural contribution, we must also define how including different perspectives and lived experiences is more valuable than just a professional experience or developed skill. When we have multiple candidates capable of doing a job, look to the questions in previous lists for guidance.

Once each person is assessed, all scorecards and interviewer feedback should be submitted to the recruiter and hiring manager within 24 hours. The longer the candidate has to wait for feedback, the stronger the likelihood everyone's experience will become fragmented or diluted.

Making the Offer

Once the questions from the previous sections are answered, it's time to create a clearly defined process for how to make a decision on the final candidate. The workflow should include the feedback collected throughout the entire process, the recruiting scorecards, and any additional perspectives or processes relevant to the workflow and the organization. Once the candidate is selected, it's time to make the offer.

Each organization will have its own workflow, but here are a few steps that are effective:

- *Verbal offer*: Call to extend a verbal offer on the position and offer a potential start date.

- *Written offer*: Within a few hours of the verbal offer being accepted, create and finalize a written offer. For advice on drafting a written offer, check out How to Create an Offer Letter Without Contractual Implications (SHRM).

- *Negotiations*: Don't be surprised if a candidate engages in negotiations during the verbal offer or after the written offer has been provided. Each organization should determine its flexibility and comfort when it comes to negotiating. We would recommend engaging with an internal or external HR professional to define parameters that work best for the organization. However, if negotiating flexible or performance based compensation, carefully consider how pay models work in different outcome scenarios to avoid unintended pay consequences.

- *Finalizing the offer*: Once negotiations have been finalized, ensure we get the document fully executed (signed by the company and the person we're hiring) and that start date is clearly communicated to key internal partners or organizations (HR, IT, security, management, etc.).

Once the candidate has accepted the offer, it's time to prepare for their onboarding into the organization, their new department, and their role. Moving beyond the recruiting process is exciting, but bringing a new employee into our organization is time and energy intensive. The relationship begins on the right foot when expectations are set up front. People do their best work when they know what's expected of them.

Next, focus on better practices for helping new employees accelerate into their new job.

Onboarding Employees

New employees experience waves of new people, places, tools, processes, and languages as they acclimate into their new role. This onslaught of new inputs and expectations can be overwhelming for even the most experienced employee. Helping new employees onboard quickly and effectively into the organization is equally as amazing as it is challenging.

Employee onboarding done right accelerates engagement and productivity. When employees onboard poorly, they are slow to adapt, leading to slower performance levels and a negative impact on employee engagement. Challenging starts to a new job are disruptive and overwhelming for everyone involved.

This section builds foundations and clear expectations for defining a successful employee onboarding experience—good for new employees, their coworkers, the company, and customers.

The Purpose of Onboarding

Employee onboarding helps new employees understand how to behave within their new organization, team, and role. Effective onboarding establishes clear operational and behavioral expectations that guide and protect all employees.

Look at organizational onboarding through four different phases:

- *Introduction*: Getting started

- *Organizational*: Mission, vision, values

- *Team/department*: How we operate

- *Role*: Goals and expectations

Each phase has different sets of opportunities and functions necessary to help new employees build the skills, perspectives, and abilities needed to do their job. Doing so in a structured manner sets expectations and helps get new hires productive quickly. This process starts with day one.

Day One Onboarding

An initial email congratulating the new employee on joining the organization and expressing excitement for them to become a part of the team goes a long way. This email may seem obvious and straightforward, but being welcomed before starting makes a massive impact on the employee and is often not done, which leaves those hired feeling like they're in an ambiguous state. We cannot understate the impact clear and straightforward emails can make on reducing anxiety for a new employee.

A couple of template emails can set clear expectations for what a new employee should expect on day one and help get everyone on the same page. This includes things like: Where do I log on? What should I wear? Where do I park? What do I need to bring? Who should I ask? Keep in mind that new employees could take a job at a competitor or take offense to certain words and post them on social media, so make sure everything written down (and this is true with everything that involves communication) can withstand the scrutiny of the public and/or human resources regulations.

Impactful day one onboarding clarifies expectations and paths to support a new employee as they begin their journey. This email also establishes a point of contact for new employees and outlines expectations and actions for their first day at work. Here are a few topics to consider when sending an initial email:

- Where to go or dial into (and how)

- Who to ask for and expect when arriving or logging on

- The time to start

- Where to park (if in person)

- What to bring (e.g., a copy of a driver's license or passport)

- Guidelines for lunch and breaks

- Anything specific for accessing the facilities

- An itinerary for the first day

This will give new coworkers a feeling that the company is on top of things and that they are a priority. Flowing from there, the first day of a new employee's experience should be organized, defined, and shared with everyone involved. This includes meeting with HR, IT, the manager, and the team, as seen in the following "Day One Mock Itinerary":

- 9:00–9:30: Arrival—initial meeting with the hiring manager and review of itinerary

- 9:30–10:30: HR onboarding—paperwork, agreements, and benefits

- 10:30–11:30: IT orientation—tools and access to technology

- 11:30–1:00: Lunch with the team and hiring manager

- 1:00–3:00: Meeting with the manager—onboarding expectations and career path

- 3:00–4:30: Solo work and reflection for the new employee

- 4:30–5:00: Recap and planning session with the manager

There are a lot of stops and new experiences on an employee's first day. The better those are clarified and aligned, the more likely a new employee will have a great first day that sets the tone for a fantastic career at the company.

Organizational Onboarding

Organizational onboarding is the part of onboarding that all employees participate in. Completing a successful day one sets the stage for effective organizational onboarding. Organizational onboarding focuses on helping new employees understand the mission, vision, values, products, services, and customers of an organization.

Organizational onboarding then scales based on the size of an organization and often the complexity of the position being hired. Larger organizations may require several days of onboarding, where smaller companies may accomplish onboarding through a few hours of conversation. Further, each team may add additional onboarding processes given the added intricacies of various roles. If hiring quickly, consider creating cohorts of new employees for organizational onboarding - this can streamline the process and help cohort members create natural connections with each other that make the organization stronger across teams or departments. At the end of organizational onboarding, an employee should be able to easily answer the following questions, regardless of the organization's size:

- *Mission*: Why does the company exist?

- *Vision*: Where is the company headed, and what are the goals?

- *Values*: How do employees behave within the organization and why does that matter?

- *Products*: What products are provided to the market? Why do they matter?

- *Services*: What services are provided to customers? Why do they matter?

- *Customers*: Who leverages the products and services? How do those help them?

Team or Departmental Onboarding

Small startups might treat organizational and team onboarding as the same, but should do so assuming they'll be split up as the organization grows and onboards more people. Team or departmental onboarding builds on top of the work completed during organizational onboarding to help new employees understand how the team or department supports our mission, vision, values, and customers:

- What are the departmental goals and KPIs (monthly, quarterly, and annually)? Why?

- What are the products, tools, resources, and workflows the department uses? Why?

- What are the rituals and meetings for the team? Why?

- How are decisions made? Why?

- How does the team communicate? Why?

- How does the team collaborate? Why?

- How does the team execute? Why?

- How does the department onboard? Why?

- What does continual development and growth look like? Why?

Team or departmental onboarding clarifies the operations and expectations for employees. This stage of onboarding will also scale up or down based on the size and complexity of the role. At the end of team or departmental onboarding, an employee can answer the preceding questions, regardless of organizational size.

Role Onboarding

Role onboarding is the last step in the process and helps new employees accelerate into their new responsibilities. Role onboarding is usually spread out over a three- to six-month period and contains performance and behavioral milestones. Role onboarding requires the most time, effort, and energy of any of the phases.

The first step in the process is to ensure that both employees and managers are in alignment when it comes to roles, goals, and expectations. This can involve the same three simple questions asked throughout the book:

- *Roles*: What is this job? Why does it matter?

- *Goals*: What are the goals/KPIs (monthly, quarterly, and annually) for this job? Why?

- *Expectations*: What expectations does each party have for the role? Why?

Helping new employees onboard into their new role is a real journey. When done right, those who organize the onboarding can learn as much from the new members of the adventuring party as they teach. This helps a company to be better and to iterate and improve the process so that it's better each time. This onboarding roadmap helps document and define several phases of the new employee experience. Here's an example of a week one onboarding:

Milestone One WeekOne	Goals: What are two goals for this milestone?	Example: Make 25 phone calls or update your personal record in a system.
	Performance Objectives: What are they able to do?	Example: Use the phone system to make calls or access the internal records systems.
	Training Needed? What is needed?	Example: Video training on how to use the phone systems and expectations for the phone call.
	Experience Needed? What is needed?	Example: Actually making a call out on the phone system
	Coaching Needed? What is needed?	Example: Manager listening to initial phone calls and providing feedback on what worked and where they can improve.

Beyond week one (or month one, if there's time to plan it), consider having the 30-/60-/90-day milestones defined by the end of a new employee's first week. Know that goals and milestones will shift over time. Better we begin our journey aligned on potential milestones than be oriented toward nothing!

Milestone Two 30 Days	**Goals:** What are two goals for this milestone?	
	Performance Objectives: What are they able to do?	
	Training Needed? What is needed?	
	Experience Needed? What is needed?	
	Coaching Needed? What is needed?	

Milestone Three 60 Days	**Goals:** What are two goals for this milestone?	
	Performance Objectives: What are they able to do?	
	Training Needed? What is needed?	
	Experience Needed? What is needed?	
	Coaching Needed? What is needed?	

Milestone Four 90 Days	**Goals:** What are two goals for this milestone?	
	Performance Objectives: What are they able to do?	
	Training Needed? What is needed?	
	Experience Needed? What is needed?	
	Coaching Needed? What is needed?	

Taking a step past that, consider having the 6-/9-/12-month milestones completed by the end of the 90-day milestone. These goals and performance objectives should be aligned with the full expectations of the role across this final series of milestones.

Milestone Five 6 Months	Goals: What are two goals for this milestone?	
	Performance Objectives: What are they able to do?	
	Training Needed? What is needed?	
	Experience Needed? What is needed?	
	Coaching Needed? What is needed?	

Milestone Six 9 Months	Goals: What are two goals for this milestone?	
	Performance Objectives: What are they able to do?	
	Training Needed? What is needed?	
	Experience Needed? What is needed?	
	Coaching Needed? What is needed?	

Milestone Seven 12 Months	Goals: What are two goals for this milestone?	
	Performance Objectives: What are they able to do?	
	Training Needed? What is needed?	
	Experience Needed? What is needed?	
	Coaching Needed? What is needed?	

Getting employees started with the correct perspectives, orientations, and understandings builds healthier companies. Taking the time to define these experiences for new employees increases the odds of success in their new roles. Keep in mind that managers must commit to helping coach, guide, support, and grow new employees through onboarding and beyond. These tools and perspectives should help build employee onboarding experiences that accelerate talent and grow organizations in an appropriate fashion.

Performance Conversations: Aligning Performance, Growth, and Priorities

Performance conversations are the foundation for effective and healthy organizations to exist and grow. Performance conversations focus on current, past, and future employee performance, growth, and engagement. Without consistent, common, and continual communication, we will struggle to build the relationships and clarity needed to drive employee performance and growth. Without communication, no relationship can persist.

Performance conversations can be weekly, monthly, quarterly, midyear, and/or year-end interactions that focus on an employee's

- Performance (current, past, and future)

- Development, career, and growth (current, past, and future)

- Engagement, motivations, and rewards

Performance conversation frequencies are organization-specific but are always led by managers to help employees and organizations improve and grow. Healthy organizations build unique cultures, and through these cultures, incredible results are produced. By creating consistent, thoughtful, and intentional conversations, people and organizations can grow to solve today's realities and tomorrow's challenges.

Talking About Performance

Performance conversations start and end with performance. Our objective is to discuss and review past, current, and future performance. Conversations about performance help us identify behaviors we need to adjust, keep, and grow.

Productive conversations about performance assume that there is role and goal clarity between the employee and manager. Review the section on role clarity to ensure that the right expectations are defined and aligned. Here are a few performance conversation starters to explore:

- What would you consider to be the greatest contribution and successes you/they are currently making to the team? Please provide examples and the impact these behaviors make on the organization.

- When looking back, what do you believe were the biggest performance challenges/opportunities you/they experienced? What can you both do to help implement the necessary changes and behavioral adjustments?

- Do you feel there is enough time for you/them to successfully complete the work assigned? Are you/they overwhelmed or requiring more time to focus?

- On a one-to-ten scale, how productive are you/they? What would it take to increase your/their productivity?

- What's one project you/they would love to focus on for an entire week, but don't have time to accomplish?

- What are you/they spending a ton of time doing that has the least impact?

- What would you consider to be the greatest contributions and successes you/they made over the past (add a timeframe)? Provide examples and the impact made on the organization.

- How well did you/they prioritize and manage your/their workload? Where did you/they find success? Why? Where could you/they have improved?

- What are your/their goals over the next week, month, quarter, or year?

- How do these goals align and drive the company's strategies forward?

- What do you believe are the biggest opportunities to improve team and organizational performance? What would you recommend? Why?

The current performance is only one part of what should be covered in these conversations. We also want to help our teams grow.

Growth Conversations

Growth conversations focus on developing the skills, perspectives, and abilities of an employee to directly impact performance. This is similar to how attributes (e.g., strength, dexterity, constitution) and skills (e.g., proficiency with a weapon) are gained in a role-playing game, although that can just happen automatically when a player goes to add new points to a given skill. Skill leadership might involve working on strength, and people leadership might involve charisma. There are lots of ways to improve a character. In real life, it requires much more work than in a game.

Growth conversations also focus on career path development as the topics align to performance. The best path to expand one's career development is through growth and performance. Helping employees develop the skills and performance necessary proves an ability to grow, adapt, and master a current set of responsibilities. This mastery allows an employee to expand their duties into new opportunities. Career development needs to be focused on skill development, not titles.

Here are a few growth conversation starters to explore:

- Are all employees currently working on either skill leadership or people leadership development? Why?

  - *Skill leadership*: Expanding technical or specific skill development in a focused area of the business (sales, marketing, engineering etc.)

  - *People leadership*: Expanding skills and abilities focused on leading, developing, and managing people

  - How has each employee's skill development made positive contributions to the success of the team/company? Please provide examples and impacts of these behaviors.

- Moving forward, do you want to focus on skill or people leadership development? Why?

  - How will this make a positive impact on your goals?

  - How will this make a positive impact on your growth/career?

- What skills are you/they struggling to develop? Why? And where do you/they need help?

  - Do you/they get to use your/their natural strengths within your/their job? If yes, what are they and what examples and impacts can you share? If no, what impact is this having on your/their performance and experience at work?

  - Over the past *n* weeks/quarters/months, how and where have you/they grown skills and abilities as an employee or leader? What impacts has this development made to the organization?

- As a manager, what could you have done to have helped this employee build greater levels of success through their development?

- What skills and experiences have you/they gained that align with your/their career development and progress? What did you/they learn? What has changed for you/them?

- What new skills do you/they want to have by this time next year?

- What skills or abilities would you/they like to focus on over the next *n* months? Why?

- How will developing these skills impact

  - Exceeding goals?

  - Driving the organization forward?

  - Supporting customers?

  - Developing your skills and career?

Every organization is different, and these conversations can go in a lot of different directions. They must be positioned in a way that involves the different motivations each employee has (and so there's no single approach).

Engagement, Motivations, Rewards, and Recognition

Understanding employee engagement, motivations, rewards, and recognition can accelerate employee growth and performance. These elements can be challenging for many managers and employees as they require conversations that are both personal and beyond simply the work. For managers that can bridge this gap, employee performance can accelerate beyond expectation.

Engagement looks at an employee's level of commitment, passion, belonging, and focus on their work, team, and organization. Engaged employees significantly outperform disengaged employees, but a majority of the workforce is disengaged with their work/teams. Motivations focus on individualistic (intrinsic and extrinsic) motivators that drive employee behaviors. Motivations are dynamic and change with employees over time and as their realities shift.

Not every player is looking for all their rewards in the form of gold pieces. Rewards and recognition focus on the rewards systems and styles of recognition that individual employees appreciate. Cash is not the number one way to reward/motivate all employees, and not everyone wants to be recognized in a public manner. Each of these areas requires time, attention, and conversation between an employee and manager to be fully understood and leveraged. In the following we have provided conversation starters for engagement, motivation, rewards, and recognition:

- *Meaning*: Does my job provide me with a sense of meaning and purpose? How?

- *Autonomy*: Do I have the freedom to choose how to best perform my job? Why does this matter?

- *Growth*: Do I feel challenged and stretched in my job in a way that results in personal growth and satisfaction? Why does this matter to me?

- *Impact*: Most days, do I see positive results because of my work?

- *Connection*: Do I feel like I belong here?

Additionally, we want to cover motivators and how they are formed. For this, we recommend having teams select three to five from the following list and explain why they matter:

- Compensation

- Strategic thinking

- Culture

- Leadership

- Relationships

- Achievement

- Creative work

- Security

- Autonomy

- Balance

- Stability

- Clarity

- Communication

- Growth and development

- Connection

- Recognition

To unpack that last one, let's look at how people want to be rewarded and recognized. Consider how they (and not just you) like to be rewarded when they are successful and why. Also consider how they like to be recognized when they do good work. Once motivators (and ways to meet them) are aligned and defined, we must ensure that goal priorities are established. Both managers and employees should understand which goal is the most to least important and why.

Ensuring there's alignment on goal priorities supports the most important work and ensures appropriate time is allocated to these top priorities. Moving forward, keep the following in mind:

- Each organization must develop performance conversation cadences that work best for their realities. The more frequently, intentionally, and consistently a manager and employee discuss performance, growth, and engagement, the higher the chance performance will grow, skills will evolve, and engagement will rise.

- We must all remember that none of us can read minds, and due to this, we must find ways to communicate openly, honestly, and frequently. When it comes to growing employee performance, growth, and engagement, there are no shortcuts, only conversations.

Employee Reviews

A standard review process maintains an equitable review of teams. Let's start with a deceptively simple question: Should the organization keep and retain a given employee—and why? To help answer that, first consider the following questions:

- How has this employee helped get the organization to this point? Why does that matter?

- What are their greatest contributions for the leadership team/company? Why does that matter?

- What does the manager appreciate most about this individual? Why?

From there, let's dig into what the current realities are for the individual:

- How are they doing professionally?

- Where are they performing?

- What do they need to start doing?

- What do they need to stop doing?

- What should they continue doing?

- Where are they struggling?

- How can management accelerate performance and reduce their struggles?

- How are they doing personally?

To get into their motivations, analyze what rewards keep them satisfied and engaged and those that help their future career:

- What matters to this person's career?

- What type of work do they enjoy doing?

- What type of work are they good at?

- What type of work do they struggle with?

- What does *career* mean to them?

- What matters most in their career?

- What are the three things that keep them working at the organization?

- What are the three things that push them away from the organization?

- How do they like to be rewarded for great work?

- How do they best receive feedback when things aren't great?

An often-underrepresented aspect of management includes the relationship and interpersonal dynamics. Let's look at some questions that can help get to the heart of those:

- To improve the relationship and communication, what do they need their manager to start, stop, or continue doing?

- What do they need from the leadership team?

- What does the leadership team need from them?

Honesty and candor in the responses should be front and center with teams. This doesn't mean to be rude or mean—but also don't pretend things are great when they aren't. Don't hold back for fear of making people complacent. Check out books like *Radical Candor* from Kim Scott. No summary would do her work justice by offering up just a page of her wisdom.

Improving Performance

People performing at a high level are easier to have reviews with—provided they are compensated appropriately. Those financial aspects are covered in the section "Compensation Structures." As discussed in this chapter, financial considerations are just one aspect of total rewards. Those who aren't leveling up fast enough because they are performing at a low level need more help and provide more opportunity to earn loyalty by helping others to be their best self. This is where a performance improvement plan comes in. A performance improvement plan is exactly what it sounds like. They can be codified—and are often needed to protect the organization from a lawsuit if the organization separates from the employee. That can come off as aggressive in a startup, but it's better to have a low-performing employee leave than stay.

The performance improvement plan should include a list of performance issues and then how they will be addressed with the employee. This is a collaborative effort. It often helps to start with why behaviors exist. Here's a pretty big, important note: it's often our fault.

Once there's a list of issues and reasons, put goals in place to improve the performance. The places where it's been our fault might go back to when an employee was hired or onboarded—but more often than not, it's simply that the right expectations were never set.

Once expectations have been reset or gaps in training corrected, many middling employees become high performers. For those who don't, it's important to have consistent, documented evidence that the organization helped the employee as much as possible. The most important aspect of the performance improvement plan, though, is for it to be an honest attempt to improve performance—otherwise, save the heartache and part ways as quickly as possible.

Help Employees Find a Better Fit

Once the character has enough experience points, it's time to raise the level of the character. They get to pick up new skills and better attributes. Careers work in much the same way: most people work their butts off and then plateau, get a new job or position, work their butts off again, and then plateau again. Provided employees continue to level up when ready, their career is likely to be full of learning and new adventures at every turn, just the way it should be.

Managers need to stay on the lookout for when people are ready for more responsibilities. Maybe the employee can be retained within the company, or maybe the company helps them find a new position elsewhere to recognize the hard work and dedication they lent to the cause. Unlike a game, this happens gradually rather that all at once. Here are a few ways to tell if some has earned enough experience and it's time to move up to the next level:

- *They're bored*: Once someone has learned everything they can learn in a position, they are likely to get bored (cyclically so per level), no matter how much work comes through their desk on any given day. This is as it should be. Some employees may be motivated to sit in the position they are in for a while. Provided they're good at it, let them know that whenever they're ready, others at the company can help them get to the next level.

- *They know what to expect*: Other members of their team know it and consistently go to specific employees for advice about the job. Once an employee gets good at a position and they know how to do all the things, who to call to get something expedited, and where to kick the jukebox in order to get a song to play and overall they feel good about their accomplishments, they need more. Anyone even remotely observant should feel it in our bones (with or without a perception check). Where possible, help prepare employees for what's next on their horizon; if some who are higher-up at the company doesn't recognize the high performers who are ready for a promotion, someone else will!

- *They're frustrated*: Answering routine questions can get old after a time. High performers can start to resent the organization, the team, and everyone but themselves. This means they stayed too long in a position and it's time for them to move on (and hopefully up if they didn't get too toxic). Don't let them start hating the job; that will do no one any good. Instead, look for ways to challenge staff and keep hiring from within to keep the momentum going.

- *People tell them*: Sometimes a manager at another organization tries to recruit an employee, or they get asked to work with customers directly. Team members might start to point out other positions. Either way, if their humility or fear of change hasn't allowed them to apply for that next job yet, it's probably time to push them into it. If it's not in the startup, then at least they will remain friends to the cause.

- *Money*: Capitalism means that most people take a new job that pays more money when they can. The staff may love the team, the people, and the freedom often provided to high performers. But after they realize there's much, much more for them in other positions, if nothing else has caused them to move on, cold hard cash will. One of the hard parts of being in a startup is that there's a financial plateau for employees as there's an organizational margin that needs to be maintained. Founders can offset that with equity, but keep in mind that exceptional talent might be able to motivate others. By amplifying what teammates can accomplish, those who are otherwise topped out in compensation might be able to justify much larger salaries.

Finally, there are going to be times in everyone's career when they're not collecting experience to level up at work anymore. That might be temporary. New parents, those caring for sick loved ones, team members who have side projects, those spending all of their free time out on a lake at a cabin, and so many others are in a state of coasting. And that's fine. There is nothing wrong with pressing pause on a career provided that the output at work is what's needed for the employer, both the organization and the employee are aware of the pause, and everyone is communicating about where they're at. Communication is key. If there's an employee who needs to level up, dedicate time to review that—and where to go next.

There are also times when an employee doesn't work out. The interviewer might have missed that they were a bad fit in the interview process or that there is too large a gap between what they know and what they need to know, or bad behaviors were allowed during onboarding and continue to persist. Whatever the reason, sometimes an employee needs to be exited. Never do this alone. Use the services of the outsourced HR (or HR staff, if we're to that point) to have a second person sit in on the exit interview and make sure that all laws for a given country, state, or municipality are satisfied.

These conversations can be hard. Make the transition gentle but make sure they understand how they can avoid this situation in the future (in other words, tell them why they're being let go). Try to be kind but firm. Immediately think deeper about how this happened and add that to one of the many feedback loops in the organization.

Building Feedback Loops

This section offers a foundational approach to develop feedback loops for programs, people, and everyone else in the organization. This section is not a definitive guide on feedback; these are simply productive approaches. They help collect, reflect, and process insights and perspectives to improve programs, people, and, with a little humility, those who develop the feedback loops.

Intentional and consistent feedback loops clarify and challenge perspectives, assumptions, blind spots, and beliefs. Getting and giving feedback is easy when everything is going well, but hard when it isn't. Specific actions uncovered in feedback loops allow those who design experiences to upgrade them. There are specific behaviors to help improve how feedback is requested, provided, received, and processed. Creative solutions require reliable, consistent, and helpful feedback loops to develop and deliver valuable solutions.

Feedback loops should be a constant part of any organization. They are continual feedback cycles that help us improve our perspectives and ideas. We build these loops around projects, programs, people, and ourselves to help make things better. We often use surveys or forms to collect feedback and data in a reliable, repeatable, and controlled process. Feedback loops begin by understanding what is important and why. The example examines one simple feedback loop. Reducing the number of variables helps increase clarity, make it easier to provide feedback, and understand whether we are accomplishing our goal. Here's a simple example question to reduce complexity:

Q1: Did this section help you identify one simple feedback loop you can implement?

Yes, No, or Maybe.

vs.

Q1: Did this section help you identify one simple feedback loop you can implement?

Disagree 1 - 2 - 3 - 4 - 5 Strongly Agree

Is the number 4 any better than a simple *yes*? Readers who are software developers might note that a Boolean value certainly takes less space in a database. In this case, moving to an integer or varchar would add space, increase the time a database lookup requires, increase complexity of the code, and, in exchange, provide little to no value. Turns out hacking computers to communicate more effectively is pretty similar to hacking humans to do the same. In a board game, a flip of a coin might require fewer parts for a game to be lost than a polyhedral dice!

Having said that, certain statistical requirements might provide a 90% success rate vs. a 4.5 out of 5 and so may yield different responses and conversations when presenting to diverse audiences. Whatever is decided, it should make sense for our organizations and those we engage. For every quantifiable piece of feedback collected, we should also capture qualitative feedback.

Quantitative feedback can be counted, measured, and expressed using numbers. Qualitative feedback is descriptive and conceptual. Traits, characteristics, or observations can organize qualitative feedback. Blending quantitative and qualitative feedback then helps us expand our perspectives and provide a more holistic view of the feedback we collect. That could be as simple as asking a follow-up question to the previous question, like "Please provide feedback on how this was or wasn't helpful."

It's also possible to allow for a *maybe* response. A *maybe* is not a *yes*; it is closer to a *no*. This idea might be dramatic, but it allows an approach to the feedback from a growth perspective vs. a success perspective and calibration on that approach. A *maybe* can become a *yes* or a *no*; actions and the antics of the rest of our adventuring party determine how that feedback shifts. Approaching a *maybe* from the perspective of *no* encourages the assumption that there is an opportunity for improvement and engagement with the work vs. assuming a passive posture.

Giving and receiving feedback is a full-on neurological assault on minds and emotions. Everyone can recognize that feeling when someone says, "I have some feedback for you" or when there is a semiannual performance review. The psychic "pain" might be more real than realized. Studies have shown that giving and receiving feedback can even spike heart rates. This is where we can make a staggering difference in ourselves and our organizations, though. Now let's look at some of the things to think through before instigating feedback loops:

- What is the goal? Why?

- What does success looks like? Why?

- What programs are measured? Why?

- How are people measured? Why?

- How are we measuring ourselves? Why?

Again, the goal is to always get at the why (a theme of this book and a potentially great growth hack for anyone). Be open, honest, and grateful—even if the feedback is grating. It's still an opportunity to do better. Look for honest feedback. No one is perfect, but the faster feedback can be requested and processed, the faster improvements can be made. Be accepting, process the feedback, and then appropriately adjust and communicate how it was helpful. Feedback helps us build systems that adapt. Nothing is static in startups, and if there's no intentional feedback, then systems won't improve.

Compensation Structures

One aspect of running an organization where there's plentiful feedback is compensation structures. This is a huge aspect of an equitable total rewards program that keeps teams engaged and sticking around. Compensation doesn't always appear at the top of the list of motivators feedback is requested—but whether it's there or not, it's on the minds of every adventuring party.

There are a few aspects of the compensation structure in a great total rewards program. The first is a static base salary. The adventuring party needs to be able to buy iron rations to survive a long journey through the Underdark. That's where the base salary comes in. The second aspect is variable compensation. That includes bonuses and commissions (the latter being most common with sales teams we bring on). The following table shows a few ways that the two combine to form on-target earnings (OTE).

YO!

This model provides equal payout on variable pay based on quota attainment. i.e. if you accomplish 90% of your goal you get 90% of your payout.

There are a number of ways you can build this out - such as releasing less variable at lower quota - i.e at 90% of quota you only get 50% of variable - and this can ramp on both sides of the variable comp. I've provided a second model below that shows this in action.

Whatever you do - it should align with your compensation philosophy and approach.

This model aims to set clear performance objectives and goals and then reward them in a consistent and controlled manner for the business. This helps create predictability for employees and the operations of the business.

The model also should provide controlled upside performance that is fair and encourages continued performance.

01 | Quota Attainment & Payout Are Equal

Base, Variable and OTD - Model | Leveling and Range Structure |

Base			Variable			OTE (On Target Earnings)		
Entry (LV 01)	Entry (LV 01)	Entry (LV 01)	Entry (LV 01)	Entry (LV 01)	Entry (LV 01)	Entry (LV 01)	Entry (LV 01)	Entry (LV 01)
$40,000	$50,000	$60,000	$20,000	$30,000	$40,000	$60,000	$80,000	$100,000

Entry - LEVEL 01 - VARIABLE % & OTE BASED ON QUOTA ATTAINMENT

QUOTA ATTAINMENT	85%	90%	95%	100%	105%	110%	115%
% OF VARIABLE PAID OUT *	85%	90%	95%	100%	105%	110%	115%
VARIABLE PAYOUT	$17,000	$18,000	$19,000	$20,000	$21,000	$22,000	$23,000
BASE PAY	$40,000	$40,000	$40,000	$40,000	$40,000	$40,000	$40,000
OTE	$57,000	$58,000	$59,000	$60,000	$61,000	$62,000	$63,000

Mid - LEVEL 02 - VARIABLE % & OTE BASED ON QUOTA ATTAINMENT-1

QUOTA ATTAINMENT	85%	90%	95%	100%	105%	110%	115%
% OF VARIABLE PAID OUT *	85%	90%	95%	100%	105%	110%	115%
VARIABLE PAYOUT	$25,500	$27,000	$28,500	$30,000	$31,500	$33,000	$34,500
BASE PAY	$50,000	$50,000	$50,000	$50,000	$50,000	$50,000	$50,000
OTE	$75,500	$77,000	$78,500	$80,000	$81,500	$83,000	$84,500

Sr - LEVEL 03 (SR) - VARIABLE % & OTE BASED ON QUOTA ATTAINMENT-1-1

QUOTA ATTAINMENT	85%	90%	95%	100%	105%	110%	115%
% OF VARIABLE PAID OUT *	85%	90%	95%	100%	105%	110%	115%
VARIABLE PAYOUT	$34,000	$36,000	$38,000	$40,000	$42,000	$44,000	$46,000
BASE PAY	$60,000	$60,000	$60,000	$60,000	$60,000	$60,000	$60,000
OTE	$94,000	$96,000	$98,000	$100,000	$102,000	$104,000	$106,000

02 | Quota Attainment & Payouts Ramp

Entry Base, Variable and OTD - Model | Leveling and Range Structure |-1

Base			Variable			OTE (On Target Earnings)		
Entry (LV 01)	Entry (LV 01)	Entry (LV 01)	Entry (LV 01)	Entry (LV 01)	Entry (LV 01)	Entry (LV 01)	Entry (LV 01)	Entry (LV 01)
$40,000	$50,000	$60,000	$20,000	$30,000	$40,000	$60,000	$80,000	$100,000

Entry - LEVEL 01 - VARIABLE % & OTE BASED ON QUOTA ATTAINMENT-1

QUOTA ATTAINMENT	85%	90%	95%	100%	105%	110%	115%
% OF VARIABLE PAID OUT *	70%	80%	90%	100%	110%	120%	130%
VARIABLE PAYOUT	$14,000	$16,000	$18,000	$20,000	$22,000	$24,000	$26,000
BASE PAY	$40,000	$40,000	$40,000	$40,000	$40,000	$40,000	$40,000
OTE	$54,000	$56,000	$58,000	$60,000	$62,000	$64,000	$66,000

Mid - LEVEL 02 - VARIABLE % & OTE BASED ON QUOTA ATTAINMENT-1-1

QUOTA ATTAINMENT	85%	90%	95%	100%	105%	110%	115%
% OF VARIABLE PAID OUT *	70%	80%	90%	100%	110%	120%	130%
VARIABLE PAYOUT	$21,000	$24,000	$27,000	$30,000	$33,000	$36,000	$39,000
BASE PAY	$50,000	$50,000	$50,000	$50,000	$50,000	$50,000	$50,000
OTE	$71,000	$74,000	$77,000	$80,000	$83,000	$86,000	$89,000

Sr - LEVEL 03 (SR) - VARIABLE % & OTE BASED ON QUOTA ATTAINMENT-1-1-1

QUOTA ATTAINMENT	85%	90%	95%	100%	105%	110%	115%
% OF VARIABLE PAID OUT *	70%	80%	90%	100%	110%	120%	130%
VARIABLE PAYOUT	$28,000	$32,000	$36,000	$40,000	$44,000	$48,000	$52,000
BASE PAY	$60,000	$60,000	$60,000	$60,000	$60,000	$60,000	$60,000
OTE	$88,000	$92,000	$96,000	$100,000	$104,000	$108,000	$112,000

Keep in mind that OTE can be a negotiating point. Let's say the company will bring in three sellers early on. An offer of increased OTE in the form of commissions means increasing commission percentages in exchange for a lower base salary. Sellers need to buy those rations if they're going to last through the quarter, so make sure they're appropriately incentivized on the lower end as well. The possibility of a larger commission check doesn't mean they'll be able to close, and there's nothing worse than having a seller bring in a windfall of business a week after they quit. It's better to keep them than start the process over with another seller once it's known that they could sell.

It's also important to know what a competitive salary looks like in a specific geographic location. Sites like glassdoor.com can be used to find comparable salaries (and there are paid services that get much more targeted compensation information). To get competitive, consider stock options, better benefits, training, and other aspects to the total rewards provided. Next, consider a system to track total rewards.

HR Tools and Technology

Remember that tools are simply that: tools. Tools and technology should help accelerate our plans, goals, and intentions. Many believe that tools are the entire solution, but this is rarely the case. Owning a hammer doesn't mean someone can build a house just as owning a scalpel doesn't mean someone can perform surgery. Tools might require plans, resources, skills, abilities, permits, and many other items to be useful.

Tools and technology are the same when it comes to talent. Once goals are identified, tools can be mission-critical. Just remember that a tool is not a solution (something important to remember during a sales process as well). Shortcuts are never short, and this is truer when it comes to selecting and onboarding talent. That being said, great plans and foundations make the right tools a game changer in the way people engage and work.

Here are some tools that can help accelerate HR plans:

- **Human resources information systems (HRIS)** help centralize and streamline many human resources functions (onboarding, performance, payroll, benefits management). They can also integrate to other systems (ATS, LMS, PMS) to unify data about organizational structure. Examples: Gusto, Zenefits, Bamboo, and Workday.

- **Applicant tracking systems (ATS)** help streamline and scale the recruiting process for organizations, from posting jobs, candidate communication, pipeline management, and much more. Examples: Greenhouse, JazzHR, and Lever.

- **Learning management systems (LMS)** help organizations build, share, and scale training within organizations. From organizational onboarding to role-specific training, learning management systems help centralize, direct, and track learning progress for individuals/teams/organizations. Examples: Lessonly, Litmos, and Trainual.

- **Performance management systems (PMS)** help set, track, share, and update goals and development for employees/teams. Often HRIS will include PMS solutions as part of their offering. Performance management systems help create clarity across organizations, teams, and individuals. Examples: Lattice, 15Five, and Reflektive.

- **Employee engagement platforms (EEP)** take the pulse of an organization to help uncover and track the levels of engagement within an organization. Research shows that an engaged workforce outperforms disengaged talent. These tools help give voice to the organization and help increase action and accountability. Examples: Culture Amp, Lattice, CultureIQ, and TINYpulse.

- **Internal wikis or knowledge bases** help centralize and share information, operations, plans, and policies within an organization. Wikis help unify focus, develop single sources of truth, align teams, and increase collaboration. Examples: Atlassian Confluence, Notion, and Basecamp.

- **Chat or communication platforms** allow individuals, teams, and organizations to chat and connect via multiple communication channels. From messaging, audio, and even video, chat platforms help reduce geographic barriers and centralize communication. Examples: Slack, Microsoft Teams, and Google Chat (G Suite).

Mindset and Approach

Everyone looks for hacks or shortcuts when it comes to growing business and talent in virtual environments. Organizations that best develop talent in a virtual environment have clearly defined fundamentals and select tools that accelerate this work. These organizations understand the *why* behind their actions and select resources that help accelerate toward their goal:

- Why is a position necessary?
- What is the goal of each interview question?
- Why is this person a part of the interview process?
- Why does a new employee need to understand the mission, vision, and values?

The *why* is about increasing clarity and accelerating the right behaviors. This level of intentionality is not geographically dependent—it's leader dependent. The best leaders get the fundamentals right, and they understand the *why* behind their actions. Remember that it is okay to slow down to go fast, and getting fundamentals right helps grow amazing organizations in-person and virtually.

Conclusion

There are two sides of human resources. The first is mechanical: make sure people get paid, take care of benefits administration, and protect the organization from itself by limiting liabilities. The second deals with the issues that arise in the beautiful and frighteningly complex interpersonal relationships that form in companies. Most early-stage companies should outsource the human resources mechanical pieces. Organizations like Gusto can help take some of the mechanical aspects, or, if there are deeper needs, a larger outsourcer can help (or an outsourcer that's industry specific). That gives founders time to think about hiring, onboarding, and retention.

A lot of the mental math that should be done before the first employee is hired was done throughout the chapter. That's important; if skipped, there won't be a culture the founders are proud of (which is much harder to fix later), teams won't be as productive as they could be, and there will be long-term retention problems. Much of this chapter was spent on retention. Humans are one of the most expensive parts of any organization. Other chapters covered leadership and management, but none of the other chapters were possible without the characters in the adventuring party to fill the necessary roles in a company. Companies are most effective, and a more fun place to work, when they can retain the humans. When people leave, so leaves institutional knowledge about the *what* and *why* and *how* regarding systems.

It is possible to overanalyze retention, if only as a means to avoid conflict. If someone isn't effective, we need to coach them better or make a change. Keeping substandard performers on board lowers the morale of the whole party. These can be tricky and should be done with the assistance of an HR professional. Now that we've gotten through how to intentionally build a company that people want to work at, think through a product with a good market, and lead the organization, it's time to finally turn the attention to the actual technology used in Chapter 8.

CHAPTER 8

Technology

An adventuring party is formed and has a goal they need to accomplish. Maybe they make it through the adventure, or maybe they don't. If they don't, hopefully they try again. Sometimes, the adventure turns into a series of games, often with an overarching theme and many of the same characters. A campaign in role-playing games begins with a single game, and some of the decisions we make early on have interesting repercussions as the games unfold and the party levels up. Some companies start that way as well.

We often start building a company and the technology that company delivers based on what we know. In the early stages, it usually evolves over time. There's a general idea of where it's going, but we build features, options, and integrations and focus on aspects that allow us to acquire new customers based on our individual perceptions or insights. And that's important—but we should ask ourselves several questions about the technology and techniques used routinely. This is what we explore in this chapter.

We've long felt a good annual planning meeting (even in a company of two) helps us make sure we don't just build tons of new features without spending some of our time working on the foundations of our products. If we do that, we will eventually slow down the development of new features as the technology atrophies. Aging technology, or technical debt, can also become a liability as security problems crop up in libraries or services that don't get patched.

© Charles Edge, Chip Pearson, Amy Larson Pearson 2023
C. Edge et al., *The Startup Players Handbook*,
https://doi.org/10.1007/978-1-4842-9315-7_8

Leveling Up the Technology

Many products begin with a simple line or three of code. Developers add some functions and classes. From there maybe microservices, apps, and web apps. And from there, well, who knows. Every organization is different. A business productivity tool might be a database with a pretty GUI on top. Or a SendGrid might specialize in the ability to provide an API for others to get some aspect of programming for free (like email and texting). We then develop more and more technology to try and meet more customer demands. While many products mature differently, most mature in similar fashions. Let's look at a typical progression we might see from a later-stage organization:

- *Level 1*: We outsource the development of a product or have a technical founding partner who sprints toward an MVP (Minimum Viable Product) alone. Here, we begin with a person or two developing technologies.

- *Level 2*: We bring in another person to help. Maybe this is a growing outsourced team, someone on staff to take over what was done by an outsourcing agency, or a helper for the primary developer. This person likely owns a part of the code, and everyone building technology still wears several hats (like QA, DevOps, etc.)

- *Level 3*: We reach a full Scrum team. We've now got a little technical debt (keep in mind that a little technical debt is a good thing, which we'll get to later in this chapter). We've also got people with a little more of a specialty in certain areas like DevOps, machine learning, etc.

- *Level 4*: Once we reach four developers, rather than bringing on more people to contribute to the main product, it's good to start looking at offloading things the main developers don't want to do (or that are specialties). Here, look to hire someone in QA (automated and manual testing), DevOps, or hyper-automation, or split the app/application development, back end, front end, and database development of the tools.

- *Level 5*: It's good to start to think about compliance, so when we hit $1,000,000 in sales, six developers, or twenty people or when customers need it to close deals, the discipline is in place, and it doesn't create a cultural nightmare to change the process to publish code. This means tools like Tugboat, Hyperproof, Apptega, StandardFusion, or Secureframe. The new processes involve things like writing down the processes used to develop software, host software, access customer data, etc. Some of these can be a culture shock for developers, but it's important to start developing technology like a mature company so we don't leave our customers at risk on several threat vectors.

- *Level 6*: If we didn't start as a contract-first or API-first company, we'll need to shift in that direction to continue maturing scalably. This means we take a feature, mock it up in UX, document how endpoints will work to support the feature, and build the APIs and then the front end based on the APIs. It's important to make sure the code and services are as modern and object-oriented as possible (or intentionally functional according to the language). That allows an organization to develop less cyclomatically complex software (e.g., there are fewer duplicitous functions). Hopefully we started out this way, so it's a matter of getting back to it. If we have a monolithic application, we might have a pretty big hill to climb, but if we're going to grow, we have to do so.

- *Level 7*: Scale is hard. We produce less features, and we uncover defects and address the technical debt of mature products. We have product teams feeding us features and sales teams asking when a feature will be done to convert a customer. Here, we need a technical roadmap to go alongside our product roadmap, and we need to decide what percentage of the budget goes to each.

Scaled development is hard. Beyond level 7, if we haven't already, we'll experiment with Kanban, scaled Agile, and every other task management paradigm under the sun. All will come with some successes and some failures. This is a problem that goes back to the 1960s when the first large development teams were forming at IBM. That resulted in a book called *The Mythical Man-Month* and Brooks's Law from that, which can be paraphrased as adding incremental people to projects make those projects take more, not less, time. However, every startup seems to need to learn this lesson the hard way.

The way out of getting less done with more people is to think more deeply about how we want our organizations to build software and how to allow smaller teams to work more independently toward common goals. In the 1960s, this was moving toward waterfall programming (where we focused our efforts on a big project plan). Then as the decades of understanding of each paradigm for development practices came in the ensuing years, we got Extreme Programming, Scrum, Agile, etc.

The next thing or development in programming or hosting will come. We need to focus on the present but with an eye to the future. One of the best ways to do that is have our team split time between the product roadmap, covered earlier in the book, and a technical roadmap. Think of this as a budgeting exercise, where we budget technical resources. Negotiate annually or quarterly how much of the time the development organization will spend on each and review at regular intervals using a standard rubric (quantity of code, story points, etc.). That technical roadmap can be different based on the type of technology we use, but there are some commonalities, which we'll get into in the next section.

Technical Roadmaps

The technology covered in that annual review often comes in a variety of themes for web applications, namely, around getting smaller and smaller services that can be more easily and economically hosted. Smaller services can then be more easily developed as the application grows, additional logic is added, etc. The questions posed in this section are meant to provide a good starting point for that annual review for earlier-stage startups—and maybe even for some larger organizations as well.

The answers should provide a workstream for development teams based on how we prioritize a gap analysis between the answers of what we have today and where we'd like to be in six months, a year, or even three years. We'll start with one of the more critical aspects of software: how we store and access data.

Data Access

- Is the back end developed based on the API?

- Is the database schema version controlled?

- Do we use an API gateway?

- Is there a REST API to access the data?

- Is the API versioned?

- Is there a Graph API representation on the data (or one planned)?

- Is there an API style guide?

- Are grammatical rules for the API consistently applied?

- Do we employ any kind of "contract testing" on API endpoints?

- Is the front end developed based on the API?

- What third parties have access to that data?

Code Maturity Level

- What languages are in use and where?

- Are there any classes with more than 1,000 lines of code?

- Is an ORM (Object Relational Mapping) being used?

- Are we planning for microservices to be leveraged in the environment?

- What type of dependency management tool is being used?

- Where are user identities stored? Is that accessible via an IDP (à la OAuth, SAML, etc.)?

- Do we have any automated testing? Manual testing? What is the testing environment like?

- What is the process for onboarding new customers into the environment post-sales?

- What technical debt do we see needing to be addressed in our software over the next few months?

Data Center Operations

- Do we have an on-premises offering, cloud offering, or both?

- Where is our data stored?

- What services are being used?

- What is the containerization strategy?

- What is our process like for continuous integration/ continuous delivery?

- *Hosting costs*: What is our average spend on compute time? What is the average spend on storage or other hosted microservices?

- Is there anything in use that is outside of our control?

- How many requests per second are processed?

Compliance and Security

- Can developers access the database?

- Can a single developer post a product change directly, or is a review process required?

- What version control tools does our software employ?

- Is there a comprehensive list of all third-party projects being used in projects and the license used for them?

- Do we produce any open source tools?

- Do any third parties integrate into our solution?

- Have we run the code through any security analyzers or manual penetration testing? Do we do so automatically upon commits?

- Do we perform any automated or manual penetration testing on servers?

User Experience

- What's the process for planning new features?

- How do we test new features?

- Do we provide support for multiple languages? If so, which languages?

- Are leads from the pre-sales efforts connected to accounts in the product database?

- What type of drip campaign do we employ for leads?

- What type of tracking and logging products are we using (e.g., Pendo)?

- Are we properly notifying users of these?

Product Management

- What is our roadmap like for the next year?

- Of the items on the roadmap, which are commitments that have been made to customers?

- What type of quantifiable results are expected from each item on the roadmap?

- Take any example of recent software changes. What are the qualifiable and quantifiable expectations for that change?

- What are our release management processes like?

- Do we do standups? Agile? Scrum? Kanban?

- Are there any areas of the code that only one person knows?

In no way are these meant to be universally applied. Every organization has a different stack and so different words that matter. Nor should the conversation end with a simple answer. As the organization grows, new engineering hires will want to be included, and the scope of an annual meeting of the minds will naturally increase. The fall or early winter is one of the best times to have such a meeting, so we hope this helps you get started deliberately planning for next year!

Create a Platform

Books like *Platform Revolution* and *The Business of Platforms* tell teams to make our products "platforms" or that we want to build a business model where in our products we can facilitate the exchange of data with other products. In doing so, we gain access to more customers, make customers stickier, and, ultimately, do more of what the promise of computing in general is meant to do: we make the people that choose to use our products more efficient (which in turn makes our products more valuable).

So we want to create a platform. There's just one problem: every build takes valuable time away from features we want to create and then makes our products more expensive to own and further develop–that is, unless we can sway other organizations to integrate with our product. The more users our product has, the easier this becomes.

We see this most acutely when we talk to product teams or developers at other organizations. I can't tell you how many of these calls have ended with a vendor in an adjacent market agreeing we should build an integration but leaving it up to the company that has the smallest user base (and so the most advantage in the relationship) to build the integration. Often, neither company has a great stack of technologies for building an integration, and so the project just dies, even though both parties see a lot of potential benefit in an integration. But it doesn't have to be that way.

API Strategies

An API, or Application Programming Interface, is a set of functions and procedures that allow access to features in a controlled way. Sure, we could allow others to write directly into our databases (or disks, if it's an operating system), but that can be dangerous, so we need to provide a way for other developers to do so following rules that reduce the risk of having others interact with our software.

In modern SaaS architectures, the API is usually a collection of REST endpoints. Each allows a tool to Create, Read, Update, and Delete objects in our software. Those operations are camel-cased because they're often referred to in SQL as a CRUD framework, and while there are more mature ways to conceptualize these, they represent a good basis of understanding without getting overly technical.

Let's look at an example. Let's say we have a database of parts in a warehouse at an organization called Pretendco. We might create a REST endpoint called Parts and allow another vendor to look up a list of parts by calling `https://pretendco.com/parts`. We could then return a list of parts, and if they then wanted to view information (or Read the information) on the part with an ID of 1130, they might call `https://pretendco.com/parts/1130`. We can then allow them to Update the information or Delete by sending different parameters. To allow for different data structures and more complex operations like authentication and authorization, we then get into more detailed REST commands, but that's a basic explanation of an API endpoint.

Why We Need an API

When two software companies exchange data, it's usually done with an API. This allows engineers to specify rules to interact with software in much the same way we do when users put data in. If we have a required field on the front end, GUI, or web interface, then we would want that same field required in the API. If we require a number in the phone number field, we'd also want to require a phone number in the API. That provides consistency and so keeps the integrity of the data. If the web interface uses the API rather than direct calls, then it doesn't create additional work to remain consistent.

We also provide rules for which vendors (often represented in the form of a unique API key) have access to various pieces of data and what types of operations they can perform. Consider this: When we take a photo using a third-party photo app on our iPhone, we get prompted to grant access to that app. If we accept, we've allowed that vendor's app (and so domain or key) access to the API that makes the camera work on the phone. This way, Apple has provided a means for vendors to access features on our phone safely and only when we grant the level of access required. The same becomes true when providing access to one piece of software in another, and each endpoint is programmed in a way that allows for that access to occur when authorization to do so is present or accounts for what happens when that authorization is not present.

There are other reasons to build a good API:

- Allows customers to automate processes around our product.

- As we grow, our customers will demand it.

- Provides a better framework for testing our own tools.

- Gives us the ability to create more interfaces for products faster.

- Breaks apart monolithic blocks of code.

- Reduces the code required for various functions.

But for the purpose of this section of the book, let's keep our eye on the value of the API to external vendors for a bit.

API Strategies

The API is where the rubber meets the road in becoming a platform company. This is also an area where an upstart company can outshine incumbents. Companies like Stripe were able to grow to over $30 billion by appealing to developers more than anyone else. And they did that by being API-first.

Microsoft rose to dominance over superior operating systems in the market at the time. They didn't do so through subterfuge, as many at competitors might argue, but because Microsoft copied the APIs from an operating system called CP/M when they built DOS. This meant that upon the release of DOS, every application built for CP/M worked on DOS. And the initial versions of Windows allowed for a protected mode that ran all those applications, giving them over ten years' worth of apps that ran on their operating system. They became a platform based on borrowing a great API and making it better. They then leapfrogged the market share of the Mac with Windows by providing an open platform with more options than the competitors and being an early proponent of making that API object-oriented. Thus, they won over software developers, and there was more software available for the platform.

The API-First Strategy

Organizations build software in a lot of different ways. An API-first strategy is one where we build the API endpoint and then we build the various ways the people that use our products access them: a mobile app, a web front end, an integration with another tool, etc. We build an endpoint or collection of endpoints that facilitates the operations required by those tools that consume the output of that endpoint.

The Stripe documentation offers great insight on what it means to be API-first. When we read how to do something, we see how the API works before we see the graphical screens users see. By building the endpoint first, we are able to make sure that every task a user might perform in our front ends is available through the API—and by being in the API, able to be used by other products.

Over the years, several API strategies have been employed at various organizations. Each has their pluses and minuses. But API-first is usually the best for net-new applications. This makes applications less monolithic in nature (and so cheaper to maintain over time) but also forces developers to treat the capabilities of third-party integrations as first-class citizens even compared to how we handle our own sites and apps.

The API-first strategy starts with understanding how our application is architected. In the SaaS world, there is usually a database where the data lives (e.g., MongoDB, SQL, etc.), and then there are the aspects regular users interact with, which are accessed through a front end. The application connects the front ends (web apps and apps on devices) to the database. That has a bunch of endpoints as described previously. Rather than have a large application that does both the front end and the back end, developers might have a front-end web app built in (let's say React) and a back end built in (let's say Java). React then calls endpoints provided by Java, which Java then processes.

That's pretty simplistic, but to make sure every task the front end performs is available as an endpoint is central to being "API-first." If we're already building logic into the front end that can't be performed by a third party using those endpoints, then we're starting to drift from the goal of being API-first. Developers and architects should avoid software that violates that manifesto and keep a running list of areas in software where we built something just to get out the door quickly that needs to be remediated. Further, many apps have been maturing for a decade or more, and so there are other strategies to employ (like move a monolithic piece of code to microserviced endpoints as each needs to be updated), albeit hopefully just en route to being API-first.

The Workflow-Based API Strategy

The next strategy we'll look at is workflow-based APIs. Here, we try to think of a list of everything we want another vendor to do with our data and build endpoints to facilitate those transactions. The really great thing about a workflow-based API is that vendors who are doing the tasks we thought of usually have a curated and easy approach to build integrations with products. Third parties can get up and running quickly, and, provided they only do what we think they're going to, we can easily build the facilities to enable their tasks and keep them updated. They don't have to decipher an architecture built to support a front end to perform standard operations.

Over time, a workflow-based API is really telling a fragmented story of how our products can be used. We don't know what kind of innovations others will create with our products when we expose the whole products to APIs. We've seen companies reinvent themselves based on how their products get used. Some have become hubs that facilitate tasks in other products; others have realized huge value in areas they never considered. Public APIs make it easier to pivot when needed.

A drawback of a workflow-based API is that organizations have to maintain endpoints built for the express use of third-party integrations. When we build new features, those become second-class citizens, and interacting with those features is often put on the backlog. We have to maintain a workflow-based API when we update features, and so we might end up breaking third-party integrations in regular updates if we aren't testing for every way a third party might interact with our APIs; we have little to no control over how that happens. This becomes dangerous as we grow and as our integrations get used more. The value of the increased productivity ends up potentially getting offset by the negative value of having that productivity unavailable while we fix what we broke.

Still, companies with monolithic apps and a lot of history behind the logic in those apps might need to start a platform strategy with a workflow-based API—given the huge amount of work required to move into an API-first-based approach to software architecture.

The Data API Strategy

Most software is just a front end to a database. We put data into the database and recall it. One common practice when building an API is to just wrap the database in a REST interface. Here, we build a 1:1 map of our database in endpoints. We'll refer to this as a Data API.

Data APIs also don't consider much of the logic we create in our apps. Over time, we add logic. We define certain fields as required, we transform data as it's entered (e.g., from a date stamp to epoch time), and we present data differently when it's recalled in screens. We also break initially simplistic representations of data up into multiple tables and add operations where various tables update one another when needed. In short, our app gets complicated.

Data APIs can expose too much data or too little. We can cause too many requests to construct an appropriate representation by forcing users to perform too many queries to find all the pieces of information we might have otherwise exposed in a workflow-based API or documented well in our own findings building a front end if we were API-first. We also might forget to limit what's allowed in our database and allow for inconsistency in the data, causing what our front end might consider a bug.

Data APIs can be great for simple apps, but most apps aren't simple. Even if an app is simple, it's not likely to stay that way as we create additional value for customers. Anyone embarking on adding an API on top of the database schema should do so with careful deliberation, not only around what gets exposed but how another vendor might be able to represent our data. Often, if a Data API will be employed, it should be paired with a workflow-based API.

Graph APIs

Every few years there's a new hotness in software development. The latest hotness in the API world is a Graph API. A Graph API is an API that builds on the concepts of a REST API but allows for a more object-oriented approach, with a focus on the relationship between various resources and their related objects. The concepts required to understand a Graph API need their own section. But suffice it to say, it can be incredibly efficient and useful. Any organization without an API that's looking to implement a new strategy should rule out a Graph API before moving to any of the other strategies.

A Graph API is also great to ease into. Developers can build an endpoint that exposes several options, and then as partners need additional fields, we can expose those as well. Especially if we've already begun to leverage an ORM (e.g., Hibernate), once all the internal developers get trained on it, we can begin building our front end using the Graph API as well. Again, anyone that doesn't yet have a customer-facing or partner-facing API should start their process of considering an API strategy by eliminating the option of a Graph API before moving to any other strategy—and consider that the best strategy is often to have a combination of all those considered.

Additional Considerations

Along the way in building out a clear API strategy, there are finer points we'll discover. Often we don't understand the importance of various aspects until we get bit by not having them. Let's look at a few of those implementation details now:

- *Authentication*: How will other vendors authenticate to the app? Plan for more than a basic key. We should also plan for tenants in a multi-tenant architecture to either distribute keys or preferably leverage federated access solutions out there (e.g., Okta or Azure Active Directory) to distribute keys to access their tenants. Those solutions might be ones we consume, or the tenant might bring their own. Unloading the liability of keeping keys in the database is always preferred, even if we're salting hashes and all that good stuff.

- *Authorization*: Some vendors can call this something different. Once a process is authenticated, authorization is what that process has access to. Apple calls these "entitlements" and prompts users the first time an API is called that needs access to specific resources. The Microsoft Graph API has a global authorization that a tenant owns. Each user then provides authorization to given resources. The security posture of an organization will mature over time, and the way authorizations are granted to given resources will become more complicated. If we plan for more than a run-of-the-mill CRUD framework when initially building our app, we can build parts as we mature and not redo much of the work to ship the first versions of our APIs.

- *Rate throttling*: Other developers shouldn't hit our endpoints too much. This allows for DoS or DDoS attacks but also presents a concern around the ability to brute-force keys.

- *Pagination*: It's inefficient to give more data than necessary. It's also inefficient for others to get more data than they need. We can limit the results in a query and what information is provided with each query. Once another vendor has processed the first set of results (or page), they can move on to the next with a subsequent call.

- *Response codes*: We need to know when a process worked and when the process didn't work. Response codes can tell us all those details much easier than unstructured JSON in a payload. If we stick with common response codes, other developers will quickly be able to understand what's happening. At a minimum, try and include 200, 201, 204, 400, and 404, and stay with the way those are spec'd.

- *Documentation*: It can be frustrating to develop against another organization's API. Much of that frustration could have been resolved with better documentation. When a company is ready to use an automated documentation repository like Apigee (`https://docs.`

apigee.com), first read up on OpenAPI (we used to call
this Swagger) and build the framework to automate
API documentation early. The later we wait, the more
it will seem like a heavy lift, and the more we'll be
reaching in the cobwebs to remember how we meant
for something to work. It may seem like more work,
but it makes us a better partner to third parties, and it
makes training new people on our own front-end teams
much easier.

- *Webhooks*: We've mostly covered working with our own
  API. We can also create webhooks, which allow us to
  send information to the API of another web application
  if some action happens in our app. Think of this like
  APIs are organizations pushing information to us
  and webhooks are them receiving event-driven data.
  Hopefully, by providing a great API, we can use better
  and more modern techniques to interact. Check out
  tools like Zapier (`https://zapier.com`) to see how a lot
  of different services can be daisy-chained together to
  do some cool stuff with webhooks.

- *Versioning*: Our app will mature. We will need to
  decommission endpoints and alter the output
  of endpoints. Versioning with a /v1 or /v2 either
  globally or per endpoint will allow us to do so without
  introducing breaking changes to our own assets that
  consume endpoints or third parties that consume
  endpoints. We can then set a time limit for how long we
  will maintain old endpoints and communicate changes
  to developers.

All of this might seem like a lot. But in many cases, we can just get a solid understanding of what each is and write our code around building aspects later. For example, just add the versioning in the URL scheme at first. This gives us the ability to version later without changing URL schemes. The point is to do a little planning to potentially save a lot of effort later.

Marketing the Platform

Now we have an API strategy. As we build endpoints (or expose them if they're already built), we can have more meaningful business development conversations with third parties. If they don't have an API, then even if they're larger than us, they'll realize it's more logical for them to build some of the integrations. Becoming a platform means we create value by owning the exchange of data. This will be a must as our user base grows. But facilitating these exchanges can also create a network effect based on having multiple other organizations working with our data and getting additional customers by cross-selling and cross-marketing with our new partners.

Once there are integrations, it's time to push the platform strategy. Doing so means aligning sales and marketing with those same groups at partners. When on those business development calls, look for ways to get in front of sales teams and systems engineers and get the brand represented in the marketing assets like blogs, social posts, articles, help desk FAQs, etc. This follow-through to the technical innovations solidifies us, and the more integrations we have, the clearer we are the platform the other vendors in adjacent markets should build integrations with.

Create Value with Machine Learning

Machine learning is one of those things that practically every investor seems to ask about these days. The reason is that there is so much information and code available for free that at this point, if we come up with some good strategies, they won't take years to implement. And we can finally improve the productivity (and joy) of knowledge workers in the ways J. C. R. Licklider first laid out in his 1960 paper "Man-Computer Symbiosis."

Some of the tactics and strategies can be built on top of simple machine learning libraries. These might be tools like Python libraries that could be imported into a web app without much fanfare. Others are much more laborious and/or expensive to develop and compute. All will grow in terms of both complexity and training (and, hopefully, end user benefit) as our apps mature.

A Rough Look at Implementation Strategies

This section of the book looks at a few machine learning techniques that can be universally applied for a lot of tools that use large blobs of text inputs. These can easily be summarized in a few options, detailed in the next few sections.

Sentiment Analysis

Sentiment analysis scores text based on a model that weights words. Text can be entered into a field and most easily scored upon commit. This provides a score that could be used to sort, look for anomalies, and even color-code feedback (typically in larger varchar fields).

- A proof of concept (PoC) might be planning one sprint with the goal to get a sentiment analysis score into the database per record. This information doesn't have to be presented to users yet, but should allow developers to refine the follow-up estimates in order to do so and help product teams conceptualize how to leverage sentiment scoring in various parts of the app.

- Implementation should plan for a minimum of two sprints to plan a minimal test implementation. The first is to allow users to train the model—for example, provide a list of words that the system doesn't know how to score and have users enter a score. The second sprint would be to implement how the screens appear and how we help make faster decisions based on that (e.g., color-coding of scores on screen as we'll review later in this chapter).

Once the initial implementation is complete, have a cooling-off period to get a better understanding of what other options we might build and the cost in terms of development, compute time, and training the model required to go further.

Categorization

Categorization predicts the appropriate category for records, based on text or other metadata in fields.

- A proof of concept could be to vectorize all existing categories/titles of articles/pages/records provided at the time of implementation into a table and run simple scripts to see how accurate predictive categories are.

- Implementation might include planning for a sprint to surface category selection in the interface and another to allow users to help train the model and then a cooling-off period to capture performance data and plan what a larger amount of work might look like.

Tagging

Here, we predict tags for information as it's being entered. This is like efforts in categorization, so should not heavily impact the cyclomatic complexity of a given app; however, given the way tags are often implemented, it could be less performant and require more work on the front end to make as interactive as many might expect (especially given how well tools like LinkedIn have implemented tagging systems).

- A proof of concept could be to again vectorize all tags provided at the time of implementation into a table and run simple scripts to see how accurate predictive tags are and have product teams and/or subject matter experts help train models.

- Implementation plans should account for a couple of sprints to surface tagging in the interface and then a cooling-off period to capture performance data and user research around how users of the product would like tagging to be improved upon.

Similar Items

Similar items is a well-documented machine learning outcome that predicts which items are like others, for example, a record that has similar characteristics to another record, aspects that are like others, a "Similar Posts" option in a blog, or "Similar Articles" on a news site.

- A proof of concept can be slightly more complicated than the previous options. The PoC would involve using a tool like ELKI (`https://elki-project.github.io`) to match similar items, and so the PoC would be a fork of a web app where ELKI is imported and requirements determined.

- Implementation is based on the complexity of the app and how we choose to surface findings in our interfaces. Many blogging systems like WordPress have this as a plugin, but that isn't incredibly complicated from the machine learning side. To get much more accurate and useful results, models need a fair amount of refinement.

We'll start with sentiment analysis, as given the logical layout of many a web app, this would provide the highest return on investment (ROI) from development efforts.

Sentiment Analysis

Sentiment analysis is the automated analysis of content like text or speech as positive, neutral, or negative. That positive or negative analysis can be considered looking at the polarity of the words, and a result of sentiment analysis is often a polarity score. This type of scoring allows organizations to better understand how constituents see them. This might mean analyzing Twitter or Facebook to ascertain how people feel about a given subject or tagging a sentiment score on blog posts or comments on posts to determine how people feel about a given topic.

Using technology like sentiment analysis, we get insight into how people perceive something. This is usually done using the natural language processing part of a body of work we tend to generically call machine learning. Sentiment analysis has become key for many industries to figure out what people think and to then improve the experience with products and address any branding concerns or promote positive branding when possible.

While natural language techniques in computing began all the way back in the 1950s with Alan Turing's amazing article, "Computing Machinery and Intelligence," the philosophies, models, articles, and software grew steadily into a body of work over the course of the next few decades.

The explosion of data in the last 20 years then became impossible to analyze manually. Suddenly there were much broader uses for the techniques already under development, and we could isolate and classify content and even score feelings, which is where sentiment analysis comes into play.

How Sentiment Analysis Works

Sentiments are subjective and usually refer to opinions and emotions. This means we put a quantifiable overlay on top of otherwise qualitative data. Still, these aren't facts. For example, the word "bad" might be considered to have a negative polarity, but "that's not bad" might be considered a bit more neutral.

Because sentiment analysis has grown as a discipline over the years, different branches have different needs, therefore a variety of strategies to identify exactly what sentiments are contained in text being analyzed. Subjectivity/objectivity identification involves classifying sentences into a subjective or objective grouping. Feature- or aspect-based is another branch of sentiment analysis that isolates what opinions are related to an entity and so picks up on nuance rather than just isolating a score. Neither is simple, but scoring subjectivity/objectivity is much more common.

The uses of sentiment analysis have become more ubiquitous. Once considered ground-breaking, these days with frameworks available for popular programming languages and example code spread across a variety of social coding websites, organizations can get started relatively quickly. While the implementation can be quick, removing unnecessary information or training code to interpret information in a way specific to a need can be fairly time consuming. This is usually referred to as training a machine learning model.

The more we train a model, the more significant the findings, or insights, can be. This means an organization can go from a generic lexicon of words and their scores to a more specialized analysis. This isn't necessarily required as we can easily quantify opinions and accept a bell-curve type of approach where the typical response becomes a baseline. This allows us to quickly start tracking the normal reactions and comparing others against those. But over time, most organizations begin partitioning that information and looking for specialized data to train.

Models can take a long time to get accurate. A well-trained model for a given industry can be more valuable than a company that creates the model—one of the many reasons investors look for machine learning projects to get started early.

A Quick Sentiment Analysis Win

Let's look at one example of quickly getting started with sentiment analysis and how that use case might expand to include training a more complex model than what comes stock with an implementation. Let's say a television company meets with people in focus groups to ascertain their thoughts on new television shows. They record interviews and transcribe the findings. That data is qualitative in nature. We can export the data and then analyze the sentiment of each interaction generically using a simple process like the one we wrote up at `https://krypted.com/ux-research/batch-process-sentiment-analysis-for-ux-research-studies/`. This is a script available to anyone to use for free.

That company doing the research caters to an industry that uses some pretty specialized words to describe things, as do most companies. In the preceding project, there is a data.json file. In that file, we can define a blurb of text and then identify whether it's positive or negative, giving it a polarity score. This impacts the scoring of future interviews by altering the way the algorithm interprets specific bits of text and can be used to then get a score with a higher confidence interval.

Drawbacks of Sentiment Analysis

Machine learning isn't perfect. Vannevar Bush described what would become computers as devices that supplement humans but don't replace them in his 1945 *Atlantic* article, "As We May Think." That article inspired many of the original pioneers in computing. Sentiment analysis is similar to what he meant by computers that help people do more; it helps guide us in research and helps us process findings faster but does not replace human interpretation. Quantitative and qualitative review of data should always overlay one another. As with most research findings, interpretation is key. And that interpretation is often represented in the model for the machine learning project (e.g., the data.json file in the earlier example).

There will always be subtleties that machines can't pick up on. We can analyze more data with the help of machine learning, though. Sentiment analysis can also be dangerous if we don't train the model. Using a baseline is fine but requires a lot of review to see how accurate the machine's findings are. The better the training, the less human intervention required. However, the cost goes up so exponentially for each percentage point of accuracy, so it often becomes less expensive to hire larger teams of humans to analyze data. However, poorly developed models can lead us to inaccurate findings and therefore bad decisions. This is one of the areas where such projects have bogged down for decades.

Another concern with sentiment analysis is that humans create models to do machine learning. There are a lot of tools available, and each is as good as the person who wrote it and similar to the use case the tool is being applied to. Test multiple tools and models to find one that works well.

Finally, clean analysis requires clean data. Data often needs to be consistent, and the humans that put data into databases or forums don't always have that consistency in mind. Errors are always a concern with machine learning but more specifically when there's bad data. Most of the time spent on many machine learning projects has been to get data into a consistent and analyzable fashion. The more structured the data we're working with, the easier that process and the quicker we're able to develop solutions.

Despite these drawbacks, machine learning is likely to be an integral part of any organization as time goes on. The ability to leverage deep knowledge to interpret data faster is where we realize the true potential of many an organization, especially once there are products to surface that data into databases.

Advantages of Using Sentiment Analysis

We can learn a lot when we have a machine help synthesize data. We could always do such things manually, but it can be time consuming. Using sentiment analysis, we can quickly see how customers feel about granular areas of an organization much, much faster than manually combing through our databases or just reading through a whole lot of posts on the Internet or forums. The more reactions to our products out there, the harder it is to find how people really think about things, much less analyze that data.

Tiny robots help us get further, faster. We can then drill down into very specific questions we need answered by combining sentiment analysis with recommender and/or classifier machine learning projects—and do so without bias (unless we amplify our bias in our models). Findings and uses are far-ranging, and, in some cases, the value of the machine learning tools is more than the value of entire companies.

Sentiment Analysis Implementation Strategies

One of the hardest aspects of any machine language project is to get started. Then a lightbulb goes off, and we scrap our initial forays into a subject and start over. But a little basic guidance can go a long way. Most software involves people entering information into a system and then calling that information back up later. Seems simple at first. When they give us information, we commit that information into a database. Then we display it on a screen, modal, or dialog later. These are the two main places where we can process data. Over the years, we've found each machine learning information processing technique to be implemented at a different time when users work with software.

Sentiment analysis can easily be determined when the user is giving us data. The project we linked to earlier uses an export of the data, but we probably already perform some sanity checks on data entered into our software prior to committing the data into a record (or a bunch of records). At the time we are committing data, we can quickly process it. This could be a simple service like a lambda that calculates the polarity score and then adds that into an additional field or column for the record in the database. When we then display the data, we can also display the polarity score (and go from a range of –10 to 10 to a range of 0 to 10 or 0 to 100).

We also have a lot of options for how to surface our findings. The color of the field can change based on the score. For that matter, the whole screen or modal that displays the record can change as well. Or we could pop up another screen that warns that the sentiment is bad. We could instead display an emoji. We can pretty much go anywhere we want.

Recommending Tags and Categories

Another quick win that's easy to explain is finding items that are similar to other items. This is most commonly done using what is known as K-nearest neighbors, a simple algorithm developed in the 1970s that converts strings into vectors, then maps those, and looks for similar items based on distance. As with sentiment analysis, understanding the statistics is not required, as it's mostly handled by the libraries we import into our projects.

Here, we can import basic libraries in Python to process the data. The natural language training kit (NLTK), Pandas, Matplotlib, TensorFlow, and sk-learn libraries are great for these types of operations. NLTK can be used by itself as there's a tag library, which can be seen in this project we put together to showcase it: `https://github.com/krypted/lightweighttagger`. And since we're training a model with sk-learn, `https://github.com/krypted/lightweightcategorizer` shows how to do that and then process how far neighbors are.

K-Nearest Neighbors Implementation Strategies

Now that we see how easy it is to predict tags and categories, let's look at how we might implement these into our software. We calculated sentiment at commit time. Tags are often preemptive, so we might want to derive recommended tags when we present a tagging modal. As users type, we can present a list that tries to predict based on the letters they have typed as well, so we may keep an array of tags we think are appropriate and then present only the ones that match the data being typed. If we are working with a list of static, predefined tags, then this is straightforward—just capture the tags when entered. Don't forget to train the model when new tags are created.

Free-form tags are a bit different. Users can enter new tags as they go, so we'll constantly be updating our model, and we need additional layers of learning to aid in making that faster. This points to the need for more of a deep learning option. At this point, it's best to investigate machine learning libraries or services available for the languages used in any given project.

Categorization is a bit easier than tags. This is because many products have a single category (or at least a smaller number of categories) per record. We change categories less, and the closest single neighbor to other objects with a given category is usually more accurate. Categories, as with sentiment, can usually be calculated at the time that a record is committed. We should plan on users entering tags as they go, though, and so account for them in all screens.

Keep Going with Machine Learning

We've only covered a few of the dozens of forks in machine learning thus far. Do a little research for the specific stack of software in use for a given project and investigate other languages. If Python isn't used anywhere else, there's no need to suddenly become a polyglot-type of product. For example, a Java shop can have plenty of options as well. There are tons of other languages. Whether using Swift, Ruby, Go, or even COBOL, there's probably a wealth of information on how to quickly import libraries and implement basic options in software projects.

This is not meant to be a comprehensive strategy document, but instead to get developers and product managers started in thinking about how to implement machine learning. Ultimately, each piece of software is unique because developers are trying to do something new and different. Or so we hope.

The various options available can help go far beyond simply storing and recalling information pertinent to a given cohort and into processing that information to truly aid in human-computer symbiosis. This allows software to predict, diagnose, and detect anomalies and commonalities in data in ways that, given specific knowledge of what that data represents, will benefit users by saving time, surfacing information faster, and helping people perform and react more quickly in ways that are unparalleled.

Machine Learning on the Edge

Machine learning doesn't have to be done in a data center; it can be done in apps or software on desktop computers as well. This helps keep costs at a minimum and helps simplify implementations in small and targeted applications. When using AI or machine learning at the edge (in apps on devices), account for architectural differences both in terms of pipelining data to the endpoint and how to process data, as the syntax is different (e.g., CoreML vs. TensorFlow) and personally identifiable information needs to be protected.

The biggest opportunities are around processing speed, the ability to process when the device is offline, and reduced cost by not deploying expensive gear in a data center. That gives a ton of possibilities, provided we can operate in the constraints, which include needing to be more careful about what data we can send to a device (keeping in mind that any data we send to a device can be accessed using various means). This gives us less data in many cases, as we can't just run a K-nearest neighbors algorithm against account data that might have personal identifiable information in it or use keys that could potentially allow someone to process or take the data and use it elsewhere. Some have approached this with technology like protobuffs, but keep in mind that any data on a device can be accessed.

Each platform has its own technical requirements. The latest devices from most manufactures have chips equipped with a neural engine that can offload machine learning workloads. Any ARM8-based CPU or better (like the Snapdragon, Apple A13, or M2) performs great with a number of machine learning techniques. Beyond that, we look to frameworks provided by each operating system to enable us to run workloads most efficiently. For example, CoreML relies heavily on the endpoints in the Apple OS, and while there are other frameworks that can be imported into a Swift project, they usually can't run as efficiently as those that run at a lower level than Apple's. ChromeOS has a similar machine learning service, and Android has ML Kit. These are purpose-built, so there are APIs for vision, face detection, text recognition, etc. We can still bring in simple Python frameworks to crunch a Jupyter Notebook, but as workloads increase, native is usually best—which might mean a little refactoring.

Machine Learning as a Threat

According to some investors, software is eating the world. The industry has evolved since that movement began in the 1960s. First, we digitized processes, then enriched them with additional information to provide more telemetry, and put them online. Now the knowledge of the world is just an endpoint away from any app we are developing if we just know where to look. All that information can now be combined and synthesized to produce the types of insights that wouldn't have even been considered just a couple decades ago.

Along the way we got a cadre of computer scientists, mathematicians, and statisticians developing new and interesting ways to take increasingly complicated mathematical questions and put them into computational algorithms and effectively turn each into a series of Turing machines. The resultant explosion of machine learning capabilities as we found the intersectionality between hundreds of diverse fields has now given us the capability to generate predictive models at a cost and speed that now makes doing so profitable almost immediately for internal use cases.

Let's take the simple example of a basic categorization tool. These frameworks took a couple of days to develop for generic categorization uses (`https://github.com/krypted/CoreML_CLI` or `https://github.com/krypted/lightweightcategorizer`). Within only a few hours' worth of work, a developer can take one of these (or many others) and ship a tool that analyzes text and creates a recommended category for a given object. Nifty, but basic tools should be limited to basic, and internal, uses until models can be trained to be accurate and so not be misleading.

Once there's a basic implementation, it's time to manually train the model. This means each time there's a correct match for a category, the model file should be edited. Maybe this means identifying why our brains chose to categorize an object with a given label and trying to create an entry in the file that weighs the parameters that guided our choice. If the model produces a result that makes sense to our brains, we add a line or multiple lines into that file that weigh a category to a given set of parameters. If the model predicts the wrong category, we add additional information that indicates why. This allows the model to incrementally become more efficient.

The time it takes to train a model until it's in a mature state is different for each use case. Maybe the model was 60% accurate on day one and becomes 80% accurate within a few days. Maybe we consider 80% accurate mature for a use case (especially when a human has to approve a score before information is committed to a database). Or maybe there are medical implications that mean we need an image analysis tool to be 99.999% accurate. Either way, we can quickly see machine learning augmenting the ability of a human by enabling us to make choices faster, provided we're still hitting a button before committing to a given result and the possible outcomes of that result.

Now, let's take a few examples of some areas where machine learning can be useful:

- Predicting how news about a company impacts their stock price using a sentiment analysis tool (e.g., gradient boosting)

- Identifying suspicious network or logon traffic (anomaly detection)

- Forecasting purchases in a supply chain using linear regression analysis (logarithmic or polynomial) and bolting on additional variables to get to logistic regression

- Detecting stenography using a Support Vector Machine (SVM)

- Using Convolutional Neural Networks (CNN) to perform facial recognition to open and close doors

- Detecting credit card fraud using K-means (e.g., K-nearest neighbors)

- Blocking spam at the organization level with a naive Bayes algorithm

- Predicting marketing trends using a Gaussian Mixture Model (GMM)

- Determining an insurance rate using Principal Component Analysis (PCA)

In each of the preceding examples, a combination of algorithms will likely work better than one alone, but it's usually best to start with one before getting into more combinatorial logic. A simple model might be able to augment our human ability to make decisions for each of these. Consider the potential threat that an overly simplistic approach to machine learning can produce if put into production. Let's say that a competitor, attacker, or even nation state realizes which machine learning models are used to make decisions and takes an action to see what our results are. Maybe they put out a bogus press release with a lot of negative sentiment about a company to drive down the stock price. Maybe they block an email from a supplier by tricking a spam filter into blocking emails with certain words (like the supplier's name) in them. Maybe they reverse engineer the supply chain purchases a company makes to cause them to over- (or under-) purchase in a given area when prices are at a peak or valley. Until the models become mature, the outcomes for simplistic machine learning implementations still need a human to approve actions rather than automate tasks.

The more simplistic algorithms and models, the easier it is to reverse engineer actions based on given data sets. This danger is amplified if we sell access to the data we make decisions based on. Security through obscurity has long been considered in poor taste—and yet the more data points we make publicly available, the easier it is to reverse engineer other data points, our decision trees, and ultimately our actions. If a hedge fund attempts to short a stock based on an algorithm, they may find others attempting to profit from outmaneuvering them based on their ability to pull in machine learning models that are accurate with a limited data set.

Now, let's say we train our data internally for a year and get to 90% accuracy with our models. Two years to get to 94%. Three years to get to 95%. Five years to get to 97%. And along the way we've enriched our data sets and likely added a custom algorithm that leverages multiple models to derive the same results. We've gone from importing a whole tool like TensorFlow to bringing in much more custom (and so performant) tooling. We're efficient, likely moving further into deep learning, and we have made it far more difficult for others to predict what we will do with a level of accuracy that is weaponizable against us. The ability to make decisions in an automatic fashion can then cut out latency, reduce cost per transaction, and become a competitive asset for the organization.

Many organizations incur a fair amount of cost in anonymizing and preparing data for use in machine learning, and some choose to pass that cost on by making that data available to other organizations for a fee. We won't argue that the adventuring party shouldn't sell data. There are scenarios where data sets can make the whole world better or lift up an entire industry. But before selling data, understand the full impact in risk management. It is important to make sure data is compliant; it's also important to consider how the data helps derive algorithms and models. If used by others, those reduce competitive advantages, but can also become a threat. Further, consider what various customers who own that data would think if they knew even some of it was shared. In fact, go a step further and inform them. Transparency breeds trust.

Imagine ordering 10,000 times the number of widgets we need, recommending offensive content to people, buying thousands of shares of a stock that's about to tank, giving high-risk loans, becoming the underwriter for a block of people about to file tons of insurance claims, or any of the examples from the list of great use cases for machine learning earlier in the section. To be competitive, we need hyper-automation based on machine learning. We just need to control our expectations for how quickly to expect results.

Machine learning is an important part of computer science's quest to augment the human intellect. We didn't learn calculus in the first grade, and we can't expect machines to learn too quickly, either. It's better to be patient, train models, be deliberate about where and when we implement automation, and define when a model is accurate enough to predict an outcome given the risk threshold involved. Computers may have helped our decision making—but they certainly haven't made us more patient.

Scan Products for Vulnerabilities

There are about as many reasons to test apps for vulnerabilities as there are apps and vulnerabilities combined. For the purposes of this section, we'll look at testing both as a creator of apps (and so trying to reduce the likelihood of an escape defect on our side doing harm at our company) and a consumer of apps (being harmed due to a defect).

The Open Worldwide Application Security Project (OWASP.org) is a foundation that sets security standards for application security testing. We strongly recommend checking out their testing guide available at `https://owasp.org/www-project-mobile-security-testing-guide/`. Some of their techniques are architectural, like making sure that anything that is in an app is absolutely needed and documented and that those dependencies have good security controls. Others include how apps communicate. Many of the controls from OWASP will call for vulnerability testing and/or scanning at some point. Luckily, much of this can be plugged into automated build trains used to compile, test, and submit apps to their destinations.

Types of Scanning

There are two main types of vulnerability scanning, which can easily be automated—static and dynamic analysis:

- **Static analysis** is scanning the source code of an app, analyzing it from the inside out. Because we need the source to complete static analysis, we either have to decompile an app or have access to the source, and so it's typically done by an application developer as a part of the pre-compilation step of the CI/CD process.

- **Dynamic analysis** is scanning an app for vulnerabilities from the outside in. This involves looking at the app as it's running and/or decompiling the app to check the frameworks and libraries in use—looking for any potential vulnerabilities.

Both have their place in a security-minded CI/CD implementation. Static analysis might see things that dynamic analysis can't. Not only does dynamic analysis provide run-time analysis but it can also uncover problems that came in due to a flaw or attack on the CI/CD infrastructure itself.

And it turns out that many of the tools available do both, so most of us don't have to pay for two separate tools. Whether an internal app development team or one who builds tools destined for the consumer or enterprise app stores, scanning (even a hardened runtime) should be done by most organizations.

The more complicated topic is which is the specific tool to use. If there's a seasoned application security expert on the team, MobSF is a great tool that can do both static and dynamic access. We have to build out our own infrastructure to use it, and there's a bit of a learning curve—but anyone with the skills can use it free of charge (unless we want to pay for a support contract or training). More on MobSF can be found at `https://github.com/MobSF/Mobile-Security-Framework-MobSF`.

For those that just want to plug a tool into the build system or into a device management infrastructure if just consuming apps (and so relying on dynamic vulnerability scanning), there are a number of tools available that each have their own pros and cons. Given that every environment is different (some can't use SaaS providers, some have privacy restrictions, some need compliance, some might rely on a specific endpoint availability, etc.), we'll just provide a list here and say "YMMV"—build a list of requirements and check each:

- *App-Ray*: Based in Austria and one of the more MDM-friendly of tools (`www.crunchbase.com/organization/app-ray`).

- *Codified*: Based in London and one of the older toolsets on the market (`www.crunchbase.com/organization/codified-security`).

- *Ostorlab*: Built by a former Google security engineer and based in Morocco (`www.crunchbase.com/organization/ostorlab`).

- *Quixxi*: Based in Sydney and has an additional feature of phoning home to check for unlicensed use of the software (`www.crunchbase.com/organization/quixxi`).

- *ImmuniWeb*: Based in Geneva, also scans web apps (YMMV based on the language used) (`www.crunchbase.com/organization/immuniweb`).

- *Appknox*: Based in Singapore, can also scan our API endpoints (`www.crunchbase.com/organization/appknox`).

- *Data Theorem*: Based in San Francisco, they offer an expansive product and a full support and services infrastructure (`www.crunchbase.com/organization/data-theorem`).

All of these vendors do Android and iOS app (.ipa) scanning. For those integrating with a device management tool and scanning when purchasing apps, Ostorlab and App-Ray have the most integrations with other vendors. It's easy to imagine a workflow where any .ipa added gets a dynamic analysis done upon upload and those from the app store are checked before making them available for distribution once they're seen in Apple Business Manager or an enterprise managed Google Play Store account.

Note   None that we looked at currently support scanning Mac apps, but some do support scanning Windows and/or Chromium apps.

Many of the code pipeline tools do some forms of security scanning (e.g., dependabot alerts from GitHub), but none get this in-depth or provide the pipelining for consuming and building. In the future they likely will, given the prevalence of OWASP and public vulnerability feeds—but we can't build our plans around "someday." Every developer needs to help protect the reputation of their organization. Nothing will destroy a reputation faster than a CVE or worse a zero-day vulnerability that gets exploited and results in a breach of customer data. None of us want lawsuits. This type of scanning can take as short as 15 minutes per build, and some of the tools out there allow doing so on a freemium model. There's no reason not to check code and runtimes before they leave our environments, even if we're trying to get new features or bug fixes to market quickly. The time and focus doing so takes away from other projects will be paid back with a high ROI when the organization doesn't get pwned.

Bring New Vendors on with Intention

As any company grows, they can't do everything anymore. As our needs become more complex, we end up with data sprawled across a lot of different places, and a few steps early in the life of a company save us a lot of time later down the road. This section looks at how vendors are brought on in large organizations.

Understanding how mature organizations onboard new vendors helps young companies who need to work with larger organizations that have more complex and often regulated engagement processes in two ways. The first is to understand what, if our endeavor is successful, those processes will look like for us someday. The second is to understand what our larger "enterprise" customers will need from us and what challenges they will face. Next, let's look at how our needs will evolve in order to help us plan how we'll handle vendors from early on in the life of the company to when we find ourselves in that mature state. We'll start with a playbook.

Why Having a Vendor Management Playbook Is Important

Once upon a time, we downloaded software, and our relationship with a vendor was over until several years later when there was an update that was hopefully cool enough to justify buying the new version (or until the old version wouldn't run on a new operating system). Software developers wanted to release updates faster. In a newer age of software, we moved from buying software to buying access to software. Now, we pay for our software on a monthly or annual schedule.

Another difference is that people used to buy software that sat on our machine. Data lived there or on servers on local networks. Now, we buy access to software that sits on a cloud, often with data that also sits on shared servers. Cue the security problems with hastily developed online services and the fact that data stored in that software no longer lives just on our computer but in servers that are potentially far, far away. As any organization grows, it becomes too dangerous to let any old employee fire up new projects and buy software, even if doing so is within already agreed-upon budgetary constraints.

We could break an existing process, or there could be compliance issues around a service. Therefore, having a playbook on how to spin up a new service can help do so in a deliberate and consistent fashion, where teams aren't surprised by the introduction of something that might impact them. Many of the aspects of this involve licensing third-party products or services (generally, web apps) for teams to go to market quickly with a new concept. However, these guidelines for developing externally facing products and services can also be used to inform our playbook on internal initiatives.

Note   This section was originally meant to help keep projects on track for the SOC2 compliance process rather than an instruction manual for others. But as we were working on it, we realized that many of the organizations we work with are going through some of the same things with growing teams and thought it might be of use to others.

A Software Vendor Onboarding Checklist

What follows is a software vendor onboarding checklist, split into two parts. The first covers internal considerations, and the second is for initiatives that are external (or customer facing).

Internal Considerations for Onboarding New Vendors

- **Are there dedicated teams for procurement, vendor relations, and management?** Many organizations have one but not all. If there are people dedicated to each of these responsibilities, it makes the process much easier. If not, then the remaining steps will be key.

- **Does the vendor need to sign our non-disclosure agreement (NDA)?** If so, many organizations have what is known as a mutual non-disclosure agreement (MNDA). It may be available on an internal wiki, like Confluence. Depending on your policies and tools available for obtaining signatures, you might share it in PDF format or using your organization's e-signature solution, like DocuSign. Some vendors will need to edit the document, as they can't abide by various terms. In these cases, they may request an editable version, like in Word. It's good to have both versions available to speed up the process.

- **Does the vendor have a contract we need to sign?** If so, is that submitted through a service desk or to an email address for a legal team? Usually, this same onboarding address or ticketing system will be the

319

same for both the MNDA and the vendor contracts themselves. Keep in mind that while getting a contract executed is usually not necessary, the process can take weeks. It's often worth getting this part started as soon as we have made a purchasing decision.

- **Will the vendor host our data or customer data?** This is where things often get specific to different types of businesses. Any organization that builds SaaS solutions or software will likely be well acquainted with filling out Data Processing Agreements (DPAs). These provide clarity on the relationship and how the data provided is handled. These are a must in any organization that handles personally identifiable data.

- **Does the IT team need to have the vendor fill out a security questionnaire?** Again, if the vendor is hosting data, this is usually required. Sometimes it's required with or without that. Either way, it's best not to fly under the radar and just get all these agreements knocked out as soon as possible. Many compliance teams are running a few weeks behind, so doing all of these in parallel helps keep the progress flowing.

- **How will the vendor be paid?** Accounting and finance teams are increasingly automating their processes. This might mean that we can more easily get budgets approved, but we still need to engage with the people that will pay the monthly or annual invoices to vendors—usually someone in the accounts payable department—even if the purchase is small enough to be put on a team member's company credit card.

- **Do we need to integrate with a federated login?**
  This is what enables single sign-on and just-in-time
  provisioning of accounts (through SAML, OIDC, etc.).
  The important thing an IT team is usually looking for
  here is the ability to have the disabled account and
  password change actions (actions they take from a
  centralized repository of accounts) be applied to all
  the web apps and servers in use in the organization. If
  every team has a solution or three that they're using, we
  can all sympathize with how much work it would be to
  provision or de-provision accounts without this type of
  centralized functionality. At the very least, the IT team
  needs a login in case we get hit by a bus.

- **Will the data be integrated with other systems?** This
  is where things get fun. If the tool will bring data in
  or the data placed in the tool will be used by other
  systems, then planning for that data flow is next. This
  is an area with a lot of potential to deliver value to all
  involved. By integrating data across systems, teams
  can gain better visibility in, understanding of, and
  control over task management, ERP, data visualization,
  analytics, and any number of other valuable areas. In
  some organizations, getting data copied into a data
  warehouse will be a requirement.

- **Does the rest of the organization need to be
  informed?** If someone gets a call from a customer out
  of the blue, how might they find information about
  how the organization is working with a given vendor?
  A clear and comprehensive page explaining what a
  vendor does on behalf of the organization can go a long
  way toward helping others provide an awesome service
  experience to both internal and external stakeholders.

External Considerations for Onboarding New Vendors

The internal considerations are common to just about any new vendor relationship. External-facing solutions are generally more of a concern for situations where the new vendor provides a solution that will be experienced in some direct way by the people our organization serves, for example, charts that load into a tool from a third party. If it's a tool that doesn't integrate with our products or that users will never see, these considerations are less important. For those external-facing solutions, consider the following:

- **Will this be a standalone product or an enhancement that can be sold?** If sold (e.g., a white-labeled service), then an SKU (Stock Keeping Unit) is usually required. No matter how big an organization is, there's usually just one or a handful of people that manage those. Most of the projects that teams take on aren't for an entirely new product the organization will take to market, but it happens.

- **Will the product be resold by third parties or distributors?** Any new SKU is likely sync'd every month or two with distributors or resellers. This is usually handled by the team that creates SKUs, but any teams that deal with resellers should be prepared, when possible, unless that activity is handled by sales or marketing enablement teams.

- **Is there an integration where the product needs to be put into another product?** This might be a tracking code or a single pixel or even something much, much larger. If that's the case, then product management probably has a deep pipeline of needs, and the new tool being used needs to get prioritized against those.

- **If the product will receive any changes, is there a documentation or technical communications team that needs to be updated so they can put things into their backlog?** This should be addressed as early as possible, especially when internationalization is involved, as that tends to take a good amount of time.

- **Do training materials need to be updated or produced?** Training is different from technical communication. Training often involves in-person or virtual classes. It could involve production of video content, such as would be hosted on a YouTube channel. The education arm of any organization will need to be made aware of product changes so they can determine if they need to make any corresponding changes to training materials.

- **Will the professional services team be impacted?** To ensure they're able to continue providing great service, it's important to make sure these team members know what's coming and how it will change or enhance their service options and processes. This is especially important if a valuable process will be disrupted.

- **Will the support team receive any calls because of a new vendor?** Even if it's a minor change to the product, make sure support staff have information available about that change. There are a variety of ways to support the support team—enablement training, providing test accounts, information on working with the vendor, etc. It is also often helpful to have a specialist become the subject matter expert, curating wiki or internal support enablement pages when possible.

- **Will international teams be impacted?** If so, then take a pass back through this checklist with those teams in mind. As our organizations become more and more geographically distributed, make sure to cover your bases in those various regions.

- **Will the solution be accessible through a different web address or site?** If so, this usually involves getting a change to the DNS for the organization (e.g., domain. pretendco.com). Those should take a maximum of 72 hours to replicate through the Internet, but internal change control processes could take months to complete the same change.

- **Will there be cookies?** GDPR requirements are usually handled during the information security review, but if the site uses cookies for sessions or even retargeting, then there will likely need to be a code snippet with the organization's policy on processing those.

- **Will third-party developers interact with the system?** This is where enabling a developer relations team will eventually be a requirement (but if it's successful, it'll pay for itself).

- **Can sales or marketing teams use the tool to better compete in the market?** If so, then there's probably a sales enablement team the initiative should coordinate with. They'll know best what should be socialized and how. Make sure to establish whether a press release

or another form of communication necessary. This
may include

- A one-sheet for account teams to hand out or email
  to potential or existing customers

- Blog post on the company blog

- Post on any user forums

- Social media mentions (Facebook, Twitter,
  Instagram, etc.)

- Pay-per-click AdWords buying or retargeting

- Sponsorship at conferences

- Webinars

- Email campaigns

- Meetings with sales teams to demo the new
  features or products

This is a lot of stuff, right?! As a startup we just need to know about
what's required for many organizations and build our early processes in
a way that they aren't overly taxing for us but do set a standard that lets
us work with the types of customers we want to work with. We should
also know what we'll eventually grow into if everything works out, but to
deploy that capital when needed. Along the way, we might find our target
customers step on toes to get our initiatives put on the priority list of other
teams. We all have our priorities, and we can all empathize with how much
goes into big ideas or little ones.

Conclusion

Most modern startups are technology-oriented; thus, our technology is as much our core focus as anything else we do. However, we often get wrapped up in the features and feature expansion to win customers and forget to consider infrastructure, automation development operations, security, and other aspects of our technology stack.

It's important to build innovative features, but it's also important to innovate at every function and discipline in a company. That means keeping technical debt low and thinking of new ways to think about and automate operations. We looked at that from the lens of what an investor might want to see in this chapter.

Understanding how investors think about our technical viability provides insight into what boxes we need to be checking given that they've been around and seen a lot of things that we might not have seen yet. But we all have blinders from time to time. It's important to remember, technology comes in phases and the primary phases of software evolution these past few years have gone along the following path for most industries (vertically and horizontally):

- Moving paper to computers in a rudimentary form that would resemble spreadsheets today (effectively digitizing business processes onto computers)

- Moving from those rudimentary spreadsheets to databases that have logic applied to the fields and triggers to further automation

- Enriching the data with other sources and thinking of it three-dimensionally, referencing tables to find trends

- Taking our data online so we can monetize it and amplify sales

- Overlaying existing data sets with machine learning and artificial intelligence to help people do more and cope with the massive amounts of data now at our fingertips

- Rethinking an industry now that we have all these advancements in the previous stages—often referred to as disruption

Some industries comprised of technological laggards can skip a stage or two here and there. Some industries have several sub-steps to get between stages, but these are the main buckets. If we encounter those that haven't yet hit a point, then we can think of the next step or two beyond where they were.

Technology is always changing, so we have to watch for trends to know what's next in our path. This might mean moving our monolithic web application to a microservices architecture, or it might mean adding a chat widget to our site or app. Each of these small and big enhancements simply makes us more scalable as an organization. We should also be thinking about our own operations from this perspective too. That extends from how we build products, sell products, and package our offerings to how we deliver support and run our financial operations, which we'll cover in the next chapter.

CHAPTER 9

Accounting and Finance

It's important to know that there are enough gold pieces so the party can buy the supplies required to make it through the next stage of each campaign. There are the known costs and there are unknowns. A good accounting of what any adventuring party has and a good idea of where and how new endeavors will be financed allows the rest of the organization to expand with confidence and in ways that don't potentially risk everything through poor planning. There are a lot of hurdles to run a company, as with a role-playing game–but one of the most important aspects of executional excellence is to get a grasp on the finances of any organization. We need to know where all our gold pieces are and where they need to go, have a snapshot of the financial well-being of the adventuring party months in advance, and know how fast we're burning through hard-fought-for cash. This allows us to grow safely, to have peace of mind, and to speak knowingly to all the stakeholders in our endeavors.

For the purposes of this chapter, we'll break the money discipline down into two main aspects. The first is accounting—to get a grasp on the basic cash flows and reporting systems needed to run a company. The second is finance—reporting on the past and planning for the future. The younger the company, the more indexed on accounting we are, but as we grow we need to get better and better at finance and understanding how and why we use each type of financial instrument at our disposal.

© Charles Edge, Chip Pearson, Amy Larson Pearson 2023
C. Edge et al., *The Startup Players Handbook*,
https://doi.org/10.1007/978-1-4842-9315-7_9

Leveling the Accounting Team

There is a fairly standard journey that a lot of accounting disciplines and organizations grow in companies. Although some grow fast and burn through a few levels at once, many take months or years to go through each stage. Often products with higher cost need fewer accountants per dollar of revenue earned, so there's not a magic number for how many people we need based on a metric of revenue or staff.

A great accounting firm might also get us through a couple of levels without having to bring on staff or with outsourcing certain functions. The longer we can wait, the more savvy we should be in hiring our team when it comes time. But pretty much every company will end up in a similar place with accounting around the later stages. Consider the following as we grow and need those gold pieces tracked. Let's look at a common growth structure for the financial management of a company:

- *Level 1*: Nearly every organization begins with an outsourced bookkeeper (except accounting firms, of course). Most also start off by outsourcing the tax filings. So, until a company hits four or five people at a minimum, accounting is outsourced and likely remains outsourced indefinitely, at least in part (we'll eventually need third-party auditors). Once we hit our second or third person in a company, we want to make sure we practice good financial prudence and are legal. We'll still likely need a little help transitioning to a good revenue accrual model and some light modeling as we start preparing for board meetings. Finding a blend of what founders do and what certified public accountants (CPAs) do helps us keep our costs down while also flexing a more mature financial muscle.

- *Level 2*: Once we hit a few people on the team, we start needing someone to do light operational duties. Maybe this is a bookkeeper that can also manage some of our vendors and keep up with the payroll. Most of us are self-sufficient, but if we can forge alliances, sell products, or write code and let some of the repeatable tasks go, this is a perfect early hire and often less costly than another engineer.

- *Level 3*: The first person we bring on staff in the accounting organization is usually a bookkeeper. As we grow, this individual is likely to shed various responsibilities they might have incurred along the way to be dedicated to accounting. Beyond that, as we scale, they might grow into a bigger position or might take on part of the accounting duties, such as paying the bills, but as we grow, we will need someone to handle the basic day-to-day financial needs.

- *Level 4*: If we don't have an accounting manager, then as we grow past about 100 people, we likely need someone to manage the tasks. The founder can usually manage tasks for up to a few dozen people, but having someone who can manage the people who are doing what that original bookkeeper/assistant did is going to free up founders to raise money from customers (through sales), sell to investors, and manage the roadmap. We know we're moving into our next stage when the existing team has troubles maintaining daily accounting needs, covering all the expenses, making sure customers get invoiced (or that our monthly Stripe accounts reconcile), etc.

- *Level 5*: More money, more problems. Once we start to see our financial systems break down and need more sophisticated reporting than we can do even with the help of our existing accounting team, it's time to hire a controller. This individual also helps with internal controls and process management and often gets pulled into those types of tasks if there isn't anyone else in operations.

- *Level 6*: Once we are talking about more and more money and more complicated financial structures, it's time to bring in a chief financial officer (CFO). This individual can sit in board meetings and explain the aspects a founder might otherwise stumble over repeating. Therefore, somewhere between a Series A and a Series B, if not sooner, many organizations need a CFO. They add more mature long-term budgeting assistance and KPI development, help with fundraising, and, when we're ready, also work on mergers and acquisitions (or at least, the financial modeling of them). We cover the CFO in more detail when we discuss scale and bringing on an executive team later in the book. The CFO will also shape what the accounting and finance disciplines look like long term.

- *Level 7*: The accountants can seem like they're always around as we grow. They need things signed all the time. Maybe we're doing SOC2 compliance, which also involves accountants. Maybe we've decided to nest human resources under the CFO. Maybe they also end up with legal, internal IT, and even compliance. This is in part due to the sophistication they have to bring in order to do all that reporting and budgeting. That leads to trust. Most leaders want to help out—let's just try to keep an eye on the long term and not allow the CFO to overburden themselves by being too helpful. Eventually some of those duties will be shared with a COO (unless the COO is a more sales-oriented position).

Beyond level 7, the CFO is likely one of the most important people in any organization (probably more important than the founders eventually). Public companies often have the CEO and CFO on calls with investors, and that scales down to having them in board meetings, even as a ten-person company. Accounting can seem foreign to founders (especially before we have a trusted source in our party). In the next section, we'll begin the journey to level up our financial discipline (and acumen) with some basic accounting concepts every founder should understand.

Basic Accounting Terminology

A successful startup founder doesn't need to be an accounting expert; that can be outsourced. Founders do need a solid grasp of basic accounting concepts, though. As a small business owner, we need more than an intuitive feel for the performance of the business. Understanding a few basic Accounting 101 concepts goes a long way toward keeping the goals for a company in alignment with performance. Here are five accounting concepts to get started.

The Balance Sheet

A great place to start when evaluating the performance of an organization is how to decipher a balance sheet. At a minimum, we should understand assets and liabilities and how they relate to one another. Assets are what we own, which include signed contracts we haven't taken payment on. Liabilities are debts, as well as goods and services that we have taken payment for that we must contractually deliver.

A basic equation to calculate the worth of the company is to take the assets and subtract the liabilities, with what's left being the equity. Putting this on paper results in a balance sheet. This provides us a quick overview of our organization. Lots of cash on hand and little debt means a strong balance sheet. High debt and low cash means a weak balance sheet. The balance sheet drives long-term decisions on where to invest resources.

The P&L

A profit and loss statement (or P&L statement for short) provides a good idea of how the organization is doing at any given point in time. The P&L indicates the cost of sales, margins on each product, and costs that impact margins. Those costs include inventory, shipping, manufacturing, etc. The more granular these become, the more data-driven we can get with establishing the cost of products. Every P&L includes net income. The net income is a statement about the profit made—the reward for the time and blood, sweat, and tears we invested!

The Cash Flow Statement

In startups, cash is king. Cash is a cushion for when, not if, the business suffers a setback. Cash should cover the operational costs to run a business for a period of time. (Each organization has a different outlook on how long that might be.) The key to understanding cash flow is the cash flow statement.

Consider the cash flow statement as the connection between a balance sheet and an income statement. The cash flow statement explains how our net income transformed into net cash over a given amount of time. The cash flow statement divides activities into three categories: operations, investment, and financing. Initially, organizations have cash from ongoing operations, but as a company grows, we'll also manage cash from investments and operations. We usually pay taxes on at least some of that cash and take deductions from those investments and operations.

Taxes

As a founder and therefore business owner, we need to understand taxes. Most organizations seek to minimize their tax burden as much as possible, and that's where our knowledge of accounting can really pay off—we should understand the tax advantages of different legal structures (e.g., a corporation vs. a sole proprietorship) and the potential tax savings that are available to small business owners. This isn't something we should do on our own, though—hire a great tax advisor. They will help with quarterly tax payments and keep companies out of trouble.

Pro Forma Projections

Accounting is a story of the past and the present. The pro forma is a projection of future performance based on past performance. Pro forma projections enable us to project how the business will do in the future. Projections are critical, as they allow us to make informed decisions about staffing, delivery, and the value of each line of business.

At the end of the day, most small businesses will outsource accounting, so don't get too hung up on all the accounting jargon or the finer points of different depreciation methods. A basic understanding of the three core financial statements and a good idea of what they tell us about future performance will set you on your way to becoming a solid founder!

Accounting Software

Every company needs a good accounting and finance team to grow effectively. The most central piece of accounting is the general ledger. That's not a physical book like it was before personal computers came to be, nor is it a large mainframe like *Warhammer* players might expect. There are a lot of pieces of software that can be used to track simple credits and debits, and many have transitioned to SaaS business models. The best solution for many organizations is probably the one the person leading the finance team wants to use. They know the organization best and know if it's critical for a given type of business to use a specific package or if the organization should just use a tool like QuickBooks. If the finances are outsourced, as is the case with early-stage companies, the one the person keeping the books wants to use is probably best, within reason. Make sure data can be imported and exported through standard data formats as it's likely that the software that works for a three-person company won't be used at one with 300 people.

Even though each company hopefully has a trusted advisor who can guide the decision about what accounting software to use, it's important to at least try to be involved and engaged with the process of selecting a tool. There are some attributes that we'll all care about as time goes on, so let's look at a few to help participate in the process:

- All information should be exportable to a new platform when and if the time comes. For example, it's common to use a solution like QuickBooks online for an early-stage company and then grow into an Intacct or NetSuite around the time of a Series A or Series B round of financing. This is worth reiterating.

- There should be plugins or integrations with other solutions in use at the organization. If we use Salesforce, then we want to make sure each tool we short-list supports integrating with that. If we use Stripe to accept payments, we want that information to flow into the accounting software for easier and eventually automatic reconciliation. If we have employees who need to submit expense reports, we'll want the tool to integrate with Expensify or another similar software package. Pluggable software also denotes that a package is big enough to warrant other vendors wanting to work with a provider.

- We need the ability to build custom integrations with existing tools. Maybe we have a web app and can wire together a workflow using a simple webhook that eliminates hours of duplicative work. Maybe our CRM doesn't support the tool, but both have simple REST interfaces. An API that covers all the data we put into our accounting software, at least as read-only, is key to future-proofing automation ideas.

- We need to be able to export granular reports and files. These support the individual doing our taxes and are used for routine board meetings, sent to investors, reviewed by auditors, etc.

- We should understand how much work is involved in the customization of the software to work best in our environment and what that cost is. Many software packages are not "customer installable" and so can cost tens of thousands of dollars just to get set up and integrated with bank accounts and others.

- We should understand the long-term implications of our selection. That means the availability of contractors who can help us with basic routine tasks, more experienced advisors, and staff when the time comes to hire them.

- Make sure working with the tool doesn't suck. A founder needs a basic understanding of the accounting software in the early stages of the company. Maybe we have a read-only account so we don't mess anything up—but we should be able to log in, look at reports, spot-check how things are coded, and look for ways to improve the flow of information where needed. This might come in handy in that next board meeting!

Much of this is about automation and extending what tools can do. In software we tend to think we can bend rules where it's possible because we can write a few lines of code to do so. Avoid doing so when it comes to accounting. There's a reason that generally acceptable accounting principles (GAAPs) exist, and we want to not only stay within legal frameworks but also just do business well!

Once an accountant recommends a piece of software, we want to make sure we're using common tools. Some of the more traditional products available include the following (but there are hundreds of others):

- QuickBooks

- Xero

- FreshBooks

- Simply Accounting

- MYOB

- Zoho Books

- FinancialForce

- Peachtree

- Intacct

- NetSuite

We can certainly use others, but maybe do additional research if a tool isn't on this list. Once one is selected, there are countless online training videos and classes for any of the preceding tools. Every founder needs to have a finger on the pulse of the finances—and there's no better way than just being able to navigate the software that tracks where all the gold pieces are going, where they are coming from, and why. This is important at every stage of the company and simplest when we're using down-market accounting solutions.

The accounting software that gets us from five employees to a Series F company with IPO aspirations is very likely going to be a different solution. Some of the ecosystems are better than others. Some are closed off from other tools in one ecosystem. We want and need our accounting team to be best able to support us, but also want to make sure we are protected from having massive amounts of work to upgrade to a tool later. That's one reason we want to be able to export all our data. This includes how we code expenses, custom codes, the table of debits and credits, a chart of accounts, etc. Beyond that, it's not uncommon for those who lead accounting or finance teams to have strong opinions about what product to use, so that's something we should identify during the interview process and make sure there's compatibility. A final aspect of the tool to consider is if we're just starting and doing cash-based accounting; then we'll want to make sure it supports moving to accrual-based accounting and makes that process simple (with or without third-party plugins) and clear about where that line was drawn for future reports so it doesn't appear that we have a mixture of cash and accrual methods to confuse investors (which is much more common than it might seem).

Accrual- vs. Cash-Based Accounting

Most begin their journey with accounting on a cash basis. We receive cash and consider it immediately available to spend. A customer gives us $120, and we provide a good or a service. This is easy at first, and, if we're bootstrapping our organization and it's just us, that's not a big deal. This is known as cash-based accounting.

Then we level up, and we have money coming in monthly or weekly and going out at about the same rate. The second we bring on an employee or get investors or owe customers for goods or services that we haven't delivered, it's time to change the way we accrue revenue. Accrued revenue is money that we've *earned*. If we take a payment to provide access to a piece of software or hosted environment for a year, then we only earn as much as how far we are into that year, typically split into a monthly percentage. So, if the customer gives us $120 and we're in the third month, we've likely earned $30 of that.

This is known as accrual-based accounting, and it's best to move to running the books that way as quickly as possible in any startup. This is why QuickBooks has a little button that says Accrual and another that says Cash for every report.

Let's map out why things work this way as the numbers grow. Let's say we have $1,200,000 per year coming in based on annual contracts. We "earn" $100,000 per month. If a customer demanded a refund for remaining services or if for some reason we had to turn off services, then we would owe those customers their money back. If we haven't spent the money but instead have it sitting in a separate account for unearned revenue, then we won't have to go bankrupt when that happens.

Accrual-based accounting is a little more complicated than just using a spreadsheet or a bank statement to run the books. This is a point where we should hire an accountant—if only to help get the books in order on a routine basis.

Hire an Accountant

Every organization needs to account for all the gold pieces that flow through their doors. Many founders can usually handle the basics of a general ledger, but even for a sole proprietorship, they will likely need to have someone to do taxes at a minimum and often end up with a second someone to help with basic accounting tasks throughout the year.

The easy stuff includes things like tagging receipts to categorize expenditures and entering money as it comes in (at least with a little instruction). But there are a lot of complicated aspects of accounting that career professionals will need to handle, especially if we find success and there's real money being made or raised. As those trusted to run a startup, we shouldn't have to deal with all the accounting minutiae (and in fact, some checks and balances are a really good idea). Instead, we should immediately hire someone to help us get our books in order.

We often find that a good accountant will not only get what we've done in the past in order but set up a better system for the future. And our first accountant is likely to also act as a financial advisor of sorts. Later, those roles will diverge due to an increasing level of sophistication for both. When hiring an accountant, look for someone that doesn't let us just do what we want. This means we need to listen. Yes, we are our own boss. But they're our boss, too, now—as are our employees and customers. It might have been easier when we just had one boss...

The bookkeeping functions of a small business are not the same as those performed by an accountant, financial advisor, or tax preparer. We need someone (and at first, it is likely to be you) to enter receipts, enter receivables, write the checks for payables, reconcile bank statements, reconcile credit card statements, and maybe deposit checks for receivables that come in the form of physical checks. There are now SaaS tools to automate much of this, so a good accountant will show us how to do as much as they think we can be trusted to do and define a delineation of responsibilities between us.

As we grow, the accounts receivable and accounts payable often split into responsibilities carried out by two different people. But for now, let's keep the setup simple. We need to bring on a tax preparer and likely an accountant to come in at least once a month to help us get the books in order. Before we hire them (or pretend we don't need to), here are a few things to keep in mind:

- Before we accept our first payment, we need to choose what kind of company to start. At a minimum, we likely need to form an LLC to get some level of liability protection. See Chapter 3 for more information on what type of business to start. An accountant can often help us file the appropriate paperwork.

- Accountants can work in person or remotely. We should interview them with video at a minimum.

- We need a tax preparer and to understand when we should plan to make our first quarterly estimated tax payment and how much to set aside for that payment before we accept our first payment.

- Based on the person we choose, we also need to identify which tool will automate the business. This is important because it needs to integrate into the accounting solution we use. For example, if the accounting system is QuickBooks and our bookkeeper and tax preparer both use QuickBooks, then we should make sure a Shopify store (or whatever tool we like to use) integrates with QuickBooks.

- Build good checks and balances. We need someone to keep us honest with spending, forecasting, and taxes. Many an accountant won't have access to our accounts. We need to check their work anyway, to make sure they got things right and are good stewards of the business.

- Categorize receipts immediately. If we let our receipts build up, then we'll have a mountain of work. If we do them upon receipt of a delivery, when the charge hits our accounts payable, or at least once a week, then it will be much simpler. The tax preparer will sort out what we can and can't claim. This includes services, travel, subscriptions, and the cost of the office—which at first might be a part of the costs of a home.

- If we get financial advice about a business arrangement, think long and hard before proceeding against that advice. We all screw this up and learn the hard way eventually.

- Don't ever, ever, ever write your own accounting software. Been there, done that, bad decisions, and making up your own GAAPs will ensue.

- Keep all the records pretty much forever.

Every business is different, and we can't provide a universal truth with how to structure business finances. But hopefully some of this chapter information helps frame things the way each startup needs them framed, to help us hire someone we can trust—probably someone we aren't related to. And we should plan to get additional services (insurance, legal advice, etc.) from other vendors every now and then.

Taxes

Taxes pay for our governments to run. They fund schools, fuel defense spending, make our roads drivable, maintain social programs, pay down national debts, fund research, help our fellow humans when needed, and much more. Putting politics aside, taxes are necessary for every organization, and most organizations look to minimize the tax liability both for the corporation and for the individuals paid by the corporation.

The tax code is complicated. Individuals can often do their own taxes or pay a minimal amount for someone to help them do so, but organizations usually need help. This comes in the form of paying someone to file business taxes. Let's go through a few important aspects there. Every organization needs to file tax documents every year in order to maintain their business license. It doesn't matter if the organization lost money, if it didn't cross a certain threshold of income to think it matters, if we're a nonprofit, or if we didn't raise any capital like we thought we would. If the organization has been incorporated, we need to file our taxes. Not doing so has been the downfall of many a successful enterprise.

Previously, we looked at how incorporating a company impacts fundraising. The first thing a tax professional will help with is to explain how those articles of incorporation impact how (and when) we pay our taxes. It's always great to consult with a tax professional on the repercussions that each method of incorporating a company will have on our tax burdens before we file those articles of incorporation. If we didn't, we can always change things for future years if need be. But for the previous year, we have what we have.

We'll work with that tax professional once a year to make sure we're legal and all the appropriate paperwork is filed. More than likely, they will have specialized software to help with the process. We'll also likely meet with our tax professional (or someone in a firm) to file and, if we have a tax burden of income, to pay quarterly taxes. We may even combine the bookkeeping responsibilities with the firm handling our taxes. We should immediately start keeping our books in a way that the filing and bookkeeping are easiest for those we outsource those tasks to. Many accountants and tax preparers have software that integrates with

QuickBooks or other popular bookkeeping software packages. The person we hire should like and, if possible, have software that integrates with the systems we're using.

Part of filing taxes is to take expenses out of income, where the appropriate expenses are known as write-offs. We've all thought some things should be write-offs that aren't appropriate or considered various expenses as inconsequential that when added up grew to the point that they impacted our profit and loss. A lot of things can offset our tax burden, like a research and development tax credit. However, the tax code can be incredibly pedantic about such things, and our tax professionals are there to help navigate those icy waters.

Over time, we all build up assets. These might be computers, office equipment, office space, and even code. These assets depreciate on known schedules that, despite the word *before* in the acronym, can impact EBITDA (earnings before interest, taxes, depreciation, and amortization). We might defer tax deductions until we are profitable, or we might pay the tax immediately and carry certain aspects over. This is an area where we should keep a spreadsheet of everything owned (as a check against what's in our accounting systems) so a tax professional can help us figure out what goes in which column and how.

Research and development (R&D) is one of the more difficult aspects of taxes many software organizations navigate. We all know that the second we commit code, that code becomes technical debt. We also know that many of the features we build and innovative ways we figure out to maintain legacy code could be research or could be not. Most states allow us to account for research and development costs differently than maintenance of products. This is another place to work closely with a tax professional. Again, keeping a spreadsheet (or exporting from Jira) of where all development time went (and the cost of that time) helps arm a tax professional with how to account for our R&D costs vs. our maintenance costs.

Lastly, ask tax preparers a few questions about how products impact the tax burden of the customers. For example, for organizations working with small businesses, we might want to provide a simple export of our receipts annually or quarterly for customers to use in their tax filings. Or we might market differently at tax season, especially if we sell larger systems that might be considered capital expenditures. This helps provide special marketing content for customers around tax time. Those promotions can go a long way in propelling a company forward in what might otherwise be hard months for SaaS companies!

Insurance

It's never too early to get insurance for the business. Even if incorporated as an LLC, there are limits to that protection. Even if we're not charging for products, we can still be liable for damages occurred in their use. The answer for this is usually errors and omissions (E&O) insurance. E&O insurance, as we end up calling it, is a liability insurance that protects the company and the people that work at the company against lawsuits over negligence or other liability claims. Like most for-profit companies, insurance companies need to make a profit. To do so, they protect us financially against a known set of possible things that can happen. Some are bundled into a standard policy; others cost extra. They track variables that help them determine the likelihood. Sometimes those algorithms are dated, but often they help us uncover ways to make the organization better—if only to get a cheaper rate on a policy.

The policy is an agreement that we will act in a certain way, and if something bad happens and we get sued (or there's a claim against the policy), the insurance company will help with, or completely cover, the damages. Selecting a policy isn't a simple task. Most business owners won't understand a tenth of the words in a policy. Selecting the right type of policy can be complicated, and selecting how much we spend to extend coverages in different areas might be difficult. But we need the safety net that insurance provides, so we have to get started somewhere.

We also have a responsibility to be efficient with how we deploy the limited funds in any startup. Our personal needs might be different from those of the company. Some organizations will sell products and have offices and so need more than E&O insurance and need general liability insurance with certain wavers based on their state and city.

Almost every business needs insurance. If it's the first time, the hardest part is to just pick up the phone or go to a web page and fill out a form. From there, it gets pretty simple because there's someone that has a quota on the other end, and they'll be calling us to sell us a policy. So let's go through a few things to consider:

- **Write an End User License Agreement (EULA).**
  There's an important aspect of the EULA (or EUSLA for specialized software license agreements) that is a cap on damages. The cap should be less than the mount of insurance being purchased. Some industries or sizes of companies have standard caps required for damages, and so this will be different for various types of companies.

- **Talk to at least three agents before buying a policy.**
  The old maxim is "shop around," but a couple of different things happen when we talk to multiple agents. We get better pricing, which is never a terrible idea with limited funds, and we get educated on the industry and what we need. We also get more opportunities to find someone we can trust for the next decade.

- **Try to find a broker that immediately builds trust.**
  This isn't just about money. Especially due to all the
  complexities that are entailed with insurance, lack of
  expertise in most business owners means we must
  trust the broker. They should build trust by being
  knowledgeable and, well, by being trustworthy.

- **Ask how the agency calculates their quotes.** We
  should shop around for different insurance agencies
  to get the best quote. But remember to make sure
  that they are transparent throughout the process.
  For example, don't forget to consider the size of the
  company, amount covered, and industry. Knowing all
  the facts and figures about how the agency assesses
  the business will allow us to stay more informed. If one
  policy is cheaper than another, ask why. They should
  already know the policy is being shopped around, and
  so this should come as no surprise.

- **Choose a plan that scales.** When trying to buy
  company insurance, see if the quoted prices work as
  the business scales. Some specific insurance agencies
  have per-employee costs, making the overall scaling
  process more and more difficult. Or to sign a deal with
  a new customer or to add a feature that we didn't have
  before, we may need a $2M policy, so understanding
  what we'll have to do and what it will cost is important.
  It's a great problem to have, provided we're charging
  large customers enough to fund the policy changes.
  Planning for overall growth is helpful in all areas of a
  business, so researching for insurance is no different.

- **Look beyond general liability insurance.** We want
  to cover a number of different aspects of the business
  potentially not otherwise covered. It is important to
  read all the insurance-related documents and contracts
  in as much detail as possible to get an understanding
  of what is covered and what is not. Usually, small
  businesses start out with general liability insurance
  while doing their own analysis in order to find out what
  they need to get additional insurance.

Believe it or not, there are some great side effects to getting E&O insurance. To get a policy, we'll have to fill out some paperwork. That paperwork will see us checking boxes for things we have in place, and the policy gets more expensive the less of those we have. Therefore, if we add certain security protections that we probably already knew we needed, our policy gets cheaper. Checking some of those boxes can take our focus away from building features that inspire customers, but at least we aren't building software that's dangerous for our customers to use.

While looking for insurance, remember that a single policy might provide comprehensive general liability coverage and even separate coverage for property damage owned by the insured. Getting the correct insurance type and amount of business insurance is a key layer of protection that should never be avoided, even though it's money and time that takes away from features that help us close clients. The lessons we learn about protecting the company while acquiring and renewing insurance are critical to protecting ourselves as we blossom into an amazing company.

Don't Look Too Far Ahead: Cash Flow and Burn Rates

One of the jobs of a finance whiz is to keep us from spending too much money. Seems almost silly to say it, but it's true. As our adventuring party grows, we take on additional humans with unique skills that help amplify the impact we have. But we need to pay them. That might include some equity but more than likely also includes an actual paycheck. If we take on an office space, then we have additional debits. We probably have hosting bills and software fees or licenses and insurance and much more.

Bootstrapped companies usually operate in the black—which is to say they self-fund growth so usually spend less than they make. That can come at an opportunity cost given that spending more on growth often leads to faster growth and, when there's competition, we need to outpace competitors. That's life in a startup, or it is for most. Yet we still have a responsibility to those who joined us on our adventure (and those who helped fund it) to be good stewards for everyone's well-being.

Every CEO or founder should know how much money comes in every month, how much goes out, and the balance in the accounts that keep the company running if the money dries up. The money that's coming in and going out is referred to as cash flow. Many startups have more going out than coming in. That difference is known as a burn rate. And we all need to know how long we can sustain losing money, or operating in the red. The finance team should be able to project, with a fair amount of certainty, how long the company can operate at the current levels. They should also be able to project, if given an infusion of cash from an investor, how many people can be hired, how many services added, and what will be required to sustain existing customers.

Grow too fast and the burn rate can't be maintained. Grow to slow and competitors take the market away. It's a fine line and the hardest part of planning for scale. But if it were easy, we wouldn't be making the big bucks (which in the beginning likely isn't even enough to buy drinks when we go out).

Awesome Charts and Graphs

Images are incredibly impactful tools in storytelling. Corporate finance is as much about storytelling as it is about number nerding. Graphs that show costs and expenses and trendline out projections can be powerful ways to communicate the state of a company. We just need to make sure we're trying to show reality and not cherry-picking numbers that promote a certain view.

The spreadsheet is one of the most widely used and useful tools in the arsenal of anyone in finance. This makes projecting and analyzing trends in Excel or Google Sheets one of the most valuable skills we can have to project cash flow, income, and other items on a balance sheet.

The process can be as simple or as complicated as we want it to be. For example, let's say we have two columns—one with a year and the other with the number of net-new employees or customers we bring on in a year. Given enough years, we can use that information to project out how many employees we'll be hiring or customers we'll be onboarding in future years.

From Excel, we can add a trendline to our simple spreadsheet. To do so, select Add Chart Element ➤ Trendline and then select More Trendline Options...

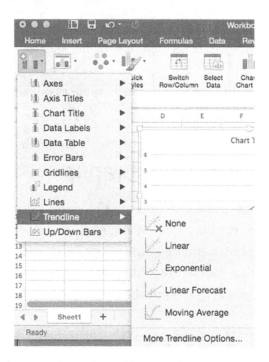

At the Format Trendline pane, click Polynomial and check the box for
"Display equation on chart." Copy the equation onto the clipboard and
paste it into the formula bar for the next row.

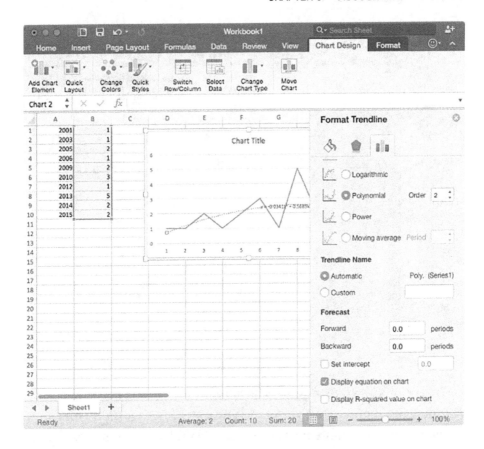

Next, we'll remove the y and convert the symbols into formula elements.

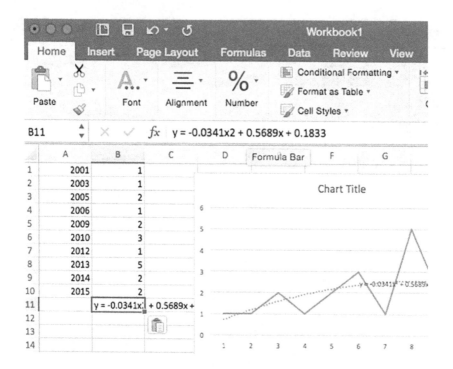

This results in wrong numbers because we've got years instead of ascending numbers and we've got missing years when we didn't hire any new employees or acquire new customers. So we'll convert the years into a number starting with 1 and going up (where 1 is 2001 and so on).

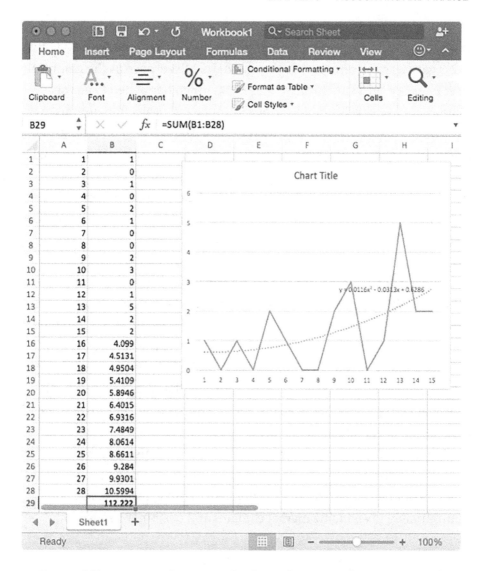

Keep adding rows and copying the formula into each new row, and you'll find how many employees you expect the company to have in 2035.

Finally, keep in mind that you need data to build good trendlines. The more data points we have, the more accurate the projections. Also keep in mind that anomalies happen (like pandemics) and those changing behaviors (like the impact reorganizing the sales team has on customer acquisition) can alter the course of trendlines!

Imagine life before the spreadsheet. It wasn't that long ago. The modern spreadsheet came along in 1979 with VisiCalc, and by 1983 Lotus 1-2-3 gave us charts in spreadsheets, and then Excel gave us the graphical user interface on a spreadsheet in 1985. So much happened in just six short years. We slowly added various formula and projection options over the next couple of decades, and then Google came along and brought us into a modern era in 2006 when they bought XL2Web so multiple people could work on a spreadsheet at the same time. And this is yet another example of the technological determinism of modern computing. We had a tool built for the personal computer. Then we got tooling online and then rethought the whole thing and infused it with collaborative elements.

There are several tools that go far beyond the capabilities of Excel. Some, like Snowflake, Splunk, and a host of Amazon tools, can pull data into a repository and then provide mechanisms to dynamically generate graphs on the fly. Or look at time-series data of numerous CSVs and the drift in our "big data" over time. That solves two issues: getting a central big data repository and developing dashboards that provide us with critical information about the health of every aspect of the company where data is available. Tools like Domo go further down-market to automate some of the steps of developing those charts.

If a team has an idea of their goals and expectations—and we can track key performance indicators that show how we're progressing toward meeting our targets—then we're better able to run a business and react appropriately to changing market climates and customer needs.

Conclusion

Every startup needs organized finances. The faster we get every piece of money coming into the company and going out of the company into a system, the better. The more credit cards, lines of credit, and bank accounts we end up with, the harder to keep track of everything. This is why we likely need a bookkeeper, tax preparer, and business advisor early in the life of a company that's being built to last. Luckily, they are good at money so can help us to budget for their services!

Once we can plot out what's coming in (whether from investors or paying customers) and have a holistic understanding of money going out, we can then turn our attention toward understanding the impact every purchase, monthly service, and hire that we make has on our burn rate. We can also build charts that look at the past and even project future performance. Never forget the basics of how many gold pieces it takes to buy enough rations and supplies for the party, though. It is important not to get caught up in too many synthetic numbers and forget that if we can't make payroll, our adventuring party will fall apart.

No matter how good we are at tracking our finances, we'll need income to continue operations. Products don't buy themselves. Yet! Therefore, we'll likely need to bring on sales and marketing. The next chapter begins that journey with sales—because for many we want to get a deep understanding of the buying motion before we go on to spending marketing budgets and because founder-led sales is so impactful compared with less direct means of selling.

CHAPTER 10

Sales

Sales is critical for any organization to survive. The revenue generated from selling products is raising capital from the most important source: customers. Paying customers validate our existence and provide non-dilutive income. Sales don't just happen on their own, though. They require someone to help potential customers (leads) see our vision and value and hopefully convert them into evangelists for our mission.

Many see sales as an arcane art that we either are born with or aren't. Others (often the more technical founders) consider sales a dirty word and salespeople a necessary evil. Maybe it's because when people think of sales they think of that cliche of the guy trying to sell us something we don't need, at a price that is unfair - maybe a trickster rogue. The first step then is to change our mindset about sales itself. Consider that our product and our company have been created as a solution to help people do what they want to do faster, better or with more ease. Therefore, sales should be a critical step in forming a beautiful business relationship - not the last part of a deceptive process. There are so many ways to sell and to do so ethically. In this chapter we're going to go through the main stages of an organization's journey through sales.

Levels in Sales Organizations

The journey begins with founder-led sales, when it's just us out in the world trying to spread the word, and goes through to a mature, layered sales organization. The growth of an organization comes in stages, which shape

© Charles Edge, Chip Pearson, Amy Larson Pearson 2023
C. Edge et al., *The Startup Players Handbook*,
https://doi.org/10.1007/978-1-4842-9315-7_10

up according to the type of sales we make (deal size, customer type, length of sales cycle, etc.). Yet, most organizations evolve along a similar path:

- *Level 1*: Founder-led sales is where most organizations begin. As with many disciplines we cover, the founders wear a lot of hats. They find their own route to close deals, often with unconventional means.

- *Level 2*: Some of the first hires we make in companies are in sales or marketing, according to the type of product we create. Based on where a founder has forged a path to successful sales outcomes, we can then start to train others to sell our products.

- *Level 3*: Once we see where we're successful, we can start to define sales cycles and journey maps more clearly. We probably implemented a Customer Relationship Management (CRM) tool back when it was just us, but at this point, we should re-evaluate that tool and see where we can integrate apps and web apps with business process automation.

- *Level 4*: Once we get past four sellers, we should be able to predict performance of a sales organization. We should also be hiring a sales leader if we haven't already. This might be someone we promote from within the existing sales team, or it might be someone we bring in from an adjacent industry externally.

- *Level 5*: Now that we're learning more about how to sell our products, there are certain aspects we put on an assembly line. We create buyer personas to map leads in the CRM, we have more required settings in our CRM to move sales along stages, and we start to see different sellers focus on different parts of the sales process.

- *Level 6*: Scaling a sales team means aligning sellers on similar methodologies used. Implementing a methodology doesn't mean we can't allow for flexibility, but it does mean we find a selling approach that we can then put as a requirement (or more easily train new sellers).

- *Level 7*: Our sales organization needs to be international so we can meet more customers where they are. This means contract negotiations in different countries, the ability to transact in local currencies, and go-to-market activity in a lot of different languages. That's capital intensive, and now we're better able to understand the ROI for each dollar spent in sales.

One important aspect of how a sales organization evolves is how transactional the sales cycle is. An organization that appeals to consumer or prosumer users and charges a small monthly fee (even an in-app fee) is likely to focus more on marketing, and so the sales organization might not begin to evolve until there's a few million in annual recurring revenues.

A sales organization that has survived beyond level 7 is a machine. This force of nature seems somewhat unstoppable. In fact, we may even find ourselves referring sales to other companies when they aren't a great fit. And yet, it all starts at most companies at the same place: a founder hitting the pavement and closing some deals.

Founder-Led Sales

Many founders have no experience in sales—and yet selling is one of the most important aspects of a founder's job. It's often the difference between making money and not making money. While we're building a product, we might ask for feedback from people we consider potential customers. At some point, we release a product into the world and need people to give us cold, hard cash (or the digital equivalent) to buy or use the product.

This is a make-or-break time for any organization. Most founders will start off by emailing the people we worked with during the development that the product is finally ready for them to use. And we expect perhaps that not only will those early users give us gobs of money but that they'll tell their friends all about how amazing things are and we'll get more money and they'll tell their colleagues and so on. This usually isn't how things work.

Instead, we each have to find our own way, and many will have different styles. It is okay to play to our strengths provided we keep trying to sell. It's about tenacity and sincerity more than charm. So here are a few things to plan on and put into action:

- **Allocate time every day to do sales.** For some, this will be emailing prospects to setup demos. For others, this will be picking up the phone and calling people. Within each industry, the different personality types of employees and customers, as well as different types of products, lead to a myriad of approaches to sales. The important thing is to plan time and experiment with different approaches. If we have verified our product market fit, we know we can help our potential customers, but making the connection is our responsibility.

- **Get a CRM early.** We don't want to reach out to potential customers too often, but we do want to reach out routinely. A good CRM will help us see whom we've communicated with and set follow-ups. Many a founder can focus too much on the mechanics of a tool. The most important thing here is to pick a tool and start capturing information about potential customers and every interaction with them. As we get more experience and learn what's working, we can customize the CRM to better accommodate whatever selling motion is working for us.

- **Find a mentor.** This is important. We don't know what we don't know. Other people have done whatever it is we are doing. They can share some of what worked for them and some of what didn't and provide guidance, fresh perspectives, and new ideas and keep us honest with ourselves.

- **Sit in on demos for other companies.** When we sit in on webinars or demos from other companies, we pick up ways of speaking confidently or things we can say that are impactful, hear how potential customers ask questions, see how experienced sellers show different parts of products, or pick up even just a simple turn of phrase that pushes prospects to communicate with us further. We shouldn't creep on the competition—think about an adjacent market. We can also keep in touch with sellers or presenters we really like.

- **Build a network of sellers who sell to similar customers.** Not only can they give us tips on better communicating with potential customers but they can also be valuable potential future employees.

- **Ask around about sites, blogs, and methodologies.** When we're talking to other successful people in our industry or sales, make sure to find out where they're getting their information. Not only can these become valuable sources of understanding for us, either about our industry or about sales, but they can also uncover valuable places to try to find influencers to talk about our products and later advertising opportunities.

- **Write an outline of a demo or sales call.** Now that we've worked with mentors, discussed how to sell with sellers, sat in on demos, and researched sites, let's write the outline of a demo. We don't want to seem scripted, so don't write a full-on script. Instead, just write an outline. Start with questions about what the customer wants to get out of the demo and leave room to make sure all of their issues are addressed. According to the complexity of a product or what we want to show, let's focus on a 45-minute demo where we front-load everything we want to say in 30 minutes and then provide a 15-minute question and answer session at the end. Have enough content to run for another 15 minutes if there are no questions.

- **Dry run the demo with people who can provide critical feedback.** Don't just run through a demo with an employee who will smile and nod the whole time. We want to get better. Record the demo and watch it as well, since we're all our own worst critics! If possible, find someone to do a dry run of a sales call. Role-playing these things makes everyone better at it.

- **Provide demos to a small number of small- or medium-sized prospects.** Now that we've practiced, let's run through a demo with a small, hand-picked cadre of customers. Every single person who has ever done a demo gets better with more repetitions. We are never guaranteed a second chance. If we don't do well, we may regret front-loading the biggest and therefore riskiest potential customers.

- **Ask a lot of questions.** Can you describe how your organization currently handles this? How might this fit into your current workflow? How much time does your team currently spend on this? These are some simple and generic questions. The more tailored to a given industry and function, the better.

- **Document responses.** Categorize responses into themes. Keep it simple at first. Check Airtable for won-lost call templates and think through what prospects tell us about our product and try to create categories for responses. If every single call is different, we might have a problem. But if they all fit into a few buckets, then we might be able to either find ways to handle objections with the words we use or find ways to address issues in product or pricing.

- **Be willing to experiment.** Try different approaches and double-down on the ones that work. The larger the circle of people we're working with (be they mentors, peers at potential customers, or sellers in adjacent markets) and the more we research, the more chances we have of uncovering awesome strategies.

- **Be patient, but not too patient.** It's not possible to hit a home run every time. It can take a dozen or three-dozen attempts before we get the chance to turn a prospect into a customer. Additionally, no matter how good we are, the larger a customer or the newer (and so more innovative) an industry, the longer a sale will take to close. So be patient, provided of course there's a cash runway to keep in business. At some point, if we aren't getting traction, we might have to pivot either in approach or product.

Selling is one of the hardest parts of starting a new company. But it's about just getting in there and doing it every single day. Get prepared for the grind. Under study, we find the sales process only seems like magic after gathering our components, studying our books, and saying our magic words (and maybe praying to our gods). As the organization grows, the time we spent selling early will pay off not only in profit, but because we'll better understand our customers, be able to hire an amazing sales team, and be prepared to manage them.

Seller Onboarding

A young company with founder-led sales doesn't need a lot of internal systems. Before new sellers can work on leads, they need infrastructure to keep efforts organized. This becomes more important the bigger an organization gets. Tools can help keep sellers aligned. There are also a number of frameworks used for these, but none should be universally applied. Instead, to meet the needs of most startups, let's break down what is necessary for most organizations into a few basic points:

- *Mechanics*: Manage sales using existing technology. A how-to guide could be a simple Confluence page. This helps us all get aligned and be on the same page. That guide should be simple, but go through what to put into each field. That should be guarded, so every week, go through the leads a seller is working, check the data integrity, and then review the status of each. If things get to the point that you don't have time to go through each, re-evaluate reporting structures.

- *Assets*: PDFs, links, and other assets that sellers can send to customers to help respond to questions that map their priorities to a product. For this, it's good to have a page on Confluence that lists available assets and when to send each. That will expand over time, but a single page with a table connecting sellers to assets is a great start.

- *Train on a basic framework*: There's a chance that pulling a framework out of a box (e.g., Solutions-Based Selling, Sandler Selling System, etc.) is a good long-term solution for hiring purposes, more rapid onboarding, etc. With a smaller team, having a lightweight framework might be best. Looking at some of the existing frameworks, let's look at a simple structure to lay out a sales call:

  - *Understand priorities*: Define what customers need out of a product. These evolve into the questions a seller will ask to qualify a lead (potentially in a quantifiable fashion based on the answers to these questions). For example:

  - What are the priorities potential buyers have for the product?

  - Which can we impact? How?

  - *Define initiatives for the customer*:

  - How is the customer advancing their priorities? *We're hopefully hiring two new team members and creating a template to add notes into Confluence.*

  - Is there a defined initiative to address the priority? *We're waiting to get budget to hire those team members.*

  - Has the department approved any initiatives that can help? *The executive sponsor is the VP, but we haven't gotten the other VP stakeholder on board yet.*

  - *Business impact*:

  - Define customer business impact clearly.

- Define how that impacts links to existing initiatives and executive priorities.

- *Legitimate authority*:

- Why should the customer believe we are well-positioned to help them solve the problem? A valid response might be: *The founders lived and breathed this problem for decades and solved it with a portal that gives customers their experience without having to hire someone that's been around so long in a growing industry.*

- What evidence increases the customer confidence? A valid response might be: *We have hundreds of customers that have shown a huge uptick in productivity using our solution. Would you like me to put you in touch with one?*

A good seller will be differentiated by how much they can tailor these quotes, statements, and objection handling to the responses from customers. Having a quiver full of these quotes that they've made their own will allow them to overcome many objections. Building a collection of assets sellers can send to customers comes in many forms. One of these is quotes in various press outlets or those approved by customers to post on a website.

Customer Relationship Management (CRM) Software

CRM stands for Customer Relationship Management and is a piece of software organizations use to store information about customers and sales prospects. Once upon a time, we had a piece of software to track trouble tickets in support, another to track inbound sales leads, another to track email list subscribers, yet another to track outbound sales leads, another to store vendor information, and the list goes on. But these days, we often use a single piece of software for all of that. And that software, more often now than not, is Salesforce.

We also used to buy big complex software tools that took days to set up. Now we can get started in minutes with a number of simplistic SaaS tools and then customize them over time to do a myriad of tasks. From tracking support tickets to building inventory, many of the solutions can not only easily end up acting as a way to store contact and communication histories but also run other aspects of our companies. Given how much of the company we automate in the CRM, the package, or service, that we use is likely to be one of the more important decisions we make in starting a company. Having said that, provided we choose something where the data can be exported, we can always move to another tool when we grow into it. A common workstream we see here is to move from a fairly accessible tool like HubSpot to a more comprehensive tool like Salesforce.

What We Need in a CRM

The tool should allow a company to go from a simple sales paradigm to one that is complex and automated (and not just automate the sales process). This might be simply exporting the data prior to such a migration, but hopefully includes the following abilities:

- *Store information about customers and prospects*: The original CRM was Act!, a digital rolodex introduced in 1986 that did basic contact management. Siebel Systems rose to prominence after releasing the first true CRM in 1993, which did basic sales tracking. From there Oracle, SAP, and PeopleSoft quickly entered the market, adding other aspects of enterprise resource planning (ERP). But that original tracking of information about prospects that moved from spreadsheets to Act! included contact information and the various attributes of a contact that are important for a given industry (and so preferably extendable).

- *Ingest leads*: It's important to flow data from web forms on our sites directly into our CRM. This might mean an embedded form that's copied from the CRM into the site or APIs that move data from our CRM to capture information on those forms and put them into our CRM.

- *Assign leads to sellers in a programmatic fashion*: Each time a new potential customer comes in, we want that lead to go to the most appropriate seller. This might be assigning leads based on geography, company size, revenue, or vertical market. The more this is automated, the quicker leads will be assigned, and the faster we can get to working on converting leads to paying customers.

- *Score leads*: Each time we communicate with a prospect, communications should impact the score positively or negatively for the prospect. That way we can focus different activities on those that nurture at various stages of their journey with the organization. For example, if a prospect looks at the pricing page, we might add 10 points to their lead score, whereas if they opt out of our email newsletter, we might remove 20 points.

- *Automate communications with leads*: A key aspect of nurturing leads is to automate a set of emails that go out when a specific trigger is reached. This might be after an in-person sales meeting or when a lead gets a high enough score to change the type of communication we have with them. If the lead opens the email, responds, or clicks a link in the email, then we want those actions to impact the scoring automatically as well. This responsibility typically lives with a marketing team, but once the leads reach a threshold, they become "marketing-qualified leads" and are turned over to the sales team.

- *Synchronize contact information into other solutions*: We increasingly live in an app-driven world. We likely benefit from some of these apps connecting to and leveraging the data from our CRM. This might be automatically connecting to Outlook or Gmail to import emails with leads, report on LinkedIn Ad performance, connect to one of the hundreds of automated messaging platforms out there, or connect to surveys, a social network, POS systems for retail, or anything else we can think of.

- *Produce bids or quotes*: We want to do as much of our bidding and quoting in the CRM as possible, to keep all sales data in one place. This helps keep from double entry and helps with future reporting efforts. If order fulfilment isn't done in the CRM, then when deals are closed, the information can be manually updated into other systems as a check and balance until the deal flow quantity reaches a point that it needs to be automated.

- *Provide detailed reports on conversions and quota attainment*: As organizations grow, we can't rely on our perceptions. Qualitative analysis should be backed up with quantitative charts and graphs that complete (and prove or disprove) a given story. Most modern CRM solutions come with reporting options, but make sure to actually build the charts necessary—and look to the developers to explain how they've built tools for others in order to support initiatives to build more mature workflows. Those reports should extend to financial forecasting as well, once there are enough conversion metrics to build meaningful forecasts.

- *Accessibility*: Making sure the tools work for everyone in the organization. This helps make a fair and equitable place to work for everyone. Make sure there are text options for all non-text fields, make sure users can navigate from a keyboard if needed, make sure that the software works well with the accessibility features on computers, provide descriptive text for form inputs, verify software still looks acceptable after zooming, and anything else we might put on an accessibility matrix for our own products.

- *An app*: Today more than ever, organizations need to anticipate that sellers will look at their computers and an app on one or many of their devices. This means being able to easily see information. But importantly, we also want sellers getting alerts when deals change, when conversions happen, etc.

- *Compliance*: Software should make an organization compliant and not be a liability when the company begins the process to get certified with various compliance frameworks. Making sure to understand opt-in options and GDPR is important to make organizations compliant. Look for software that is SOC2 compliant or software that maintains the compliance upstream customers will rely on. Start thinking of any Data Processing Agreement (DPA) required to provide to customers, especially if the CRM will track information beyond when the quote is provided (e.g., synchronizing a list of users in a tenant or usage data to a CRM).

Looking to the Future

The preceding information represents what could be considered the modern basics of a CRM. But as mentioned, the CRM is now asked to do much more than back in the days of tools like Act! and GoldMine. Today, we also need to

- *Track customer service issues*: The sales process should not end when there's a PO to make a purchase. Many sellers will want to keep in touch with customers, not only because they want the customer to renew but also because they genuinely care about making sure the company lives up to our promises from early conversations. Most CRM packages have moved into also providing ticketing systems. As a result, many ticketing systems have also started to do CRM.

- *Do enterprise resource planning (ERP)*: An ERP as opposed to just a CRM manages every aspect of the organization, from inventory to human resources. Chances are that a single tool will not do everything well, and startups have increasingly looked to link together a number of relatively inexpensive tools rather than try to buy a single large monolithic package to do everything we need (often because we're used to breaking up monolithic code into microservicey code). A CRM that can grow into an ERP will be necessary at various stages of development, even if various disciplines eventually choose to split their own needs off into tools built for their needs.

- *Sync to financial systems*: Tools like QuickBooks track a company's finances. Tools like Avalara calculate taxes that have to be paid as sales come in. Tools like Stripe allow companies to take payments on sites and process them automatically. As we grow, we will think through not only how customer relationships flow but also a lean and automated approach to how money and revenues flow. These are often handled as plugins to popular CRM packages. Just make sure when selecting each platform that there's a known path for integration later.

- *Pull in additional data*: There are several data providers that can enrich or supplement the information available on a prospect. These often have automated integrations with CRM tools. Maybe that's getting the phone number, a job title, an email address, the department a contact reports to, etc. These can be used to improve lead scoring but also to allow sellers to better communicate with the leads they're assigned and to do so when appropriate based on those lead scores.

Popular CRMs

We mentioned a few CRM solutions from early in the life of the industry earlier in this chapter. Today, most will be SaaS tools that might be available in a freemium model. Some that early-stage founders should make sure to check out include

- *Salesforce*: Starts at $25 per user per month. Salesforce is the gold standard and pretty much unlimited in terms of flexibility and third-party tools on their marketplace. Salesforce is also easy to train new team members on, as most sellers have used it at this point and as Salesforce has a considerable amount of training materials online.

- *HubSpot*: The basic CRM functionality is free, and as the needs grow and organizations look to add the things that can't be tracked in a Google Sheet, like marketing, the cost goes up. There aren't a ton of customizations beyond adding new fields, but setup is fast, and it's a great way to at least get all the data in one place as we prepare for larger sales teams once we mature beyond founder-led sales organizations. It can also do integrated chat and support flows and has a large marketplace of vendors that provide integrations.

- *Act!*: Starting at $25 per user per month, this Act! is very different than the original stand-alone application. It goes from just tracking user information to marketing automation, email management, etc.

- *Agile CRM*: Starts with basic features, free for up to ten users, and then grows in cost from there as plugins, support, and integrations are added. It's simple to get started and easy to track but seems limited as you get more advanced in needs.

- *Close*: Starts at $21.25 per user per month. Close comes with pretty good custom email sequencing and reporting. Close can help with the phone call aspects and automated voicemails, and they also have straightforward integrations with tools like Zendesk and Mailchimp.

- *Copper*: Starts at $19 per user per month and is probably a tool needed by every organization that has centralized around using G Suite for other services, not only because of the way it integrates with Google but also in the shared design philosophies.

- *Insightly*: Starts at $29 per user per month and has a lot of great built-in integrations, especially for reporting in Microsoft's Power BI. Not a lot of custom fields, so we'll run up against customization limitations fairly quickly if that's needed (and it usually is).

- *Freshsales*: Part of the sprawling Fresh empire of applications. Starts at $12 per user per month and seems a little clunky. If using the rest of the Fresh ecosystem (Freshmarketer, Freshrelease, Freshsuccess, Freshchat, Freshservice, Freshdesk, Freshteam, etc.), it's a no-brainer.

- *Keap*: Starts at $49 per user per month. Keap is one of the more user-friendly tools in the beginning. Keap is great for small businesses and freelancers and has lots of built-in features but has limited integrations.

- *Less Annoying CRM*: Starts at $10 per user per month. It's easy to use; easily integrates with Google, Mailchimp, etc.; and doesn't have a lot of frills.

- *Monday*: More of a board-driven product, but if using a tool like Monday for project management, might be used for CRM as well to keep costs contained (as could Airtable or Trello, but that misses the point of a CRM by shoehorning tools like that into a use case they weren't developed for). Starts at $8 per user per month.

- *Pipedrive*: Starts at $12.50 per user per month. Easy to use and good sync for Google shops who can grow into it (but make sure to use the Chrome extension to integrate with Gmail).

- *SugarCRM*: Starts at $40 per user per month and a minimum of ten users. Sugar has been around for a long time and does a good job displaying customer journeys and helping sellers stay on top of tasks. It's also one of the few that do GPS integration on the apps.

- *Zendesk Sell*: Starts at $19 per user per month and integrates well with the Zendesk ticketing tool. Great API support, good email templates, and the channel-based sales options are pretty sweet. Oh, and a great app.

- *Zoho CRM*: Free for three users and then $12 or more according to how many of the sprawling Zoho services we may choose to use. Good lead management options and great built-in social media options, but to look at stages and use integrated intelligence, might seem a bit unwieldy.

Note   Many freemium products have limits, like on the number of contacts created. Make sure to understand when each will force an account upgrade, especially if API access is to be used.

There's no perfect CRM out there. Most are built to work with any industry and any sized company, so each will require a bit of customization. The important part is to test them and then see if any customizations we can think of up front are supported. Use the list of attributes earlier in the chapter to see how many tools that were tested actually map to necessary features or business logic.

One point: DO NOT build a CRM (unless it's the core product). You will hate your life. Same goes for building an accounting solution. The off-the-shelf products make us work in a way that builds on lessons learned by generations of sellers. That's a good thing. If we want to go down the custom tooling road later (once we have a lot of experience and knowledge about running a sales and marketing organization), fine. Don't start out that way–stay focused on the mission instead.

Starting a company can be expensive. Keep costs lean in the beginning. Start tracking sales data as early as possible, though. Choose software packages that can be grown into, especially as dedicated sellers are hired. Don't build a complicated solution when there might be a pivot, but do get in front of leveraging automation once it's needed. Developing the CRM shouldn't take valuable time away from development, product design, marketing, or actual sales time. We do need to know that as we grow we will need to devote time to building out the CRM fully.

A good sales team paired with a good CRM can move fast. We can build sales processes around the CRM that match with the values of our organization. We can automate the aspects of working with leads that feels right for our organization. When we meet to review the pipeline, we can do so in a way that puts data at the center so we can focus on the soft skills for selling and how we want the market to perceive our products. In short, we can sell better, and our teams will work smarter, knowing what we expect of them.

Customers

It's easy to get into a mindset of winning sales—but it's better better to be in a win-win-win mindset. As described earlier, this means the customer wins, the startup wins, and the employees at the startup win. That means fair pricing for a quality product. When a company is focused on just winning sales, it shows, and when the focus is on a long-term relationship and community building, we build fanatical customers willing to help us with our cause.

Still, we have revenue goals and targets that we'll need to hit to build a lasting company. On the way to keeping the customer first, let's look at defining some information about who they are and what they need using a buyer persona. The buyer persona is a fictional representation of a buyer—maybe a composite of multiple people we know. It's best to start with three archetypal customers whom sellers will talk to—and then check back in during won-lost calls to see if the persona matches the actual buyers. This will include things like the type of content a lead is likely to engage with, how they prefer to engage, and problems the product helps solve that actually resonate with them.

As with the personas built in Chapter 4, this should have some personal details—maybe age, marital status, and the part of town they live in. It should also include some psychographic data such as attitude, values, personality, and interests. It's easiest to build personas if we know a lot of people in the communities we serve. This means taking what we think we know and matching that up with a little persona research. Here's a sampling of some of the attributes we can survey or discuss with existing or potential customers:

- Name
- Position
- Type of organization (or industry)

- Location of the organization

- Size of the organization

- Approximate age

- Size and type of family

- Personality type

- Challenges (pain points) they have in their position and how they are important

- Solutions found to those challenges

- Where they go to find solutions to problems

- How do they make decisions

- Typical news outlets and industry trend outlets visited and when

- Social media habits

- Types of technology used in the job

- Communication style

Getting a customer to open up usually requires it be clear they're not being sold anything, so make it clear this is about research. This information can get put into a free-flowing text document, a template, or a battle card (possibly using the template from the "Personas" section of Chapter 4).

Once there are personas, a Persona field can be created in the CRM to match customers with personas. This allows us to tailor communications to them based on personas and use information discovered to better discuss pain points and how tools address those during the sales process. Training sellers on using them is part of developing a great sales team. Another aspect is to provide great career and skills development.

Sales Cycles

A sales cycle is a series of events that occur when selling a product. These typically involve finding leads, connecting, qualifying, presenting, objection handling, closing, and nurturing. But each organization and type of product might have their own flow. That flow can be considered a journey—and rather than take a prescriptive approach to cycles, we'd rather do something far more custom and begin by looking at this process from the customer's perspective.

Map the Customer Journey

The customer journey is the general process followed by a person when becoming a customer. Here, sellers group customers into four primary stages and then dig deeper into managing customers in HubSpot or another CRM using lead scoring. In the beginning, the lead score and staging will be used to help focus on the leads that are the furthest along. As teams grow, these help define who's working on a lead, where leads are getting stuck (so we can develop ways to get them unstuck), and ways to automate communicating with leads so sellers can swap out those manual tasks with tasks that require a human.

The general stages of a customer journey include the following:

- *Awareness*: People are looking for answers, insights, resources, and education.

- *Consideration*: People are looking for justification, determining if we're a good fit.

- *Decision*: People are making a final purchase decision.

- *Nurturing*: People are now customers and should be retained.

381

There are two sides of the customer journey: that of the customer and that of the company as they deal with the customer. The seller maps these activities to stages is HubSpot, which can require some work in engineering and will likely end up displacing some other items in the roadmap. The insight will be invaluable, and this is one of many cases where telemetry into sales and marketing vs. new features is a tradeoff.

The following is a modified SiriusDecisions Demand Waterfall that has been tailored for an example company use. In it, we removed the TAL and SAL stages common in the Demand Waterfall model to accommodate for a much smaller sales team, and there was no split between sales development representative (SDR) and account executive (AE) roles.

Stage	Definition	Object	In	SLA	Disqualification
Known	Has personally identifiable information in HubSpot used for marketing. They may not be aware of us, but we are aware of them.	Lead and contact	Trigger: Lead is created in HubSpot.	None.	Unsubscribe
Inquiry	Prospect has engaged with the company, so we are aware of one another.	Lead and contact	Trigger: Clicks link or visits web page.	None.	Unsubscribe

(continued)

Stage	Definition	Object	In	SLA	Disqualification
Marketing-qualified lead (MQL)	Prospect reached a score of 100 points (this includes account creation).	Lead and contact	Trigger: Lead score exceeds 100.	Marketing will trigger delivery of lead or contact once lead score reaches 100 points. Sales: HubSpot will assign lead to appropriate rep.	SPAM Duplicate Incomplete data Existing customer Competitor
TQL	Prospect is qualified and accepted by a rep.	Lead and contact	Trigger: Lead status/contact status is set to True.		SPAM Incorrect data No budget No authority No need No timeline No response Existing customer Competitor Blacklist (no forever) Good with free internal use / partner Missing feature Missing integration Other

(continued)

Stage	Definition	Object	In	SLA	Disqualification
SQL	An opportunity is created.	Contact	Trigger: Opportunity created.		

Those experienced with the SiriusDecisions Demand Waterfall model may note that the first three stages of this lifecycle are nurturing a customer into becoming a marketing-qualified lead. We can shorten this by having a rep reach out sooner and thus inorganically moving leads through the funnel faster. Given the stage we are in, this makes sense; however, we should have the technology put into place to allow for a more granular funnel before it becomes too difficult to do so. It's important to treat each model as a guide but to customize it to make sense at the development stage any company is at.

Once a lead is worked on by someone on staff, how to deal with each lead is part of what's covered in the daily meetings. Listen in on at least a couple of calls per week in the beginning, providing a great time to take notes and offer feedback on how the seller is doing at working with each customer. Be careful not to interfere so as to let the seller grow in their discipline. Additionally, workshop various product ideas with the people making those calls and sending those messages.

Inbound

Inbound leads should be the easiest to convert into paying customers. Here, we got someone's attention with an ad, a go-to-market partner, or word of mouth. The legitimate authority of a partner or word of mouth referral is invaluable as it comes with a high conversion rate. Drumming up business through these seemingly passive outlets involves knowing the customer and where they are approachable. A few of the places we can then generate these inbound leads include the following. This is by no means a comprehensive list but will hopefully spark some creative ways to find other outlets:

- *The online marketplace of a larger vendor*: Here companies can develop integrations with third parties that increase the value of a solution. This chapter covers a number of CRM solutions, most of which have similar marketplaces of apps that integrate with the CRM. Maybe an app integrates with one of them (or a different SaaS app) or exchanges data in a similar fashion. Marketplaces often mean the company gives up a percentage of money that comes in but has a ready-built route to market and sometimes doesn't have to deal with taking payment.

- *Retail outlets*: Many organizations send someone to a retail store (Apple, Microsoft, Best Buy, etc.) to buy devices when they need something. The people who work there form relationships with people and products from companies that they then refer business to when a customer has a need matching what's offered.

- *Trusted consultants or managed service providers*: MSPs often focus on supporting devices at their customers. Products that align with the type of customer being supported can then see increased business by getting MSPs, or consultants, in that industry to refer business. Here, we likely need an offer specific to the customers or provide the ability for the consultant or MSP to make money from the referral.

- *Blogs*: Customers often find solutions to their problems on websites run by others in their field. Getting bloggers to write about products is covered further in Chapter 11 but can be a great way to get the word out about a product and sometimes a direct referral from influencers.

- *Other people in the same or similar positions*: Word of mouth referral is a growth hack that harkens back to the early days of commerce. We cover incentivizing referrals in Chapter 11, but think of ways to make it simple for people to post about products on social media or give out a referral code and what they might get in return for doing so.

One way we can amplify any effort we put into any of these is through evangelists. These are employees (or just friends and family) whom we turn into raving fans about what we're up to. Hiring evangelists is a great way to scale the grassroots "get out the message" efforts we discussed in the preceding list. Much of this involves what we might think of as dark social, or conversations that we don't have analytics about. This can be frustrating, but there are ways to get information. For example, if we hire evangelists to visit every retail outlet of a partner, we can track web traffic and conversions from those geographies they visit. Whatever the source, the goal is to get the word out and ultimately increase transactions.

Transacting

Once a customer is on our site, we want to nurture them into a paying customer. This means being ready to convert and making that transaction as frictionless as possible. We discuss analytics a lot in the book, but there is a balance between how much information we acquire about prospects and customers and how much data we can collect without causing them to abandon our sign-up page(s). Build a rubric where a customer can transact potentially without any involvement with humans. But when nurturing a potential customer and there isn't a conversion, sometimes it's best if someone just picks up the phone and calls them. Maybe their name and email are on a web form, and a seller can now get a phone number using public or paid sources. Now it's time to nurture them or call to see if we've found a great match.

One thing we don't want to get in the way of winning customers is cost. We do still have a margin to maintain, but if we provide a small haircut, then we might be able to get a loyal customer who turns into a supporter by promoting our mission on social media or blogs. We should arm sellers with objection handling materials. These are phrases that a customer might use to turn down an offer and ways to address those issues as they arise. We also want to arm sellers with sales and marketing assets that can be sent in response—or even proactively—to objections.

We want to stick with non-financial incentives when possible. Money-back guarantees are one way of providing a low-cost alternative to discounts. But the last line of resort is those discounts. Custom offers, if provided, can become a billing nightmare, so we want to make sure the tools we develop allow for custom pricing just in case we provide it. This might mean a cost field in a table that triggers a different billing increment. That keeps us from manually running billing in Stripe, PayPal, or whatever billing solution we're using.

Sellers do what we incentivize them to do. If we provide a revenue target, then they will go after that at all costs. That's human nature and to be expected. But if we provide margin, customer satisfaction, or customer loss goals, even as kickers, then the sellers are more likely to practice behaviors that align with the mission. Consider those when scaling out a sales organization or bringing on a net-new sales team. Just don't make the algorithm too complicated, or potential hires might be turned off from seemingly synthetic targets.

Working with Big Companies

Discounts are expected at scale. We often refer to huge new customers as whales. In sales this usually means a customer that is ten times the average sale. Working with big customers isn't just about the money; we usually think of the value of having that logo on our list of customers and as a means to legitimize our products and efforts. Sometimes we start with a big name. Other times we grow into it. Larger customers are a natural point of growth for small- and medium-sized businesses, and it's thrilling to get a chance to work with them. Suddenly, it seems like we've really made it. Our other customers will feel vindicated, our investors will increase the value of the organization, our team will be energized, and our parents will be proud.

But hold on just a second. Now that we have a big customer and contract, the work is just beginning. There are a bunch of things that we need to be real and proactive about in order to not let them ruin our business. Instead of thinking of these types of organizations as high-paying customers, think about them as partners. Let's look at some of the ways we're going to need to adapt (if we haven't already) to such a partnership:

- **Prepare for more meetings.** Large companies need collaboration by a number of teams, or stakeholders. This can be hard to understand in a two- or three-person company, but it's important for the champion who brought us in to gain acceptance that they're doing the right thing across all the stakeholders who will use our products. The more people have to be in meetings, the further back they push. Having dozens of meetings will take us away from our core objective, although they can teach us a lot about our product and how customers might want to use the product. One way to prepare for the meetings is to simply ask about the cadence of meetings when acquiring larger customers.

- **Be prepared for latency.** Larger contracts require more people to make decisions, and that takes time. Additional time needs to be allocated for budgets. For example, many companies need to wait until the beginning of the year for new contracts. Once budget is allocated, the terms are usually such that we don't take payment for 90 days (or further out) after we invoice larger customers. And of course, an invoice can be stalled while it just sits on someone's desk for months during a routine audit. We need to plan cash flows around these longer account acquisition cycles.

- **Factor additional costs to negotiate contracts.** Our contact at a company usually can't just accept our terms—they need attorneys on staff at their company to review terms and often have their own contracts or master service agreements we have to agree to. Most startups don't have on-staff legal teams like they do. But we can't just agree to any contract without first understanding the terms, and there can be some pretty stringent requirements that impact how we run our companies long term. Maybe this means we can't sell equity in the company without a big customer approving the sale or that a customer contractually requires us to meet a certain service level or they get credits. Or they could end up owning the rights to certain features they help us mentally model. All the back and forth to negotiate large contracts requires time, and we're usually paying by the hour, so make sure to plan for that.

- **Know the impact to business processes.** Compliance means that we may end up needing to plan time to fill out security questionnaires and be prepared to change our own business processes to be compliant with the needs of larger customers. For example, developers might not be able to access data in a database. This can complicate testing and troubleshooting, but in general these requirements are there for a reason (even if we don't understand them in the beginning). Knowing the guidelines up front reduces latency while making sure that we're a good fit for some of the bigger customers.

- **Understand fiduciary requirements.** Larger organizations often require additional insurance, audited financials, and a more mature outlook on accounting. It's important to know all of the aspects of working with a company before agreeing to increase those third-party contracts. Once done, though, we'll be better prepared to work with the next whale (although each is a little different)!

- **Get ready to compete.** The larger the contracts, the more competitors are willing to reduce pricing. This means we can easily end up selling our products for less than half the going rate to win and retain the largest of contracts. Most true enterprises have buyers on staff who make a living by getting better deals from vendors. Don't let the contract sizes cause decisions that might be detrimental to the business, though. Stay mindful of requirements and the time associated with winning a large opportunity to preserve margins.

- **Be understanding.** These big new customers need the kinds of requirements we're given. It's important not to get resentful of the hoops we must jump through to close deals. They have evolved because they have had to, and we cannot know all of the reasons each requirement exists. As partners, it's on us to understand the requirements and evolve our business to meet them where they are or back out as quickly as possible if we cannot.

As we've shown, there are a lot of places where an "enterprise" company can crush us if we aren't careful. The contracts seem large. But we have to take the extra effort, legal requirements, and compliance needs into our pricing. This usually means the signup page for products needs an "Enterprise" option that is open ended if we want to allow for enterprise buyers.

A big new relationship comes with a potentially big price tag, branding opportunities, and legitimizing our authority in our space, and how we meet their requirements sets us up to be able to work with other large organizations. Landing a whale doesn't come without a number of challenges, though. The key is to go into these with our eyes wide open, so we can leverage the relationships to take our organization to the next level rather than let them nickel-and-dime us right out of business.

Contract Negotiations

Contract negotiations are potentially one of the larger expenses a startup can incur, especially when selling to large organizations. Anyone selling into enterprises and other large organizations should anticipate the occasional $10,000 agreement that takes six months to iron out, just to win a customer in the Fortune 100. Sometimes we get away with skipping it, but rarely.

There are a lot of great contract attorneys. But we often get what we pay for. One reason many organizations provide an "enterprise" package is that attorney review of contracts can run around $500 per hour. This eats into profitability and in some cases puts us losing money when working with larger customers. A little-known growth hack is that many organizations can win deals simply by being flexible in contract negotiations. Here, we allow red lines (or changes to an existing contract or EULA) where other organizations might no longer do so for any old customer.

Eventually we may reach a point where we have to put a minimum on deal sizes that qualify for a red-lined contract. But once there, resist the urge as by then there will be competitors who are willing to do so. Instead, think about ways to be more efficient and reduce the cost to negotiate while still moving sales forward. One of the most effective ways to do so is to spend some time thinking about what is important in contracts:

- **Limit liability.** As any company grows, it will need errors and omissions (E&O) insurance (for more on insurance, see Chapter 9). Our contracts should limit the extent of our exposure in the event of a lawsuit filed over our negligence. Mistakes happen, but as we grow we want that E&O policy to grow as well and protect the company, especially as more and more people rely on us for salaries to feed their families.

- **Define the rules of engagement.** Social norms aren't enough to define how we work with customers (especially when dealing with different geographies). Set expectations for what is provided and how accountability works for the expectations we set. This includes service-level agreements (SLAs), standard hours of operation for support teams, account management, and other aspects of day-to-day operations. These can be in the contract or EULA or as standalone documents referred by and linked to from the contract.

- **Protect intellectual property.** We don't want anyone who uses products to copy products, steal code, decompile and then steal code, etc.

- **Protect against competitive action.** In addition to protecting intellectual property, when possible, restrict a customer from engaging in competitive action–which includes not hiring staff, developing a similar product, etc.

- **Make sure to get paid.** Notice this is last. That's because while we want to grow and make money, we only want to do so provided the rest of these are taken care of. We typically include invoicing terms, late fees, remediation options, legal jurisdictions, and other aspects of what happens if the customer doesn't pay their bills in a timely fashion.

Once we know what matters, and where we're willing to be flexible, we're more easily able to make concessions in a clear and focused way. When a seller comes to us asking for a red line to be accepted, it's good to have already made this mental math—and thinking through these things in advance keeps those legal bills down, as we won't be thinking through things on the phone with attorneys. Some other suggestions to keep those legal bills in check (and it's never too early or late to start on these) include the following:

- *Versioning*: Contracts change over time, so make sure to version them, just like we might with software. For those who hate version numbers, a date stamp is fine. Version numbers show how contracts evolved over time. In the event that customers automatically agree to a EULA when signing up for a product, keep a record in our ERP of the version that was agreed to so it's easily looked up.

- *Provide standard contracts to customers upon request*: Many organizations need a non-disclosure agreement (NDA) or a Data Processor Agreement (DPA). It's a good idea to have these that can be provided to customers upon request and preferably e-signed and stored in the CRM.

- *Compliance*: It may cost upward of $100,000 to get a SOC type 2 compliance, but in the long run, doing so will bring in extra customers and potentially reduce legal expenses, as some language required in contracts is hammered out during the process of getting there.

- *Work with associates*: Many firms have day-to-day tasks done by associates or those newer to the firm. This often comes at a lower rate as the associate is junior to a partner. For some of the larger initiatives, a more seasoned staffer might be required to work on projects, but keep in mind that associates become an assembly line for red lines and so are actually more efficient while being cheaper.

- *Make concessions in exchange for... something*: It's common to want concessions in contracts. Keep in mind that some of these companies have more attorneys than a startup has employees. Therefore, some of the protections we demand don't end up meaning much. It sucks, but complaining about it doesn't help close deals. And think of the revenue we could have accrued during the months that these

agreements can go back and forth. Sometimes, it's best
to make a concession and then ask for a customer story
in return!

- *Get all parties on the phone*: One of the biggest time
  savers in getting a contract executed is ending the cycle
  of back-and-forth red lining. If we can get all parties
  on the phone when we see this start to happen, then
  we can avoid getting nickel-and-dimed and get to the
  heart of what each party wants in a negotiation.

- *Don't get emotional*: Emotional attachments or getting
  worked up about something can cause us to dig in
  where unnecessary or make concessions when they
  weren't needed. Don't get defensive. We want to
  bring our whole, authentic self to work—but when the
  lawyers get involved, it's time to compartmentalize.

Make sure to keep a copy of every single custom agreement and
start getting them into a database as early as possible. For example, if
using Salesforce as a CRM, get a standard naming convention in place
for executed contracts based on the version number of the contract and
add either a field in Salesforce or an area in the namespace of the file
to indicate it's a custom agreement. Not only is this important as we're
dealing with the occasional issue that might arise with a customer, but as
we grow into an organization with a dedicated legal team, we'll be able to
provide them with the resources they need to inherit the legal duties of the
corporation.

Finally, we want to have a good and trusting relationship with
customers. Most of the items in this section deal with business-to-business
sales. We don't want the stakeholders at customers to get off on a bad
footing with us. We also want to close deals. However, we want to do
these things in a way that doesn't put the company at risk. Mature, great

customers will understand this. Once we've done the work to get contracts sorted out, there's a larger barrier for them to move to a competitor as the oceans get redder over time. Each protracted legal squabble should use all of this as part of the litmus test for identifying the perfect customer.

Developing Sellers

We hire people and expect them to perform at a role. We can't always find people with tenure in a given role to go exploring dungeons with. The more training we can provide, the faster a discipline can be mastered, and so the whole organization levels up. Every team benefits from skills and career development. This might be technical skills like how to write code in that hot new language—but it also might be soft skills development, like objection handling.

Most startup founders aren't amazing sellers with a strong track record at the skills required to sell. Nor will we all have experience building sales teams and developing the skills on those teams. As we grow, there will be other people to fill those voids. In the meantime, when transitioning from founder-led sales to having a team, it helps to understand some of the common sales methodologies and the parts we can take from each (or leave on the shelf as they don't match up with our values or buyers).

Methodologies

We looked at founder-led sales earlier in this chapter. Any organization that finds success in selling then needs to scale a sales team. We've looked at basic steps to help founders find success, but the ability to grow means finding a sales methodology that works. This can be custom, but in the beginning it helps to use a canned methodology and then customize it as needed.

We don't operate as an island and can learn a lot from those who came before us. A sales methodology is the phased, or staged, approach an organization takes to selling products. There are about as many documented methodologies out there as there are successful sales teams. This is because every organization is different, and most are best left to pick and choose aspects of a methodology that work from existing sales methodologies.

It's not likely that any methodology will match the needs of an organization completely. But some of the existing methodologies might work well with the personality of our sellers and customers. If we haven't hired anyone in sales yet, let's focus on the seller and the customers and look for a canned methodology that helps kickstart developing our own process. It's good to know what's out there and what bodies of knowledge have been documented. Keep in mind we can always learn new tactics, no matter how successful we might have been up to this point. This doesn't mean we have to use the aspects of any methodology that don't work for our environments, though!

To help start researching sales methodologies, let's look at a few of the most common that have been kicking around, sometimes for decades (and are common in the startup world).

Target Account Selling

Target Account Selling is a standard in the sales world, with over 650 thousand sellers trained to convert smaller customers (or smaller groups within larger environments) into bigger and more permanent customers. Target Account Selling, which as a documented methodology is around 30 years old, breaks larger deals up into smaller components. Using a strategic plan throughout the life of the sales cycle, Target Account Selling deemphasizes the politics of an account.

Target Account Selling is popular due to the ability to automate the whole sales process via Salesforce. This makes it easier and simpler to integrate with existing workflows. The cost of training the staff for Target Account Selling can be high because we're teaching about various strategic plans. We can hire a ton of experienced sellers who already understand this methodology and focus training efforts on the specifics to selling our products.

SPIN Selling

Neil Rackham wrote the book *SPIN Selling* in 1989. He probably didn't realize then that his methodology would still be in use over 30 years later. *SPIN* is a word we might not want associated to our sales process these days, but that doesn't mean the methodology is a bad one. SPIN is short for Situation, Problem, Implication, and Need-Payoff. At the heart of it, we ask questions and then match up the situation a buyer is in with the issues and consequences of their situation, respectively. The questions are supposed to establish trust. Responses are meant to be aligned to the solutions provided. Matching their choices and preferences surfaces their needs.

As with sales in general, SPIN Selling requires pretty good communication skills. This can make it seem more like good communication techniques. Everyone likes to be heard. While there aren't concrete steps and phases sometimes, SPIN Selling does help us learn to establish a stronger bond with customers without making them see like we're overly indexed on closing a deal. This methodology is great when we can pair it with lighter, transactional sales with multiple stakeholders.

SNAP Selling

Jill Konrath developed SNAP Selling in 2012 under the assumption that everyone is busy and frazzled. SNAP stands for Simple iNvaluable Aligned Priority. The goal is to have a simple framework that makes us invaluable by aligning with the customer's needs. Then we can get them to prioritize the product or service we are selling.

We do that by getting "in the head" of the customer. We have a debate at the office of whether it's possible to control where on the priority list a product falls with a prospect. We can try to do this by building products that reduce cost, by hastening a customer's development cycles or time to market, and by providing discounts to move sales up. But SNAP selling is a good, focused read that is more about aspects a sales team can control than product teams. Everyone in sales should read the book *SNAP Selling*, even if the sales department doesn't leverage it as a methodology. It doesn't work for large, complex deals, but it's a great look at focusing on the value chain that it demonstrates.

The Challenger Sales

The Challenger Sale is one of the most popular methodologies for software sales teams. It came from a large research project performed by Matthew Dixon and Brent Adamson, which resulted in a book called *The Challenger Sale* and then a methodology and training series. *The Challenger Sale* breaks sellers up into five categories: Relationship Builders, Hard Workers, Lone Wolves, Reactive Problem Solvers, and Challengers. The reason it's so popular is that the Challengers are the more successful closing sales in large ("enterprise") environments.

Instead of unraveling the needs and demands of the customers, the Challenger Sale builds consensus in larger teams with a lot of stakeholders. This methodology involves delivering a consistent, static message to the decision makers and helping guide them toward specific products by challenging the customer to see their needs in a different manner that aligns with our value propositions. This involves teaching customers about how we define our problem space. Sellers research market trends and customer preferences so they can stand out. There's not a clear strategy for larger sales instead focusing on bundling large, complex solutions to meet the needs of a prospect. Today's buyers are more educated than ever, so being prescriptive is a strategy that works for many.

Value Selling Framework

The Value Selling Framework was developed in 1991 out of a need to reduce deal customization. Here, a process is built that can easily be harnessed by teams with basic sales skills. There's more documentation, which involves asking boilerplate questions to get to the needs, mapping each opportunity to a predefined set of capabilities and developing a plan to close.

Solution Selling

Solution Selling was developed by Mike Bosworth in 1988, a message to sell solutions, not products. That seems simple and has become pretty standard, but has substantial impacts into how we approach customers. Given the timing, several other methodologies are loosely based on Solution Selling. Solution Selling provides more insight into increasingly informed buyers. The great thing about Solution Selling is that due to the large number of people who train on the framework, the methodology has evolved to meet the changing needs of sales teams.

Conceptual Selling

Conceptual Selling is more about understanding the buyer's process and managing the stakeholders involved in that process. Developed by Robert Miller and Stephen Heiman, Conceptual Selling focuses on listening and information gathering to provide the right information about products and services to get a commitment at each level of a potential buyer's organization.

The underlying idea of Conceptual Selling is that buyers don't buy a given product but instead buy the concept that the offering represents. This means that once we've gathered relevant information, we can move on to five categories of alignment:

- *Confirmation*: Review any information obtained and get confirmation from customers that the collected data is correct.

- *New information*: Explore exactly what customers want to achieve.

- *Attitude*: Understand the connection each stakeholder has to the sales cycle and so the needed product outcomes.

- *Commitment*: Understand how far the customer can go or how committed they are to seeing the sale and implementation through.

- *Issues*: Look for roadblocks in the sales process, including commitment, attitude, logistics, legal reviews, etc.

The most important aspect of Conceptual Selling is to listen, as with all methodologies. Listening to the customer tells us what they need and allows us to then categorize those needs and their status into categories and provide known, scalable responses to each.

The Sandler Selling System

The Sandler Selling System has grown since it was initially introduced by David Sandler in the early 1960s to franchises across 250 offices and 23 languages. The Sandler Selling System was so popular because at a time when sellers told customers what they needed, Sandler advocated for uncovering the needs of a customer and then customizing a pitch to them. Most modern selling methodologies customize this but espouse the original concepts.

Zig Ziglar and others did inspirational speeches on sales, with a similar focus. Sandler went further to emphasize having the buyer invest equally in the sales process. This means having sellers bring up blockers early and getting enough buy-in that buyers get options and assistance in overcoming those obstacles. This doesn't completely end up with a bilaterally equal investment but does allow us to show that we are committed and aren't wasting the customer's time and that they aren't wasting ours on a deal that will never come to fruition. This strategy effectively leverages obstacles and increases the customer's time commitment until they end up convincing themselves to buy.

Sandler is more about being professional than being a slick seller. Some parts of the Sandler System can work in any organization, but keep an eye on the target audience and (as with all methodologies) avoid being manipulative.

MEDDIC

Jack Napoli and Dick Dunkel developed MEDDIC, which is an acronym for Metrics, Economic buyer, Decision criteria, Decision process, Identify pain, Champion. MEDDIC is about creating a plan to close each deal and then monitoring where sellers are on that path. Good automation (e.g., using HubSpot or Salesforce integrations) directs the best person to each customer and helps them message appropriately when managers are prescriptive in making a consistent delivery of the methodology.

This most heavily involves qualification, key messaging, and then working with the customer (bringing in a sales manager when needed). The result is often more tightly controlled sales pipelines for larger customers. Many of these methodologies are for larger customers, but knowledge of the processes can be adapted to smaller customers as well (think of any methodology with the word *lean* in front of it).

CustomerCentric Selling

Another methodology for lengthy sales processes (and so usually applied in larger deals) is CustomerCentric Selling. Here, we build trust by being collaborative advisors to potential customers. This means we match our process to the timelines of each customer—which makes it difficult to bring sales forward in pipelines. But the tradeoff is assumed to be increased trust and a higher close rate.

One reason for this is that decision makers aren't the same as those who buy in larger organizations. There are often lots of stakeholders, so we need to find the ones who will be key to our success and put the product in their hands (be that through hands-on demos, trial accounts, etc.). Then we find out what the customer needs and tailor our presentations to that, rather than being prescriptive. The focus on solution building is customer-centric and meant to build trust and rapport with the buyer rather than trying to leverage a false sense of prioritization. In other words, sellers look to help customers and in doing so they will buy our products, rather than convince them to buy our products.

Select and Customize

Most organizations will implement a sales methodology when hiring someone to lead sales. Founders should learn the basics of each methodology while still sitting in the sales chair (e.g., engaged in founder-led sales activities) and then as what types of experiences the sales leader has had during the interview process. Most of these methodologies aren't how to manage a sales and marketing funnel—they're about managing customers once the customer gets to an actual seller. A lot of modern relationship management is done using frameworks like the SiriusDecisions Demand Waterfall, which takes each stage from the time we get information about a customer and then brings the customer through a scoring funnel, where they eventually become sales-qualified leads (SQLs). This is where the traditional idea of a sales methodology becomes most important.

There are about as many sales methodologies out there as there have been successful sales executives. Most revolve around building a connection to a product, establishing a worldview that necessitates the product, and establishing the product as part of a solution. Part of the key to success is customizing methodologies to fit new buying patterns and specific industries. When applied properly, these strategies become an important ingredient to scaling a team. They do require training, competence, natural abilities, and soft skills development. They also need to be watched and modified as we find success with various customers.

No methodology is perfect for every business, or no business would fail. Many seem similar and emphasize listening more, talking less, respecting the buyer's time, operating at their pace, respecting them, helping everyone and not just the decision maker, and being helpful even if they don't go from prospect to customer. These are just great ways to do business. No matter the methodology, it all starts with arming a good seller with a great product. The methodology helps align the team and shorten training cycles (think of all the training materials easily available out there for methodologies that go back 20–40 years).

Methodology Implementation

One great thing about working with an existing sales methodology is that we can hire teams who have experience working in that type of paradigm. That makes the implementation so much smoother than it otherwise might be. The next steps are to decide if it's best to hire a sales leader or someone new to selling who can be groomed. The answer to that question is often in the resources available.

No matter the choice, don't make any promises—just in case things only half work out (in sales we pretty much always assume things will work out beautifully). Instead, hire for aptitude, not seniority. Companies might hire someone that sold them a car, someone straight out of school, or someone from a customer that has the perfect personality to sell into our other customers. When hiring for capacity rather than a book of customers, we'll often hire someone into their first tech sales job.

People new to industries are often among the easiest to train. They typically don't come with a preconceived set of notions about how things are supposed to work, and they usually have a lot of skills that you might not otherwise think of—often helping innovate the way the business, or even the industry, work. Think of this as rookie smarts. When hiring someone new to the industry, implementing a sales methodology requires that we read some books or take some classes on that methodology. When hiring someone with experience, we can often provide a minimum amount of documentation and let them run with it. Either way, it's time to start writing down a guide for selling products, based loosely (if not entirely) off the methodology selected. Many begin that process by mapping the sales cycles.

Conclusion

Sales is one of the most complicated aspects of starting a new company, especially when looked at together with marketing. No matter how good a product, no matter how well the product resonates with a market, if the product doesn't sell, then the mission can't be fulfilled and the adventuring party starves. Many journeys by technical founders start by reading all the books and blog posts about sales—even getting certified in various sales methodologies. But there's no substitute for sitting in the chair in sales and shadowing great sellers.

Most sales teams need to be built from the bottom up and then managed from the top down. Unless we work closely with sellers, we can't build the team to then manage it. We the authors could have saved years of acceleration across multiple companies by understanding that the journey to develop a sales team begins with hiring two sellers and studying their performance to understand the sales motions that work. Once there's an established flow, then founders can start to manage and lead teams in a more traditional manner. In other words, we can't just bring in sales leaders from established companies and expect them to build a sales organization.

As we've shown in this chapter, startup sales is different. It's hard, but really, really important. Sales needs air cover. This is where leads come in through more passive means, get nurtured, and then get handed off to sales once ready–often using the SiriusDecisions framework mentioned earlier in this chapter. Chapter 11 gets into more of the nuts and bolts of developing a great marketing organization.

CHAPTER 11

Marketing and Advertising

The brave adventuring party has built something special. We want to spread the word about our creation throughout the lands. There are so many places to do so. We call those "channels" to market through. There are so many ways to talk about the problem the adventuring party can solve. There are a lot of rubrics to review the effectiveness of how to do so.

We covered sales in Chapter 10. Selling is typically a one-to-one relationship. A good seller might be able to work a few dozen leads at once, but many startups either are further down-market from where a sales team is effective or need to keep fresh leads flowing to sellers to keep them engaged without seeming desperate. Marketing researches the market and promotes products to spark interest in the offers the organization has. This creates inbound leads that have a more authentic relationship with the company and so higher close rates. This has become so much the norm that many no longer expect to receive a cold phone call from sellers.

The mix of sales and marketing is different for every organization. In general, organizations that sell into larger enterprises will spend around 20–25% of their overall budget on sales and marketing. The Small Business Administration recommends 7–10% of *gross* revenue should be spent on marketing and advertising specifically. Taking on debt or diluting equity to propel growth might make that 12–15% of revenue for some or incalculable for a pre-revenue company.

© Charles Edge, Chip Pearson, Amy Larson Pearson 2023
C. Edge et al., *The Startup Players Handbook*,
https://doi.org/10.1007/978-1-4842-9315-7_11

Marketing Levels

The budget balance between different go-to-market activities (especially when it comes to sales vs. marketing) means that a lot of companies level up the marketing discipline differently and at different stages in their development. Some might be at millions in revenue before they engage in any kind of meaningful marketing and/or advertising initiatives. Others might spend heavily early in the life of a company but be in a more mature state before they bring on sellers. Most companies need to engage in meaningful expenditures for one of the two in order to meet the growth targets investors expect. Therefore, take the following levels to track the maturity of the marketing organization as an example, rather than an expectation:

- *Level 1*: Market where it works. Most founders should try to spend small amounts to buy some keywords, build a blog, and optimize all publicly facing site pages to make them more appealing for search engines. The important thing here is to get as many good analytics as possible early. Those ad hoc efforts can be tracked against later-stage efforts. Founders should also create accounts on pertinent social media outlets and document the credentials—even if they won't be used much until later.

- *Level 2*: Those social media accounts should start picking up followers as the first leads are converted into customers. Think about podcasts to be a guest on, whether to launch a new podcast (especially if the software appeals to emerging industries), what might go on a YouTube channel, and a social media strategy. We want to experiment with buying keywords and documenting the results.

- *Level 3*: Review what worked in earlier attempts and consider the mix of sales and marketing budgets. Based on that, work with consultants or hire someone on staff to help figure out where money is best spent. Maybe that's with conferences or print ads. Most should consider lead generation opportunities with mass appeal. Keep in mind selling through partners goes under sales and marketing. So, whether selling through resellers or alongside a larger organization, make sure to test marketing dollars here as well and look for ways to get good analytics for all efforts.

- *Level 4*: By the time there are 20–30 paying customers or there is $20,000 per month in recurring revenue, it's likely time to bring on the first full-time marketing hire. This person might do SEO (search engine optimization), ad buys, drip campaigns, or any number of other activities including those that might be considered guerilla marketing tactics. One of the most important aspects is that they'll manage the lead generation funnel, whether automated or manual. Here, we want to see a lead scoring system and stages and be able to track where potential customers are falling out of the funnel and why. That makes parts of the job fairly technical.

- *Level 5*: Once the initial costs to acquire customers are known, see if it's possible to pump more money into marketing efforts results to gain more paying customers at the same per-capita cost. Experiment with larger and larger advertising campaigns, a higher frequency of content, and different messages, and, given the historical numbers, try to better identify what's working, what picks up traction, and why. Split lead generation and more passive forms of marketing into their own roles. For example, maybe someone is in charge of content (socials, blogs, TikToks, or whatever the specific customers look to), another person is in charge of social advertising (ads on LinkedIn, Twitter, Facebook, etc.), and yet another person does sales and market enablement based on the faster pace of updates to the products. These are all unique skillsets, and in earlier stages various people can do them all, but as organizations grow, the needs tend to stretch individuals who try to do it all too thin.

- *Level 6*: Once there are a few hundred customers or a company hits a Series B, it's time to experiment with how to turn customers into advocates. Help promote them when they do. This can be as simple as a retweet, but as the pool of advocates grows, consider how some could be rewarded for their efforts, especially with an advocacy portal. Consider a manager or director of the marketing team. There might be a certain friction between the lead generation efforts from marketing and the conversion rates in sales; that's natural. If not done already, this is when marketing personas, better lead scoring, more mature drip campaigns, and much more will need to get put in place to prepare for scale. But now it's possible to do so in a data-driven manner.

- *Level 7*: Guerilla marketing tactics might still work but aren't scalable. They also come across as petty if there are smaller competitors (which a Series B or later-stage funding often inspires). Early results can be great, but the conversions trail off as organizations pump more

money into campaigns. The human capital layered
on top (the person to buy pizzas and others) becomes
too expensive to run smaller grassroots campaigns.
Sponsoring podcasts, radio shows, creating more
mature forms of media, sponsoring conferences, etc.
are all things we can do to spend the money we got
from investors to spread the word about our solutions
while providing analytical results that the board will
certainly want to see. Investors will have no shortage of
opinions about how to scale marketing, but make sure
to stay true to the customers served and mission of the
company.

As our group of heroes begin the adventure in marketing, it's quite
different from the journey to level up a sales discipline from founder-led
sales to a large sales team. Much of that has to do with how technology
has evolved the discipline of marketing and advertising over the years.
It's far more technical than it's ever been, and the price of tools can
reflect that. For example, consider the difference in price between a
tool like Mailchimp and one like Eloqua. The relationship between
marketers and customers can also come across as a little mechanical
when not done authentically. Scale doesn't have to dilute that just
because it usually does. The founders and early hires who are experts in
a given field can be solicited for input on where a company chooses to
advertise.

Once brave explorers surpass level 7, there are entire subfields
that quickly make themselves known. Founders might tinker with drip
campaigns and SEO and SERPs (acronyms will be unpacked later in the
chapter). Eventually people will be hired who have dedicated their entire
careers to just one tool that helps automate those tasks. Some specialize
in the various ways to get a message out. Think of these as channels a
marketing message is sent through, hoping for a great return from the

denizens of the realm. They analyze to increase the amount of time, effort, and spending in a given direction or stop an adventure and pick up something new that's more exciting for potential players (er, customers)!

Evolving Marketing Channels

Once upon a time, in a land far, far away, advertising meant an ad in a newspaper, an entry in a phonebook, and maybe some space in magazines. Over the ensuing weeks, maybe money showed up in the mail, or the phone rang and orders flowed in. Maybe enterprising marketers also went down to a local organization that sold a list of names and addresses or a government office and sent a mailer around to each. As technology evolved, marketers and advertisers could buy radio and then television ads as well. Direct mail, call centers, radio, television, and their modern analogs are considered channels.

There's little risk of rejection in most types of passive marketing. Marketers blasted out a message and waited to see how the market would respond. No one looked the marketer in the eyes and said "no" or not to ever call them again. They could hire market research to survey customers, but analytics weren't big in offline media. Then came digital marketing. Gary Thuerk from Digital Equipment Corporation (DEC) sent an email in 1978 to a high percentage of the early ARPANET users (ARPANET was a precursor to what we now call the Internet). People weren't stoked, but DEC made sales. Then came the Web, and AT&T bought an ad on HotWired.com (now called *Wired*) in 1994 that had a 44% click rate. Digital ads were born. Then came search engine placements in the early 2000s. Archie was an early search engine and later Google, who effectively gave us an entire industry on search engine optimization and buying ads that appear in searches.

Today, the modern marketing machine is mostly digital. Those early users figured out that we could look at the logs on our web servers and see what ads were resonating and with whom. Google provided tracking codes to make that even easier. We can now react in seconds instead of weeks. Considering the ways to reach customers in the preceding quick history of the realms of advertising and marketing, there are a few types of marketing across channels. Each company finds success with different types of initiatives over different channels based on where their customers are and their routes to market. We'll cover those types of marketing and the connection to customers before we get into the nuts and bolts of where and how to find potential buyers.

Types of Marketing

There are a number of ways to go about marketing—sub-classes, if you will. These include growth marketing, brand marketing, and product marketing as specific disciplines. But let's not overthink that. Most startups engage in opportunistic marketing—which is to say that money goes where there are results. Early on, most companies experiment, find growth hacks, or engage in various forms of guerrilla marketing. Then results are measured, and more resources pour into places where initiatives worked out.

The most important takeaway that most find in those early initiatives is to focus on customers. Early-stage companies are more apt to meet potential customers where they are at or display ads that they will actually see and hopefully click. Those ads should have a call to action or prompt people who see the ad to do something that can be measured. There should be a journey from marketing asset to marketing asset that leads visitors to a place where their interactions with the assets and whether they ultimately buy products can be analyzed. No matter how great the engagement, though, keep in mind they eventually need to buy, or the organization will run out of money.

In case that wasn't enough, we want to engage with potential customers (which we often call leads) authentically. Hopefully, they get a good product, and marketers talk about the product in a way that gets the right people to try it. It sounds like a lot, but with the marketing automation tools available, it doesn't have to be. The journey starts with customers.

Customers

Every company needs customers to survive. Part of how to reach those customers is to figure out where they find products, when they engage with companies, what they need, and whom we plan to reach. Who are the buyers of a product? Maybe the villagers in the game have banded together to put together some gold pieces so they can pay a team of adventurers to defeat the nearby trolls. Or maybe the queen of the realm has summoned a party to protect the throne. The first adventure can be fun and rewarding and in the context of a company often involves work for hire rather than a software sale. How do we find more people to pay us to access products after those first adventures?

There are plenty of questions to ask to get closer to how to find more customers. Where do potential customers go to find something like what we're providing? Is it online or in-person? Do the people that use our product read the same website or listen to the same podcasts? Do they attend the same conferences? Do they listen to public radio or go to the beach regularly? The more we know about our customers, the better we'll be able to get an ad in front of them. The better we understand their motivations to potentially buy our product, the more targeted the words and images in those ads can be.

Chapter 4 covered how to make personas for product management. Sales and marketing personas are a bit different. These focus on what makes the customer buy. This is somewhat adjacent to what makes the product work for them but looks deeper at what separates them from their gold pieces. A company will need to continue separating customers from their gold pieces in exchange for something of value to grow. That's a mutually beneficial relationship. Always put the customer first. This means companies should build features customers and prospects want and then market the solution, experience, and features the product provides in existing channels that customers engage with. The words should resonate with them as well. To know if the efforts are working, be analytical. There are existing frameworks to help be disciplined about that. We'll start that journey looking at the channels we market through using an existing framework.

Marketing Channels

Conjuration, divination, necromancy, illusion–these are schools of magic in role-playing games. Marketing channels can be a bit like that. Channels define how a lead or visitor of the site or web app was sourced. How did the queen find the party? That's a simpler question than to try and figure out how 1,000 villagers did so. Tracking how customers and leads found a product provides focus and results in more success with budgets. Every business is different, so the mix of time and other resources will vary. Think of the channels as follows (as with the previous chapter, following the SiriusDecisions model so we can hire for this easier later):

Channel	Channel Name	Definition	Examples	Statuses	Success Metrics	Notes
Default	Web	User visits site without a UTM.	Finds website or dark social	Member Converted Filled-out form	Member Converted Filled-out form	Web programs result in converted or "filled-out form."
Default	Paid media	Paid advertising tactics.	Syndicated content Cost per click Cost per lead	Member Converted	Converted	Success is measured via what type of conversion, represented in the paid media tag value.
Event with webinar	Webinar	Online event hosted live or on demand used to educate our prospects and customers on particular subjects.	Leading a great study Tracking data in a UX tool or CRM	Member Invited Registered Attended No show Attended on demand		

Engagement	Nurture	Messaging and content targeted to stages in the buying cycle.	Member Opened Clicked Engaged Exit	Engaged	Member of nurturing program who opened or clicked an asset within the program and who has moved into a deeper stage of the funnel.
Default	Email nurture	Basically the Mailchimp emails.	Member Exclusion Delivered Opened Clicked Engaged	Engaged	
Default	Email campaign	Non-operational email, content of which is usually considered marketing content.	Member Delivered Opened Clicked Converted	Converted	Used for A/B or one-off campaigns rather than nurture.

(continued)

Channel	Channel Name	Definition	Examples	Statuses	Success Metrics	Notes
Event	Tradeshow			Member Invited Pre-show appointment Visited booth Attended session	Pre-show appointment, visited booth, attended session	
Event	Event	In-person event that's not a tradeshow.		User groups Roadshows Happy hours	Attended	
N/A	Direct mail			Member		

Channels force a company to consider where time is spent and help isolate the return on investment of time, money, and effort. For example, paid media might include PPC, CPC, paid search, podcasts, email, LinkedIn, Facebook, Twitter, syndicated content, radio, Bing, and Yahoo. We'll get into the acronyms later in the chapter. But for now, keep in mind that each should be tested. Some are not likely to net short-term gains, but as the disciplines mature, our earlier attempts help focus on the words that convert customers, spread the brand, and fill the sales funnel with at least a few leads. That also provides sellers the assurance that once they work leads currently in the funnel, more will come later (and so their jobs and financial well-being are secure).

An important, and somewhat technical, aspect of analyzing channel performance is to add a UTM code to all efforts. The link at the end of a blog post might have a code of "blog_selling_to_your_boss," or if it's an ebook on UX best practices, it might read "ebook_best_practices." There are a lot of different strategies for naming UTM codes. Once we see campaigns automatically broken out in Google Analytics (or a future analytics tool once Google is outgrown), then the options will start to make more sense, but the earlier we begin, the better later employees can track efforts.

Email Marketing

Email marketing is one of the top ways for software companies to maintain connections with customers and nurture those relationships. In fact, sometimes it seems like every time we turn on the radio, there's an ad for an email marketing automation tool like Constant Contact, Mailchimp, iContact, and even Salesforce. It also probably seems like every time you open your email, there's an email nurturing you to buy something. Emails can make it easy for small- and mid-sized businesses to automate beautiful messages and build logic around the interactions a user has. Larger organizations can find a lot of success with more enterprise-class solutions like Marketo, Adobe Marketing Cloud, and Eloqua. Sometimes it's too easy based on how many emails we end up deleting every morning. Yet it works, or companies wouldn't still do it.

The ads from big companies with large email marketing teams can make it sound like these messaging campaigns write themselves. They don't; there's a lot of art in communicating with customers authentically, effectively, and in a way that resonates with the journey they'll have with our products–like a great adventure module where the back cover explains exactly what they'll be running into.

Email marketing is a delicate business. On the one hand, you don't want to be an evil spammer. Avoid lawsuits that could come from doing so. On the other hand, email automation is one of the only ways to communicate with a lot of customers with any kind of frequency. Along the journeys to align email marketing with a great customer experience, there are a lot of great techniques and some pretty bad ones. So here are some lessons to take note of:

- **Be timely.** Did a customer start a trial? Get them some tips for how to use the type of product they signed up for. Is it budget season? Help them prioritize. Build systems before having people opt into lists, so too much time doesn't expire and they forget the name. Messages that appeal to what a reader is going through at the time they receive them are likely to resonate and be opened.

- **Be authentic.** We all have a voice—the humans and the products. Give the product a voice or let sellers create their own custom campaigns. Be authentic with that voice and try to establish a great relationship with customers with consistent messaging that reinforces a kind and helpful stream of content.

- **Map the customer journey.** A map of how a customer interacts with a product has a lot of great uses. One is that at each stage along the journey with a product, the customer can receive meaningful and tailored content for where they actually are—even if they haven't yet become a customer, if they're evaluating the product, or if they're on a trial. All of these can be used as attributes to help get the appropriate content out at the appropriate time.

- **Don't send any emails that don't provide value.** Each person perceives value in their own way. Keep in mind that we always want to be worthwhile in our communications. To some, that will mean learning more about the product, but for others, the human getting the email might not ever become a customer but could still have a positive impression of a brand based on those communications we send them.

- **Choose an email automation tool that fits the size of the marketing team.** This might be to use a prosumer email automation product early. Keep in mind that robust, enterprise-class products need a staff person at the reins. Organizations that can't afford someone in that position should self-identify with an appropriately sized product. And that might be whatever is built into the Customer Relationship Management solution, like Salesforce or HubSpot.

- **Use a third-party tool instead of Outlook.** You know that Unsubscribe button? It doesn't usually come for free. We don't want to violate laws like the European Union's General Data Protection Regulation (GDPR). We also don't want to hit rate-limiting controls like those in place at a lot of mail hosts and Internet Service Providers (ISPs).

- **Protect personally identifiable information.** Those email addresses and other contact details are hard-won. And no one wants to be the cause of leaking that confidential data. Use strong passwords with multi-factor authentication with the email marketing platform and never sell customers' information unless there's a privacy policy that explicitly states it's okay to do so (and even then, it's still probably a bad idea).

- **Don't take things too seriously.** People are inundated with a lot of emails. Boring, dry emails get old fast, and people will almost invariably unsubscribe (except your competitors). We should have permission to be ourselves and conversational. We should be free to poke fun at ourselves every now and then. It resonates and makes each organization a little more human. It also makes our jobs a little more fun.

- **Automate syncing contacts with the CRM.** This isn't always necessary, as many a Customer Relationship Management (CRM) tool has leaned into features that allow teams to manage email communications. Syncing those events (opens, clicks, replies) gives us valuable insight into how the content in our messaging gets interacted with by those receiving it. Sure, syncing this data can be labor intensive and cause technical misfires that end up adding people who have unsubscribed back in or sending people duplicate emails. Those issues can be addressed as they arise and go above and beyond to make things right when it happens.

- **Use email automation to cross-sell goods and services.** One of the most important aspects of email automation is to convert leads to customers. Customer retention is critical as well. As companies grow, other items from portfolios can be sold. Don't be too salesy or constantly bombard customers with offers for more stuff. Instead, drip content out that is fresh and pertinent to customers to keep from overlapping between adjacent products.

- **Use email automation to improve products.** Don't use email just to hawk products. Send thought leadership content such as an interesting industry report to stay engaged with customers. Use existing customers and even leads that haven't yet converted to help improve products as well.

- **Have a call to action.** Each message we send a customer should provide more pathways for the customer to interact with us. This might be a "Read more" button, a "Try free" option, or a link to see similar content. The key is to use each piece of content we provide to drive engagement to another. Provided the content is timely, relevant, and authentic, we should be able to stay engaged with customers by providing podcasts, blog articles, templates, and other content that keeps them on the journey we want to help them along.

- **Pay attention to when people unsubscribe.** That is a pretty simple message usually: stop doing what caused them to want to disengage with you. If people click through content, things are working. If not, maybe they aren't. If they click Unsubscribe, things are definitely going poorly.

- **Don't forget about social media.** A lot of email gets disregarded, but social networks like LinkedIn are great to make new contacts and nurture them. Several messaging tools and CRMs now provide customers with the option to integrate various social media accounts. This provides both a free and paid approach to managing messages sent to leads at scale and insights into how potential customers are engaging with content. Again, don't be spammy—be authentic and look for mediums that match the type of messages being sent.

Ultimately, email marketing is one of the most powerful tools companies have in an ever-expansive arsenal to convert leads to customers. Once we have a solid messaging solution in place, we can start to keep those conversations going and have them in ways we never could have before this era. Picking a tool isn't permanent. Start small and work your way to a more complex and rewarding experience. There's no rush to message everyone in a database at once. Experiment and find the right ways to communicate with customers. Keep the conversation honest and authentic. That will win the hearts and minds more than anything else!

Content Marketing

Content marketing is putting content out into the world in order to drive traffic to a website. There's no doubt that content is a great way to attract potential customers to our sites. There's also no doubt that the right kind of content can drive the right kind of customers. But really, almost any content is good content.

It can be challenging for early-stage startups to take the time to focus on generating content. There are so many things pulling at founders. Many will already be well versed in talking to the audience that products are targeted at. Communicate with our customers at their level and with depth and sincerity and in a way that resonates (and so is authentic). It's easier to write about things that are known. With growth, bring on marketing teams, but they will need to learn the domain knowledge to write effective content. Let's focus for a moment on a few ways to plan for a good long-term content strategy. We'll just approach this as we might an introduction to creative writing!

- **Set goals.** Start light, maybe an article a week. Set aside time to be able to generate content. The closer a company gets to releasing a product, the more content as a marketing strategy impacts those goals. Let's say the goal is to release one article a week–once we hit five, start promoting the content (after all, that's when this stuff becomes more real).

- **Set aside time.** This is crucial. Two or three hours blocked off in the calendar here or there gives the space required to focus on content generation. As writing skills improve and the content becomes more clear, articles might get written faster. Some won't be able to focus for more than an hour at a time and so need to do an hour a day three days a week. Hopefully, that can get down to an hour per article. Things can be a little chaotic in a startup, so have permission to move the time slots when other demands eke into the allotted time, but be diligent about the content if that's a channel for the market.

- **Make a plan for content.** Start by brainstorming some words that describe the product. Don't stuff too many words into articles, but do sprinkle them into titles and headers. This helps bring focus to the products as they're developed and sprinkle unique thoughts around those products. People might naturally find the content organically when searching for areas meaningful to them. Don't focus on contrived ways to fool search engines, though.

- **Consider the mediums.** There are so many ways to put content out there. Some people are natural writers and bloggers, others prefer podcasts, and others might choose to focus on instructional videos. Founders can't do it all when also trying to keep up with the accounting, sales, marketing, public relations, product, and development responsibilities in a startup. Choose one medium and get a good cadence before moving to others. Spreading ourselves too thin will do no one any favors!

- **Brainstorm 20 titles.** This gets the creative juices flowing. Think about the biggest issues from the words that describe the product and ask "what is that" and "why does it matter" and "what can we say about adjacent topics." Those 20 article titles could be organized into a thread of articles, as a series, or could stand alone. These first articles can also be useful to get those creative juices flowing later, in case the ideas dry up as thoughts on some topics can mature over time.

- **Write an outline for one article.** Once there are some article ideas, try to focus on writing just one. Pick the one that's the easiest to get the confidence up. Go back to the most valuable articles once there's a following. Try and get an introduction, three to five key points we want to get across, some arguments to back those points up, and a conclusion. Keep in mind that articles can be as short as a few hundred words, and short articles can be as valuable as longer ones.

- **Write or record.** Armed with an outline, it's time to write an article. The reason this option is "or record" is because that outline could be used as the outline for a podcast episode if writing just doesn't work out. If writing, put the article to the side once you've moved those bullets in an outline into text and edit the article the next day.

- **Solicit feedback.** Whatever kind of content being produced, give it to someone trusted to review. Take the feedback honestly and openly and use it to make the article better. Don't post it yet.

- **Repeat the process four more times.** How many podcasts are out there with just one episode? How many blogs with just two articles (maybe three if the stock "Hello World" article they come with is included)? There's no magic number for when content creation starts to become muscle memory, but five is usually a good start—if a blogger or podcaster can make five, the asset is on its way to 50 posts. Once there are five, plan an appropriate cadence to release the content. Usually once every month to once every other week in pre-release stages or weekly in later stages for software companies is a good cadence to start with.

- **Find a good platform to host.** This might be a blog that comes with the web hosting package, a WordPress instance, a Libsyn account, or a number of other places. Things to think about are whether it can benefit the main site with search engine optimization, cost, and complexity to design. Don't worry about getting the branding perfect (that's likely to change once there's dedicated marketing staff anyways). Focus on content, content, content.

- **Socialize the material.** Most organizations will want to syndicate content on LinkedIn, Facebook, Twitter, newsletters, etc. This is important, as more eyeballs on the content, more backlinks, and in general, more reach is what everyone tends to want.

- **Solicit more content.** Cofounders, new employees, and others should feel comfortable and welcome to submit content. Again, the early content doesn't need to exactly follow a plan. But it should be quality material that people will want to engage with. Be kind with the material received, though, and don't apply pressure for others to produce content unless doing so is part of their job description.

- **Analyze the reactions.** It's simple to see what gets retweeted or reshared. Take a look at the time people stay on pages as well as the pages people go to after they engage with the content. This can be interesting as it can help understand what to talk through in sales or in a roadmap. The same is true for any paid search engine advertising we do. The more content that aligns to the search terms purchased, the cheaper those words will be. This also guides feature decisions.

The most important thing with all of this is to have fun with it! Don't get lost in search engine optimization and overthinking the analytics and branding of the site in the beginning. After all, the blog or podcast might not take off. Starting a company needs to be fun sometimes, because it can be rough as well. And if we have fun with our content, then we'll want to make more of it. That means not letting it be overly salesy. That means finding our true, authentic voice as we create the content. That means doing it over and over until we love it!

Blogs

Sometimes people actually try out products based on unsolicited emails. As writers, about once every couple of years we might end up writing an article about one of those products as well. And we've even put some of the products that came in unsolicited communications in a couple of books. And some of those we still use and even pay for. Some have even told us that they got a fair amount of business through our posts, which we love to hear.

Advertising to bloggers can work, be it through unsolicited emails, social media, or some other way to reach out. If that's all we wanted from bloggers, we'd be better off spending those advertising dollars on something more transactional. Many bloggers (who aren't us) are influencers, so one aspect of reaching them is that there's a higher rate of conversion. Services or products can also end up getting picked up by people in the media that follow those bloggers, which can then end up with mentions in various media outlets, even if those are industry specific.

Blogs also provide backlinks. It stands to reason that if backlinks are what give sites high listing on search engines, then the more of those we can get, the better. Getting a good natural listing in the search engines has a lot to do with being relevant. And having a site with a good page ranking mention our product or brand is a great way to get those backlinks and thus increase the page rank. Companies can also buy mentions in blogs, although that's less legitimate. Avoid purchasing backlinks, though. Not all backlinks are created equal. Supposedly, purchased backlinks should be tagged as "No-Follow," which means that search engine crawlers don't count the link toward a page rank. This is mostly true. Track the links that come into a site, but don't assume that those links tell the whole story of the impact of the effort to get mentioned by bloggers.

Bloggers are a weird bunch. Companies can usually reach them with emails (check the website or registrar for addresses if they aren't otherwise available), connect on LinkedIn (chances are you aren't too many connections away from them if you're in the same industry and need an introduction), message them on social media, etc. Being that we get a lot of these, let's provide some tips:

- Personalize the communication.

- Be nice.

- Explain why your pitch is pertinent to the audience.

- Include a link (but not, like, eight of them).

- Make sure the pitch fits in the first couple of lines.

- Use language similar to the language the blogger uses.

- Avoid repetitive emails.

Anyone who thinks that blogs are a good place to advertise and can't get anyone to write about a good or service can also consider buying some advertising on the site. This can usually be done directly with the blogger or through an advertising network (maybe even Google AdWords). Another way to get the message out there is through creating a new blog. Nearly every company has a blog today. Blogs allow creators to make content and put it out there for the world to see. This gets picked up by crawlers and allows us to help educate our market. We covered content creation earlier, and the blog is likely a primary vehicle for the distribution of that content.

Creating a blog can be as simple as setting up an account with WordPress or adding a blog feature to an existing Content Management System under the company marketing site (e.g., Wix and most other low-/no-code web CMS platforms have a blog feature). Reaching out to bloggers is a great way to get mentions. Creating content that aligns with a content calendar is also great, and opening up blogs for anyone in the organization to write about topics important to the industry we serve is another fantastic way to get a lot of content out there. Another way is to run webinars and embed those into posts.

Webinars

Web + seminar = webinar. A webinar is just a presentation streamed over the Internet. Webinars are usually hosted by an organization looking to sell something. Webinars educate potential buyers about how to do things in a given industry or with specific products. Notice that the sentence stopped there. It could have said "in order to capture information about potential buyers or move them down the sales funnel," but it didn't. Many no longer go to conferences or do in-person seminars. Instead, if they weren't always, webinars are now a key aspect of the modern business-to-business sales funnel when done right.

Webinars should be educational. Teach viewers how to do things with products or in our industry at large. Talk about the philosophies that drive decisions on how to build better products in the category. Help people make mature, smart decisions about how to think about the industry. Full stop. Now the second part of that earlier sentence. Capture information to inform people further about the industry and provide helpful content. Continue to provide educational content in other mediums, such as emails that help people make the most informed decisions about which product to buy if they're comparing a competitor's product. Marketers should want the best for them and can expect that even if they ultimately buy another product, they will appreciate that.

There's still a pressure to keep the pipeline moving. The larger the purchase of a product, the longer that will take, and the more gently people will need to be nudged to transact, or they'll opt out of the campaigns. Educating consumers doesn't mean there isn't a call to action; just build authentic campaigns and explain the thesis along the way. The effort to put on webinars can be put to other great uses as well. A library of webinars can work like a podcast or used as gated content. Potential and existing customers can get links to each when they have specific questions through a support portal. Webinars can be leveraged to position individuals as thought leaders. Webinars can be transcribed and used as content in other mediums.

Webinars can be a great part of our cycle for potential customers and put marketing teams in touch with potential new customers. The hardest part with a lot of creative content is just to get started. Here are some of the steps involved in the journey to help in that process:

- **Pick a date.** This is the easiest and most important aspect of developing a webinar muscle at any organization. Practically every organization knows a webinar will benefit them, but we just need a nudge to get started. Pick a date a month in the future, on a day that works well for a given industry. Divide the following tasks into weeks 1 through 4, allowing for at least two weeks from the time the invitation is sent to the day of the webinar.

- **Set milestones.** Milestones are important. In a smaller organization, this could be as simple as four milestones. In larger organizations, there could be a dozen people involved. It's best to start small, with a small group, and then allow additional tasks to complicate the process as we grow and realize a need to do so.

- **Develop a list of contacts**. A running email list is a great start to build a list of contacts to announce webinars and other assets. If there's a CRM in use, everyone who meets certain criteria should get an invitation (e.g., "lead score > 20" or "active opportunity"). This usually means an email with a link to the asset and potentially other similar assets. This is one reason to focus on building a list of people to invite early on.

- **Choose a moderator**. Someone who is engaging, a good public speaker, and knowledgeable about the product should moderate the first webinars. Everyone tends to be a subject matter expert in the early stages of a company, so there's probably no need to look too far. Sometimes it's best to have a pair of people lead webinars or have one person deliver the content and another manage questions as they come in. Experiment with a few different scenarios to find the best one.

- **Select a topic.** Remember, the topic should educate people who may buy a product. That education could be about the industry at large, cover a workflow, or be about a specific feature. A general litmus for a good topic is whether or not the same topic could be used by a competitor as well. From there, help viewers understand the value proposition without making a sales pitch; webinars should not be too salesy. The output of this step should be a catchy title and then a short paragraph that describes the webinar.

- **Sign up for an account to deliver webinars**. Zoom, GoTo Meeting, and other sites have great how-to documentation on how to set up an account and deliver a webinar. It's not free. Choose a platform based on which has the best experience and the best integration with the CRM being used. When in doubt, use Zoom.

- **Test the webinar technology.** This is important. Pick another person, set up a webinar in the platform, have them sign up, and noodle around. Share screens, try to abuse the platform, ask questions, grant presenter permissions, etc. Do all of the things an attendee or co-presenter might do. This helps educate on the settings used when running the webinar and helps keep from embarrassing distractions when the webinar is delivered. Then, document the settings to be used (e.g., in an internal wiki).

- **Set up the webinar**. Now that the platform has been thoroughly tested, use the information documented to set up the first webinar. There should be a signup link so the webinar platform can take over communications or a link to the webinar to be used to send invitations from within the CRM or messaging platform.

- **Message the contacts.** Now that there is a list of contacts, a title, a description, and the link, put this into a message and send it. Also arm sellers with a template email used to send an invitation when on phone calls.

- **Socialize outside the standard message list.** Distill the description down to a size appropriate for Twitter, LinkedIn, Facebook, etc. This is best if sent through the CRM (e.g., the LinkedIn feature in HubSpot) so we can see where people that might want to sign up drop off.

- **Test the webinar technology again.** Pick someone else and run another webinar to work out kinks. Have them yell at the cat and try to take over the screen and abuse the platform. Make sure all the settings are the same as previously documented, and if they need to be changed live, make sure they're changed in the documentation and the planned webinar as well.

- **Write a presentation.** Now that there's a description, build a Keynote or PowerPoint. As previously noted, the presentation should not be a sales pitch. The presentation should be roughly 75–80% of the advertised time, allowing for questions and answers at the end. Pick a call to action at the end and build toward it while authentically helping someone understand the topic selected. Don't put too much text to be read from slides or notes to keep from too dry a presentation; bullets should instead be short and remind the presenter what they want to say.

- **Perform a dry run of the webinar.** Now that there's a presentation, do a dry run. Have viewers save questions and feedback until the end to get the timing and flow worked out. The goal here is for someone with good presentation skills to get confident with the platform. In other words, make sure there's no to need to ask, "Can everyone see my screen?"

- **Validate the technical bits.** Once some people signed up for the webinar, make sure the team sees the signup in the CRM and for the dry run. It's important to see that they attended and that marketers can impact lead scores or message them a thank you and perhaps more content following the webinar.

- **Rehearse.** Every person who presents should rehearse. The content shouldn't come across as over-rehearsed and so dry, but should be delivered confidently. The amount of rehearsing needed, and whether it's done in front of an audience, is different for everyone. It's hard to go wrong with recording a rehearsal and watching it to help work out some of the finer details.

- **Plan for questions.** Allow for 20–25% of the time for questions. Seed a couple with people who will be attending just in case other attendees don't ask any questions but try and answer real audience questions first. After all, it's for the viewers. Don't worry if there's a question without a good answer. "Give me a day and I'll get back to you on that" is a great answer if needed.

- **Have fun.** All this work is done. Don't get stressed. Have fun with it. After all, after rehearsing and planning, it should be a well-oiled machine. Have a joke in the back pocket for when something goes wrong (and always assume something will go wrong at some point).

- **Document findings.** Following the first webinar, write down thoughts on how it went. Document what went well, what went poorly, and what gaps were there in the technology. These are important and help us deliver better webinars as we go.

- **Provide a link to the recorded webinar.** The more
  people that sign up, the more likely some can't make
  it. The link allows people to view the webinar even if
  they couldn't make it. Try to capture information for
  people that couldn't make it anyway, though, so plan
  to publish it as gated content (or even spin it into a
  monthly podcast).

- **Set up a routine schedule.** Now for the fun part. We
  did all the hard stuff. We can now set up a schedule of
  webinars. Pick a new topic for each and run them on
  a set schedule–first Tuesday of the month at 10 AM
  or something like that. Play with the times to pick a
  time that works best. Be flexible with the topics but sit
  down and write out at least six and plan to deliver them
  weekly or monthly.

This seems like a lot of steps. It *is* possible to go through all of it in an
hour. For a sole proprietor, assume it will take a day. For a larger team,
assume maybe four or five meetings one or two hours long will work out all
the bugs before delivering that first webinar. Any organization with larger
teams will have individuals responsible for each piece, and they'll likely
just need links, titles, and descriptions.

Webinars are one of the most impactful things to move people down
our sales funnel. Provided webinars are authentic and help potential
customers in their jobs, they should result in increased demand, content
that gets reshaped, more finely tuned messaging, and people who come
back for more. It can seem like a lot at first. Just don't overthink it (but
make sure to be prepared). And remember, educate and have fun!

Company Podcasts

The first time we do most things is usually the hardest. Once we get through one or two repetitions, most tasks get easier. First, let's look at why organizations make podcasts:

- **Humanize an organization.** Perceptions of a company are usually based on the interactions people have with companies. That means the attitudes of one person or a few people reverberate. The more transactional relationships between people and companies (as is common with SaaS companies with low-friction sales processes), the less likely there ever is a person customers interact with. This is a drawback of an instantaneous sales process, but can be combated. Despite efforts to build solid cultures and work to define values, the interpersonal relationships formed within an organization can't scale with external perceptions as an organization grows. By putting humans from the organization in front of an audience, organizations can allow the audience to connect with those humans and so see the adventuring party as a collection of humans rather than a faceless army whose purpose is to take advantage of them.

- **Educate.** Every type of organization is different. One commonality is that all benefit from a more educated industry. A company podcast should educate customers from every vendor in a given industry. If that education leads to taking customers from competitors, great. If not, that's fine as well.

- **Update.** A podcast can keep people informed about developments at an organization, new features in products, and lots of other great or important news. This is different from educating people about an industry as some episodes should be meant to distribute specific information about the organization—so consider special episodes categorized as such to talk about features or a news segment after covering a given topic.

A podcast can do all of these when done right. Marketers love to quantify attribution for new customers and think of a podcast as a marketing asset. Podcasts should be as much about creating an authentic connection with customers, the development of our teams, teaching people about valuable insights, and keeping them informed. Now that we've talked about why companies start podcasts, let's jump into the mechanics. To start a podcast, let's bucket what's needed into a few categories: preparing, recording, editing, posting, and marketing.

Preparing

It's easy to get into analysis paralysis. Don't. Podcasts routinely change direction. After reading through this chapter, just set a date for the first episode to release and then get to planning. With that date in mind, define a mission. That mission might be to introduce the people in an organization to the people the organization serves. The mission might be to provide short updates on what and how the organization is doing. As with the Red Hat Command Line Heroes, the mission might even just be to teach people about random topics that may or may not be connected to what the organization does. This mission should reflect an unwritten (or maybe written, for posterity) contract with the people that produce the podcast on why the podcast exists.

Preparation also means going into an episode understanding just what will be involved in production. It can take as short as half an hour to write each script and an average of 15 minutes to schedule time in participants' calendars. Find an editor to do the sound leveling and spend one to two hours cutting out the "ums" and making sure the content complies with our values. It can take maybe half an hour to post (write notes, message people links, convert files, add metadata, and upload to the hosting platform). An episode could be turned around in a few days if needed when there's timely content, but the process usually takes up to two weeks. The actual time to record is usually an hour with two hosts and one to two guests. All in all, this means approximately six hours per episode across everyone involved in addition to the editor who does the finishing work. Some podcasts take more and some take less time to produce within a company, but this makes for a decent baseline.

Next, get everyone on board with the content. Brainstorm between five and twenty-five episode titles. If there is one, allow a marketing team to help identify any areas where episodes should be added or removed and provide guidance around timing (e.g., when an episode matches up with content in a marketing calendar). The podcast shouldn't entirely be a marketing asset, nor should it operate outside of a marketing organization. Marketing teams can also best inform a release cadence (although people consume podcasts by subscription and listen at their own leisure, so don't overthink when to release episodes). One thing a marketing team will be needed for in larger organizations is to approve the use of the name of the organization in a podcast—not an issue in smaller startups.

Once there is a calendar of sorts, a list of episode ideas, and a general idea of what to accomplish, let's get consensus that it's a good idea. To do this, talk to as many people in the organization as possible and get feedback. Maybe this is a post in Slack for organizations with more than 20 people. Maybe it's at a weekly company meeting for smaller organizations. Feedback is good; analysis paralysis is bad.

While listening to people in the organization, also listen to their voices. Look for a voice that enunciates well, a voice with dynamic tones, for someone that doesn't say "um" a lot, and for someone that others emotionally connect with when they speak. Yes, we're looking for a host (or cohost). Put the ego to the side (perhaps the hardest part). Maybe the host is someone just starting out in their career. Maybe the host is a mid-career professional. Maybe we choose to rotate hosts. If the host is one person, they should be considered a temporary host. Do a few episodes and see how it goes. Two hosts is better than one, but more might be a challenge.

Incorporate the feedback and then book the first episode. Open up the list of episode ideas that were created, pick one, open the calendar, and invite everyone that needs to be there to record. We'll get into the specifics of recording in the next section. Pick a platform like Zoom or Google Hangouts to meet and include the link as well as a link to a script, which might just be a title and the brief description for now.

Recording

Guests are a great way to run a podcast. Guests should feel comfortable with the technology and logistics. To help with the latter, develop a guide that guests can read to get particulars about the recording process (an example can be found here: `http://podcast.macadmins.org/recording/`) and any tips. The choices made in the technical aspects later in this section should impact what appears in that document.

Next, make sure to have the right recording equipment. Microphones are an investment. Plan to have everyone record a local track, preferably with a cardioid microphone, such as those from Røde (`http://en.rode.com/microphones/studio`) or the Shure SM7B or MV7 (`www.shure.com/en-US/products/microphones/mv7`). A cheap cardioid mic is still likely better than an omnidirectional mic. The goal is to cut out as much background noise as possible so there aren't too many filters and edits don't sound choppy. When looking at microphones, keep in mind that XLR microphones will require a box to get the sound into a computer, such as the Scarlet from Focusrite (`https://focusrite.com/en/usb-audio-interface/scarlett/scarlett-2i2-studio`), perhaps even paired with a device to add gain, such as a Cloudlifter (`www.cloudmicrophones.com/`

`cloudlifter-cl-1`). The Shure MV7 is a USB and USB-C version of the
same mic, meaning less cables and boxes. But feel free to experiment with
a few; everyone is different, so it might take trying multiple microphones to
get the exact mix right. Guests within a company might use a second of the
same microphone, but guests at other organizations might use AirPods or
another consumer headset. Make sure all guests have headphones.

The files listeners download from a podcast hosting service are usually
.mp3 or .m4a. High-end recording software is fine, but built-in tools like
QuickTime Player, free tools like Audacity, or upgrades like GarageBand
or Logic Pro are fine as well. Once the equipment is hooked up, do a
sample recording. Maybe read a passage from a book. Listen for heavy
breathing and try to cut out a sentence in GarageBand or Logic Pro and
see if there's a hiss in the background that drops off when doing so. Reduce
that possibility out as much as possible by reducing the gain, getting closer
to the microphone, backing away from the microphone, making sure the
microphone is facing the correct direction, etc.

Podcasts should try to cut down on background noise. Guests and
hosts will want to find a quiet place to record. Pop filters are a cheap device
to attach to eliminate popping sounds. But consider an isolation shield
or booth as well. Keep in mind that hot water heaters, HVAC systems,
children watching TV in another room, and airplanes passing overhead
can introduce more background noise. Watch sound levels and listen
for that when recording and back up and restate something when noises
crop up. That's way easier to do than trying to edit around noise later. If
recording at home or an office, then some will have to settle on good audio
at some point. If we can't get to a place we're comfortable, it's time to find
a recording studio, which is usually overkill for a podcast, but not always.

Guest audio is always a concern as well. Keep in mind that guests
should probably be in other rooms even if in the same location to make
editing easier (each on their own track with no audio bleeding in from
others). Guests are probably not going to have equipment that's as

awesome as the hosts. For example, not everyone interviewed will have a high-end microphone. Every person with a voice on the podcast should create a local recording. Again, this might be done with a studio-quality tool or just their local instance of QuickTime Player. Also, keep a backup recording (e.g., record a Zoom call) just in case a local recording isn't started or crashes when a hard drive runs out of space.

Once the recording process is documented, write a script. This should just be a set of questions to ask a guest (or talking points if there's no guest). Don't let the guest read answers. That's boring. Guests should be allowed to collaborate on the questions. If there are two hosts, maybe questions are asked round robin between the hosts. The important thing here is to follow an outline that defines a story arch. If the conversation just roams, then the listener is likely to get lost. Don't bury the lede. Start with a tweet-sized description of the episode right up front. Then finish by restating the manifesto. Then have a structured conversation breaking down the idea and rebuilding it. Don't write too much; leave plenty of room for the conversation to have a natural progression. Just keep the conversation in bounds so it doesn't meander too much. Beyond that, don't take things too seriously, have fun, and try to laugh a lot!

Editing

Find an editor or learn to use editing software like Logic Pro, Adobe Premiere, GarageBand (which is really just a gateway drug to Logic Pro), Hindenburg, etc. There are whole books on editing, so read up on the best techniques for the selected software. Less is more and filters are helpful. Don't overproduce the episode.

Plan for how the podcast gets cut. If doing a few episodes to decide if the podcast is a good idea or not, look for someone internally in the organization to do the editing. If the episode needs to sound professional, then plan for $200 to $1,000 per episode to have it professionally cut. The final edited episode should come back in the form of a wave (.wav),

MPEG-4, or MP3 (.m4a) file. Most podcasting platforms will provide the option to add metadata and tag on uploads. That can also be done using an encoding tool (like https://apps.apple.com/us/app/to-mp3-converter-free/id983472324?mt=12) or within Premiere, GarageBand, and Logic Pro when exporting.

Posting

This section will be short as instructions for posting can be found at the sites that host podcasts. Libsyn, PodBean, Buzzsprout, and SimpleCast are sites that host the files for a podcast. These are structured in an RSS feed that parses the metadata from a file. The metadata is then crawled by the apps people use to consume podcasts like Apple Podcasts, Spotify, Amazon Podcasts, Google Play, iHeart Radio, Overcast, Downcast, and even SoundCloud.

Those apps then point to the audio file that's referenced in the feed. Each site has a different process for posting, so pick a platform and then upload the file as a test (test episodes can always be deleted). Take screenshots and write a how-to so the upload is consistent and the person who posts the episode doesn't forget something simple, like the image file. Keep in mind the podcast hasn't been shared with anyone yet, so tinker around—delete, readd, and find the best experience. Eventually this part will take five to ten minutes but plan to tinker around for an hour or two just to get all the kinks worked out. Never, ever, ever bother to try to build and host this stuff—the feed requirements and categories change over time, and it's best to just give someone else $0–20 per month to host the stuff.

Marketing

At this point, there's a podcast file sitting on a site somewhere. There's a collection of other episodes to run through. Now it's possible to figure out about how much time it takes to record moving forward and budget time. The full costs to build this marketing asset are known. The next step is to decide if the juice is worth the squeeze. The work done thus far could be an audio blog post and the initiative abandoned. There's been no commitment just yet. Chances are there are enough people at an organization with enough to say that it's time to make the commitment to routinely ship episodes, though.

The first few episodes will take much longer to produce than those that are published once the podcast has been going for a year or three. Evaluate the lack of focus on other projects against the morale boost often seen by letting teams have a little fun with a podcast. Provided the podcast is a good idea, now it's time to put a little push behind it. This comes in the form of posting links to social media accounts, embedding episodes in blog posts (provided the security and compliance is up to snuff), and giving credit to those who put the work into making the podcast into a reality. This is when the podcast becomes a commitment.

Solicit feedback. Conduct a survey to give listeners (and others at the company) the chance to identify what they want to hear about. This might be a short SurveyMonkey form or just poling people at conferences or online. This feedback (like most feedback) is invaluable. Feedback can be used beyond the context of the podcast and even drive feature development. Keep in mind though, when we put ourselves out there, we have to expect some hard things to hear. But it's better to know what people are thinking and address it than to be oblivious.

Consider using the assets created to compliment other efforts. Maybe an episode finds its way into a newsletter or at the bottom of a blog post (e.g., a CTA of "Listen to our team talk about this on the podcast"). We can even bring webcasts in as episodes. At most organizations a podcast should be run with a little help, refinement, guidance, and amplification from marketing but not be a pure-play sales pitch. Be transparent. Be nerdy. Have fun.

Content

Every organization struggles with the right mix when it comes to where we invest our time, money, morale, and focus. Podcasts can increase morale but take time and of course a little focus away from day jobs. They are also a great way to socialize initiatives within an organization. Look for a diverse cast of guests who can talk about their jobs and how they contribute to the purpose of the organization. Showcase people of all types and from all areas of the organization. Do so while educating the public on a given topic, how industries are being shaped, and occasionally news from within the organization. Episodes should be as much for internal teams as they are for customers. As others who work in the company get a voice, the company becomes less a faceless website.

Don't exclude anyone. Each person in each team should bring their whole selves to work. There are areas we should avoid with professional podcasts (looking at you, 2020s politics). Keep this word in mind when moving ahead with podcasting plans: authenticity. The most important part about a company-run podcast is to give current and potential customers a glimpse into the inner workings of an organization. This isn't to say that trade secrets should be given away or non-disclosures violated. But we do want to connect. In a time of learning to work in a fragmented world where new ways of connecting are evolving, a podcast is a great way for the individuals in a company to connect with those the company serves. Companies don't make those kinds of relationships; people do.

Finally, if the organization chooses not to run with the podcast, make sure the individuals who want to are empowered to do it on their own (maybe with a company email address so there's a little control). Might just turn out great, even if we ultimately end up with less control if that happens!

YouTube

A lot of digital marketing plans include YouTube as part of the plan. When those who wrote the plan discuss how YouTube fits into the plan, getting started again seems to be the hardest part. This might be because there's a gap in understanding what to expect from running campaigns on YouTube, or it might be due to trying to weaponize a digital medium we don't fully understand. The next sections help guide those conversations.

Set Expectations

Let's start with what to expect. YouTube is a place to post videos. The title, description, and metadata for those videos are then picked up by search engines. Do not expect to post videos that have millions of views unless there are millions of followers or unless promoting the videos millions of times. When promoting videos, expect to pay $.10 to $.30 for a click, if not more.

The cost for those clicks will go up or down based on the production value and how closely the video matches what people search for. Production value means quality. The quality of a video is not just the resolution (although that is part of it) but extends to how professional and interesting the video is. This is because Google analyzes trends to see how many people watch the video and for how long. The cost for a click is then adjusted based on what drives eyeballs to stay on the YouTube site. Search engine optimization (SEO) works the same way.

A common misconception among marketers is that if they post YouTube videos, people will magically find them. They might, but they probably won't. If people do find them, they might not be the people who are going to buy specific products. So then, what should the expectation be? Expect YouTube to be a great place to store videos to embed into a site. Beyond that, expect YouTube to drive traffic to a site based on how well the content that's uploaded manages to capture and retain viewers. That will require a strategy and some luck.

Strategy and Tactics

The strategy should be based on what is known about the people that want to watch our videos. This is different for every persona in every industry, so there's no one-stop shop. Most companies benefit the most from a strategy that helps inform an industry (keying off the consultative sales approaches outlined in the previous chapter). The more generic the content, the more a strategy there is about brand awareness, the more granular the content, the more a strategy is about nurturing existing contacts in the funnel.

A good strategy can be summed up in a sentence, like a mission statement, but including a purpose. These might resemble the following:

- Create content that informs <insert any old industry here> technologists about up-and-coming news to increase overall awareness of the brand.

- Build explainer videos that show how to use each feature of the product to cross-post to knowledge base articles.

- Develop content to showcase features around upcoming releases.

- Interview key industry leaders to help lift the acumen about the space for the whole vertical.

- Provide necessary training to prepare viewers to take a certification course.

- Develop videos that show how to perform common tasks to increase service calls.

At this point, there are a few ideas for how to capture new viewers but also provide helpful content. We don't want vanity metrics, though. If a video produces a million views but converts no leads, then the company might make a little money off content rather than products. That's a fine strategy, if that is the strategy. Just make sure to be deliberate (while willing to pivot if needed).

Don't attempt multiple strategies at first. Pick one thing and do it well. It's easy to add more content later (expand the strategy) if there's a good return on our investment, or initiatives can be cut back if not. Don't overpromise. If something is promoted as a monthly news update, then plan to produce content monthly. It's usually best to start at two- to four-week intervals and increase provided the commitment isn't too much, once there's a good rhythm and reason to do so. First, let's look at some common strategies to drive traffic based on YouTube:

- *Explainer videos*: In the past couple of years, we the authors have rebuilt the carburetor in a lawn mower, written complex *Dungeons and Dragons* campaigns, replaced the springs in an oven door so it closes properly, and sweated pipes to install shutoff valves in a bathroom. Maybe we're more adventurous with home projects than we've ever been before. That's because enterprising companies posted videos on how to do these tasks. Now, we're probably not going to need to buy their services in the future. However, we might recognize their brand in the future if we need something similar.

- *Industry news series*: These are often little ten- to thirty-minute weekly or monthly updates on happenings in an industry. They work like a news channel. These are most effective in industries where a vendor keeps tabs on the goings-on a bit more than the professionals who are in the field and too busy shoveling poo to buy a shovel. The key with these is to be vendor agnostic in a given space but maybe to end each with a call to action (CTA).

- *Product updates*: Inform customers about updates to products (e.g., a video about those spiffy new features) every few of weeks (on a sprint cadence) or monthly.

- *Interviews*: This is likely better as a podcast, unless they're just customer testimonials we can embed on our site as quick quotes. Most podcasting networks allow posters to cross-post to YouTube when uploading videos as well. Try to get guests to help spread the word about products. This is what marketers often refer to as "reach."

- *Training videos*: Take videos (maybe even product explainer videos) and bolt them together in a way that follows a learning plan. Usually there should be a page on the site that takes viewers through the order to watch videos, like a lesson plan or syllabus.

- *A final destination for miscellaneous content*: No content ever really needs to die. Sure, that bad haircut might look dated, the branding might have been updated since a video was created, or the video might be a little grainy—but someone might find it valuable. It's more important to be valuable than to improve vanity metrics. Dead links to old content also hurt the site's optimization. One great piece of content to include in a YouTube channel is any webinar over a certain age, like six weeks.

There are hundreds of other ways to develop a YouTube presence. But again, to get started, pick one for a minimum of a couple of months and then re-evaluate. Keep in mind each strategy, tactic, or product can have its own collection of videos in what YouTube calls a channel. After there are a few repetitions and the time, money, and focus commitment are better known, more channels can be added later. What each company chooses to build depends on the goals, target audience, and industry. Those should align with the values of the organization. Once the decisions of what makes the most sense for the organization are made, it's time to start building.

Execution

There are some basics we want to knock out before we get started. These will help us avoid early mistakes. This is important: start by creating a brand account with Google. Anyone can create a YouTube channel, but in an organization, multiple people will work in the account eventually. Learn how to set up a brand account at `https://support.google.com/accounts/answer/7001996`.

Once there's an account, set the images and description. Here, state what the purpose is and whom it's for. In the beginning disable comments; once there's some informal feedback, those can be turned on. In a previous section, we laid out some broad instructions on microphones and other equipment for podcasting. Those apply to recording for YouTube as well. Now it's time to create a video. Consider these types of videos:

- *Talking heads*: These recordings are of people talking about some things that matter to an industry. These could be as simple as a Zoom call with a pair of people talking about a subject or the news or as complicated as cameras with people in the same room with rich graphics used in transitions. Usually think about something in the middle. Try and refrain from just using a recorded Zoom. A recorded Zoom call can seem like just watching people have a meeting. Instead, consider enriching the media with slides, screen captures, and/or video clips to be more engaging.

- *Screen recording*: These are most effective when showcasing new features of a product. Try to switch back and forth to the camera every now and then as it keeps a viewer interested. A good rule of thumb is that when talking about a button, where to click on a screen, workflows, or what to put in various places in an app, show the app. When talking about the philosophy behind a feature or the general concepts, show the speaker. Just make sure the audio levels don't seem disjointed.

- *Slides with narration*: PowerPoint, Keynote, or Google Slides makes it easier to create great and compelling presentations than ever. Mix video in natively rather than embedding it in and trying to capture a screen recording. And try to put an image of the presenter (or video of the presenter) into the slides at key places, if not running in a part of the screen the whole time. With or without video of the presenter, this allows for powerful delivery of content without needing a studio. Pro tip: Apple's Keynote comes with a feature to export a deck to a QuickTime movie.

- *Filmed*: For corporate video, there are few things more powerful than footage of a customer in a product into a video. When adding historical context, consider stock video provided proper attribution and licensing is used.

- *Animations and images*: These are usually animated explainer videos, animations in presentations, animation snippets that can be purchased, and even stock animations with an open license. Tools like Apple's iMovie make transitions between these simpler and more compelling than ever. Just don't forget to read the licensing if using existing content.

- *Music and sounds*: Extra audio can make content more interesting. Just make sure not to infringe on any copyrights. This might be an intro song, some audio in a bumper, or sound effects. For this, YouTube has content available at `https://studio.youtube.com/channel/UCitOdZPPipSfa88y9ls3DiQ/music`, or there are plenty of royalty-free sites out there to pull music from. Having said that, we all have friends who are musicians, many of whom would love an excuse to create music that will be used in cool ways!

- *Mixed*: As a team's skills increase (or good outsourced editorial inspires ideas), mixed media content is usually the most compelling and often ends up with the most engaged audiences. Each type of video content can be used in different ways when storytelling. This is more time consuming, but just like when watching the news and seeing a lot of different types of videos, it is often the most interesting to watch.

- *Live video*: The great thing about live video is that viewers rarely expect a high production value. A live interview with a customer or a developer/engineer of a product is a great way to get people watching at a specific time. Just make sure to record it and keep it as someone is likely to always consider it valuable.

A new video can easily be created using the camera in most modern computing devices. A physical, separate camera is often best. Cameras on phones are usually better than those on computers. There are several pieces of software that can be purchased or downloaded to aid in great screen capture video, as well as built-in tools (e.g., the screen recording feature built into QuickTime Player on a Mac). These can also be used to play a slideshow and talk over it. Filmed content can be mixed in, giving a viewer a more real view of what we're discussing. There are plenty of great free or paid image repositories to grab images or short video clips from as well.

The best answer if there's time to produce quality content is usually to create some kind of mixed media that incorporates elements from all these types. Consider a tool like OBS (or Open Broadcaster Software) available at `https://obsproject.com`. OBS can create content with slides or video in the main screen and a still in other areas, switch between them on the fly, have an audio track recorded at the same time, and record talking heads. Simply use a logo in an image file and cut out areas where we'll put boxes for transparencies. It's a great little tool—and free.

Post the First Videos

Each video needs a great title. Don't create clickbait that tricks people into watching videos, but do want to grab the attention of potential viewers. Keep titles to about half the size of a tweet at the max and make sure they're accurate. Keep in mind that around 70% of Google searches include a YouTube video and the title will be what searchers see.

The description should include the desired keywords. Don't stuff keywords where they don't belong but do include them where they can be put in organically. Also consider using them in categories and tags. As more videos get posted (and more importantly, the path from a new lead to a converted lead is clear), we can always home in on the words that drive the type of engagement that converts. One way to get a great description is to add links to timestamps where each new slide starts along with the title of the slide. This will take a few extra minutes for every video posted but is a great way to get more people seeing content.

Make a great title and thumbnail. Thumbnails are the images a viewer sees when looking at a bunch of YouTube videos on YouTube itself or another search engine. The default thumbnail used when posting is often just a random frame. But pick something more eye-catching from the video when possible. Also create a call to action for the video. Every video posted should have a link in the description. Mention the link in the video. For example, "To learn more, click the link in the notes" is an effective ask, or "Sign up for our newsletter using the link provided." Be informative for people watching content but get to a point where they can be messaged to access more content and try to build a more lasting relationship with viewers. One way to reduce the per-video work is to add a video watermark with a Subscribe button. For more on doing so, see `https://support.google.com/youtube/answer/2972003`.

Don't post too many videos at once. If there are four that are finished, consider dripping them out once a week. Future content can come every other week if needed but set the expectation of regularly released content so more people follow a given channel. This might mean using a tool like Sprout Social, those built into Hubspot, or another alternative to schedule content to be released at various times.

Communicate the Content

Some channels cost more than others to run. Once there are a few pieces of content, creators should have a decent understanding of what kind of commitment is being made. The risk is low because there are some videos that can at the least be embedded in a site. There aren't a lot of followers yet. That's next.

There are a number of ways to inform people that there's some stuff they should go watch. Focus on a sampling of those specific to video:

- *CRM*: Most organizations likely have a list of contacts (e.g., a CRM like Salesforce or HubSpot). These can either be leveraged as messaging platforms or synchronized with dedicated messaging suites like Mailchimp. Typically, it's best to just add a snippet about videos to existing campaigns where they are complementary rather than run a campaign for the video. A great way to go about marketing a new channel is to simply write a survey asking what people want more of. A lot of people will go watch, and it won't seem like pandering for views.

- *Collaborators*: Interviewing people with strong followings will get more people watching. That might be their coworkers or professionals in the same industry. Not everyone works at an organization where they're allowed to speak publicly. Look for "thought leaders" and especially customers who are. Look for people who you can help make a thought leader— maybe the ones who are awesome and others just don't know it yet!

- *Embedded players*: Each video can be embedded in other content. This is where the web pages can also display a video. This can allow designers to place a video as gated content or embed it in a blog where more people might find it.

- *Newsletters*: A single video in each newsletter is a great way to keep readers tuned in and get them to open more newsletters later. Any organization not doing a newsletter already is missing a great way to communicate with customers and leads just waiting to get nurtured into customers.

- *Social media*: LinkedIn, Twitter, Facebook, WeChat, Reddit, and other social media outlets provide a route to potentially reach a lot of customers. Social media sites typically embed YouTube videos well. Even if there's not a huge following on social media, it's always good to flex the muscle to automatically post there. Just tailor the message to the intricacies of each social media network.

- *YouTube followers*: At the end of all videos, have a call to action to follow the posting account or subscribe to a channel. This doesn't help to get eyeballs on content in the beginning but helps drive further engagement.

- *Contests*: Not all industries allow gift giving. YouTube loves gifts. These can be used to get others to create content, like a video, leave a comment, share a video, subscribe to a channel, or even fill out a form linked in a description. Just keep an eye out for people just trolling YouTube for freebies.

- *Paid advertising*: This is last as organizations will want to use the other mechanisms to distribute content. Identify content, keywords, and titles that drive the acquisition of new customers. Otherwise, money just gets spent on YouTube or Google ads, and organizations just hope for the best. Experiment with what YouTube calls bumper ads, display ads, overlay ads, and sponsored cards to see which is best for each persona.

Most humans consume content differently than one another. Various personas in each industry might follow similar patterns, but those who create content often consume that content differently than those who consume it. Therefore, our initial attempts may or may not resonate with potential and current customers. Be humble and don't be afraid to ask people what they think and what could be better.

Keep Getting Better

Asking people how to be better is one way to produce better results. Another is to measure the results and produce content that is tailored to the audience. Tools like Google Analytics and Hootsuite will help get there, and the time invested in seeing how viewers interact with content is always time well spent. As the YouTube channel matures, also create a channel trailer. This explains how a brand is impactful to customers. Once there's engagement, spend time customizing channel banners, adding captions and translations, and really digging into YouTube analytics.

Don't just look for numbers that validate opinions when measuring content. Show humility and look for where a result didn't achieve the goals of an initiative. It's easy to look for the successes. They should certainly be celebrated, but keep looking for ways to help people in an industry get better at what they do, to reach more customers, to gain visibility into their organization, to put products in markets faster, to produce less errors, and to be more efficient. That starts with looking for ways to do the same for ourselves, even on YouTube.

Search Engine Optimization

SEO is short for search engine optimization, sometimes referred to as organic search. This is where organizations look to increase the amount of traffic to a website and specifically look to get the type of desired traffic. There are a lot of sites out there—and even more people who look at sites.

458

Having a site that gets people who want to buy a product is a huge part of the success many a startup sees at the top of their marketing funnel. SEO is one way to get higher natural search results without paying for ads or other forms of display advertising.

There are a lot of books, guides, pages, and courses to help guide creators who want to have a page that jumps up in rankings. The tactics change quickly, but the strategies remain constant after more than 20 years of emerging technology. The most important strategy: content. Bill Gates said it best in the title of his 1996 essay, "Content is King," and then a couple of Stanford students Sergey Brin and Larry Page added high-quality links back to a site as a part of the strategy a little later when they created BackRub, named after those links. They would rename that graduate student project to Google (which they ironically thought through in a building named after Gates).

Content and Links

Search engines index content and then use machine learning (originally using an Eigen matrix) to match search queries with content that matches what people search for. They rank the information based on complex algorithms that are mostly focused on the content of sites and the links that point to and from the site. The more links and the more content specific to the search terms, the higher a listing. Simple.

Simple until you get into the mechanics. Then it's ever-changing, and anyone that thinks they truly know what to do to maintain high listing is just kidding themselves–although, for those true to the strategies, there's a good shot at maintaining high rankings when each round of changes happen. Given that search engines like Google and Microsoft's Bing have constantly evolving algorithms, making the site easy to crawl and user-friendly is really where the rubber meets the road. There are entire books on those mechanics.

Define the Audience

Be clear about who the target customer is. This often includes terms like "cohort" or "persona." When we said "type" of traffic earlier, what we meant are people in the target audience. If selling a piece of software for a given industry, this would be the people who would actually buy or influence the decision to turn them into a customer. Be as specific as possible when defining an audience. Some things to think about are the type of company, the job title, and how the audience uses the Web to find content. From there, establish some goals for how the audience should interact with sales and marketing efforts. Also define a customer journey through the lens of the site.

Define the Goal

SEO is constantly changing and requires work to maintain rankings. So why bother with it? That's going to be different for every organization. The more an organization can define that, the more tailored the flow of the site to achieve those goals. "We want more customers" isn't specific enough here. Instead, get a little more depth and be deliberate about the journey the person searching for content should take on becoming a customer.

Here are a few common goals:

- *Sales*: Capture a lead for sales using a contact form for nurturing or a demo.

- *Downloads*: Download a piece of software (e.g., direct to an app page on Apple or Google) or download gated content (e.g., a white paper).

- *Direct purchase*: Buy a piece of software or service.

- *Email signup*: Capture a lead for nurturing (e.g., to sign up for a newsletter).

- *Phone calls*: Have a potential customer call to make an order or get more information.

- *Locale*: Get people to visit a location.

Once each site's purpose is understood, it's time to map the journey from content people search for to how a visitor will become a customer. If knowing the audience's intent is one side of the SEO coin, delivering it in a way search engine crawlers can find and understand is the other. One way to plot the trajectory is through the call to action from each point to the next.

The Call to Action

Once a person finds a site, a goal is to follow their journey. A simplistic path might be to go from reading a blog post to viewing a pricing page and then to signing up for a demo. Or the journey might have a number of other steps. Marketing got them to the site amid the billions of other pieces of content out there, and now it's time to help them on their path to becoming a sales lead, downloading an app, or signing up for a trial.

Each piece of content then needs a call to action to the next leg of the journey. At the end of each blog post, add a simple paragraph, sentence, or button that points visitors to the next piece of content to read or direct them to click a button like "Request a Free Quote." The form or page is then the next leg of the journey. All the crawling, ranking, and indexing isn't going to do much good if we don't tell the visitor what to do next.

Crawlers

There are tons of tiny robots out there called crawlers. These crawlers don't really care about calls to action, audiences, or goals. Instead, they read the content on a site and put the content into a database. The search engine that sent the crawlers then indexes the content. It parses out headers, page titles, text, tags, URLs, and links (incoming and outgoing), follows a site map if there is one, and catalogs anything else the crawler can get access to. Without doing any work other than to make sure the site is available to crawlers (e.g., from a backlink or a manual submission to the search engine), a site naturally starts showing up on searches, although probably low in the order of results displayed in the beginning.

The more links that point into the site and the more relative the search to the words on the site, the higher the rankings in search orders become. Keep in mind that the reason most love the big search engines is that when they search for content, there are good results. Most want that from a site. Headers and tags (somewhat synonymous with keywords) help further define what the site is about.

Don't exclude searches. It's better to have ten people come to a site and click a button to buy a product than to have 100 people visit a site and only have one buy the product. The way to improve conversion rates is to make content relevant to people whom the site resonates with and make it clear what they should do. That clarity is provided by writing relevant content and then optimizing that content with headers, tags, categories, etc. Another is to have sites in the same field or topic link back to sites.

SERPs

One way that search engines display what crawlers find is SERPs, or Search Engine Results Pages. These are more dynamic forms of search results that show answer boxes. We've all seen these when we search for sports scores, weather, definitions, etc. These are places where a search engine can parse content from the Web in a way that the content can be displayed without someone needing to click a site.

The reason these are important is that sites like Wikipedia, sports franchises, or IMDb will always appear in an answer box before natural, organic content. It's best not to worry about competing with that type of traffic (unless it's the goal of the site). Instead, focus on how to appear in the top page or three for given search results that can be competed with.

Research the Competition

Most are not going to enter an entirely new market. There will either be incumbents in a market, or there will be other organizations adjacent in a market. Use their hard work to catch up to them, see what works, and hopefully get a little insight into how to improve.

Competitors for clicks who might be friends or partners in adjacent markets have sites as well. There are plenty of tools that can isolate all the backlinks to their sites, search terms people click to find them, pull a list of blog titles, and see what headers or texts on sites work. These can help jumpstart efforts. Yes, every company should feel they are different and special, and that messaging can be added to the site—but just because we think we're better doesn't mean we shouldn't pick up where they left off.

Find an SEO Consultant

Now that some informed and deliberate decisions can be made, many should outsource the SEO mechanics. Unless there's someone on the team that's an SEO guru, this probably shouldn't be done in-house initially. A day or a week of time from an expert is far better than spending weeks or months trying to do this stuff alone as going up in rankings takes time. The sooner the process accelerates, the better.

The best SEO experts come from referrals. Friends or colleagues who have had good luck with search engines are good resources to ask for a trusted resource. Those who helped adjacent companies or ones in other successful industries are a good start as well. Marketing teams are often happy to share whom they worked with. Keep those people in the rolodex to help hire internal marketing experts in the future. People who are happy to share are some of the best marketers to stay in touch with for a variety of reasons.

There are a lot of charlatans in the SEO world. Finding someone trustworthy who can understand the target customer and communicate easily is important. Always talk to at least three to five consultants and make sure they can show how they've successfully worked with companies to achieve the desired outcomes. Look for specific recommendations like improving page loading times, adding headers, editing headers to match search terms, putting an SSL certificate on the site, building a mobile interface, improving URL structures, and adding images. If there are questions about what something means or the value, simply ask. Don't be afraid to look like a novice. This should be a great learning opportunity for founders.

This is important. Great SEO is one of the highest priorities for any company. Once the outsourced group provides instructions of what to do, complete their tasks in a timely manner. Building a sales and marketing funnel that works is often even more important than new features, because the revenue generated is the air companies breathe. Treat it as such.

Content Is King

Now it's time to build that content. That can be outsourced as well, but to make good content that resonates often requires deeper knowledge of the industry. Start with a grab bag of titles (which might be similar to those generated for the webinars, YouTube videos, and podcasts earlier in this chapter). They should match search terms in phases of the customer journey. Make content for users to read, not for search engines to crawl. Don't just stuff keywords into articles. That won't get backlinks to content or further reach for social media that promotes the content. The goal is to get others to want to come back for more.

The competitive analysis helps understand what competitors write about and what drives visitors to their site. Now it's time to provide better content! Be succinct and use accessible language (e.g., by reducing acronyms and complex sentence structures). The content should match the intent of the person who searches for it. Find ways to align that intent with good, succinct answers that brand the company as experts while also making a pitch to buy products or services.

Think of intent as informational (looking for information on a topic), navigational (looking for more content or where to have a need met), or transactional (looking to make a purchase or obtain a good). Match each piece of content with fulfilling one of those intents to keep visitors on the site. For example, if someone is looking for vendors in an adjacent market, supply them with a fairly vendor-agnostic list of great vendors. This gets them further on their journey to make a purchase while branding the company as an expert in the market. If the intent is to make a transaction (buy what's being sold), then reduce the friction to do that as much as possible. That might include a landing page to buy or to get a quote straight off a page that's been optimized to provide information about products.

Aligning content with the intent of the person searching means understanding the journey to buy. The ability to leverage SEO to capture the eyeballs of people who look for information about a given subject matter is the first step—but the rankings will shoot up if they actually find what they need on the site. Anyone who captures eyeballs with clickbait without fulfilling that social contract will suffer in the long run. Always be able to answer how any content published is valuable to visitors. In other words, be as deliberate as possible while experimenting with different words, structures, and topics. Note the purpose so it's not forgotten later.

Now that there's a list of articles to write, block off a couple of hours a week for someone on the team to produce that content. It's usually best to spread this across people on the team so no one gets burned out on producing content. Others will appreciate the ability to make a name for themselves. Release content on a schedule (like every Tuesday at 10 AM) that matches when the cohort has time to browse the Web or look for what's offered. Put content creation and release into a calendar, known as a content calendar, when there's seasonally applicable content, when content can align to events the company participates in, and when content helps promote releases or changes to products.

Don't copy content from other sources, hide text in content, hide links, or cloak (show crawlers something different than what is rendered on a page). Those create red flags for search engines. Instead, do the work and focus on what makes the product valuable and learn to engage with customers. Content generation is a muscle. The earlier in the lifecycle of a company where the muscle gets trained, the better.

Getting Links

It's time to start getting people to link back to our content once content generation is on autopilot. There are a lot of ways to do that. In general, avoid any trickery or link farms/schemes. Instead, make titles that are simple and relevant to a person who looks for the topic. It's also important to make sure to stay within the guidelines of Google and Bing:

- *Google*: https://support.google.com/business/answer/3038177?hl=en

- *Bing*: www.bing.com/webmaster/help/webmaster-guidelines-30fba23a

Use the list of links from competitors and adjacent partners to contact each and ask them to add the site to a list or write about the product. In exchange, offer an extended trial or free product. Continue to look for net-new sources long term, especially those with high page rankings. Focus on getting social media mentions. That's a good sign the marketing efforts are working, and search engines will pick these up (although a mention on a post is better). Social mentions are also validating that the product itself has legs, and influencers in micro-markets are important to win over to the cause. Social media also helps with morale.

Notice that getting links was last on this list. This is because the priority is to be deliberate about the content created and how the product is positioned on pages, and the research about how others go about the same helps inform those. Define the customer journey and be clear and honest about the intent rather than just haphazardly waste time. Guide people through the top of the funnel with concise calls to action. Have an engaging presence that appeals to the desired buyers. Once that's all locked down, the links will often just need a little nudge in the right direction.

The Long Tail

SEO is one of the best marketing tools available to any company. It continues to provide a return on investment long after the efforts are done. The SEO work also helps refine the search terms companies buy when it's time to spend money on paid search and display advertising. Organic search is more authentic and more credible, and people click the organic results at a much higher rate than paid results. Paid search trickles off when companies stop paying, whereas the good content produced for organic search is much more timeless.

SEO has other uses as well. Arm sellers with the search terms that work to close actual paying customers. They can be sprinkled into product pitches and help define the product roadmap when in the hands of a savvy product team. To get there, it's important to see who is following along the predefined journey and spread that information internally. This means analytics. Each search engine has a great analytical engine. After all, the more they help, the more likely companies are to spend money with them.

Advertising

We've discussed SEO and more organic forms of making sure potential customers find a site on the Internet. That's a task a founder can do on their own, but one that might be more targeted if outsourced. As with pretty much every discipline in this book, the more advanced and costly the initiative, the more likely companies will build, buy, or borrow resources to get to the next stage of growth.

Companies level up, and the disciplines within the company level up right along with them. Or at least, they need to. One of those disciplines that often gets outsourced early on and then brought in-house later is advertising and marketing. These become more hyperspecialized and sometimes mechanical processes where large sums could be spent developing an organic skillset in-house if existing experts aren't leveraged. In short, companies can make content like blog posts, videos, podcasts, and other creative assets, but when it's time to spend money to promote that content, it's often best to let specialists do what they do.

Early forms of online advertising involved buying banner ads and paying a monthly sum to have the banner on a site. The demand quickly outstripped the supply. Banners got dynamic, and advertisers paid for a given number of impressions. Then came paid search, now the dominant form of online advertising.

Paid Search

Paid search is advertising a good or service in the search results of a search engine. The most common vendor of paid search is Google through the Google Ads platform (previously known as AdWords). These are those listings in a search that have the word *Sponsored* and represent a large portion of advertising spent at many startups.

Google also has product listing ads, which are the carousel of products that match a search, but as this book is geared for software, let's skip that and go straight to buying a spot on the page with all those search results, which is referred to as a Search Engine Results Page (SERP). It's also worth mentioning that while Google has well north of 95% of the market share for search traffic, many have found success with Microsoft's Bing, and the buying motion and results are similar to those of Google. Advertisers can also buy display ads on most social networks, including LinkedIn, Twitter, Facebook, Instagram, etc. With all these options, it's hard to know what will work for a given company or product.

Start small—but big enough to be able to measure results. One important aspect is to get an idea of what to expect from a larger campaign. That's likely to take spending a few hundred dollars a day or week to get enough clicks to be able to analyze the results. Much more and there's likely to be lots of waste; much less and it's likely not to get enough traffic. The work done to research what content to create is a great starting point. Another important step, covered further in the section called "Measure, Measure, Measure" of this chapter, is to get as much telemetry as possible about who is coming through a paid search or display advertising channel. That means something on the site like a Google tracking code to be able to get insights into what terms are working based on how people navigate through the site once they visit.

Starting small doesn't mean not being deliberate about what's done. Set a goal, for example, to get a base cost to acquire a customer through advertising efforts. A simple set of goals might be to get a certain number of leads to click ads and then a percentage of those to fill out a contact form so they can be nurtured, open a live chat, or make a purchase. The first two are often steps to the third. Don't let great results for the earlier goals hide the fact that every company needs customers to buy their products.

Next, analyze the keywords to bid on. Notice that says bidding. The incredible innovation that made Google what they are today was that the Google ads system works by having parties bid to buy which ads are displayed. The more people that compete for the words, the more expensive they get. The more that click the ad, the more that companies will pay, so be clinical in the bidding process and limit the spend every day. When using Google, start that journey at `https://ads.google.com/home/tools/keyword-planner/` and compare it with third-party tools. Keep in mind the more targeted a given set of keywords, the less likely there will be a lot of organizations who bid on them. Brainstorm a lot of keywords and then experiment with different combinations of them.

The keyword planner will help get in front of a baseline for how much will be spent. Before any words or phrases are purchased, build landing pages for specific sets of keywords to provide more targeted messaging and test how effective the next steps in the journey work. Many Customer Relationship Management (CRM) tools have landing pages with features built into them, so get tracking codes on those and set up a contact capture form (like "See more information about our amazing products by giving us your email address"). Getting the tracking codes early will provide more historical context. Integration with the CRM will likely have a second view to see analytics as well as keep from duplicative data entry tasks as leads flow through the journey laid out for them to become customers.

Once the basic pieces are in place, it's time to buy a few keywords and see how they work. If there's a lot of traffic coming in and the conversions just aren't there, the next sales stage is to optimize the landing pages. Think through what the experience is like to visit the landing page after searching for the given keywords. Is the offer enticing enough to provide information? Is there too big a jump from each phase to the next? Test different orders of information and buttons and consider gated content (described later) as a means of capturing customer information.

At this point the hope is to have gone beyond the baseline costs established earlier. If click costs can get down by 20%, then that are 20% more clicks that can be purchased with the same budget. Hopefully those convert to even more customers. A/B test campaigns to see which work better than others. This involves creating two campaigns in the Google Campaign Manager—and likely pointing them at different custom landing pages. At this point refine the language and images displayed and possibly the offer (e.g., test pricing, what the customer is sent if they provide an email address, duration of trials, etc.).

Practice good habits early. Analyze the traffic and take steps to develop better calls to action every day. Hire a consultant to at a minimum help get started—that will save countless hours building campaigns and lots of gold pieces to bid on keywords that don't work. If the plan calls for staff to manage display ads and paid search, then focus the time with the consultant on acquiring the knowledge to manage such a person. If the plan doesn't call for a staff position but instead for outsourcing, cycle through working with a few consultants until one is found that might be able to take over the whole process as a managed service or using a retainer.

There are entire books dedicated to search engine and display advertising, and every founder should read two of them at a minimum, no matter how quickly hiring or outsourcing happens. The ability to talk the talk at a minimum will help better manage whoever is actually clicking the buttons once the return on our investment to start pumping more and more money into campaigns is understood.

Social Media

The social media thing isn't just for millennials to complain about their dungeon master. Anyone can build, own, and run a presence without the help of a nephew or a snotty hipster consultant. Help is always welcome, and input should be solicited. For over a decade, people have talked about "social strategy" or been asked what is being done with "social." Can social media really increase sales? Yes. What are the best social media outlets for various goals your company has? That's according to what the goals are, which should initially be to add a lead to the top of the funnel.

Let's look at some examples of ways that real organizations can use social media to bolster sales:

- **Get all the social properties for the name of the organization.** Try to use the same name across social networks like Instagram, Pinterest, Facebook, LinkedIn, Twitter, and even emergent networks like Clubhouse. Even if they aren't used, get the accounts before someone else does.

- **Run a photo submission contest on Instagram.**
  Provide a hashtag that people are supposed to use to
  enter a contest and then post the winner when the
  contest is over. This type of outreach helps expand the
  funnel and get the brand in front of more eyeballs.

- **Create a Group on LinkedIn.** LinkedIn Groups are
  for professionals who share common interests to
  communicate about them. This is a great way to find
  leads. Just don't be too spammy.

- **Use geography to bring business to us.** Post a
  temporary location to get a free prize or entry
  in a drawing on Twitter, Swarm, and Facebook.
  Additionally, consider running a special giving the
  mayor of a location on Swarm (or whatever the modern
  equivalent is) a special deal, as an added little bonus
  for repeat business.

- **Use smaller networks to get the message to micro-
  markets.** For example, a beer company should have
  a special badge for Untappd. Okay, not many people
  reading this will be from beer companies, but the point
  is to think of analogs for the specific industry. Is there a
  social network (or Slack, Discord, or Telegram channel)
  for the industry? Can something cool and interesting
  be done to promote the brand there? If there isn't a
  network or channel, creating one might be a great way
  to reach the market as well.

- **Drive business to the website.** Tweet blog posts,
  post them to LinkedIn, add hashtags, and keep track
  of which of the hashtags drive people to the site. Yes,
  that means a blog will be required. And, no, don't post

any tweets on the company account about upcoming elections as we don't want to potentially turn off any new customers we might be able to go off and win.

- **Stay on top of trends.** Vines are gone. There are newer trends, such as Cinemagraphs, and being on those trends can bring a little extra boost to get the organization in front of companies who might be looking to purchase service similar to ours. At the very least, they'll give the staff pride when done right.

- **Claim the address with Google.** If there's a retail front or people might find the business based on a physical location, make sure it's correct across all the networks, including Yahoo, Facebook, Google, etc.

- **Solicit feedback on networks like Yelp.** Everyone wants to think their businesses are perfect. Make sure to have a thick skin since it's not possible to please all the people all the time. For most, it's helpful to have some good feedback for people to read. More important, those stars. Give people a good experience, and they'll give us some great reviews.

- **Analyze the results.** Get software that aggregates and possibly analyzes the responses from efforts on these networks. That cuts out guessing about what's working and what isn't, which can cause people to think what they want rather than look for real insights.

Most of these networks make their money from social networking, which can be a great way to bolster other activities. Even more impactful, once there are followers on these networks, is to provide a clear and concise call to action for each thing we do, as well as a larger, overarching social strategy that fits with your customer base. Make sure to represent authenticity and, again, be okay with any negative feedback that comes back through the social channels, as negative responses will be unavoidable.

Dark Social: Old-School Paid Advertising

The advertising industry has evolved rapidly over the course of the past few decades. Many often over-index on newer models of advertising or forget the fundamentals of old-school advertising that are still true today. But the quant (short for quantitative) in each of us loves to try to employ growth hacks through online ads, even if privacy options on many devices now block advertisers from getting creepy amounts of information from people. On one hand, this is to be applauded; on the other, it's harder to sell sometimes.

Unlike the chaotic evil characters, err on the side of not being creepy. The power of digital advertising however is offset with the intrusions into privacy that we are finding increasingly problematic. So many networks work hard to sell ads and not data (or at least, avoid ads based on ill-obtained data). The timelines and streams of data shown are built to place relevant information at the top, backed by machine learning based on posts, taps, and searches. That data is also used to display ads. As advertisers this is great. As people who consume content, the jury might still be out.

Not all social networks are on computers. *Dark social* is a term usually applied to the shares through text messages, private instant messaging apps, word of mouth, and other places where it isn't possible to see where a link came from. This often just says Direct in analytics platforms. It can also be used to describe a brand as seen through some more traditional advertising. Figuring out which is which is important as it helps decide where to put more and more of those gold pieces (especially as they become platinum pieces) when buying ads.

Buy Ads on Podcasts

Some organizations pay obscene amounts of money to large podcasts for advertising products. Well, some people do it because they love a topic as well. Founders are often subject matter experts and understand well what podcasts are popular for their customers (or potential customers).

This should hopefully sound redundant: when advertising on podcasts, do so in places where customers listen. As with most advertising, organizations that serve a specific geography should stick to local media outlets. Look for podcasts that talk about the specific city, or cities. The analog in software is to look for podcasts that cater to the industries supported. If the software appeals to a specific vertical industry, then chances are that there are podcasts for it. Remember that just because a founder or someone in marketing likes a podcast doesn't mean that there will be a good ROI from sponsoring it. Vanity can be dangerous when buying ads.

Speaking of ROI, many podcasts can be thought of as dark social. This basically means that listeners of the podcast who visit the site don't come from the website of the podcast. Instead, they'll be attributed as "Direct" traffic in Google Analytics. Marketers should want to track all of the things! A great strategy to try to track the impact of an ad campaign on a given podcast would be to have the URL used to visit the website reflect a URL specific to that podcast. This isn't natural, so consider offering a deal to use that special URL. For example, visit myawesomesoftware. com/nameofpodcast to receive 10% off your first purchase. Everyone who listens to podcasts has heard this with other podcasts already, but it's worth calling out specifically and try to quantify results.

Podcast sponsorships usually come in three types: pre-roll (before the podcast), mid-roll (in the middle of the podcast), and post-roll (at the end of the podcast). Go for one of the first two when possible. Expect to pay between $100 and $10,000 per episode, and always run the ad for a few episodes. The pre-roll is usually the best (although that can be different per podcast). Additionally, consider offering to support specific initiatives, like to fund making a text version of the podcast for accessibility.

Any ad purchased will require a script to be read for the ad on the podcast. For early-stage companies, these are usually introducing the company like what is done in an elevator pitch. Keep it short so there's room to mention the custom URL for the podcast the ad is running on and the offer. It's usually best if the podcast hosts read the ad, so make sure to listen to it once before it goes out to see if there are any errors in pronunciation (if possible). Later-stage companies often tie each read of a sponsorship into a given campaign. This helps tie it into other assets created to align with the podcast.

Podcasts will have an email address. That email address will likely respond with a rate card if asked. Most podcasts desperately want to sell advertising, so they'll cut a deal if advertisers just ask nicely. Always ask for discounts, as it can't hurt to ask. Not doing so can just leave money on the table.

Radio

There are a lot of places to put an advertising budget. One of the most traditional is radio. Radio can be a tough sell given all the much more data-driven options we have available as advertisers today (especially for software companies with data-driven leaders). As with all forms of advertising, consider this: does the persona we want to buy our product listen to the radio? If we think potential customers listen to specific radio programs, then sponsoring programs with a show can be a great place to spend that advertising budget.

Consider this: Mailchimp sponsored NPR shows for years. It's hard to listen to an episode of Marketplace on NPR without hearing about at least one site or piece of software. That's because advertising on the radio can work. It can be expensive, and some studies indicate listeners need to hear a brand three times before they'll look for it, which means that many an ad will need to be run three times to get the full impact.

Radio also doesn't provide an immediate form of analytics for a site. Yes, if there are 1,000 searches for the brand a day and then 3,000 on a day when there's a radio promotion, it's easy to ascertain that the additional traffic is from the ad (given it was the only ad). Don't attribute all 3,000 hits and the new accounts created from them to those ads unless the visitor indicates they came through the ad. A lot of factors can come into play, like someone might have mentioned it online and they were where those visitors came from. This is why a compelling offer that helps obtain information as to how people found the site is important. For example, let's say the first month or two is free for people that use the special URL like mygreatsoftware.com/marketplace.

Radio advertising isn't cheap (well, some hyper-local advertising can be cheap). It's hard to get quantifiable metrics on dark social like radio. If it's a challenge to work with, why is the medium still around, given that most radio is paid for by advertising? Because it still works for certain industries. Those with a limited budget should probably focus on online advertising, especially when there are great sponsorships that are niche to a given set of customers. When there's money left over or when the company has grown to the point that it costs more to pay a staff member to uncover niche areas to spend advertising dollars than it costs to pay for larger spots, then look at mediums like radio and print.

The nice thing about radio advertising is that a lot of people who work in businesses are trapped in their cars while getting to and from work. Repetitive brainwashing to a captive audience like that will over time build brand awareness. Another nice aspect of radio is that the sellers are pretty old-school and often capable of providing substantial discounts. When a great place to advertise has been uncovered, call to get pricing, and no matter what they say, simply respond that it's outside the budget. It's easy to say found extra dollars were found later, but chances are there is a lower price point to be haggled to. Never feel bad calling for pricing—it's what their sales team is paid to do and can be surprising both how cheap and how expensive spots can run according to the station.

Print

Print advertising usually includes ads found in magazines, newspapers, and other printed mediums. It's hard for a software company to get print advertising right. Print can work better for a local brick-and-mortar store where a mass mailer can drive foot traffic. No matter how good a job is done to create the ads, many print advertisements go straight into a trash receptacle.

There are exceptions when it comes to print advertising. An invitation to an open house is a great way for a support company that operates in a community to make contacts or help find bootstrapped outsourced development work to fund product development. The concept of an invitation can be extended to a movie night, axe throwing contest, or other marketing events. Another exception would be to send a thank you card as a reminder we exist when making new contacts, especially if the thank you card is handwritten.

Another aspect of print advertising is trade magazines. Most have moved to online versions, but some still ship and can be a good way to find customers. Founders will likely be domain experts in a given field and able to navigate the best places to purchase ads. However, as covered through each section of this area on offline advertising, make a compelling offer to get people to type in a special URL to a landing page to get some analytics on performance. That provides the ability to track the performance of each ad in each channel over time.

Finally, have any print advertising professionally prepared. At a minimum, have ads (print and digital) professionally reviewed. Unlike online ads, the smallest details can be blown out of proportion when found in a newspaper or magazine (or if black and white, there are special considerations). As with radio ads, there's probably a lot of haggle room, so always try—and at a minimum, try to get the magazine or newspaper to do any graphic design work as a part of the package.

Coupons, Sales, and Specials

Coupons work for some industries and types of customers and not others. Apple rarely provides coupons or discounts off the cost of a given product. But most of founders aren't starting the next Apple (no matter how lofty the rhetoric with investors). When just getting started out or building out a new company, it can be useful to get a few new customers by offering some kind of a public-facing discount. When flush with new customers (like Apple), there's never really a reason to offer discounts. Or is there?

That doesn't mean there aren't promos to drive customers to a special landing page when using offline advertising–or even online ads. The offer doesn't have to be some game changer, but it should be enticing and have a sense of urgency that drives the desired behavior without seeming desperate. Examples include

- *Something for free permanently*: Dropbox gave extra drive space to users for using special URLs or referring friends to the service.

- *Temporarily reduced prices*: These could be an extended trial or half off for a period of time.

- *Badges*: There was a time when every site looked to gamify their experience. For anyone who has built such a system, a landing page could have nothing free, except a badge, skin, etc.

- *Physical giveaways*:These might be T-shirts, tote bags, or another marketing swag.

According to the type of work done or service we provide, a site like Groupon can fit the need of landing some sweet new clients. The conversion rates on those are low, as follow-on business, but might be worth an experiment. There also aren't many companies that leverage those types of sites for business services, so assume a primarily consumer customer, which might be the target customer. Even people in businesses are consumers.

To get into larger businesses, try offering a discount on an annual contract instead. Consider using an ad in a business journal, print advertising, banner ads on a site, or even a listing for a journal. Again, use a special URL or UTM for each medium so the ROI is easily tracked and the follow-on activities easily reported on in different ways. This is key. Let's say there are hundreds of clicks on an ad but no transactions. That usually means the messaging or price is off. The same can happen when the wrong types of phone calls come in if there's a phone number in a listing, which is covered in the next section.

The Wrong Calls

Every adventuring party turns down the wrong hallway in a dungeon here and there. One problem that can arise with advertising is that the phone or emails light up with tons of customers—but they all want something totally different than what we're selling. When this happens, there are a few options.

If all those customers want the same thing, then some companies will go ahead and offer that. After all, the offer is right, and an addressable market with an appropriate product is hard to find. Pivots happen all the time for exactly this reason. If all the customers want something different, then the message might need to be tailored to get more detailed information about the offer and why it exists. Too many random inquiries are a great problem to have but something that should be fixed pretty quickly, or the cost to acquire customers will be far too high due to cost per click and the lead qualification cost.

Whether they are good potential customers or not, make sure to respond to every person who reaches out. For starters, it's the right thing to do. If that's not enough, if there's no response, a bad impression can be made on someone that might be a potential customer someday. Even if the response is that they're not the right potential buyer, they'll appreciate it and may be able to put the company in touch with the right buyer at their organization.

To simplify responses, use a standard template in the CRM. Also, if there are enough to warrant it, look for a vendor to redirect these inquiries to. Forming relationships with other organizations is a great opportunity to understand the ecosystem we play in and get a better understanding of market conditions. That can help with comps for valuations and potentially with mergers and acquisitions way down the road. Finally, forming alliances with another vendor can establish bilateral referral business including the potential for additional kickers like marketing development funds (MDFs).

Marketing Development Funds

Chances are that companies who have customers can sell products for or align with a partner. Many of the largest tech companies like Microsoft, Cisco, and Apple provide something known as marketing development funds (or MDFs) for those who do sell their products. They can also help sell our products through marketplaces.

Sometimes all a company has to do is check in with partners to see if they can get MDFs for a campaign and could end up getting all or part of the campaign paid for. Additionally, co-marketing with a larger company can increase the legitimacy of the campaign in ways we couldn't do on our own. Most MDFs will come with strings. Maybe the partner wants to attend an event with us. Maybe the partner wants a business plan. Most of these strings attached to MDFs are actually as valuable as the funds themselves, though (if we think about them as assets and not liabilities). Business plans force more deep thoughts about a campaign before money gets wasted. They can also teach founders new words or tactics. Neither of those are ever a bad thing. Sometimes the structure required helps founders to think of things in a new way.

Having marketing staff from a partner attend an event is always a good thing as well. This helps learn more about products, better understand the ecosystem, and even get case studies or other marketing assets started. If they're sales staff, it helps align sales teams with those from partners or find a great person to improve those bilateral referrals. Sellers talk, so if a company helps make their deals larger or make them stickier, then the relationship is likely to pay dividends.

There are no sure things in advertising, so there's always risk. MDFs can be a great way to share the risk of a campaign and learn more about advertising and marketing along the way. It's all these little bits that earn the experience points to level up and create more mature outlooks on business. Another way to level up fast is to measure the performance of activities and do the things that work out well a bunch more. This also provides plenty of treasure to help buy new levels.

Measure, Measure, Measure

One of the most important aspects of any advertising or marketing campaign is the ability to measure the results and react quickly. Google is arguably one of the best advertising companies ever founded and has created a tool called Google Analytics to help companies get better at advertising and marketing efforts. There are probably tools built into CRMs, web hosts, and each outlet or channel leveraged as well.

The first step to get a good data analytics practice is to make a list of all the assets that leads, prospects, customers, staff, and competitors have access to. This includes blogs, web apps, marketing sites, ticketing software, etc. Then get an account with a tool that can look at the traffic from each (or multiple accounts with multiple vendors if a single tool can't do so). A good method might be to catalog them all in a spreadsheet and make sure the tool we select (much of the world uses Google Analytics) can provide good analytics for each asset we have. This involves a little research searching for how to best get information about the activities of each. Our last pre-stage event is to eliminate internal traffic, so don't skew the results with internal development and review traffic.

If using Google, set up the Audience Overview and Acquisition and Behavior reports. Define a funnel that steps through each call to action defined in our customer journey earlier in the chapter. Hire someone to help with this if needed or possible, but look for a coach rather than someone to do all the steps. That coach might become someone that given tasks are outsourced to later, but in the beginning, consider the goal of their help to be self-sufficiency.

Each of these has a different technique that changes, and so stepping through the technical pieces will be out of date by the time this book goes to print. The information is readily available in the documentation of the specific tool selected. The gist is to see every step from the customer journey, where people dropped off, and which paths lead from the beginning to a conversion over time. Companies want as much information as possible about where traffic dropped off based on the code of each marketing activity on each channel to know where to spend budget to get the biggest bang for the buck.

One of the most important parts of any founder's journey is to better understand the various charts and graphs that show how an organization is performing. Treasure is finite, and understanding how it performs when spent on marketing and advertising is critical. That shows what messages resonate with potential customers and how the organization can best serve them. To get better, check out the Google course at `https://learndigital.withgoogle.com/digitalgarage/course/digital-marketing/module/10`. There are also analytics courses available on Coursera and other apps. The goal is to keep prospects, leads, and customers coming back and use information collected on behaviors to do so. If they come back enough, maybe they even become some of the best advocates for the company!

Customer Advocacy

Customer advocacy often starts in the most authentic of ways. A customer tweets something nice about a company, and the company retweets it. It feels natural, and in exchange for promoting the company, the company promotes the individual. Maybe another customer posts a link to a blog post on LinkedIn, and the company shares that. There's no quid pro quo. There's no expectation; it just happens naturally.

Over time, people at the company get busy, especially in startups where people have to wear a lot of different hats. Competing priorities pull the people that work at the company in different directions. Maybe the person in charge of social media doesn't open the social accounts during a mad dash to get a new feature out, get a round of investments, or close some sales. The interactions with customers go in fits and spurts. Yet organizations look for feedback in more and more places. Companies want as diverse an outlook as possible and need it quicker than ever. The customer advocacy programs run at a lot of organizations can be a great place to look for more people and to find them faster. These have become almost universal in large companies but are used increasingly in startups as well.

What's an Advocacy Program?

Advocacy programs are systems that motivate customers to take an action. This can be as simple as a spreadsheet or an elaborate portal we create or outsource. If a vendor were to offer an employee at a customer cash to take an action on their behalf, that would be inappropriate, probably unethical, and possibly criminal. A lot of people who use our products will become fans of what a company is doing. Many will naturally share that.

As a product grows, the company who makes it naturally gets more and more people who take small but beneficial actions on their behalf. Those actions get noticed and promoted. People notice these interactions, and the company might subtly drive behaviors based on those reactions. The value of those actions is that they can attain a desired result (think a CTA) and help achieve multiple goals simultaneously.

Fans are often happy to be helpful, especially with some incentives on the line. Those incentives can ultimately be structured in a way that is branded and fun. Many advocates are among the most experienced users. Their time with the product gives them some skin in the game. As the product matures in the market, the people who have been with the product the longest often have the most to gain from the success of the product. The people who have invested the most time in products can then be those with the most to tell a company about how to improve in a way that makes tools more enjoyable to use and more productive.

An advocacy program can help uncover these fans. Many who participate in those programs would be delighted to help make their lives better. Let's start thinking of advocacy by looking at our personas.

Define Personas

Personas help to get the best content in front of advocates and determine what incentives or opportunities are appropriate to provide to advocates. Marketing teams in larger organizations are likely already using those, so be careful about stepping on toes.

There's a huge question often forgotten in the zeal to get portals developed: what is the motivation to take an action as an advocate? The larger an organization gets, the more disconnected the organization often becomes with being able to answer that very question. For startups, it's often sufficient to just make two or three quick personas and a list of actions we want to inspire them to take. There are a lot of actions that can be taken, so we often just put a bunch of things in front of customers and react to what gets amplified. Being a little deliberate goes a long way. So, when using personas to creating actions, think of the motivations and so what will drive behavior.

Start with a Spreadsheet

Now that there are personas, let's take the actions or behaviors we want advocates to espouse and put them in a spreadsheet. This can be as simple as a column for actions and another for each persona. Add columns for points to be allocated for a given action (if a point system is to be used to inspire advocates) or a simple prize. That prize could just be to create a social media post promoting them, discounts, or a giveaway.

Next, think through how prizes will be delivered. An easy way to go about this is to pick a site like www.thnks.com and choose prizes from there. There are less expensive ways, so feel free to grow into a platform like Thnks. If the only item the spreadsheet has is "Refer a friend," then the prize should almost always be a free month or a free tier increase for our product. The more rows for tasks and prizes, the more difficult the system will be to manage, but for now, just have fun and brainstorm different ways customers can authentically promote a brand and the ways they might be rewarded.

A Word of Caution About Customer Advocacy

A company receives a benefit when a person advocates on their behalf. However, as mentioned, not every industry or organization can accept prizes, even if the prize is just a $5 cup of coffee. Any company serving government, education, and highly regulated organizations should probably have no prizes with a monetary value.

Instead, think of more creative ways to reward people. Those social interactions are a great start. Helping friends of the company to do more in their careers and be more visible makes a difference. Many just want the products to keep improving. So another reward to consider might be to give them a meaningful way they want the product to evolve or to have them serve on a customer advisory board. Another reward that might not actually get written down as an explicit offer is a handwritten thank you card. Hopefully, it's obvious by now that there's no need to pay a customer or advocate in order to show appreciation for their efforts.

A Simple Implementation

Now that there there's a spreadsheet of a few items for advocates, put this into action on a small scale. In the beginning, use a lightweight system and a personalized experience for the people participating. Point systems can be fine later, but for now, let's look for something simpler.

Pick one action and a reward. Stay away from monetary rewards. As programs scale that's often an option, but try to avoid a bunch of people looking for gift cards. Instead, look for a motivator early startup customers might want, one that seems authentic. Branded materials can be great for something like this: a shirt or a notebook with a logo. These are things with minimal cash value, and it might be a pain to send, but it's so much more personal and real. Get fun with gifts. Companies that work with artists or designers might do branded protractors; slide rules that are fun can be made for a couple of dollars each. Construction customers might actually use a branded headlamp that fits on a hardhat. Inexpensive but thoughtful, like the matchbooks Eisenhower gave out during elections in the 1950s.

Make the Ask

Now let's make a list of people that might say something good about the company. Think about customers who have had success, those who were involved in some of the decision making, some who got features implemented at their request, and maybe a couple of those random ones that come in whom the creators of the program have never met. A good sampling across a couple of different personas is a great start.

Then just send the list of people a request to take the desired actions and indicate what the offer is. Remember that some people aren't allowed to talk about the vendors they work with. So don't worry about rejection. Phrase it in a way that shows their opinions are valued and the company would like to share their story. Take this example:

> *We are so glad that you've joined us on this amazing journey. As we get more and more organizations using our solution, we find there are more and more stories we'd like to help share. For everyone who posts about their journey with our product today, we'll send out a branded pocket protector, and we'll be resharing the best, most meaningful posts. Just tag us in your post, and we'll do the rest!*

Let's break down a few elements of the preceding paragraph:

- **It's short.** Let's just assume customers don't read much beyond the size of a tweet anymore. After all, they have day jobs!

- **There's a call to action.** The CTA is to post something about their journey.

- **There's a clear reward.** They get the lovely pocket protector. They should also post themselves with a photo with the pocket protector in it, of course!

- **There's an added incentive to reshare the best story.**
  The company can always reshare multiple of the
  stories.

- **The asks aren't overly specific.** This is about them. As
  programs grow there's often a "tweet this exact post"
  type of ask, but in the beginning retain flexibility and
  shoot for authenticity.

There are a few things to avoid as well. Don't want to seem desperate.
Don't make any inauthentic requests. Yes, the goal is to reach more
people–but to do so in a way that stays true and within regulations for a
given industry. Don't just create a bunch of noise that complicates the
marketing and analytics. In other words, avoid incentivizing the wrong
behaviors.

Collect, Analyze, Repeat

Once an offer is out there, see what resonates. Keep an eye on the social
impacts, the clicks, the traffic, and then the conversions. Sure, the goal is to
do this all the time, but as the program gains momentum, use UTM codes
and link shortening to track the results. Bake these into the first attempts
so those can be measured as well.

Pay attention to the analytics for new traffic generated by advocacy
efforts. This helps understand what's driving people to visit the site,
where people fall off, and ultimately how to keep people interested in the
company.

Add More Structure

Once there's some success, add a little more structure to the program. In
the beginning, this might be doing more of the same: more offers, rewards,
and people who get invites. If all goes well, there should come a time when

there's too much work to handle without either more people or some software. There are a few tools that can help with scaling a program:

- **Influitive** (https://influitive.com) is a true customer advocacy solution with integrated reward systems and lots of options for centralized management of rewards.

- **Innercircle** (www.inner-circle.io) might be the simplest advocacy tool to manage. There might be more manual interaction than in Influitive, but it can still sync to/from other standard tools, and especially in the beginning, it's fine to do manual entry when tasks are completed.

- **SaaSquatch** (www.saasquatch.com/affiliate-platform/) is much more of a referral tracking tool but has some advocacy options as well.

- **Crowdvocate** (https://crowdvocate.com) is an advocacy and loyalty tool. It's great to scale up into a place where advocacy and/or loyalty programs have a dedicated person to manage them.

It's always good to test each and look for one that matches a given use case (and compliance requirements), rather than simply trying to shoehorn a workflow into a mold so a tool works. Having said this, one of the reasons off-the-shelf software tools exist is that the developers have more knowledge about a given industry (such as advocacy) and practitioners can learn a lot from the options available in the software.

As the program grows, experiment more. Providing more challenges might mean any of the following:

- Submit a customer story.

- Create or reshare a social post.

- Post a video somewhere.

- Create a video testimonial.

- Make a video to contribute to a compilation.

- Send us a photo in a *Star Wars* costume on May 4th.

- Write a script that does something with an API.

- Make a screenshot of an innovative workflow.

- Fill out surveys.

- Send a pet photo.

- Refer a friend to an open job listing.

- Contribute to a nonprofit we support.

- Submit a feature request.

- Write a guest blog post.

- Send us a recipe for Pi Day.

- Refer a friend to sales.

- Submit thoughts on a beta version.

- Meet with a product manager.

- Review a product.

- Be our guest on a podcast episode.

- Drop us a life hack.

- Create a playlist of songs that are just perfect to listen to when working with our products.

The list is endless. Some (if not most) should be fun and engaging. The programs usually become a little less impactful per capita, but more so overall. Redemption rates in point-based systems usually hover below 25%.

It's hard to keep fresh ideas flowing, especially given the constraints for working with the personas for a given organization. The person pulling the strings of these programs really needs to know the customers well.

Once there's a program that's working, protect it. The community, engagement, or advocacy manager is a critical role, and one of the biggest risks is what happens when they're ready for a new challenge.

Turnover

Employees move up or employees move on. Anyone that's developed an advocacy program is often going to be in high demand when other organizations look to build a program as well—or within the organization when the program is a huge success. We have to be prepared for that eventuality. Have a backup. This can be someone in another team who shows interest, someone at a junior level hired specifically to run the program, or someone who's run a similar program at a large organization who can hit the ground running. Either way, train the replacement quickly so the program doesn't skip a beat!

Customer advocacy programs can be awesome. Companies can use them to find and promote people who love their products and can do so in meaningful ways. The most ardent supporters can be rewarded for their efforts. Companies can connect with users in more ways today than any time in history. The advocates can also help companies build better products. However, companies can also alienate people when they are spoken to in ways they don't understand or that come across as inauthentic. Don't do anything to risk the trust it's taken a long time to win.

Like most initiatives, start small. A simple spreadsheet is all it takes. Move on to more and more complex ways to help customers promote the mission. Some could become lifelong friends, some could end up on the team eventually, and the community can grow together in their careers.

Conclusion

This is one of the largest chapters in the book. The reason is that sales and marketing represent two of the biggest leading indicators that an organization will be successful in their mission. The adventuring party needs all areas, of course, but these are the engines that fuel a company's ability to eat, equip the party, and upgrade by expanding the disciplines required and leveling each up.

Sales is a must in products that appeal to enterprises, but many consumer or small business products begin without a sales team and only bring those on when needing to go upmarket to reach larger customers. Therefore, for some companies marketing will be the focus—the earlier those efforts begin and the more analytical, the better.

Not all of the initiatives mentioned in this chapter work for everyone. There's no magic bullet or marketing system that will always work. Sometimes it's about a clever growth hack, and other times it's about knowing enough about the target customer so the company can communicate with them in an authentic way. Any success requires a little luck. If rigorous in being data-driven, then it's easier to repeat where luck is found and iterate to amplify the results while avoiding repeating the investments into routes where there wasn't any success.

Most down-market SaaS products will find that investing in advertising becomes a huge growth engine. Most upmarket products need to find a healthy split between sales and marketing expenditures. One other area that our adventuring party needs to bring in eventually (if not from the beginning) is the public relations illusionist, which we'll cover in the next chapter.

CHAPTER 12

Public Relations

Most companies neglect to include Public Relations (PR) in business plans, despite lengthy plans of how to spend advertising and marketing dollars. PR can actually bolster the advertising and marketing strategies. But be warned: if done improperly, hiring a PR firm can waste tens of thousands of dollars and months of work because we aren't able to provide the resources the agency needs to be successful.

Levels in Public Relations

PR is an industry that gets companies exposure to audiences using news outlets and third-party publishers. These can be news publications, magazines, books, blogs, and social media. Companies can buy advertising in most of these outlets, but PR is making the news and not actually paying for placement in the news. The goal is often to gain free coverage by talking about items that are of interest to the public. The best strategy is to constantly provide value. This includes value to writers (or other content creators), value to readers, and, more specifically, value to potential customers.

PR typically includes subfields like branding, media relations, publicity, event management, special events, and relationship building within an industry. A good public relations firm will match a brand with where target customers are consuming content. But we don't always need a good public relations firm for this, especially when there are industry

© Charles Edge, Chip Pearson, Amy Larson Pearson 2023
C. Edge et al., *The Startup Players Handbook*,
https://doi.org/10.1007/978-1-4842-9315-7_12

thought leaders on staff or as a leader within an organization. Most people bootstrapping a company will have founder-led PR.

PR is much less expensive than advertising but can be just as effective, adding third-party credibility to products and services. Given the power and cost-effectiveness of PR, it's often the wiser choice, especially if we lack the budget for big advertising buys, but not always—keep in mind that PR is similar to an illusionist. When sitting in that chair, we bring the ability to project a certain image of a company that can become further and further from fact if we aren't careful. We want to have an honest account of our activities and use the illusion to bring others into the adventuring party authentically.

Let's look at a typical evolution of public relations, level by level, in many startups:

- *Level 1*: Build a tool or service. That provides us with something to talk about. During the development phase, we should look at competitors or companies in adjacent spaces and catalog where they're being discussed. Think of this as a spreadsheet of future places we'll reach out to that help spread the word about our amazing solution. This is also a great time to attend local or virtual events for organizations that can help evangelize a product or where we can meet bloggers or others with a following. We can create an account with HARO (described later in this chapter) and other sites to start providing quotes to various news outlets. We shouldn't expect to win sales, but we should be able to start building a library of mentions in the media.

- *Level 2*: Once there's a tool and a marketing website, create a media kit. This can just be a page (e.g., www. yourcompany.com/press). The press page should have a simple bio for each founder, photos that journalists can use, and contact information (like a press@ companyname.com that is an alias to a founder). This is also a great location to showcase any media mentions we might have scored through a service like HARO.

- *Level 3*: Once the first sale is made, reach out to local and industry-specific media sources and tell them a little about the company and what's been done so far. This can be a standard email template, but try to make it personalized to the people who receive the email. The list shouldn't be so long yet that this will take too long.

- *Level 4*: Once the first non-founding employees are hired, it's time to prepare for growth. The local and industry media sources, bloggers, and others with influence in our space need to know our name. Part of that is marketing, but it's time to have quotes from public relations firms to help spread the word about this amazing adventuring party we're assembling and the mission we're taking.

- *Level 5*: Start interviewing a PR firm by the time the tenth employee is hired if not before then. We'll cover how to find and hire a firm in this chapter, but we want someone who's had success getting products mentioned in news sources similar to those we discovered back at level 1—but who can get a more national or global reach.

- *Level 6*: Once there's a public relations firm, it's time to start doing press releases at a regular cadence. These can be for specific innovative features or big deals if we can get permission from customers to talk publicly about our relationship with them.

- *Level 7*: Once there are around 50–100 people on staff, it's time to think about a staff position for PR. It's probably best to keep the firm on for a time, if not permanently. But the person on staff can expand to crisis management and other aspects of public relations that can become a huge problem.

After level 7 our adventuring party looks more like an army. A really good illusionist can make it seem like the army is far bigger or still like that small boutique business our customer fell in love with. They'll be able to manage a relationship that is probably low on the priority list of an executive team at this point. Aspects of PR will conflict with other teams, like going on podcasts to bolster community-building efforts. A great corporate communications team can help us tidy those lanes up and make sure the entire company is portraying the mission, vision, and values effectively.

The Level 1 Illusionist (Founder-Led PR)

Every discipline takes time out of our day. In the beginning, reading a digest of requests for quotes from news outlets might take as short as ten minutes a day, but that's ten minutes a day we aren't spending writing code, selling our product, or other aspects that are much more directly impactful for the business.

Whether an organization chooses to engage a firm or go about various forms of PR themselves, there are several things that can maximize the impact the media can have on our organizations early on—without taking up that much time. Here a few things small businesses should do when starting up their PR machine:

- **Gather all social properties in one place.** One major function of PR is online reputation management. As small business owners, make a list of all of the online profiles, platforms, and social media sites our business is on. That way, it's easy to quickly cross-check an online reputation with each of them, formulating a PR plan to potentially amplify great reviews or rectify any negative reviews.

- **Publish a media kit.** Once all the social properties are gathered into a simple list, publish them on a page. Develop a "press" page that can be easily found from the front page of a marketing site (and linked at, e.g., www.site.com/press). Include the list of social properties from earlier, as well as a company introduction with important facts, links to mentions in the press, past press releases, and company contact information. As we grow, we'll add investor relations.

- **Make local media contacts.** No matter where a business is located, it's important to aggregate a list of relevant contacts at print, broadcast, and online outlets in the given geographic region. If something exciting happens with the business, we want to be able to quickly reach out to try to gain media coverage and, more importantly, build a lasting, mutually beneficial relationship (and hopefully an authentic real friendship along the way).

- **Know the industry-specific media contacts.** Most vertical industries also have specific websites, blogs, magazines, podcasts, and stations (e.g., YouTube playlists). Put a list of those together as well, and look for a specific contact to whom you might be able to reach out should you encounter anything that might be of interest to them.

- **Have a strong writer on the team.** Statements, columns, blog posts of your own, and press releases are powerful ways to get noticed. Although professional writers can be hired, it's valuable to have someone within an organization capable of getting the first draft going, especially in fields where domain knowledge is critical. This can be someone technical or someone who understands what we do and is a great storyteller.

Developing and executing a PR plan, even if just homegrown PR, is one of the best things that can be done for any small business. Next, let's look at one of the more legitimate ways to get mentioned in the press: helping a reporter as a trusted source.

HARO

We've talked about local and industry-specific press so far, but what about getting broader coverage? For that national and web media, let's review what HARO (short for Help A Reporter Out) can do for us. HARO is a website that connects people who write the news with people that want to be featured in the news (and hopefully the reporters can showcase those that should be featured in the news). Reporters, bloggers, and others in the press can (and do) find quotes, examples, and stories for the projects they're working on. Countless PR agencies around the world use HARO to monitor these requests and connect their customers to the writers and editors involved.

HARO sends inquiries via email several times a day. After a few days of reading through the inquiries, build a filter that will show us only those that are pertinent to our business. This means focusing on the content of the messages and looking for words like "startups," those containing various topics we consider ourselves an expert on, or our specific industry. Don't forget including local geography in that filter–being mentioned in the local press is a great way to recruit amazing talent.

The biggest holdup, other than the time it takes to respond to requests, is imposter syndrome. For example, many might feel apprehensive to supply quotes to media outlets, doubting our own talent and achievements. We all have something to contribute. Don't forget that! Especially as we get code-level expertise with an industry and level up to where we know how to do more and more of the disciplines that our company grows into requiring. It's just as good to have someone else from the adventuring party mentioned in the media, as it brands the company more holistically.

The name of the game is speed. The quicker we respond with a quote, the more likely it is to get used. Additionally, since there is a finite number of minutes in a day, we have to focus on things that either bolster our credibility with local press and customers or that might generate customer leads. Getting quoted by the media just for the sake of doing so isn't really worth the effort. Still, it's a numbers game. The more inquiries we respond to, the more likely something will get used. And if we aren't checking the requests, we won't see any that are laser focused on our audience.

When to Get a Firm

We'd all love to have enough funds to have a team do every task that needs to get done. We don't. However, there does come a time as disciplines level up when every organization needs to hire a firm. Some will do so in earlier levels than we suggested previously in the chapter for a variety of reasons; it's hard to know when it's time. Sometimes it's the initial release of the product. Other times it's years later once there are 10,000 paying customers. Some successful businesses have gone decades without dedicated staff or outsourced PR at their disposal.

There are times when PR needs to get outsourced or perhaps brought in-house. There's no right or wrong answer, but there are a few factors to take into account. Will media outreach provide a substantial benefit? Can the impact of public relations be quantified? Has the organization reached a point where the cost to attain a lead isn't changing and new, broader techniques should be applied? Is the company looking to get approached by investors? Do we have a negative perception issue we should correct? Is there some kind of public policy change we need? Are investors or mentors suggesting a PR strategy? There are a lot of other factors, but these are a good place to start.

In general, PR is an important air cover to get word out about the organization. The results are often fairly passive, even in comparison to marketing. The earlier we start doing a little of our own PR, the more quickly we can get working with media outlets to help legitimize our efforts and build our personal brands to help propel the company a little faster. And the more of those efforts we've done when we hire a firm, the quicker they're likely to get us a good return on the investment.

Hire a PR Firm

This chapter includes a number of tips on getting free media mentions. These can be key to building out a truly scalable sales organization, as the passive marketing obtained not only is the top of your sales funnel but also provides air cover for all leads as they traverse through the sales funnel— further giving us legitimacy in the minds of our leads and customers.

At some point, the founders of a company won't have time to manage a PR machine, the free efforts will have less and less return on investment, or the available PR resources in a given area or field will be saturated and it's difficult to get started in the first place. This means it's time to stop going it alone. Maybe it's just a time constraint. Maybe we don't have the right contacts. Maybe we need better assistance to uncover great potential outlets. Maybe we want to reach a larger audience than we could on our own. This is when it's time to hire some help.

Hiring help doesn't mean we have to pay tens of thousands of dollars to a huge firm (although we can and might get great results from the spend). We can pretty much guarantee there is a local PR club/ organization in every geographic area. The first place to start would be the Public Relations Society of America, at prsa.org, and then from there, search on the Internet for local PR firms. In this "gig economy," we can also look for individuals to pay directly to help with PR efforts or use sites like fiverr.com and upwork.com to find vendors to work with.

Whomever is hired should make as many people on the team participate in the process as possible–whether that's writing content, responding to emails to set up appointments for interviews, connecting to local groups, or even buying that new shirt for our first television interview! Beyond that, take their plan and then look for ways to figure out if the PR function is then working for the organization, because if it isn't, then we'll need to find a different firm to hire until we manage to find the perfect fit.

How They Work

Be careful of charlatans. Public relations is challenging to quantify, because it's usually not billed to customers on a performance basis. But most agencies or sole proprietors will have an idea of what they want to do with our company and how much time that will take. They usually reverse engineer a retainer based on an estimation of how much time it will take them to deliver the results we want. Sometimes they'll luck out and accomplish more with the time estimated. Other times they will do less. As their customers, we can give ourselves permission to ask for transparency for how they came to a retainer amount. If we understand their assumptions and limitations, we'll have a better relationship.

Note   While monthly retainers are the norm, it is possible to do project-based PR with an agency. This might be a good way to get started without a lot of long-term commitment.

It can be challenging to quantify the relationship with a PR firm or agency, but there are a couple of ways to approach the problem:

- *Measurable outputs*: Quantify deliverables, for example, how many articles or interviews or placed bylines. Multiple outputs are acceptable and subject to review at least every six months.

- *Measure quality beyond quantity*: Implement an article rating system and have a goal. That way "you" can measure the quality of the placements vs. just the quantity.

When we work with someone in PR, they should understand what we do, how we want people to perceive our company, the places they should do media outreach, what's required before doing any media outreach, and the scope of the relationship we'll have with them. They should be able to build an effective plan in the pre-sales stage or at least an outline of what they'll be doing on our behalf. Make sure to see a plan and agree on it before cutting a check to anyone. Otherwise, don't.

When PR Doesn't Work

PR efforts (and firms) often need a good six months to show a return. Most will work quarterly anyways, so this is really just renewing a contract for a second quarter. After six months, we should know the impact that a given firm or rep is going to have. Performance may improve as the firm learns more about the business or may fall off once their contacts have been saturated.

After the first quarter, there should be a little buzz in the market. If we've been getting media attention but have not seen any lift in the business yet, then we're probably on the right track. PR isn't immediate like the sales and marketing efforts, so we have to be a little bit patient. The important thing is that we know what efforts our representation is conducting on our behalf and agree with those efforts–and that those have a path to bring customers into the customer journey. It seems like these things always take longer than we initially think they will.

During the second quarter, we should start seeing business coming in from PR efforts. If there's no lift at the end of the second quarter, then it's time to either renegotiate the contract or find a new firm. If it takes three of these cycles to find the right firm, so be it. It's worth it in the long term to find a good firm, so don't be afraid to start over. The right PR can be one of the biggest game changers for any company, and so it's valuable to keep looking if things don't click.

Press Releases

One of the special abilities our public relations characters should have at any level is writing a great press release. A press release is a document that informs members of the press about an event. A software company might put out a press release about a cool new feature, a really important hire, a round of funding, etc. This is usually done with the hope that a media outlet will pick up the press release and run with it. Press releases for features or version numbers usually don't get much traction, but investments, board members, or the culmination of many new features that achieve a larger strategy goal might be newsworthy.

The cost of running a press release on Newswire or another outlet isn't worth it in many cases, but it's a valuable feature of the illusionist class, and there are some basic tips we can provide on their effective use.

Press Release Tips

Press releases are a timeless way of communicating news, events, and updates regarding a business or organization to media outlets. These brief, informative writing pieces have managed to weather the test of time, with millions being emailed to newspapers, TV outlets, and radio stations. The media loves press releases. They're like tiny bundles of news stories dropped on reporters' laps. Given that the media cycle is in constant need of content, we should be taking advantage of press releases when possible and when they're worth the cost (don't forget to include the cost of the time to write them in there).

Here are a few quick tips to review before we delve into an example press release:

- *Brevity*: Reporters don't have the time to comb through two pages of a business announcement. It's recommended to keep the release between 300 and 500 words, effectively communicating a message without boring the reader.

- *Catchy title*: In order to catch the reader's interest, include a one-of-a-kind news-spun title that isn't over the top.

- *No sales language*: A press release is about communicating the news. It's not a time to promote your sales and services in an obvious way.

- *Avoid jargon*: This is always a good idea, but even more so when someone else might not go as deep with a certain type of technology as we do.

- *Stick to the facts*: It's easy to let a flourish slip into the prose, especially if we've been writing marketing docs. Don't—keep to the facts. Reporters prefer if they add the flourishes.

- *Don't try too hard*: A press release isn't a creative column submission with the local opinion editor. It's a news announcement. Treat it as such.

- *Quotes*: Including quotes from the business owner or spokesperson is a great way to humanize a press release. Be sure to take advantage of this opportunity, including one or two quotes from someone important at the business or, even better, a customer.

- *Grammar*: Those who have careers in writing appreciate good grammar.

- *Research*: Check the Business Wire site and read recent similar releases and look at which category is most appropriate. We certainly don't want to put something out to a medical stream if we're writing accounting software.

Once the release is done, there are two options: email or call it out to local news media personnel, or submit it to syndication platforms like PRWeb.com and Newswire.com. The two aren't mutually exclusive; for the widest variety of coverage, consider doing both! Also advise the reader to put it on their website or use it in social media or blogs in order to promote it even to someone not in the "media." Now that we have the general ideas out there, let's go into the different parts of the press release.

Headline

One of the best ways to grab attention for a written work is with a great title. When working with press releases, we call the title a headline. And as with most headlines, we want one that grabs attention. Let's say we're based in Los Angeles and we want to go after the emerging home automation industry using an integration we built with the HomePod as a wedge. First, we build a service offering. Then, we come up with a great headline that pretty much sums things up. Some ideas might include

- Local Tech Firm Introduces Comprehensive Home Automation

- Local Shop Introduces New Home Automation Solutions

- A New Era of Home Automation Centered Around Apple

- Local Firm Brings Home Automation to Businesses

The preceding headlines are fairly different from one another. There are some lessons to learn here. In the preceding examples, most are kept short and easily digestible. Your name could easily (and probably should) replace the "Local Shop" or "Local Tech Firm" in the headline. There should be one catchy or trendy word, but not so many as to be unapproachable, and importantly, headlines should typically be eight words or fewer.

Header

Next, let's talk about the header. This is at the top of the page and contains some pretty basic information. On the left side, there are usually two lines. The first would read when to release the information. The reason this is necessary is that some content is under embargo, which means we want someone to write about it but not actually release what they've written until the embargo is lifted.

The second line typically includes the date the release is sent. On the right side of the header is the contact information. This should include a name, phone number, and email address, each on its own line.

Dateline and Lead

The first paragraph of the press release contains the dateline and lead. This is one of the most important parts of the release, and any reader will likely stop reading immediately if you don't keep their attention, so don't bury the lead here. Start with the city the organization is based in, followed by a dash (known as the dateline), and then include a sentence that wraps up the release in a nice pretty bow (known as the lead). An example of an opening paragraph might read like this:

> *LOS ANGELES – Charles Pearson Raskin of Megaawesome-softwarefirm announces suite of new integrations that brings cutting-edge home automation technology to small businesses, leveraging the Apple platform.*

Body

The body explains what was referenced in the title. Throughout the body cover what's often referred to as the inverted pyramid. Start with the most newsworthy aspects of the release: the who, what, when, and where. Then go to the important details and wrap up general and background information, which we'll cover in the next section.

An example of the body might include two or three paragraphs that lay out the necessary details, such as the following:

> *Edge vows to bring home automation technology to every aspect of small businesses, at a rate that more than pays for itself in energy savings. George Technicianopolis has been named head of the Automation Integrations business unit.*

> *"We are bringing out-of-the-box solutions to Main Street so businesses can control HVAC, lights, and monitor energy consumption," said Technicianopolis. "And not only does it allow companies to save on energy bills, but the bridge into all other software tools makes everyone's lives easier, being able to control everything ever with just a voice command."*

> *Technicianopolis will be at Huge Tech Conference on April 1st. Here, organizations and the media can see a model home and control every aspect with standard voice controls.*

There's often a quote or two from a founder or someone at the organization in the body. An additional quote could come from an analyst or a statistic from a study as well. There's also a call to action to join the company at a showcase where more quotes can be obtained and where someone from the media could get hands-on experience with the technologies being mentioned.

General Information

We shouldn't need to provide a summary to a press release. But we can include a paragraph of background information to reuse in each press release you put out. This is typically called a "boilerplate." Consider including the following in a short paragraph:

- How long the company has been in business. Use new or a long history as a selling point!

- How many customers the company has.

- Anything newsworthy or legitimizing about the company.

- Any quotes from industry analysts or influencers in the industry about the company.

- For smaller companies, information about the principals of the company.

An example of the general information paragraph could read something like the following:

Founded in 1602, Megaawesomeconsultancy brings modern technologies to small- and medium-sized businesses. The company focuses on Apple technologies and carries the largest inventory of Apple hardware in the world, as it has since its founding. Megaawesomeconsultancy has 894 employees, with offices in Venice Beach, Calif.

"We will save the environment, one HomePod at a time," said Charles Pearson Raskin.

For more information on Megaawesomeconsultancy, visit `www.krypted.com`.

Finally, and this is worth repeating, a press release isn't a book. Keep a press release to a single page and always have someone proofread it to make sure it fits with AP Style Guides before the release gets submitted to a wire. Once the press release is built, it can be submitted via PRWeb.com, Newswire, or Business Wire or directly to various contacts in the press.

Failures in Public Relations

Getting media attention is fun at times. We can easily ruin relationships if we say the wrong thing or divulge confidential information at the wrong time. A little common sense goes a long way; however, when we're put on the spot and we need to respond quickly, we might say something we shouldn't. Sometimes, we can ask for questions beforehand, but that doesn't really cover the way conversations can meander.

This is all part of how we level up the discipline. We hire a firm and want them to coach us. Some of that might be enunciating better, but most importantly, we want coaching for content. We can guide where the conversation goes, to some extent. So have a plan. And, if we don't know how to answer a question, it is okay to ask the reporter if we can get back to them after the interview via email.

Here are some things we just shouldn't talk about publicly:

- *Financials*: Stick to what is public. Our financials can be a big topic. When it comes up with local or business press, know what we can and can't say going into an interview.

- *Politics*: Half of any country will be annoyed by anything we say about politics. Even if we agree on nine of ten issues with a given audience, that tenth thing will potentially cause friction with a customer, and there's really no need for that. We want to bring our whole selves, but the larger an organization we're representing, the more others take on our beliefs when we do so publicly. Having said that, we don't include things like sexual orientation, gender identity, or religion with politics, even though it's easy to do so, especially with how divisive politics has gotten (or always was going back thousands and thousands of years).

- *Customers*: Unless we have explicit permission in writing from someone at a customer with the authority to discuss the work we do with them publicly, don't mention specific customers. And even then, make sure to understand the boundaries of what they're cool with discussing with the media. We don't want to create friction with those we would otherwise consider to be our best allies.

- *Vendors*: There are a few issues we can run into with vendors. One is talking about specific business topics, like margins. We're likely contractually bound not to discuss these, but it warrants mentioning anyway. Additionally, make sure not to say anything that could be perceived negatively about a vendor (unless your name is Elon Musk—okay, fine, even then).

There are other things that we shouldn't discuss with the media as well. Instead of going through each (a list that could fill several books), just be smart about what is said—even when "off the record," as prefacing something with "off the record" to a reporter doesn't mean they won't put it in print. And know the intent of the author. A little background about a piece that is being written goes a long way in understanding how we can be intentional about how we can contribute to the conversation, narrative, or piece.

Conclusion

As founders, we want to expand our reach. We've built an amazing product and a cadre of phenomenal humans surrounding our innovation and are taking it to market. We are aligned on a mission, with a vision of how we're making the world a better place, and we're doing that by living values that we project into the world.

A few minutes of work every morning while catching up with our emails can net some pretty fantastic results in the early stages of our organization. This isn't likely to drive a lot of revenue for a long time (although every product and go-to-market strategy is different and it could) but lays the groundwork for a larger push later. It's likely that PR benefits our own personal brand as much as, if not more than, that of the company. But in the early days those are often intertwined to the point that they are indiscernible from one another. Such is the life of each hero setting out on a new campaign of adventures.

As we expand our adventuring party, we want to help build the brand of others as well. The sum of those parts is greater when spread out. Each of those voices coming from other disciplines or character classes unlocks new and interesting opportunities to spread the word as well. We should know our geography and our industry reporters. Those connections we make early pay off dividends in the long term. We're effectively bringing reporters and their reach into our cause when they can say, "I knew them when they were just a first-level ranger with a wild idea."

There's also a lot of reach to be gained in the larger industry media. This is where sites like HARO come in for those earlier levels—to help us not only get mentioned in pieces where we can add something new but also make those connections with reporters. Over time, we have other responsibilities leveling up each discipline in the organization like direct sales or product development that require our attention more than the media, and so we may choose to outsource PR and eventually hire someone. But even the largest of any company should be led by an executive who understands how the press is representing their brand and can help control that narrative.

PR is somewhere between an art, science, and pageantry. When it's done well, it's an authentic illusion. One of the most valuable assets a public relations firm brings to the table is their contacts. This grows our reach, helps bring our mission to new audiences, and, if we interpret every question asked as a potential opportunity in the market, helps us build better products.

Now that we've gone through marketing, advertising, and PR, we're hopefully winning customers and getting new support requests as they amble through our products. So in the next chapter, we'll look at building that part of our adventuring party out.

CHAPTER 13

Support

Support is who customers reach out to when they have problems.
Customers rarely interact with developers, executives, accounting, or
other teams in a company—and so they end up with this perception of
the organization that is often based mostly on their interactions with our
support team. And yet, the support team often ends up feeling like the
pack mules of the adventuring party rather than the tanks that allow for
forging into new territory. This is in part because we think of software
developers as wizards and sellers get rewarded with large commissions as
we expand. It's also in part because in many organizations support is an
entry point into the company and there's a perception that we can always
hire new people to support the product.

The reality is, given that support is on the phone or responding to text
feedback from customers all day, that gives them a superpower. They're
a hero to many. Few in the organization have as much empathy with
customers as those who support the customers. Product teams are better
for having their ranks include those who have supported customers.
Services teams need to train fewer from the outside when those in support
move into those roles.

Leveling Up the Support Organization

As we grow, having the ranks of support get raided by other teams (and
customers) constantly should create a hopeful spirit in support. Those
who stay and become upper tiers of support allow developers to do more

© Charles Edge, Chip Pearson, Amy Larson Pearson 2023
C. Edge et al., *The Startup Players Handbook*,
https://doi.org/10.1007/978-1-4842-9315-7_13

because they're not fielding escalations. Awesome support teams can be a secret weapon in the sales process because it turns out that when you go above and beyond for customers, they spread that perception they have of the organization on social media and to colleagues from other organizations—and any company with a great reputation for supporting their customers will have a much easier time making a sale.

Let's put this in perspective by breaking down those phases into stages for our support organization to grow into:

- *Level 1*: As many will note by this point, most startups begin with the founders sitting in a lot of chairs (or performing many of the different jobs required in the company). The founders and/or developers are doing front-line support, often using the cheapest online chat app or maybe with a Google Voice number ringing through to their cell phones. For many organizations, this is the best experience an end user will have. Either way, all cases should be logged from day one. It's extra work but will pay dividends when it's time to hire people. And we can report on what's leading to support incidents and begin mining the data required to build better and better products!

- *Level 2*: As we grow, the founders are pulled into other areas of the business and have less time to do support. So the organization evolves, and more people step in around the company. But that causes stress when cases come in that require support and people can't finish their day job. We don't have a lot of profit yet, so try a few automated techniques.

- *Level 3*: Finally, it's time to hire our first dedicated person in support. Some products are complicated and require someone with expertise, possibly from a customer or competitor, but hopefully, we've managed to get our product easy enough to use that we can cast a wide net in our hiring. If so, we can offer a lot of upward mobility to that early customer support hire!

- *Level 4*: As organizations grow, the amount of support customers require grows as well. There are more types of customers who do things with the products that developers might not have anticipated. We need to make sure we're building new features but have to balance giving the people on the front lines supporting customers a voice as well. We want to spend resources on increasingly sophisticated automation while giving customers a white-glove service, so they feel as important as they are to us. When looking at the budget, bring in software to integrate zero-tier support assets (e.g., knowledge bases, videos, documentation) into case management to reduce the time to close each ticket and enable the next generation of support staff to get up to speed as quickly as possible.

- *Level 5*: If we don't yet have a management structure in place for support, we need to do so by the time we have enough cases to justify the fourth person in support. It's usually best to promote from within when possible, but whether considering an internal or external candidate, make sure they are focused on automation and keeping the number of people required to a minimum while still providing a quality support experience.

- *Level 6*: Support organizations typically begin using solutions cobbled together from inexpensive tools or add-ons to existing solutions. For example, organizations might use a generic Customer Relationship Management (CRM) tool shared with sales at first. As the company grows, the tools are likely to need to be purpose-built for support yet deeply integrated with the ecosystem of other products we use. Further, we'll need a paid support option for larger customers and the support organization as a revenue stream to pay for the white-glove assistance they need. Finally, support needs to feed talent into the rest of the organization as they have the highest level of empathy for customers, having held their hands through tough times and likely being some of the top domain experts in a rapidly growing organization.

- *Level 7*: Support has now become its own small army. We need to be prescriptive about where support falls in the financials, and investors are going to want to see support costs go down as customer counts go up (or at least down in the percentage of our overall spend) as investors typically think of software as infinitely scalable. This means developing a strategy to be able to bring in talent newer to their careers and a great leveling paradigm if one hasn't already been developed.

Beyond level 7, support might very well be its own army to call on in the event of a land war—or perhaps just a bad patch that was accidentally shipped (which might be the same thing). A great support organization makes for fanatical customers, while bad support causes customers to disengage. Awesome support experiences brand us as awesome companies. Consider this: does the brand of an organization reflect developers more than the people a customer talks to on the phone in the event of a problem? Resist cutting support budgets as the organization scales out but stay vigilant about the best uses of automation for a given type of customer.

In this chapter, we'll start with that level 1 founder-led support, look at bringing in those first few people to support the product (some of the most important employees we'll ever hire), and then cover leveling up the team and scaling into a support army—and leveraging new technologies to amplify what everyone in the team can do.

Continued Success

A potential customer finds us through one of our many routes to market. They find something that causes them to reach out and ask us a question on our site. Perhaps that's in a pre-sales capacity, like trying to figure out if the product is a good fit for them. Maybe that's in a post-sales capacity, trying to figure out how to accomplish a given task. Either way, there needs to be a customer experience professional on the other end of that request. At this point, we were successful in getting the customer to our site. The advertising, marketing, and sales are working for them. We've invested the cost to acquire the customer, and we rely on a good product and good support to keep the customer on the journey.

The role goes by many names in different organizations: support, customer success, or customer experience (now shortened to CX). But their mission is to keep the journey the customer is on with us going. We want customers to stay with our adventuring party if possible.

Renewal Business

We work hard to get our customers. Once we have them, we want to keep them! We mostly win and lose renewals in three places:

- *Innovation*: Our ability to infuse products with innovative ideas that make our customers' lives better. This could be by saving them time, helping them get to market with their products faster, improving their quality of life, streamlining a process, increasing collaboration, etc. This typically plays out over longer terms.

- *Product quality*: Put simply, keep the bugs to a minimum. Fewer features of higher quality will always trump code that shouldn't have gone out the door. Here, rather than offer tons of buttons with complex logic, we can laser focus on just what customers need, build in testing and automation to get products to market, and, if possible, take a zero-bug policy approach.

- *Great support*: The quality of our support (and services, if those are provided) is critical. Empathetic support buys us time when there are quality issues. Educating support empowers our customers to grow (and often reduces the support tickets opened).

The fourth place that could be mentioned there is price. But for the most part, if we're out-innovating the market with a quality product and our support makes our customers feel like we care about them, price is rarely too much of a consideration.

The amount of work required to win a renewal should be less than the amount of work put into winning the customer. Small customers might renew monthly; large customers might renew annually or on three-year terms. The larger the contract amount, the more time we likely need to spend discussing the renewal opportunity with the customer. Let's begin by thinking organizationally, where renewals live.

The Organizational Chart

As with many aspects of running a startup in the beginning, renewals likely live wherever they can. If we have a product that's tapping the credit card of a customer once a month for $5, then it's likely the renewal lives in the web interface, and the responsibility is shared with email marketing and analytics so it can be automated. Maybe we begin by shipping a product that requires manual cancellation in Stripe, and then as doing so becomes labor intensive, we move to create a button-to-cancel service.

Larger, more expensive products will require more thought. For those, renewals (as with sales) often begin with the founders. As we grow, they often remain with sales in the early days—especially when sales teams are small. According to how a company perceives renewals on the balance sheet and how good a track record we have with renewals, leaders on a team will either run to or away from overseeing renewals. Renewals typically fall under sales or support but can also be their own separate team. Let's look at each:

- *Sales*: Sellers who receive commissions after the first term of a contract (e.g., for renewals) often want to be involved in the renewal process. This helps them stay connected to the success of customers and protect their own livelihood. Over time, many will realize that it can be awkward when the seller calls once a year to ask for money and forget about customers in the meantime. This is because they're often hunting for new customers. Therefore, many organizations evolve to having support teams handle renewals.

- *Support*: Support teams often end up with renewals as sales organizations scale and focus on how to bring in new business. One reason for this is that sales teams start growing faster than support teams, and when a business leader looks at the balance sheet, it's easier to justify hiring more sellers. Support teams, especially when a dedicated representative works a given account, end up talking to customers throughout the year and so seem less awkward when renewals come around.

- *Dedicated renewal teams*: As sales and support grow, renewing accounts can become a tedious task—and one with a specialized skillset very different than the specialized skills required to provide quality support for products. Therefore, larger enterprise customers often end up working with dedicated renewal teams. Once an organization reaches that level, account renewal teams likely report into the sales organization again as sales becomes responsible for the revenue line of the balance sheet.

As mentioned, smaller and more transactional renewals are often handled within products automatically, which is great whenever possible. This might simply be using a payment processor like Stripe to process a transaction until a customer cancels the service. This is obviously the method with the least amount of friction, but also with the least amount of touch. In these cases, just make sure to provide great support and continue innovating the product so there isn't a mass exodus of customers because something better comes along.

Staying Relevant

The adventuring party is growing. We've proven the market, which paves the way for other entrants. No matter which support delivery method we choose, keep in mind that to remain relevant and competitive, we need to out-innovate the competition and provide great support for customers. Let's look at some ways to make sure to do that:

- *Tirelessly attacking quality*: Nothing loses a customer faster than losing their data. Customers will become more frustrated if they click buttons that don't work or if they are asked to pay for an unavailable service.

- *Close those tickets*: Before we can close tickets, we need a ticketing system. This is the center of the support universe and comes free (or at a nominal increase in cost) with many CRM suites. Track the time it takes to close those tickets and automatically escalate tickets that are open too long up the leadership ladder. Early-stage companies often mean that service interruptions go straight to a founder. In later stages, we end up classifying tickets and assigning those escalations per the classification of the ticket type (and sometimes differently for named or enterprise accounts).

- *Feature requests*: If we ask our customers the right questions, we never need to have another innovative idea again. Feature requests (and sometimes the ability to vote those up) are a great way to uncover what customers need to get more value from our products. Providing value often means we don't have to compromise on price and makes renewals easier. The ability to vote feature requests up or down then gives us a natural quantifiable metric for the features customers might find most valuable.

- *Surveys*: Features aren't the only aspect of a software business. Another aspect is just the experience of what it's like to work with the company. Surveys that cover how the sales and renewal processes were, in addition to thoughts on the product, are a great way to uncover how we can better serve our customers. One type of survey question is simply whether a customer would recommend our product, the heart of what we call a Net Promoter Score or NPS. This can be put on a dashboard for everyone in the company to track brand loyalty and is a great early warning sign that there will be renewal challenges when it dips low.

- *Know the competition*: Innovation is often an evolution. Small features that enhance workflows are great to bolt onto products, leveraging insights a competitor has come across, but in ways that match our own ethos. Companies shouldn't actively use the products of our competitors, but we should keep an eye on images of products posted to websites by influencers and how people talk about products. We also shouldn't over-index on what our competitors are doing, but we should stay aware of what they are up to.

- *Talk to every customer that leaves*: Every time a customer leaves, people who care feel a pit in their stomach. It can hurt to lose customers, especially if we put a lot of effort into getting them in the first place or if their name provides some cache. Whenever possible, talk to them and understand where they went and why.

- *Be attentive, but clear*: We want to be attentive to the needs of our customers. This starts with feature requests and surveys but might include phone conversations and even in-person discussions. But don't leave customers expecting something we never plan to build. Hearing them and making them feel heard is important, but we should be clear about where their needs fit into our roadmap so we don't leave them waiting.

- *Pick up the phone (not just at renewal time)*: Many customers don't have time to chat with every vendor that wants to call. They have day jobs, and we are here to make them more successful at their job. If they don't have time to talk with us, they don't have to answer— but at least when we call, they know we care. And if they happen to answer, it's great to touch base and hear honest opinions of how we're doing.

Each lead is hard to find and harder to win. Each sale can take months (if not longer) to close. That's a lot of nurturing, whether done automatically or manually by sellers. The revenue derived from customers is the lifeblood of any company. Without gold an adventuring party cannot retain great talent to help the party scale. Renewals are a huge part of that. We should all understand how we want renewals to occur, what happens when customers upgrade, how we measure satisfaction, and what success looks like.

Ticketing Systems

The entire adventuring party should know what each other is up to. Each time a customer contacts us with a support issue, a ticket should be created. When done properly, that ticket contains a description of the incident, a category for the incident, the severity of the problem, each contact had with the customer about the incident, and a resolution. The severity and category are often overlooked, but provide valuable reporting data as we grow and help automate escalations.

The ticketing system is one of the more important and yet undervalued systems in use at any organization. It's simple to spin up an instance of one out of hundreds of SaaS products these days and almost immediately be tracking tickets. We often just use what we've used before. But first, consider the following:

- *The type of support*: The people that use products can communicate with us via chat, phone support, or email and through integrations with third-party tools like Slack or Microsoft Teams. Each of these routes has its own costs and considerations to plan for.

- *The experience for users*: Each route has its own impact on experience. Many organizations have shifted away from having a dedicated phone number to call for support, but that's still one of the more popular means of contacting companies for support. When providing chat support, we can with just a few lines of embedded code provide a chat button throughout our website and within a web app. If need be, our support representatives can always call customers if chat isn't getting their issue resolved. The key here is to understand and plan for the experience customers have with each route they go through to attain support.

- *Knowledge base integration*: Zero-tier support or allowing customers to receive automated responses that point to help desk articles is a great way to keep support costs low—especially for consumer or prosumer products. When looking at knowledge-based integration, also consider how that knowledge base or how-to articles get wired into chatbots and other support tools.

- *The agent experience*: Every company should want a great experience for our customers. But we want our employees to enjoy using a tool as well. This means the application or web application that support agents monitor should look modern and be easy to navigate. Also, look to have the ability to create a knowledge base from a ticket and for agents to be able to interact with chatbots, initiate tickets easily from phone calls, etc.— without complex data entry of contact information already sitting in the CRM.

- *Escalations*: Beyond agents, support organizations will (hopefully) ultimately grow to have managers run support services. As we select a ticketing system, we want tickets to be able to alert managers when tickets exceed the amount of time they should sit in a queue. This means automated escalations. In the beginning, this might mean that a ticket goes from the lone support agent to a founder—but as we grow, we want the flexibility to route tickets to different escalation queues.

There are a lot of ticketing systems out there because there are a lot of workflows, and different innovative approaches help to automate. The best place to start the search for a ticketing system, though, is the CRM we select.

The CRM as the Ticketing System

One aspect of developing a ticketing system that might not seem obvious at first is that it needs to integrate with the CRM solution. Many of the CRM packages realize this and build tools that either come free with their solution or come at a nominal cost (as compared with buying a third-party tool and then implementing a link between them). Therefore, the very first step in trying to figure out the best ticketing system should be to start by looking at what the CRM provider has.

As we've seen with CRM solutions, smaller teams might benefit more quickly from the options built into a tool like HubSpot but then find the lack of customization and automation options at scale to be cumbersome as teams grow.

Stand-Alone Ticketing Systems

Many a CRM will have everything a support team needs. Ticketing is an afterthought for most vendors, though. The big ticketing systems out there (not including those specific to MSPs) are ServiceNow, Zendesk, Freshdesk, and, for software development teams, Jira. Tools like Halp then connect APIs between Jira Service Management and Zendesk up to tools like Slack and Microsoft Teams. This is a common way to manage tickets internally within a company.

External relationships can be a little different, but there are tons of open source and proprietary integrations that can link ticketing systems to chat and contact systems. Pay attention to these costs, including the costs of integrations, especially as a smaller company, because they often rise faster than the number of users and agents.

There are some other attributes to consider for a ticketing system, including

- *API*: Even if it isn't used in the beginning, it's important to be able to create, delete, list, and manage tickets from the API. This allows developers to build whatever links between web apps and other tools needed for a customer to be able to work with tickets within software. It's always great to have the flexibility for future innovations around these, but in the beginning, just check to see which options are available to interact with programmatically—and which aren't.

- *Embedded chat*: Yes, we mentioned this already. But it's worth revisiting. Support teams will want a slick chat experience, especially if that's the only way our customers can contact us. And in the early days when it's founders and developers responding to chat requests, we want them to get bugged when there's a message so they can't pretend they didn't know.

- *Machine learning*: When we resolve an incident or write a document about how to do something, we want future incidents to be able to be resolved with those links when possible. Anyone that's asked a chatbot a question and gotten immediate feedback with a link on how to resolve an issue will agree. That requires data aggregation and often for all the systems to be linked together but is worth the work if users are willing to work with the chat system.

- *Where it's being used*: Keep a running list of everywhere that an embedded form, bot, or another snippet from a third party was used (and make sure they meet any compliance requirements).

- *Reporting*: Every organization will want to be able to track statistics over time. Think about the amount of time it takes to close a case, how many were because of defects with software, the severity of each, the frequency of new cases, etc. These are best when sliced by the category of a ticket.

- *Surveys*: When a case is closed, it's important to have the ability to ask the customer how it went. This should be done every time an incident is created.

- *Privacy*: Companies must be able to destroy any user's data if they request we do so. When that happens, we should have a known playbook for how we respond and be able to understand how that impacts the integrity of our data about cases.

Now that we have a ticketing system in place that allows us to automate several options, let's look at the agents we've mentioned and start with hiring a great support team.

Hiring for Support

Some of the original Mac team in 1984 came out of the Apple support team. Pierre Omidyar supported developers at General Magic before he left to found eBay. We never know exactly what we have if we don't look. Support teams are a great way to come into a company. This doesn't mean they're entry-level or should be treated as anything less than the face of the company to those who need us the most. But we can leverage that entry point for the company into a powerful growth engine. All of this means we want to be careful about who we hire in support.

The first dedicated support employees should be people who consider it their mission to serve people. Not in a weird way, but it's really important to hire people who are kind and patient with customers, especially when we're starting out. A great interview question is

"There's a customer on the phone for the third time and they're asking for help, but it's not an issue with the product. It's an issue with something different. What do you do?"

We want people with empathy. This identifies a few different things. Are they comfortable being on the phone? Do they want to just get off the phone and move to the next ticket or play some *Among Us*? Are they interested in the success of the customer? There are a lot of iterations to this question that might work to achieve the same goals. There are other attributes as well, although combined they might not be as important as empathy. Let's look at other attributes we might look for when hiring for support positions:

- *Patience*: Supporting customers can be challenging. But there's no reason to rush interactions. The more patience we show, the more the customers will see that we actually like them.

- *Kindness*: This might go without saying, but we need people who will be nice to our customers. Again, every interaction with the customer is an opportunity to improve the relationship. Let's not screw that up.

- *Organized*: We need to take a data-driven approach to support. This allows us to build zero-tier (or training) assets that meet customers where they are to elevate the industry and thus reduce cases. If the number of cases (and time to close each) goes down—or at least goes up slower than the rate of increasing customers— then we know we're trending in the right direction. The more organized workers are likely to become the people who build these systems moving forward.

- *Domain expertise*: The more complicated a product or industry, the more we'll need people who understand the industry. We prefer to build talent rather than buy it, but scaling support fast might mean we need to bring in people from other companies who understand the space.

- *Provide competencies in other areas*: This is important in small companies but becomes less and less so as we grow. This might mean documenting products, Quality Assurance (QA), becoming a developer, and the ability to handle renewals or even outgoing sales. For a lot of young startups, bench time (or the ability to do projects when not on support cases) is probably the number one customer a support representative deals with.

These attributes hopefully seem like great attributes for any employee. But they're amplified with support given that many perceive support teams as the face of the company. Another way to grow support without hiring more and more humans is to invest in allowing customers to support one another.

Customer-to-Customer Support

Some of the best and most legitimate support that a customer can get is from another customer. Other people using the same tools are often in the same type of job and have the same needs. They also usually find workarounds to issues we may not even think are issues.

A community that connects customers to one another can be as simple as an email list—but that's a bit 1990s. We can also use Slack channels (especially a channel within a larger community) or even develop our own community platform using off-the-shelf tools like Khoros (https://

khoros.com/), Higher Logic (`www.higherlogic.com`), or even the open source Discourse (`www.discourse.org`). There are also groups on LinkedIn or Facebook and community features in a lot of different software we use, from GitHub to our help desk tools. And many a CRM has a community add-on.

It's natural for a community to form around a product as its use grows. If the company who makes the product doesn't build a community, then one will spring up as market success is found. One way to bring the community into focus is to use software that helps to do so. The right community platform is different for a lot of organizations, but some products can emerge with a little thinking about the problem we're trying to solve or how we want the community to run. A huge aspect of business is understanding motivators. Why would customers be in a community? Why might they support other customers? Here are a few common reasons:

- *Career progression*: Establishing themselves as an expert in an industry is a great way to get a better job in that industry.

- *Ego*: Yup, sometimes people just like the recognition.

- *Swag*: We can increase community engagement by providing an incentive, as we covered in the section "Customer Advocacy" earlier in the book.

- *Badges*: Gamification was a buzzword for a hot minute. As with many a buzzword, it had great use.

- *To get support*: If a customer answers questions, maybe someone else will answer their own.

If we know the motivators, we can choose a good solution that meets the needs to fulfill those motivations as well as our own motivations. Maybe we want to reduce the cost to provide support by connecting other users or want to help users get faster responses or make the community look larger. Whatever our motivations, nearly every product can benefit from having a community of some sort.

Once we start building a community, we can drive awareness by doing things like sending follow-up emails to customers after calls that show them threads about their issue. We can also use the community to feed any machine learning tools. A community connects customers. They see that others are in the same boat as them. Maybe their adventuring parties are similar to one another. Communities can form with or without our input. If we take the initiative and do the community creation up front, then we can more effectively steer the direction, even if we try to take a hands-off approach unless needed (which is usually the right strategy when community building).

Parlay Great Support into Referrals

Successful customers often lead to much larger footprints (or deal sizes) in their second year with a product. One of the best ways to grow an account is to grow our footprint within organizations we've already closed deals with. This might mean something as simple as a freemium customer we'd like to nurture into a paying customer. Or it might mean a small customer who we think could grow into a much larger client.

Most people who do a job task that a given company helps to automate or gain more visibility into see the value in the products that the company creates. But selling that value upstream to get more budget and a larger implementation can be a challenge. There are always competing priorities within organizations for budgets and other resources. It can be hard to compete with those that have more visibility to leadership and influence over budgets. But it can be done! Let's look at a few ways to arm customers to promote a good or service within their organization.

The Value Proposition

Some companies can clearly state what it is they do and what market problems they solve. What's often far more interesting is how the person who acts as the champion of those companies talks about the product and how it benefits their lives and what impact it had within those companies.

If we know that, we can tailor our content strategy in such a way that helps them to get more buy-in, making us stickier and maybe even growing our footprint in an organization. Let's look at a few of these.

Get Products and Initiatives to Market Faster

Opportunity cost can be a killer in new product development. As teams grow, there's an increasing chance that some of what we do has already been done. Cataloging information about previous products, research, sales strategies, and results helps keep us from redoing things that didn't work and so speeds up time to market without sacrificing well-grounded decision making.

This also frees us up to answer new questions and hypotheses instead of those previously worked on, allowing us to do more.

Uncover the Hidden Connections in Our Data

A lot of the software companies use are databases for specific markets. Many could be spreadsheets, but there's more value when we go beyond a simple spreadsheet. With all the data and insights into our data tagged, cataloged, and in one place, we can start to see relationships between otherwise disconnected insights.

Many startup founders have deep experience in their respective fields. Any one insight may be interesting, but when taken as a holistic collection of data, the founder can often surface insights into that data only gleaned from years of experience in a field. That allows customers to do more faster, with the experience of a veteran on staff even without actually having to have that veteran on staff–or a lot of veterans as our organizations grow. With machine learning, we can often make inferences between a lot of data points from multiple sources. In short, there's been an explosion in the number of targeted applications for a given role or industry simply because the narrowly defined workflows and data sets based on deep experience are so valuable to organizations just getting started in each discipline.

Save Cycles

Our teams need to understand what they're building toward. They might have questions about what led to a particular state of a process they're managing or what the next step is. We also might put guardrails up that don't allow people to make mistakes. Instant insights allow us to automate tasks, but when people don't know where we are with a given task or order in a process, things can come to a grinding halt until various questions get answered.

Providing teams with easy access to whatever it is a given company is there to catalog keeps them well-informed and confident that they're on track.

Never Lose Valuable Information

Staff turnover happens. It's always a bummer to hear stories of institutional knowledge getting lost when someone leaves an organization. This is why mages have spellbooks. Accounts get deleted, and with them go a pile of valuable data and insights. Or the person is the only one that knows where everything is saved. This is totally avoidable. Our businesses and processes are an investment. We should protect it, especially when it helps future people in support teams get up to speed faster.

Increase Trust in a Discipline

Let's face it. Not everyone considers the output of a given team as valuable, especially not with given disciplines still "looking for a seat at the table" or new teams at an organization. Many tools now provide insights not only to the ones on the front line fielding calls with customers, taking orders, researching, or any other individual contributions—those tools can also end up showing each of these to people in other teams as well.

Exposing hard work and plans and the evidence behind insights, statuses, and processes goes a long way toward establishing that credibility, allowing the people consuming the output of a given team to see the context around it and verify that the work holds up.

A Product Saves Money for a Budget Holder

Almost no teams have the resources to accomplish everything they'd like to do. So leaders are always looking for ways to have the same group of people be able to do more or have more people be able to do tasks themselves. This might mean a service desk that integrates with a tool that provides built-in workflows for executing tasks for a given discipline. That reduces the time to complete a project, keeps our teams focused, allows for better scale, etc. Providing a tool that connects other teams also provides guidelines and templates so that those not in our team feel more comfortable with the boundaries and automation we provide.

Provide Transparency to Leadership

It is the nature of complex organizations to have gaps between those who run the place and those on the front lines. The most successful organizations are ones that consistently bridge those gaps, finding ways to communicate fluidly up and down the ranks. Providing senior leadership with efficient access to what a team does can be an effective way to increase demand for that team and influence strategy at higher levels in the organization.

Understanding the Needs of Leadership

The best way to understand the needs of leadership is to include them in the conversation. They may have valuable insight into how to sell ideas further up the chain or horizontally to other groups.

Leaders can certainly provide valuable insight into their own perspectives and goals. We can end up with a better understanding of competing priorities and the values that drive decision making around an initiative like those we are trying to get done. A little research on their goals and the problems they face gives us empathy for them.

Ultimately, every leader and budget holder is different. Different approaches work better with different stakeholders. Some will be interested in innovation and reducing time to market, while others will focus on cost reduction. If we aren't able to get budget approval, all is not lost.

Simply keep the champion at a customer successful, and the budget will come. But understanding which value propositions that products at a startup are in support of, or when to focus on each, is a key aspect of not only selling to a champion but arming the champion for success within their organization. A database of support tickets can be a valuable place to mine that information.

Conclusion

Early in the life of a company, the founders are likely to do a fair amount of support. Maybe we have developers split the duty as we grow as well. If we're lucky, we will grow into an organization with a dedicated customer experience (CX) and/or support team. But it's often an afterthought in all the wrong ways. The truth is that great support can make an organization. It turns our customers like to know they matter.

Great customer support comes with other benefits. It justifies higher premiums, allows us room to experiment with the technology, buys our way out of failures with escape defects, and just feels good. Great support can be a differentiator, and so going above and beyond expectations can be a great growth hack. There are plenty of examples of companies who grew their software because their support teams bought them the time to do so.

Bad support can also break an organization. Customers who can't get access to support in the early days of an organization aren't likely to stick around, especially if we haven't gotten to the point where we have a slick onboarding experience. Larger leads likely won't even convert to customers if they can't get basic questions answered quickly. The customer service representatives that work with customers set the tone for the relationship, and while support might be separate from other teams, there's often a mental image of the company formed and either improved or harmed with every interaction that customer has with support.

The prevailing wisdom is such that a SaaS company develops a product and, once the product is done, sales are infinitely scalable. This just isn't the case; we all know that nothing is infinitely scalable. Therefore, we need to build a scalable support organization that ever-so-slightly reduces the costs per capita (with that ratio being based on whatever the organization's currency is, which we set back in Chapter 4).

Every dollar we spend on support is a dollar not spent on developing an amazing product, hiring sellers, or improving some other department. Each organization will find its own path to a similar eventual realization: earmark a certain amount of margin, and therefore budget, to supporting products. This could range from 10% to 30% according to the type of organization and product we're building. Once we know how much money we have to play with, we can scale the organization reliably and scale the support organization right along with it. The next chapter jumps right into just that—scale.

CHAPTER 14

Scale

The company has found a little success. Our adventuring party managed to complete a few side quests, level up a little, and prepare for bigger and better romps through the startup universe. Here's the thing: early successes can be parlayed into huge later successes if we have a good framework to grow. That means building systems that align around intentional and deliberate actions, as well as maintaining culture and bringing on the next generation of leaders. Hopefully, that sounds like a lot because as more and more people grow dependent on our continued success, we need to be serious about the game, or horrible, evil monsters will eat us all. Okay, so not entirely serious if we're still talking about monsters.

This chapter looks at many of the common steps and questions to ask when scaling an organization. Some of these are boring character maintenance things, but many are really focused around thinking more deeply about why we're here and narrowing the focus of what we want to accomplish. We'll fund the increased risk in later chapters, but let's start by looking at what got us in a place where we should scale and what we should be doing while getting there.

Scale Happens After Success (Most of the Time)

The founders had an idea. The thing got built. We managed to get a few people using the thing. We might even be making a few bucks a year in profit by selling the thing to some people. This is a place of privilege that

© Charles Edge, Chip Pearson, Amy Larson Pearson 2023
C. Edge et al., *The Startup Players Handbook*,
https://doi.org/10.1007/978-1-4842-9315-7_14

not everyone can get to, and before we get to the hard stuff, everyone should pat themselves on the back for it. Seriously, it's awesome!

Feeling good about ourselves, let's think about what even more people using the thing and joining us on this journey will look like:

- More people using software means more people do weird things to the software. Those increased iterations uncover defects in the software that most people call bugs. The bugs need to be fixed. We keep adding features, making the code more complex, and so it takes longer to fix each bug.

- We hired more developers, and now we have them redoing each other's work, stepping on each other's toes, building software in different ways, and organizing their work in a way that is purely technical and lacks the awareness that, you know, we have customers to delight.

- More people using the software means more questions about what it does and how it works. This means we need people answering those questions. That's called support.

- More money means increased scrutiny, increased receivables, and more paid out. We also have more people spending our money and so more work to keep expenses coded properly. Small mistakes get amplified. So we need accounting and finance to keep us aligned with generally acceptable accounting principles.

- More customers means more specific ads. The ads we're running work, but we need to iterate them to amplify the success, or the words we use that appealed to early customers don't win us customers later.

- We have a tendency to stop listening to customers and just build what we think they want. Then we get confused about why they didn't like it.

- We might hire people without explaining the mission or the values, and they then run through days trying to get as much done but don't prioritize properly because they don't know the why.

- Teams may be overworked and mad, and that can show in their work.

Most of us don't think about these things until we have to–unless someone tells us they're coming. Many of the areas we discuss in this book are for later-stage companies—until they aren't. We need to see the signs that it's time to incur a cost to scale an area of the organization before we have to do so retroactively, rushing the quality of the effort, increasing the cost, and likely causing service interruptions or bad experiences with our customers.

None of this was an issue when it was just the founders. We often hear statements like "We got so much done back then" from founders discussing growing organizations. But in our experience, much of what we got done might have been incomplete by more mature standards. We also had four- to six-person companies with flat structures. One of the most notable signs of scaling up is just that: moving from a flat organizational structure to a structure with two or three or even seven tiers of management. This levels up each discipline and then each sub-discipline.

The Organizational Structure

There are teams that report to their managers, and their managers report to directors, and the directors report to vice presidents, and they report to officers who in turn report to the CEO (who reports to the board of directors and investors). That's a simplified hierarchy of a modern company.

The organizational structure of most young organizations simply means that each new discipline falls to the person most capable of leading it. Over time we shuffle teams, which become departments, underneath new leaders. But let's take a step back and look at the upper-level departments in a more mature organization, as seen through the leaders who run them:

- *Executives*: These fall under the CEO and are comprised of the senior leadership team. The HR leader will often report to the CEO directly, given how integral and important those humans are to the success of any given organization.

- *Finance*: Led by the chief financial officer, this is the team responsible for collecting and distributing funds. As we grow they manage investments and securities and investor relations, and sometimes we find mergers and acquisitions or legal here as well. This might be represented as part of the operating expenses (OE) of an organization on a balance sheet.

- *Revenue*: Led by a chief revenue or chief operating officer (CRO/COO), this is where sales and sometimes marketing fall in the organizational chart. On a balance sheet or budget, this might be seen as part of the costs of goods sold (COGS).

- *Technology*: Often led by a chief technology officer (CTO), many startups include development teams, internal IT, DevOps, and security.

- *Customer success*: Sometimes falling under technology, sometimes under revenue, and sometimes under its own officer, CX includes support, onboarding, and usually services teams such as professional services and training.

Earlier in the book, we looked at these leaders as being representative of the different character classes in a traditional role-playing game. The domain experts; product management, user experience, documentation, compliance teams, and many other job functions are missing from the preceding list. Many of these fall into the type of organizational structure we had as an early-stage company because they are often the glue that binds teams together. These jobs matter across departments, and so as organizations grow, these functional responsibilities can alternate between department leaders, who then go from managing increasingly complex budgets to managing political power and back in a cycle of politics.

There is no right answer to what structure works best for a given organization with different customer needs to fulfil, so we work to find the right balances. No matter what structure is implemented, each emergent discipline then becomes a resource to manage—a resource with a finite amount of bandwidth and therefore output.

Team Bandwidth

Most adventurers begin alone or with a cofounder. We necessarily have a limited amount of bandwidth. We put our time into writing, selling, and marketing software. We also have to put time into accounting, finance, support, product management, and even legal. We hire someone to help us write code or support the product. We are increasing the bandwidth of the whole organization by 50–100%. Yet, we make a choice (conscious or not) about where we want to spend our time.

As organizations grow, more people are hired and new disciplines form. The bandwidth of the organization grows, yet the amount of bandwidth the organization and each team has is still finite. In fact, scaling the organization often means people put in less of those 12-hour days that were fine early in the company and need to get back to family and friends and recover their lost lives. In other words, as we grow we often end up not actually increasing the time and thus output of the organization but instead reducing it if we aren't careful.

Fred Brooks wrote that "adding manpower to a late software project makes it later" in his 1975 book, *The Mythical Man-Month*. While he'd later say that this was an oversimplification, it's no less true. Brooks had come in and rescued the IBM S/360 project, which cost more than the Manhattan Project to bring transistorized computing to market (and thus the evolution that allowed for interactive computing). He included a lot of points backing up the assertion, including that it takes time for people to be able to work together as a team, the amount of time it takes to communicate goes up as teams grow, and that software tasks are often less easily divided up than other tasks. In part, we owe much of Agile and object-oriented programming to this realization.

Organizations need to improve in areas that can't ever have enough bandwidth, yet we all bring this idea of how things should be when we join or form a company. For example, many organizations save nearly half their programming time by investing in user researchers, and yet that's often a discipline that's only formed later in an organization's lifecycle. Our advice here is to think about how the organization will work at the next one and, if possible, two evolutions. Understanding the organizational chart and task at later stages helps us make investments into humans and tools that can pivot to the new structure without alienating people—or, worse, having staff turnover.

Turnover can be a killer. As we grow and bring in leaders to manage teams, early hires can easily get left behind. We go from working lots of extra hours out of necessity to distributing work across more humans. We go from chaotic members of a party to teams with methodical, predictive, and systematized expectations. And yet we want them to be innovative and productive as we scale so our margins don't disappear. One way to give teams nearly unlimited bandwidth is to allow them to innovate how they do their jobs.

Empower Teams to Innovate

Innovation comes in the form of productivity gains, pricing paradigm shifts, governance, or visibility into a market problem. The more of these the innovation achieves, the longer lasting the impact.

Innovation doesn't come easily in heavy-handed, top-down run organizations. Innovation isn't the big idea but allowing new ideas to infuse every discipline that an organization builds. We need to understand the prevailing logic that generations of people in roles and industry have spent countless hours evolving and understanding. But we also need to provide the freedom in positions to try new things—to fail and succeed and fail again. We should understand the history of initiatives not so we don't try them again but so we iterate with the findings to avoid repeating failed initiatives.

Scaling is hard. New leaders bring in new disciplines and new thoughts and ideas. The individual contributors who report to them do as well. A true innovation will be followed by competitors that either innovate faster, build on the findings of the initial innovator, or outspend to acquire market share. Thus, first-mover advantage is an illusion, and competitive advantage is retained by taking all those ideas from every level of an organization and giving them room to flourish.

It is a mistake of the ego to assume any observation is new. Ego leads us to poor decisions and, combined with inattention to details at lower levels, keeps us from taking on risks. As the power and influence of an individual character in our party grows, so grows their dependence on power, and they become more predictable. Disruption can be (but is not always) synonymous with innovation.

The larger an organization becomes, the more bureaucratic it becomes, and so the more likely the bureaucracy will slow net-new innovations. The greater the productivity gains or visibility provided by the innovation, the greater the proof those gains will require. In many ways, this is what makes scaling an organization so difficult. Bureaucracy breeds politics. When two bureaucracies collide for power over an innovation, the likely result is to create a new bureaucracy. Doing so reduces the impact of the innovation. Not doing so reduces the chances the innovation will be accepted. Picking a side creates a party to undermine the innovation. However, to avoid involving bureaucracy or to undermine and blame bureaucracy is to assure failure.

Politics stifle innovation. One reason is that the impacts of an innovation can't be separated from the social, economic, political, and organizational conditions that brought the organization itself into being. If we can acknowledge all of this and communicate it to leaders as we hire them, and if we can do so without our own ego getting in the way, then we can more predictably allow innovation by empowering everyone in the organization to innovate their own position–provided we do so with accountability. Just keep in mind that productivity gains from innovations are reduced over time. This is one reason we need to be deliberate and repeatable.

Scale = Intentional, Deliberate, and Repeatable Actions

Scale necessarily happens when sales, and therefore revenue, outpaces our ability to deliver products or when we choose to inorganically grow with funds from investors. A theme of this book is that the best way to scale is with intentionality. Not only does this put us in the enviable position to be able to scale (when our strategy aligns with market needs) but it also allows us to scale in a fashion where we understand what's going on at every level of the organization. We're also better able to react to evolving market climates and guard-change control processes.

Clarity of communication makes us intentional in our actions. Intentional actions with clearly defined requirements are then more repeatable and easier to evolve over time. Think of the organization itself like a collection of microservices where each human process should have a contract of sorts, guarding the inputs and outputs. Teams then evolve delivery of services with autonomy, provided the contract requirements are still met. Those services require deliberate, repeatable actions in order to meet the requirements—so we can train the next generation to backfill us once we're ready to move up into our lofty new position.

We want to build our pool of talent. When each generation can enable the next or automate themselves out of a job, they've earned the next position. When they can't do so to meet the rapidly changing needs of the organization, we might need to seek new talent from the outside—or buy our talent. When we can't find or afford that talent, we may need to borrow from others (and so outsource a function).

The organization is then an ecosystem with a lot of loosely connected systems operating within it. The connection those systems have with one another necessitates the change control—especially when we outgrow the capabilities for that change to be communicated over tribal communication channels, that is, those that develop organically based on friendships or acquaintances made in the organization.

Systems and Repeatable Processes

We discussed making precise and repeatable processes via intentional development of an organization in the previous section. There are a lot of ways to go about this. The best way is when we can take a process or function off the shelf using a third-party piece of software. For example, if developers need to look up tax information at the time of a transaction, an army of accountants could be hired, or just create an account with a service like Avalara that can provide all that information back in a nice, juicy blob of JSON. The latter is preferable.

Some processes can't yet be automated. Maybe they haven't matured enough for us to identify to an algorithmic model. Or maybe they are just chaotic in nature. We need to have humans do a thing, and we need to make that thing repeatable. Further, we always need to be able to answer whether a failure to carry out the process was because the process wasn't defined tightly enough or because the party failed to reach the end goal.

There are a number of frameworks available that we can learn to help us in that journey. We've mentioned the John Boyd paper "Destruction and Creation," but there are frameworks that go beyond theory and into a known set of best practices where a company can give new members on the team a book or send them through training courses, which include the following:

- *EOS*: Short for Entrepreneurial Operating System, EOS is a set of tools that get everyone in an organization meeting, planning, prioritizing, communicating, measuring, and following the same processes. There's more, but for the purposes of this section, there are aspects of EOS that focus on role clarity and processes within that. Most founders should have a working knowledge of EOS, especially as it pertains to process.

- *The E-Myth*: A book that provides a great overview of getting started with business process in small business. The premise (and ensuing empire of training materials) is that most businesses fail because we don't move from acting like technicians to acting like businesspeople. And the crux is in creating repeatable actions. This is an oversimplification, but it's a small book that is certainly worth the read. If inspired, feel free to keep going with the products in that ecosystem.

- *Six Sigma*: A philosophy that all work that needs to be done can be documented, defined, measured, analyzed, improved, and controlled. Six Sigma goes way beyond that philosophy and includes hundreds of tools to measure and maintain almost any process imaginable. It's worth noting that there is a lot of work involved and it's more a grab bag of techniques to use when needed. Further, while Six Sigma has a keen focus on reducing variations in process delivery (and thus defects), Lean Six Sigma is a variant that focuses on eliminating waste and thus making processes more efficient (often with less variation as well).

There are also Kaizen, TQM, the Theory of Constraints, Perigon, and many, many more. But these are the tools most software organizations who want to dig into proven methodologies use. As we grow, we scale in and out of them. Hopefully, we never stop learning. We can also choose to go far beyond these and empower our teams to reinvent their own work. And once we've clearly defined every process, we can look at which can be automated and the cost to automate each. A huge part of scaling is taking the processes that don't scale well and refactoring them, sometimes trading simplicity for solving for edge cases and eating the cost to completely solve exceptions as they arise in exchange for immediate and automatic transactions.

The Impact of Process to Culture

Automation displaces workers and/or existing power structures and so can create contempt. But it doesn't have to. Everyone we hire should be excited about automating or innovating themselves out of a job and into a new, better position with more authority and autonomy.

Once processes are codified on paper (or a Miro board these days), they get digitized. Once digitized, aspects of those processes become relational (e.g., put into a database with tables or endpoints linked to one another). Once relational they are analyzed with machine learning, furthering our understanding and promoting even more productivity gains. Moving an industry (or a business representative of an industry) one stage forward on this horizon is then deterministic, not innovative. The impact this has to process is critical to understand as it involves how disruptive rethinking certain aspects of a business can be—and how regulatory and societal shifts need to be considered. Further, once an industry or process has matured a stage, the previous stage goes down-market and becomes a commodity—thus, cottage or craft industries will arise so the analog variant survives.

It all begins with process, and process must be refactored each time we mature to the next stage (think "Destruction and Creation" by John R. Boyd here, circa 1976). If the culture is one where we prioritize innovation and automation (in a human way) and give our coworkers space to get creative, rethink everything, and maybe even fail a little, then we engender a sense of autonomy, collaboration, and owning successes at every level of an organization.

The impact of iterating faster and outperforming competitors makes people feel good about working at an organization. A simple analogy to this might be the use of machine learning in the early days of Google. The first search engines involved a lot of manual entry. Then came robots that would spider through sites and catalog information. That information started flat and, as the Web grew, could then be stored in relational databases. Organizations like Yahoo! hired teams of researchers to catalog the sites manually. Google used first classification algorithms and then much more complicated combinations of simple learning machines (yes, that's a six simple machines reference—thanks, Archimedes!). That permeated throughout the organization.

When it came time to sell search, which others had a difficult time doing, they were able to apply similar algorithms to auctioning off search terms using a web interface rather than getting upsold by slick sellers as was being done by Yahoo! at the time. The impact was that the best engineers in the world wanted to work there. Google outhired the rest of Silicon Valley and had a veritable cornucopia of innovations effectively allowing them to rewrite the rulebooks. It was as though they were playing a campaign in a completely different ruleset than their competitors were.

Some processes should not be automated until they're ready. Others should have been automated a decade ago. Often there's an app or simple workflow that can automate aspects of the business. If we focus on putting out quality tools, there are a number of projects to help isolate escape defects, security vulnerabilities, or duplicative code. We can also build aspects of automation and machine learning into our core product, providing value to customers. But one of the easiest areas to automate (especially if we don't want to get bloated) is the operations of the actual business.

Operate and Automate the Business

The example of Google needing less sellers is overly simplistic. They also needed less humans sitting in an operations role. This drove down the cost of doing business. And here's a clutch piece of information: very little they did isn't available on some college kid's GitHub today. Still, there are certain areas we want to semi-automate until we have a very high level of confidence they are appropriately ready to be set free from human interference.

Small problems with payroll, billing, or anything involving human resources can be detrimental to the trust our employees, customers, and investors have in our organizations. These areas seem the easiest to automate, but a check and balance where a human looks at each before they are transacted can save a lot of time and heartache.

Think of return on investment. Automation is one of the best ways to help us scale. It can help us scale well or very badly according to how much thought we've put into our organization's operations. We want to give team members the ability to rethink operations, but we want to start somewhere and then institute change controls so when there are changes to basic processes, we are made aware of them.

Let's take how a support ticket comes in as an example. A customer opens a chatbot on the site, and immediately we have our first item that might be changed as we develop support assets. Do we ask them what their question is and then try to point them at documentation, or do we immediately put the customer in touch with an agent? Every industry is different, and some will choose to skip that bot altogether and instead just have a phone number. Different products and target audiences have different expectations. Exceeding the comfort zone of our audience is likely to be met with dissatisfaction.

We need a lot of zero-tier assets (e.g., blog posts, FAQs, how-to articles) in order to have the option to provide that documentation to a customer looking for answers. We also need a ticketing system. Then we need a chatbot that ties into our ticketing system and is capable of cataloging our assets. We also probably need the whole thing integrated into our CRM to understand the needs of our customers. This means the project to provide a known automated experience has building blocks that we need to plan for well in advance of implementation.

Many startups will bring on a CRM early in the life of the business. Tools like Salesforce either can have apps in them that perform tasks not related to sales or can easily be integrated with third-party tools that perform those tasks. This includes ticketing, chatbots (Salesforce has Einstein built-in), accounting software, and almost anything we might want. Each CRM has a set of other options as well as APIs so we can develop our own automations.

All of this brings us to a simple instruction everyone should be given during onboarding: automate yourself out of a job. Routinely pick apart the manual tasks required to keep the organization running and look for out-of-the-box solutions or areas where the communication between two vendors or services developed in-house have known good inputs and outputs that allow for the automation of the process. And a diversity of backgrounds might even allow us to see places where some of the tasks we do really aren't needed as they don't benefit our customers or help protect our organizations.

Diversity and Inclusivity

We want the future workforce to experience the rich entrepreneurial tech culture that is happening all around the world. That future workforce is not like the white men in suits that made up the mainframe, minicomputer, and microcomputer revolutions of the 1950s, 1960s, and 1970s. We are as diverse as an interconnected and global world allows. And yet the technology industry lags behind most in hiring diverse candidates.

Diversity is a term that typically refers to hiring candidates from a lot of different backgrounds. Building an inclusive workplace is about making those diverse voices heard, bringing people into conversations, and providing more foundational opportunities. Equity is then making sure the total rewards for all team members are in alignment.

Diversity, equity, and inclusion (DEI) are then the programs and policies we implement so that everyone in our organizations feels they can bring their whole self to the table. They feel their abilities and disabilities, age, culture, ethnicity and race, gender, religion, and sexual orientation are assets and not liabilities. Throughout this book we discuss having diverse points of view, and that's not just different opinions about how many lines of code make a function monolithic in nature. It's about allowing everyone to be represented and participate in our organizations.

We need those diverse backgrounds, experiences, and skills and expertise they shape. This improves our performance, our level of innovation, the organization, and finances. Oh, and it's just the right thing to do. Something else we can do, take a step beyond and put *justice* at the end of the acronym (DEIJ) and become an antiracist and antidiscrimination culture. The future workforce will embrace it.

There are a lot of books out there on diversity and inclusivity. We recommend reading a few, even to founders who come from diverse backgrounds. We can all do better. If we don't, there's likely bad press and lawsuits waiting to happen. Oh, and did we mention it's just the right thing to do? As we scale an organization, the excuses like "There's a supply chain gap in hiring diverse candidates" start to fall away and become disproven. If we're mostly a homogenous team, we've failed to see what's going on in the world around us.

We need to promote diversity at every level of the organization. The leadership team sets a tone for the rest of the organization. One of the most important places to focus on inclusivity and diversity is the executive team, which we'll look at developing in the next section.

Build a Leadership Team

Growing companies can't be led by one person alone. We need to surround ourselves with people we can trust and who can run parts of a company. A leadership team, or executive team, is the top three to five senior members (or officers as we grow) of a company who help the CEO make important decisions. This involves setting strategy, culture, communication channels, and control structures and responding to bigger issues that arise over the course of doing business.

A leadership team doesn't always mean an officer or executive. It's a core group who has the pulse of the entire organization and customer base. Executives can't always contribute at that level as they have departments to run and might not have the requisite experience. And yet they often do for a variety of reasons. The best leadership teams have clear reporting, expectations, and accountability. Members should be comfortable challenging one another, accepting feedback, and thereby growing. No avoidant behaviors can be tolerated. Keep in mind these are the people who protect the jobs of those who elected to join us on a grand adventure. Those humans are important to us, and the leadership team not only provides critical feedback about how things are working out for them but also sets the goals and strategies and culture that shows we have as long term a commitment to them as they've shown to us.

This means moving from a focus on our functional areas to one that balances the enterprise needs with our functional responsibilities. This means we are given the right to look forward and so have the responsibility to do so. When we're interviewing for leaders, we need to keep this in mind.

There are a number of roles that come up in the life of an organization. The typical top structure of companies includes a chief financial officer (CFO), chief operating officer (COO), chief technology officer (CTO), chief product officer (a role a founder sometimes moves to if a CEO is hired), etc. We'll get started with a business development lead, which might evolve into a chief revenue officer, or CRO, role.

Business Development

Many founders need to show some success in founder-led sales to get to the point where they can start hiring a sales team. Founder-led sales don't scale, so there's an important question we need to look at: will the company scale go-to-market activities with investments that lean more in the direction of marketing or sales?

Software companies that have simple, consumer- or prosumer-focused products often use a freemium type of business model in go-to-market activities. This means advertising, marketing, and maybe public relations take a front seat to pure sales. Companies who make products geared toward enterprise, on the other hand, often invest heavily into sellers who can take a more solution-oriented approach to guiding customers through a funnel. Neither structure is better than the other in general, and as we grow we'll incorporate parts of both.

We won't spend that much time looking at what we need from a chief marketing or chief revenue officer like we will in the next couple of sections, because we go into much more detail about running those disciplines in dedicated chapters in this book. The various aspects of those that we lay out are more a grab bag. Some companies won't have any sales teams at all, and others will invest less in marketing—so there's no single position description or set of attributes we can provide.

There are commonalities we'll want in both. The leader should understand the customer being served and provide (or be able to implement) a solid plan to get our product in front of them in the most authentic way possible. They should agree to the key performance metrics we set out and be able to report back achievement toward them. And given a SaaS or software company, they should love number nerding. Selling is one of the most important aspects of the company, so be sure to read all three chapters to help form a view of what we're looking for in the business development leader.

Another position we'll discuss is the biggest number nerd of them all, the CFO.

CFO

Typical startups will have simple finances, maybe a credit card or the founder's bank accounts. As we grow we have multiple accounts and income flowing in and can level up to hiring a part-time bookkeeper. Then we have investors who want to see financials using generally acceptable accounting principles and taxes and accounts payables and accounts receivables, meaning it's time to scale up to a finance team. The person that sits at the top of that team is the chief financial officer, or CFO.

Let's look at what the CFO will be doing (or tasks they'll be leading):

- Manage the cash flow.

- Reconcile credits and debits in the general ledger.

- Manage accounts payable and accounts receivable.

- Develop financial models.

- Manage, direct, or otherwise lead others in the finance team.

- Keep a keen eye on where actual financials don't meet expected financials.

- Prepare reports and financial statements.

The CFO might be asked to do more according to whether other business leadership positions have been filled. The CFO might also be asked to do sales forecasting or other number crunching for sellers (like where to concentrate efforts) according to the maturity of a sales organization. Human resources might be aligned under the CFO. If there's no COO, maybe some elements of operations go there until there is a dedicated leader for that. But the key aspect of what we want in a CFO is to run the finances.

We won't include any of these in what we'd consider putting in a job description, but here are some items that might go on the position description of a CFO:

- Provide leadership and direction to the finance and accounting teams.

- Provide strategy recommendations to the executive team.

- Maintain financial forecasts, budgets, and reports.

- Advise on long-term financial and business planning.

- Review all formalized finance procedures.

We're not typically big on including degree or advanced degree requirements in position descriptions. But the CFO is one of those roles where this might be a good idea.

As we mentioned, scaling up takes time, and one of the positions where the CFO might be filling some of those gaps is the COO. Let's look at what that entails and what responsibilities might be trading back and forth between other leaders.

COO

The chief operating officer, or COO, oversees the business functions at an organization. This begins with operations, or what needs to happen for the company to run smoothly and grow. The COO might also lead finance or sales—but each of those is likely to be split into a separate officer title and executive function as an organization grows and directing those affairs becomes more complicated.

The COO carries out company policies and manages the day-to-day activities that keep the organization marching toward the targets and so becomes accountable for those. This includes

- Operational excellence

- Understanding finances and burn rates (if not managing them)

- Managing growth based on the strategy

- Facilities management

- Making sure local, federal, and state requirements are met

- Being the bridge to the staff

- Having a keen eye on eliminating wasteful processes
  and promoting productivity

- Automating as much as possible

This can be a lot, and as we grow the role will not only shape itself around the traditional responsibilities of a COO but also fill gaps in other areas while newer disciplines are forming. Let's look at a few items we might put as requirements in a position description:

- Leadership skills

- Understanding business planning and regulatory
  requirements

- Exceptional project management skills

- Solid grasp of analytics and tying those back to
  necessary performance metrics

- Experience motivating direct reports and partners

- Excellent problem-solving skills

- Strong organizational skills

As we go through the role of a COO, it might sound a bit like some of the duties of a CEO. As an organization grows, the CEO also has a board and investors to manage, becomes a key sales asset (and pushes the sales organization), needs to work on acquisitions and mergers, ends up becoming a public relations figurehead, has the technology to keep a finger on, and much more. So there's a leader for each of those areas in order for the CEO to have a trusted resource they can get the pertinent information from and collaborate on how each is run.

CTO

Founding teams often include at least one person who's technical in
nature. That's part of software. This might be a talented software developer
or someone who writes much of a proof of concept or even an app that
we take to market. As we grow we need a more robust set of skills that
no one person can have, and so we bring in other developers to wrap
around them.

That original developer may stay on to grow into a robust executive or
may just like writing code—if that's the case, we'll need to hire someone
to work with the technical teams we hire. Alternatively, a product could be
conceived by someone with a given domain expertise, and we outsource
development to go to market. We then hire an internal team to take over
once we have enough money flowing in from customers or another
funding.

Both of the preceding scenarios mean we're going to need to hire a
head nerd. In a two-person company, this might be a great developer—but
as we grow they'll need to be a better orchestrator than developer. This
means enough technical knowledge to understand how the pieces fit
together but maybe not living in the code all day.

The CTO will also likely have the technology used by people in
the organization reporting to them. This includes providing network
infrastructure services, endpoint security, patch management, technical
support, identity management, line-of-business applications, and anything
specific to the organization's needs (like those weird smoke detectors in
that one closet with the mop bucket in it)–although some startups will
move this under a COO once hired.

Other disciplines that often report into a CTO might include product
management, DevOps, research, compliance, pre-sales systems engineers,
and more. The breadth of knowledge a CTO needs in a startup is then

fairly large. Let's look at how we might put some of these requirements in a position description:

- Set the vision for how technology is used by the company and strategies to accomplish the vision.

- Establish and communicate goals for research and development.

- Provide and report on timelines to achieve technology goals.

- Establish budgets and timelines for each aspect of the technology landscape.

- Ensure projects get delivered on time and on budget.

- Lead and inspire team members to innovate their part of the technology stack.

- Make sure all technology assets adhere to regulatory guidelines and are in compliance with any necessary frameworks.

A common theme as we go through these positions is that many of the officer positions might be filling a gap for another. We should also mention that rather than hand out the lofty titles (unless we have to in order to get a good candidate), we can also use titles like director of technology for the CTO position (or using a manager or director title for any of these). This allows us to grow a great hire into that position or hire someone else without having to hand a demotion off to someone in the future.

One final aspect that might fall under a CTO (or stay with a CEO) at a software company comes into play around the time a company is typically raising a B or C round of financing: corporate development. This is really about inorganic growth at a company. And it's easy to imagine that buying experience points doesn't always provide a level-up.

Corporate Development

Investors are good at putting money to work. At some point between a larger-sized Series A and a Series C investment, the investors are going to ask what company a founder wants to buy—or what companies. What they're really asking, though, is how the corporation is going to expand—and whether it will be accelerated via acquisition.

Buying companies is an oversimplification, though. There are a number of ways a company can grow:

- Open international offices and expand into new territories. New languages also have technical impacts, like whether it's necessary to get a new data center (or Amazon instances in those countries for privacy and data reasons) and if the software needs to be localized for different countries.

- Bring on a new business development discipline. We can hire 20–30 sales development representatives to hunt for customers and win deals.

- Bring on an entirely new team to build and take another product to market. We don't have to buy companies to get new products. If we see an untapped product-market fit or want to expand our portfolio, we can build it. Here it's best to keep the newly created organization quiet and small, separate from the trappings of politics in a rapidly growing startup. But we want the team to know they'll eventually be folded into the main organization (unless the company is large enough to have a general manager per product in a portfolio).

- Buy a company to get one of the preceding ones. The most common here is to buy a company that gets us a new product, but there are some great examples of buying companies to get the developers or the sellers or, like Microsoft in their rapid rise in the 1980s, to get a sales office in other countries rather than build them organically.

- Buy a competitor.

We can certainly buy a company to do one of these. We see multi-billion dollar deals, and they're almost always product-centered acquisitions. Gains should always be plotted against the value of money over time in order to extract a true return on investment. We spent a lot of time talking about culture earlier, but one of the hardest parts of an acquisition is the impact to culture.

The Politics of a Growing Organization

Power dynamics are as old as time, and pretending they don't exist doesn't make anything any better. As an organization grows, we bring in more people with diverse backgrounds, and workplace politics happen. It's inevitable as increasing levels of specialization alienate those who see that as constraining and as those areas of specialization seek to protect their interests. It's healthy to see our roles as critical to the success of the organization. It's unhealthy to put our personal needs above those of the organization. The line between those two is often blurry, and the former is positive, while the latter is negative.

Ultimately we seek to find compromise, or common ground, when we're learning to agree to disagree. That's fine in small doses, but the negotiation and politicking can take too much time. It often begins with how decisions are made at an organization. We can maximize transparency to let those around us see how decisions are made. That can go beyond the surface level in decision making, so sometimes we need to dig a bit deeper and be able to unpack why a decision was made.

It's better to be proactive than reactive. We can do nice things for those around us and exert positive influence. We can then help our coworkers do the same. We should avoid microaggressions and be up front, if not assertive, with our feedback. Accountability is an important aspect of leadership, and we can be kind but firm with feedback. This inspires good interpersonal relationships in the company—and that improves efficiency. Not only that, it's just a better place to be.

A leadership vacuum inspires putting personal gain over the good of the company. Personal gain might be getting more than someone else or trying to get the next job. Ego and aspirations are real, and we can acknowledge them without letting them become a negative force in an organization. To help keep the company good at the forefront of minds, make sure employees are getting credit and compensation appropriate for their contributions. The other side of ego is insecurity, and between total compensation and showing our appreciation, we can take steps to address that individually.

Some people we hire bring their politics as baggage with them. We can address this during the interview process but often don't know it's a problem until too late. We don't want to reward people for being able to carve out aspects of a system to navigate. It's better to identify when people are doing so and institute process to stop turfbuilding. Fiefdoms impede creativity and innovation in exchange for a status quo.

Many leaders avoid reprimanding teams. Political behavior causes an organization to get bloated as that specific type of conflict breeds withholding information, backstabbing, harmful alliances, gossip, rumors, and other bad behaviors. Instead, we can foster an adventuring party that's professional and recognizes the work in others, where self-improvement is important but so is volunteering, and helping not only others in the organization but also the larger community surrounding us.

Another aspect of politics is tribalism. Scaling is hard, and there's often an us vs. them mentality with the more tenured members of an organization and those brought in to run it at its new size. Perhaps a round of funding infused the organization with capital to grow, or perhaps we're building a new discipline. Some organizations need things like dotted-line reporting structures in matrixed organizations—but allowing those to happen in a hyper-growth company is likely to destroy morale and productivity (the two are intertwined). Instead, we can get our teams doing what's best for the team. We can insist that new leaders and individual contributors network and get great relationships with their coworkers. We can take steps when we see cliques forming. We can discourage gossip of any kind rather than get pulled into it. But we have to pay attention and be engaged to notice any of this.

Finally, an important aspect of avoiding negative politics running amuck is to avoid a bureaucratic and politicized structure. That's likely to happen in larger, more mature corporations but will sink productivity in a startup. Get teams to buy into the mission, vision, and values. Don't let teams weaponize them against one another. Instead, stay transparent and don't leave a leadership vacuum just looking to be filled by competing factions when scaling the organization.

Reorganizations

It would be great if there was an optimal organizational structure for companies of any type and at size. The simple answer is that the structure is going to be different for everyone because part of an evolving organization is the trust we find with leaders of various disciplines and the knowledge each has of other disciplines. A young startup can't just go hire an executive for every function. The CEO or founder will take on some responsibilities and, as the organization grows, fill gaps opportunistically based on how much money is in the bank account or simply because a need arose.

Success in our adventure usually means growth. Growth means people get new bosses. Reorganizations are never easy. Or if they are easy, that's a clear sign that something is very wrong. No matter the response, any reorg will inspire anxiety in at least part of a team. New leadership and management lead to questions that require answers that are clearly articulated (which in turn require deeper thought on our parts). Starting employees off with an expectation that things will change is a proactive way of getting in front of the coming reorgs. It's not uncommon for the second or fifth person hired at a company to have a new manager or director a year throughout a decade of growth. Success is a lovely and complicated thing. It doesn't have to leave our teams anxious and so less productive while reorienting to a new structure.

A reorganization doesn't always mean something is broken. Especially in startups, it might mean that the CEO or some other leader simply has too many direct reports to be an effective leader for the given team(s) being mapped to new leadership. We've said this throughout the chapter, but transparency about the decisions should be able to inform teams that what we're doing is evolving the organizational structure in order to better align with size, priorities, and goals. This makes us stronger, more malleable, and better able to scale emerging disciplines. If the reorganization is due to a problem, that should be stated. Transparency and a clarity of communication don't just mean using more words—it means helping others to see the truth more clearly.

Here are a few more items to consider when preparing for a reorganization:

- **Communicate early and comprehensively.** This should begin with the why a reorganization needs to happen, and then include a list of who rolls up to which leaders and why. That means all of those details need to be worked out prior to communicating changes. Having said this, the second we include line-of-business leaders who we need to collaborate on the structure, we have to expect that information will leak out to every part of the organization.

- **Show how each team maps to the mission and downstream to strategies and priorities.** The ability to connect the efforts of a team to the strategies in a clear manner shows teams they're important and a priority. It also increases engagement and maintains the culture we've worked on during the previous chapters.

- **Keep teams autonomous yet accountable for results.** This is a key takeaway from the whole book. Think of a team like a microservice; whether a team writes it in Go or Node or Python, it doesn't matter provided the service fulfils the contract for an output given a valid input. The same is true with teams we build. We should maintain some form of change control, yet if accounts payable moves to a new tool or sales development representatives use a new method for qualification, then provided they meet or exceed the results everyone agreed to, leaders should be open to new and innovative approaches to getting the job done. This shows our teams we trust them, which again keeps them engaged.

- **Reduce costs and increase efficiency.** More layers of management often create additional latency in communication channels and for decisions to be made. Reorganizations should reduce the amount of time required to manage humans, direct strategies, and coordinate tasks upstream as less of a day will be devoted to them. Provided we give space to evolve, expand scope within defined lanes, and grow within careers, the teams typically accept changes when there is clear communication. If a new leader in a reorg comes in and changes these things, then the affected parties start saying things like "I guess we'll just act like a big company now," which is counterproductive long term.

- **Acknowledge when teams become further from the CEO.** This is important—there will be more layers between a group who maybe reported directly to a CEO early in the life of an organization. They now find themselves reporting through an "outsider" who was brought in because of their expertise in a given field. They need to be reassured that they are no less valued. Maybe they're so good they don't need to report to the CEO, who needs to shift the focus on fundraising for a time to product management or sales or whatever disciplines get more of the time and attention.

The simple takeaways about reorganizations are to collaborate with leaders but to do so quickly. We then want to communicate with a maximum amount of clarity and retain as much autonomy in each role or discipline as possible (obviously compliance, regulations, and a need for checks and balances in various aspects of a company get in the way). Having said all this, it's not uncommon for a team to bounce back and forth between two leaders repeatedly. This is because we don't always get it right. Leave our doors open for more ideas and follow-on thoughts and room for making further changes (without seeming chaotic) as time goes on. After all, if the company grows quickly, more reorganizations will come annually if not more frequently.

Conclusion

Different organizations scale in different ways. Some focus on distributed innovation or inspiring teams to make what they do better. Others scale more rigidly and take a more top-down and structured approach. All scale in a hybrid model across these spectrums.

Software as an industry is usually scaled in a more distributed fashion. We see it in action when a developer walks up to a Kanban board and takes a sticky, choosing what they are going to work on. While software companies have accounting and other traditional disciplines inside them, they often work similarly, according to the leader brought in to build that team. We often focus on automating everything, but as we covered in this chapter, we first have to build systems to support what we'll automate.

Growing fast means rebuilding systems routinely. As we mentioned, we can alienate fewer of our adventuring party (with whom we spent a lot of time gaining experience) by proceeding with deliberation and intentionality and by instilling an entrepreneurial spirit into everyone. An important lesson we want readers to take from this book should be that we don't have to grow fast. In fact, we can sometimes find more happiness when we stop growing. We'll get into more detail on that in the last chapter, but in the meantime, we'll move from scale to services (and funding operations and further scale through services) in the next chapter.

CHAPTER 15

Services

Companies, as with adventuring parties, often have a mission and values. This book is about how to build a software startup (although much of what we go through can be applied to any type of company). But many a software and hardware company also sells services. Every company with a household name has a services team. Some consider professional services a profit center; others consider services a loss leader done to improve onboarding or retention. This can be seen by where services reports in many larger companies–sometimes in sales, sometimes in support. And when services supports enough of the revenue of a company, it can even stand-alone as a division.

Scale means that services should either be in support of our mission and values or align with the mission to fund operations. This is one aspect of why we do services, especially in the early days of a company—to help fund our operations. Our adventuring party often takes side quests to earn experience and make enough gold to build a great equipment list that helps us amplify what we can do. This is similar to libraries of code to reuse for other projects; we use the money we make from services to hire more people and so on.

Services can also help us bootstrap a company. A great way to begin an adventure is to sell services while we build core products. After all, adventuring parties need money to buy supplies, pay henchmen, upgrade inventory, and so much more. But services can be a distraction as we try to scale up. The revenue doesn't always look the way it should on a balance sheet for a pure SaaS startup, either.

© Charles Edge, Chip Pearson, Amy Larson Pearson 2023
C. Edge et al., *The Startup Players Handbook*,
https://doi.org/10.1007/978-1-4842-9315-7_15

Services are more than revenue, though. Our services teams can also help us convince the townsfolk to band together to support our mission. The projects we take on can help spread the word about our organization. That can help us with long-term recruitment, advertising, and even finding even more customers.

Leveling Up a Services Organization

The services we provide change as our organization evolves. Sometimes it's hard to pinpoint exactly what it should be like when we hit a certain milestone, but in general, services might progress with the following level-by-level guide in many startups:

- *Level 1*: We use services to fund development of a novel new product. This usually comes in one of two forms. The first is that we do projects for cash as an outsourced software development agency, and the second is that we build the product for an organization at a discount with an understanding (the consideration in kind for the discount) that we can own the code and take it to market.

- *Level 2*: We have a product that is ready to be released or has had a soft release. Here, we have built a tool or service but aren't yet making money. We can direct funds raised from services to improve the product and find additional routes to market that start to fuel profits and the ability to redirect those profits into continual development and building a company in support of our innovation.

- *Level 3*: We have a steady stream of income and can use that to grow our development organization. Now we have some decisions to make. The product has proven market fit to a degree and can hopefully stand alone as the sole source of income. However, our services are still required either in support of customers who need help to find success with the product or to help fund more aggressive growth strategies. We have to make sure our services team understands the part they play, given that most of the attention likely goes to the product rather than their contributions.

- *Level 4*: As we grow we're likely to take on capital, even if we started out as a services organization. Now we have investors who ask about revenues and want to see different types of revenue broken out differently on financials. We have sales and need to compensate them for everything they sell. We have an organization with a leadership structure if it continues to grow. All of this impacts the margin on services, and so we want to find a structure that is sustainable.

- *Level 5*: Now that the product is a key aspect of the company, it's time to set a strategy for the services team. That likely begins with a percentage of revenue that we'd like to see services bring in as well as a percentage of the budget services consume. We need to acknowledge the intangibles that services provide: customer success, evangelism, input into products, etc. But we also need to prepare our financials to look like a software company rather than like a services organization–unless, of course, we have a business model that is centered on services (e.g., an open source software solution funded by a services team).

- *Level 6*: Software is a more scalable business than services. As the software grows, the cost to maintain it, market it, and support it does not grow symmetrically like it does with services. So the return on investment from our services team remains somewhat stagnant percentagewise. In other words, every dollar we invest in software returns more than each that we spend on a services organization. So we might want to slow the growth of services (e.g., remove any commissions or quota retirement for services in order to slow their sales).

- *Level 7*: The mature services organization now has services engineers who make more money, and so we want to look for ways for them to contribute in other parts of the organization. Implementation engineers make for awesome product managers and pre-sales systems engineers, while developers can transition into other areas of the growing team in support of the product. If we continue to sell services not affiliated with our product, then both types of services can now be delivered by those who backfill our more tenured team members. Here we're looking to build a rubric where services is in a steady state and has a predictable long-term strategy.

After level 7 our adventuring party looks more like an army (although hopefully they aren't battle-worn). The great services team supports our mission in a number of ways. They bring in revenue, help onboard large or complex customers, evangelize the mission, provide a unique voice of the customer, and can even provide flex labor to other teams when needed (e.g., QA during a big release). A great services organization can also become a crutch in each of these areas. We might not build a great onboarding experience if customers don't ask because we send services out for that, or they might mask the fact that a product doesn't achieve product-market fit.

Yet, services offer a great way to bootstrap any company—especially in a software company. We can fund the development of our own products while we hone our skills as developers, make great contacts, and learn valuable business skills when we provide outsourced development. Services that wrap around the product we provide bring in revenue, diversify revenue sources, and help brand us as experts in the field. But as we grow we need more focus on products, and that can make services delivery a difficult proposition. We'll dig in deeper on this with the mix of services revenue in mind, not because that's where we start but because if we start with that in mind, we can build a better long-term plan. That end goal helps us structure each of the steps that leads up to it in a way where, if we're transparent about the strategy, we're on the same page with those who join our adventuring party for what's sure to be an amazing campaign!

The Mix of Services Revenue

Software companies often need to focus on what we're good at: software. But we often find we build a services team and potentially compete with some of our own customers. We want the revenue, but it's hard to turn services revenue into balanced monthly recurring revenue. Per generally acceptable accounting principle (GAAP) rules, we need to accrue professional services revenue at the time services are delivered. This makes our pretty chart of the increase in monthly recurring SaaS revenue difficult to project properly and often means an asterisk in our business plan when we show investors and board members EBITDA (earnings before interest, taxes, depreciation, and amortization) over time. One of those long-term options is to hire early professional services engineers whom we move into other critical roles over time and begin to outsource our own services to another party. We do so not for the revenue, but to ensure customer success.

Outsource Everything, Right?!

We used to "stand up" (or configure) large clusters of computers to host web servers. That practice has largely moved to visualized hosting environments, like those hosted by Amazon, Google, and Microsoft. We used to host our own servers for files, business tools, and Customer Relationship Management (CRM) tools. But these days, we use SaaS tools for those services. So, in an age where we take old concepts and slap "as a Service" on them, as we grow and need focus, many software companies hire other organizations to act as our professional services arm, rather than building a large team of road warriors ourselves. Again, this allows us to stay focused on our core business: software.

But we bootstrapped the company with services, right? For some, the answer is definitely yes. The right time to make a deliberate decision about what to do with each line of business (e.g., software, support contracts, and services) is when the software business can pay the bills on its own. We have a finite amount of time and resources, and the logistics and management of a professional services department will start to compete with the time we spend in our core business. When we build a new company or try to react to hyper-growth, if we aren't intentional about where we spend our time, we won't be able to perform at the level we need to for anything, and quality in neglected areas will impact those that excel.

Services Can Be Necessary

What we choose to do with services is impacted by what our services delivery is for. Products that require services here and there may require us to have a services team forever. If we bundle services for free, we'll want to treat that as a cost of goods sold and try to keep services delivery as a soft cost. Services as individual products can often be outsourced, though. This provides us with a low-risk way to deliver services in a way that we can still capture revenue. Services could also be delivered by a third party simply with a referral if we don't need to capture that revenue. Most software companies should do services simply to earn the funds to build a product. The customers that use those services often aren't in the market the core product servers.

Choosing to move services to another company, whether branded as our own or simply as referrals, requires us to reset the expectations with customers who might rely on us. Before doing so, we'll want to find a vendor with pricing that provides us with the margin to make the effort worthwhile—or if we're simply handing them a referral, who we trust will do a good job for the customers we care about. But there are a few questions we should ask vendors as we begin to outsource our services:

- *Margin*: If we only retain about three to five percentage points, then there's likely no great reason to embark on a journey like this unless we want to streamline the sales process for the core product, or if services are necessary but billable.

- *Scoping*: Make sure to work out who scopes services when a customer needs something that isn't part of a standard services catalog, a known design pattern that acts as a mechanism for the outsourcer to accept the Scope of Work (SoW) generated, and a way for change orders to the services defined in the scope to be accepted once jobs begin (or at any point in the job lifecycle, really).

- *Lateral support*: Customers expect mastery when they pay the vendor directly, so make sure to work out escalated support for the third party as well as routine training.

- *Discounts*: Predefine how discounts will be applied when sales teams request them. We obviously don't want to go into negative margin after we've paid commission on the sale, paid taxes, covered soft costs like coordination, and paid the vendor to deliver services. We need to know the fully loaded costs to deliver services and the impact those services have on customer satisfaction, ramp time with software, and churn.

- *Visibility*: The more defined our processes to schedule, deliver, and track outcomes, the better. We should be able to see the date and time that services are delivered and, more importantly, integrate that into the accounting system automatically, so the finance team can recognize revenue properly. We also want to make sure we don't bundle services, as GAAP rules might require us to accrue revenue for software only once the services are delivered. This probably means software. If we have all of this in a software package, customers can automatically schedule and follow up on any issues, and we can run long-term reports to track outcomes.

- *Customer satisfaction problems*: Customers are often likely to call the sales team when they have a problem. We want our sales teams positive and out there selling. We don't want sellers to backpedal to deal with unhappy customers due to a services delivery problem.

So we need a standard script to deal with unhappy customers and refunds, especially when there's a subcontractor involved.

- *Customer surveys*: We don't want to just react to angry customers when they call. Customer satisfaction is more rewarding when it can be proactive. We should always send an automated survey to check on how customers feel about the services they received, and for an even more white-gloved approach, sellers can call once services are complete to see if the customer needs anything else.

- *Follow-up support*: We also want to be clear about whether a subcontractor can directly engage with customers once services through our organization are delivered. If not, there should be strict rules around who owns the customer. If they can, then sales and account teams need to understand the potential impact to future services sales and be okay with that outcome.

Necessary or not, services come with rewards (retention and success). But few rewards come with risk. In the next section, we'll look at the risks involved with services delivery.

De-risking Services

The word "risk" is one of the most important aspects of services in an organization where services aren't the core product. There is always the risk that something goes wrong with services, and if we deliver enough services, something will happen eventually. This can include travel delays that cause our resources to miss appointment times, customer satisfaction issues, accidental damage, and hundreds of other things we've seen. Services are still revenue and help the bottom line and help diversify revenue.

We've seen services carry companies during otherwise lean times. This can help us grow in ways that don't require additional debt or further diluted equity. As we grow, services may continue to be a great part of our businesses, but we want to be deliberate about our strategy. This means we need to track the mix of sales that are services related, the fully loaded costs of every line of our businesses, and the amount of attention services require from the upper levels of the company. Once we understand all of this, we can make a thoughtful decision about how we want to proceed with services over time and re-evaluate those decisions annually. As with so many other aspects of our organizations, it's all about being deliberate in how we expend our limited resources.

Bootstrap with Services

We've mentioned that services can be a great way to get a software company off the ground. Not only do we end up building code libraries we can probably reuse in the future but we raise money, get valuable experience, make friends in the community, and see a wealth of diverse projects. Let's look at a few aspects of building up services that are important to note:

- Are services only being offered to fund operations? If so, then we'll often want to limit the number or extent of services (e.g., we only sell 25–50% of our time or only engage in projects where we can reuse code).

- Will we own the intellectual property? If so, bootstrapping with services becomes much simpler (and more valuable). The contract we have a customer sign (estimate, bid, etc.) should contain language that we own and can market what we build, and we can negotiate that point on a per-deal basis. Following the project, we can decide if there are parts that belong in our other software or maybe even pivot into marketing the project we just built for a specific customer.

- Are the services an add-on to software? Many a software company is sprung from the mind of a founder with deep knowledge of a given field—especially in emergent industries or subordinate industries to established ones. That founder often surrounds themselves with people from that field, and services can become a powerful driver of revenue early on in the life of a company, given ready access to talent.

- Are services to be charged? Given the title of this section, that seems like a funny question to ask, but if the software costs $10,000 a month or more, then it's easy to just throw in a day of service to get a customer started—especially if we don't have a great onboarding experience. But we don't know if customers will be willing to pay for services until we ask. So ask!

- Can a customer pay us to add a feature to our software? This seems simpler than it is. First, make sure the customer doesn't own the intellectual property when the project is done. If they don't, then ask if other customers want it or whether it's something that can be hidden behind a feature toggle for that specific customer. Either way, don't forget the long-term cyclomatic complexity of the code and how that will impact the cost of ownership of the code over the long run. A negligible amount now might cost way more later, when the customer represents a much smaller portion of our revenues.

Anything that takes time, energy, money, or focus away from our core mission is bad. Or at least it can be when it happens too much. Services are great to raise funds without diluting equity. Services can provide a fantastic customer experience. Services are a way to differentiate and help build a market–that is, provided it's done deliberately.

Now that we've said all that, outsourced software development is an extremely lucrative business. Many companies thrive in that market and do nothing else. Finding customers either through informal channels or through services like Upwork or other portals is easy in many areas. So all that time we might otherwise spend looking for seed capital could be spent chasing non-dilutive funding opportunities. Once we start to grow the party, we'll want to put systems in place that help us run that business like, well, a business.

Operationalize Services

We like to put everything on an assembly line since the advent of the industrial revolution; services are no different. This means building packages for what goes into our services portfolio. Once we have those, we need to make them easy to sell.

Every company is going to have different areas that need to be checked off before we can consider services packages and operations as being on autopilot. Systematizing and thus streamlining each aspect of what we do is one of the more important goals of any business function. According to the size of the company, there are teams we need to meet with to explain what we'll be doing and why. A few of these will even give us homework to be done before they allow an SKU (or Stock Keeping Unit similar to those used in a supermarket) to be sold. This is part of leveling up when scaling a company.

We might be able to crank out an invoice and Statement of Work on the fly for the services we provide early on. But as we grow, here are some questions we need to ask—and if there are teams at your organization who deal with these, schedule meetings to confirm our assumptions about what they need. (Pro tip: If services are founder led, then we should do these things early so when someone inherits the services function, they won't have a mess to clean up!)

- *Legal*: One of the most important aspects of delivering services is to make sure our contracts with customers cover all the goods and services provided to customers. Any time we change or add an SKU, make an appointment with the legal/contracts team and verify that these cover what we're doing. If our legal team manages corporate insurance policies, then review these as well; otherwise, work with both the insurance/risk team and the legal team to make sure that insurance policies cover the scope of the services we'll be providing. Early on, just make sure things are good with the lawyer but try to get services added to the EULA (End User License Agreement) so it's easy to deal with and costs us less to maintain an organization as we grow.

- *Sales operations*: Most sales teams need an SKU. We'll talk about sales enablement later, but we need to equip sales operations teams with a list of product names and costs. Schedule this meeting early, as many organizations have specific change windows where SKUs can be changed due to similar windows with distributors and resellers. Typically, a change you make will not take effect with resellers for at least 60 days. Additionally, iron out any details with how communications and sales enablement are handled with partners. One important point here is that sellers sell what gets them the biggest commissions for their time, so if we incentivize them to sell services, they will—whether we want them selling a lot of services or not.

- *Finance*: We have coordinated SKUs, but now it's time to figure out what happens when they're sold. Some details that need to get worked out include the following:

  - When is revenue recognized (e.g., upon delivery of the service or spread equally across the duration of a services contract)?

  - How will finance report on that?

  - What kind of impact do costs in finance have on the revenue that gets recognized, including commissions, costs, unallocated expenses, facilities costs, subcontracting costs, etc.?

  - How will we generate reports on recognized revenue?

- *Ticketing*: This is an important component. We need to ticket in such a way that we don't make supporting customers even harder than it is otherwise. Therefore, tickets need to use the same system as that of our support teams. But the ticketing system also needs to probably track travel, costs, and reporting on the utilization of time-based consultants. Additionally, if we recognize revenue based on ticket closures, make sure to work out how finance will get those reports.

Once these details are sorted out, write them down. If the company has an intranet or wiki, put the information there. Be as complete as possible without overloading people with more information than is necessary. Then have the teams from all the meetings confirm the notes and requirements, which can then become articles in that wiki. These also act as an FAQ for when people ask about how the services operations work in the future. As we grow, sellers will ask a lot of questions. The more that are in the FAQ, the easier it becomes to just send a link.

Now that we've got a bunch of details sorted out, expect more than we can begin to prepare you for in this book. Again, all companies are different. Once those are sorted out, we can move on to get marketing and sales enablement efforts underway. Before we start working with sales teams, first make sure the marketing team has provided some good air cover to support their efforts in the form of sell sheets, documentation of what services will be delivered, etc. And if it's a small company, do these kinds of things anyway, as time permits—it'll pay dividends in the future as others take over those functions.

The Services Portfolio

There's a lot our adventuring party can do. Maybe we have a package just for a good old classic dungeon crawl and another for a much more intricate extraction of a wicked ruler. Or maybe we can build a web app or integration with another product. These can be packaged up and sold as a bundle, either alongside our software or separately.

Bundles are a great way to amplify the sale of services within a larger organization. They also reduce friction during the sales process because they're easy to explain. Once the numbers are known, the target margin should be defined, the costs defined, the percentage that can be billed vs. the percentage of time that the organization will be giving away to close sales or have team members on a bench (most services engineers can't run at a 100% utilization), subtract the reseller margin (if there are resellers), and figure out a necessary daily number. Easy, right? Let's extract margin from a daily average price vs. cost structure:

```
((NUMBER OF DAYS BILLED IN A YEAR * MSRP) * AVERAGE RESELLER
MARGIN) / ANNUAL DEPARTMENTAL COST
```

If we pull a report of the total goods sold, we start to get a pretty good picture of costs associated with running a team and the complexities that can arise. The preceding formula quickly goes into a spreadsheet or a database. It only gets more and more complicated as organizations grow and finance teams get trickier to deal with when it comes to revenue recognition and cost allotments or charge-backs.

Once we know that daily cost, the necessary margin, and the actual goals, we can build a bundle. When at all possible, work in daily increments with services teams inside larger organizations. It's a simple currency and easy math for sellers. If sitting in a meeting or needing to make a snap decision, knowing the daily cost and the daily profit gives us a great baseline with which to do so. Even if we deal in fixed cost Statements of Work, we're going to do the math to build the bundle based on an amount of time it will take to achieve the deliverables and our known margin for a given price point.

The bundle is meant to make it simpler to buy services. This makes it easier for teams to communicate what a customer is getting. There are two ways to approach bundling: days or deliverables. From there, we decide whether to bundle services with other products in the portfolio of an organization. For example, let's say we sell training classes. We might bundle five days' worth of training and five days' worth of custom services (often in a row to reduce travel costs) and apply a 10% or 20% discount to that, and a customer is more likely to buy the bundle, thus potentially getting us additional sales that we might not have had otherwise. The customer gets a good deal (or at least, has the perception they did), and we get revenue and valuable experience.

Bundles of days mean less Statements of Work need to be written (less is very different than saying none). This impacts our costs, and customers always have an expectation that they will get a discount when buying in bulk. Here are some thoughts to consider while bundling services:

- Make sure that when stacked with a reseller margin, we still meet our target margin.

- Try to bundle services with other services (e.g., training, enhanced support packages, etc.) and not software in order not to alter the ratable accounting treatment of software (e.g., we don't want to have to deliver 100% of services to recognize software revenue).

- Try to keep services being delivered remotely when possible. Travel budgets for services teams can explode, and delivering services remotely is long term better for costs and the families of people we hire and far more flexible. It can also be better for the customer as they usually get services performed more quickly.

- This isn't always possible, but unlimited bundles are the best for SaaS companies. It's easiest for training. As we deliver a paid course, we can record or prepare for a screencast and then sell an unlimited subscription. But each time we create a bundle, we should think of whether that bundle could be an unlimited service over the course of a one-year subscription, which would provide a GAAP-allowable way to recognize revenue as monthly recurring.

- Delete bundles that go unsold to keep the list of SKUs from getting unwieldy.

Once we have it in our head what we're selling, write a pretty document that explains what a customer gets. Then add what they specifically don't get. This saves us from having extra calls or messages with sellers as more and more customers buy the services.

Now that we've built out our services packages and the appropriate discounts that can be applied to them, it's time to put the processes in place that support the services component of the business or refine them to meet the new services packages. Once we've built the products and services to take to market, they should undergo scrutiny and then be put into a form of change control. The scrutiny will look different in each organization, but be thankful for it and not defensive in the least.

If no one feels comfortable providing scrutiny, go to the product management team. All product management teams are happy to give feedback on anything you might ask them of, including the product, everything around the product, the best way to make a peanut butter and jelly sandwich, and endless debates about whether Led Zeppelin or Pink Floyd was more impactful to rock and roll music.

Monthly Recurring Revenue and Services

At some point the company has to decide if it's a software company or a services company. Services can have great margins when implemented correctly. They take time, focus, and money away from other initiatives. Early-stage companies can grow without diluting equity by making revenue from services teams as product-market fit is attained and as we learn to reach potential customers and convert them. Services teams also allow us to hasten sales, book (and earn) revenue faster, and even grow the collective knowledge of a nascent industry, solidifying our brand as experts.

Over time a good services team can outpace the revenue and growth of a software organization. Services can become a crutch that allows an organization to make software that requires services and is less transactional. If we don't cycle people into other teams, the services can become a lower-margin team and end up being a drag on the books.

Services can also end up competing with customers. Managed services, customization, and other service industries are huge and, when done right, can be a permanent item on the balance sheet that we don't wince when we look at. It does take away from potential revenue from organizations who offer those types of services and could be valuable channel partners and/or resellers. Most software companies are obsessed with monthly recurring revenue, or MRR. Therefore, we have to keep looking for ways to move services into that bucket, so the revenues we recognize are less lumpy and more predictable. Additionally, look for ways to make services teams more valuable around the organization when they aren't out billing customers.

Master Service Agreements

The authors can't provide legal advice in a book like this, especially since the response from all attorneys is that "It depends" when asked almost any question. But we can say that every company who performs services for customers should probably have a service agreement. It's best if that agreement can be wrapped into the existing software license agreement as an additional section. This reduces the friction to get new contracts in place when adding services to what we're delivering to customers. The same attorney should be able to do both, and it's usually less expensive if they're done together (and sometimes merged).

Most of these agreements will include things like payment terms and warranties on the deliverables. Therefore, we might also include a Scope of Work (SoW) as well, on a per-job basis. The actual cost for services should be moved to the SoW as well rather than be in our software license agreement. Additionally, large customers may provide a master service agreement, and those should always be reviewed by counsel (as should non-disclosures and others). The net-net of this is that everything a customer signs or that we sign should go through a lawyer!

The Mix of Services

Let's say we've done a good job leveraging services to help fund the operations of a young company. The adventuring party still has a mission, and chances are that it has nothing to do with delivering services. As we go to raise funds elsewhere, someone is eventually going to ask about margin and profit. And if we don't have a good story to tell (and in writing), then the conversation probably won't go all that well. So what is the right mix?

That's a great question, but before we start to push an agenda and possibly end up doing the opposite of what's being asked of us, consider the following (which we should review with management and our board):

- What profit margin is needed from the services organization?

- How much services are going to be given away for free in order to drive software and hardware sales?

- Will free services be credited back to the services team in the form of a charge-back?

- How should sales enablement for services be handled?

- Should we plan on staff augmentation as part of our services packages, especially as we grow?

- Will the services team be involved in getting the community (resellers, consultants, MSPs, integrators, etc.) enabled to deliver services, or will the two be competitors?

These aren't that many questions, and we should be happy to answer them and have a thoughtful conversation about these topics with pretty much everything we do in a company. We should also allow conversations to expand to get a fuller picture of thoughts the rest of the company has. Services can represent a potentially large impact to profits—and engaging in these types of projects can dilute the velocity to take a product to market. The answers aren't static, either. These should be reviewed with a leader or the board quarterly and probably have a larger discussion annually as well.

Once we understand the margin goal and sales goal, we can set a rate. Approach pricing the same as we've done in previous chapters. After all, a business is a business. The difference here is that we'll set aside whatever time has been allocated for free services. A warning though, don't get too synthetic with the numbers. If we're supposed to operate at a 15% or 40% margin, that's the key metric. The more we dilute it by adding contributions to other areas of the company or monetizing bench time, the more we can end up losing money and thinking we're making money. And we can scale revenue without staff by developing bundles of services to be sold.

Staff a Professional Services Team

The first few times we implement our product for a customer, it's almost always done by a founder or technical lead. That distracts us, and so we eventually hire others so we can keep building more features or focus on sales or whatever other task is always lighting the other side of a candle.

There are three main ways people hire services teams:

- **Send people in other roles to deliver services.** This is pretty much how most services teams begin. Maybe people are doing double-duty in services and support. This can work well for a while, especially when the team is remote. Software engineers may tolerate it for a bit. Heck, we've even seen accountants sent out to deliver services. It works until it doesn't. Keep in mind that when we try to sit in too many chairs at once, we'll invariably fall on the floor here and there.

- **Hire inexpensive talent.** If the product can be taught to a group of early professionals, then it's great to have a plethora of options for whom to bring on. Here, each implementation should be similar and likely require little scripting or programming, and the rate structure should be created in such a way that customers won't think they're getting ripped off.

- **Hire grizzled industry veterans with domain expertise.** Okay, maybe not "grizzled." But people who can truly empathize with the customer are people who have walked in their shoes. Two interesting things can happen when we hire people in the industry our product serves: we gain diverse insights into that industry, and others in our industry begin to see us not only as a vendor but possibly as a potential career destination as well. People who want to work with us often become more evangelical toward our cause.

- **Hire services talent from adjacent companies.** This can be interesting if we are considering leaning into the adjacency, but keep in mind there's a premium to be paid for people with that kind of experience, especially when the adjacency is actually a competitor.

Careers of services employees in a software company are different than those of software engineers. The managers we hire for any discipline need to keep in mind that our best possible outcome for one of our staff is to leave that manager. Or replace the manager when the manager moves on to something else. The best feeling is when those who deserve to do so replace us.

All that training, all that work, and suddenly they're better off when they leave the services team. Why's this? Well, let's start with why employees would be leaving in the first place:

- *To get in front of the product*: How many people have been in front of as many customers in real-world scenarios as those who go to customers and do work? Those are often the best situations to then build product roadmaps. At some point, many in services will get tired of complaining about priorities and will instead want to get more active about the future of the hardware or software that your organization makes.

- *To get closer to the product*: Services engineers often make great Quality Assurance (QA) testers (after all, they've been testing the product with customers live after it's been released) or can easily end up moving into development teams provided they've acquired those types of skills.

- *To move into sales*: Few in services will want to admit this, but in a hardware or software company, they make some of the best possible systems engineers because they're so close to the software and customer. Those who want to move into sales can not only talk the talk, but they can walk the walk as well.

- *Travel is too much*: The previous reasons were other roles that services engineers might move into. This is a reason someone might choose to leave the company outright if we can't find a solution. Many a team member begins the job loving the travel, but then as they grow up, they want to have relationships, children, and settle down. This is another great reason to look for ways to deliver as many services remotely as possible.

There are certainly going to be other reasons. But those are by far the main ones that we've seen people leaving services roles or destinations. The reason we mention those destinations is that when we're hiring someone in services, try to envision where they'll be in a year or three. That becomes part of leveling up for them. Some organizations choose to build very small teams or not build a team at all and instead rely on subcontractors, as covered earlier in the chapter.

Conclusion

Services can play a substantial part in the early life of any startup, but especially when it comes to enterprise software. Our party can buff up our equipment and experience and learn a lot about either development or the problem space (or both). If we aren't careful, we can grow services too well or rely on services instead of building great onboarding experiences. So there's an appropriate mix. On the one hand, services help to brand us as experts in the field; on the other hand, the revenue is less scalable based on the amount it costs to hire and train a services team.

When bootstrapping off services, if all goes well, we won't eventually be able to satisfy the services and product sides of the business concurrently. We have a decision to make: do we continue or stop, and if we stop, what should we do with the book of business? There's a good chance that a solid revenue stream can be sold—yet another way to raise a round of funding without diluting equity. In the following chapter, we'll dig into lots of other ways to raise funding, the rounds of funding, and logistic and legal concerns and even maybe try to talk *some* founders into waiting a little longer to do so when possible.

CHAPTER 16

Capital

The adventuring party has been leveling up individually and raising the gold they need when necessary. But as more individuals join the party, it's time to make sure to keep plenty of rations on hand, repair armor as needed, pay for lodging, and, of course, buy the required components for spells. Or more likely, the party needs to pay these newcomers on a retainer, so they can do all the character maintenance stuff themselves. This isn't cheap and so requires money.

A common theme in this book is that the best place to raise capital is from customers who pay for a good or service. This can be referred to as bootstrapping the company. There are a lot of ways to go about it. This chapter appears so late because most entrepreneurs will benefit from building the structure of a company prior to taking a capital investment. Some have a side hustle like driving for Uber. Some keep a full-time job while starting a company. Some consult as freelance software developers. The point is that to avoid diluting equity in the company, operations were funded by bootstrapping, or self-funding, the capital required to keep going.

There are a lot of valid reasons to get funding from other sources. Maybe the idea is too big to build otherwise. Maybe some external validation will help support more aggressive growth. Maybe there have been too many encounters with kobolds who give up one copper piece each, and the traction isn't fast enough not to burn through the savings of the founders. Or (and this is the best reason) maybe the organization is growing so fast that cash flow can't meet the demand of customers.

© Charles Edge, Chip Pearson, Amy Larson Pearson 2023
C. Edge et al., *The Startup Players Handbook*,
https://doi.org/10.1007/978-1-4842-9315-7_16

Leveling Up the Organization

As the company grows, it becomes more and more important to manage finances in a way that supports what the customers need. We created these leveling guides for each chapter. None are simpler in some ways than this. Funding is one of the more mature areas where a business can be on an assembly line and grow fast or fail fast, or founders could lose control even faster. Let's quickly go through these levels while allowing for further detail later in the chapter:

- *Level 1:* Self-funding is when the company builds tools in the basement, after hours, and does so without any resources from a potential or existing employer. If gainfully employed, be careful not to violate any existing contractual obligations but sprint quickly toward a prototype or MVP.

- *Level 2:* Accelerators and incubators are startup enablers that might or might not come with funding, advice, discounts for products/services, etc.

- *Level 3:* Seed capital (and angel capital) is the money raised from friends and family, or smaller venture firms. This may come before accelerators but is the money we often use to move into working on our products full time. It comes with the dilution of equity, or how much of an organization we own.

- *Level 4:* Series A is a round of investment from a venture capital firm (or firms) that is sizeable enough that the company can probably start accelerating growth. This often comes once a product-market fit has been proven, and it's time to take a product to a wider market than, let's say, word of mouth in an industry.

- *Level 5:* The organization likely grows faster than the founders are comfortable with, and it's time to get some help and de-risk the investments founders have already made. Series B is a round of investment that often comes with an extra zero at the end from Series A. The company is growing but needs help with cash flow and, almost more importantly, the type of advice that it's hard to actually pay a consultant for.

- *Level 6:* Series C–Z are later rounds of venture capital that bring in more and more investors, more and more capital, and help scale us, usually for an event horizon in an increasingly nearer-term future.

- *Level 7:* We'll put private equity (PE) in level 7 but it could have come at any level along the way. A PE firm acquires some, if not all, of the organization. That firm then tries to harvest revenues, expand the value of the firm, or both. PE firms often buy on debt, but these days rarely hold assets forever (e.g., they may sell before the debt financing is due).

After level 7, the company is speeding briskly toward an event horizon. Maybe that's an exit, an IPO, private equity, or one of an infinite number of outcomes. Either way, there's a team of financial advisors at the disposal of the adventuring party, lawyer-balling away to find crazy and hopefully amazing outcomes. It all started with capital.

Pre-seed, incubator, accelerator, seed, Series A, private equity, IPO, and other phases of financing a company covered later in this chapter are different between industries based on how capital-intensive the startup costs. Consider a biotech company with lengthy regulatory requirements that take two years to sort out; that's a race where a patent could trigger a Series B. A consumer app may not require capital for the business to turn profitable but may choose to take on a Series A in order to expand into an adjacent market.

For the purposes of this chapter, assume (given how late it appears in the book) that there's a great idea and the product-market fit has been somewhat proven. Now the organization wants to use external capital to accelerate traction in the market. Why? Every adventure needs funds. Not just to feed the party, but to hire higher level retainers (think non-player characters) and buy cool magic items. The funds that are used can come from a variety of sources. But again notice how late in this book this chapter shows up. We definitely think it's more important to focus on building a useful product and a cash flowing company than courting investors - the investment is not the point of the company. The later a company waits, the more leverage the founders have.

Whatever the reason to raise capital, there are a lot of routes to come across it. There are family members, banks, and investors who specialize in different industries, sizes of companies, and geographies. Family members are simple enough, although it's wise to treat them as investors. Banks are usually a long-shot unless there's a personally backed security to provide to the bank. This leaves investors.

Raise Capital from Investors?

The most important difference between bankers and investors is equity—in other words, who owns what. This is the difference between a barkeep in an adventure loaning the party funds to start their quest for a fixed sum in return (the principal plus interest) and starting the party off with a sum in exchange for a cut of the treasure pulled out of a dungeon.

In real life, raising capital can get much more complicated. The dilution of equity starts with a simple capitalization table (or cap table for short). This is a listing of shareholders and percentages or shares they hold of the company. A sole proprietor of a company holds all shares, the simplest of cap tables. If there are two, then it might be a 50/50 or 60/40 split. As we bring on additional investors, and some of them use more sophisticated financial instruments to invest, the cap table can get a little more complicated. There are several tools out there like Carta.com, Gemspm.com, Astrella.com, Shareworks.com, and LTSE Equity that help to move a cap table out of a spreadsheet on our computers and into a legitimate authority. The reason this is important is equity.

Why do investors give startups money? Because companies grow and pay the investor back. For example, investing $1,000 in Amazon stock when they filed an IPO would net over a million and a half dollars today. Investing even earlier would have exponentially greater returns on the investment. It turns out when a party gets funded to go exploring the dungeon below the castle in exchange for a percentage of the loot, investors can make a pretty nice return if the party makes it back. Invest in enough parties and one is bound to do so!

The origins of the modern investment system are halfway between the startup investment climate today and that adventuring party. Derivative and stock markets really hail back to a time when the exploration of the new world and trade routes throughout the rising European empires needed funding to explore and expand. Investors went earlier stage around the end of World War II when the modern venture capital system began to evolve more quickly. Today, companies use funding to explore and expand ways for computers to make humans more productive and/or to make the lives of real humans better. Many of the startups that an investor backs will fail. But for those that survive and thrive, the returns can be great.

There are a lot of reasons to bring on investors. One is sharing risk. Founders could invest into their own company, but the derivative of shared risk helps them stay out of personal debt. Additionally, founders might not have enough in savings to fund such an adventure. Many of the companies that get funded have fairly young founders, before mortgages and families limit the attention they can give to their startup. Another is to validate the idea as a form of de-risking the opportunity. If founders can't find any other investors, then how can they be really, really sure it's a great opportunity?

Investors can also bring their knowledge of industries and building companies to the table, which can be far more valuable to some startups than the funds. That knowledge might include decades of experience running companies, deep knowledge on taking products to market, or even just a sweet network of contacts to tap into for anything and everything a new company might face. In short, search out investors for all the right reasons—not just to help fund a quest to take down a black dragon. There's more detail on choosing the right investors throughout this chapter (although very little on how to take down a black dragon). Suffice it to say that for many a startup, the investors are integral to the success of the enterprise.

Investors do mean equity is diluted. The crusade is now spending other people's money. That means transparency and often legal requirements to report on the affairs of the company. Understand the legal and regulatory requirements and hopefully go above and beyond the rights of investors so they feel inspired to continue helping beyond whatever exit happens. Some even end up with lifelong friends. To keep honest about and ahead of all these requirements that many founders don't even know are important yet, start the investor trek with the paperwork.

Lawyers, Money, and Guns

Selling shares to a company can be intricate. Each campaign starts with an idea. Technological determinism has put an opportunity to evolve some space or industry in a way that is meaningful to humans in front of a founder. Our bold traveler sets out on that journey and later decides to bring in others. The team grows and more funds will help the undertaking grow faster, smarter, and/or safer.

Before discussing investments, it's important to understand what the existing shareholders (maybe just a founder or two) are getting into. Those details are defined in a term sheet. That term sheet is a document that outlines the terms of a loan, shares, or for more modern startups a loan that will convert into shares in a given scenario. The term sheet is much more than a few words like, "I, the investor, give the Adventuring Party of Marook $100,000 for 10% of the proceeds of the loot."

Most term sheets contain a lot of nuance. For starters, if the founders agree to certified financials, expect reporting requirements that can cost tens of thousands of dollars a year to meet. For a convertible note or SAFE (covered in more detail later in this chapter), a founder could also be signing away the rights to purchase future shares for a predetermined price. The company also might be giving up a seat on a board of directors (one that hasn't yet been formed). If the company isn't a C Corp (as covered in Chap. 1), then it might not be able to satisfy a requirement for a preferred class of shares (and then once it does, there can be substantive tax ramifications). All of this can be a lot.

Most founders aren't lawyers or accountants by trade and so need to negotiate the terms in a term sheet with the assistance of one. Preferably that person has experience negotiating term sheets for startups. There are a lot of great firms out there and, it's strongly recommended to use one of repute (scallywag adventures are great, not so much for attorneys). Prior to taking on an investment, get an idea of how much the negotiations will cost (we've seen them run $10,000 even for a simple contract, which comes out of the net proceeds).

Integrity is important. Be as honest and open with investors and attorneys about everything as possible. No number fudging or misrepresenting the facts. No rounding up or leaving out a seemingly not important cost. Omissions can have dire long-term consequences. Instead, focus on bringing on lifelong friends. Make sure to bring any existing contracts to the attorney hired. There are tons of gotchas, for example, noncompetes from previous employers.

Noncompetes and Covenants

The sale of a company (or shares of a company) likely comes with an agreement not to compete with the purchaser. This might be a noncompete agreement not to start another company that does the same thing, or covenant (which is often similar to a noncompete but even more binding). Think of this as an asset that the purchaser pays for. Think of it as part of the personally backed securities held by a bank when issuing a car loan. This security is such that the adventuring party can no longer operate in a given location or embark on a specific type of quest.

When someone leaves an employer, they're often held by a similar noncompete. Noncompete agreements are more binding in some states than others, but in general, whatever the law says can pale in comparison with the legal fees to prove no wrongdoing. When working with a former customer in any capacity, try to get a waiver from whoever holds a noncompete prior to doing so (even if doing something different than what the old company does). It's always best to be above board to avoid an injunction or getting sued for damages in the future.

A word that frequently comes up in noncompetes is *solicitation*. Many may think they can claim, "The client called me first so I didn't solicit," or, "They're not being treated right by the new management." One of the things that makes many founders successful is the fact that they care about customers. Maybe personal relationships were formed with many of those customers outside of work. It will be hard to see them potentially not be taken care of in the way they're accustomed to. Noncompetes can mean the new company is legally bound not to interfere with their relationship with a former employer. So, when competing with a former employer, be extra careful. Violating that agreement may come with serious repercussions, such as not being able to get funding due to outstanding litigation (even if the litigation doesn't ultimately go anywhere). Be cognizant of the risk and the risk to former customers when stepping up to the line that could violate those noncompetes.

Methodologies to Calculate the Value of a Company

A friend was once asked how much his house was worth at dinner. He responded, "whatever someone will pay for it." It took some time to fully appreciate the wisdom of the comment. These days, Zillow or Redfin will send a report once a week with the value of a home. They're pretty close to what houses go for. Ultimately, the house is worth what someone will pay to buy it, though (whether more or less than the estimate). If sold, the seller would walk away with the sale price of the asset (the house) minus any liabilities (the mortgage). That's the true value of the home to the seller.

A company is similar: it's worth whatever someone will pay. A portion of the value can be sold for shares with the value indicated in a term sheet. There are a few different methodologies to use to get a good idea of what a startup or business is worth. Traditionally, these would mainly be the assets minus liabilities, a comparable look at other similar businesses (especially for pre-revenue companies), a multiple of the income of the business, and a replacement value. The valuation then becomes the basis for any investments or capitalization done to accelerate the growth of the company or to buy out any partners if principals exit.

Valuation can be one of the more contentious aspects of a company. When money is involved, things start to get weird, especially when that money can be taken out of a company rather than used to fund operations. It's often best to let a third party help handle investor relations. Once a company goes public, the valuation is easy. The market sets the value based on the outstanding shares and the price per share (although arguably the psychology of public markets can make them infinitely more complex). This chapter looks at a number of ways to do a valuation in a pre-IPO scenario.

Assets

Appraising the value of a company by assets is a common way to derive what a traditional business is worth. The adventuring party has how many gold pieces? This is an easier approach where an analyst looks at the assets and subtracts the liabilities, much like the example of selling the house earlier. Assets would include unpaid invoices for contracted future services, cash, furniture, accounts receivable, products (like software), property, computers, rights to patents (or other intellectual property), etc. Liabilities would include any debt incurred, unrecognized revenue, outstanding accounts payables, taxes, mortgages/rents, and outstanding salaries for the year.

There are other traditional approaches to come up with a valuation. The going concern approach looks at the value of the business if the business were to continue running as it had prior to valuation. This means no assets or product line changes and no further capitalization to introduce new big changes. This is great for private equity where a business will continue to run to provide monthly recurring income. Liquidation is an approach that looks at the value if the business were to sell some or all the assets and satisfy any outstanding liabilities with the proceeds. This is usually lower because the business is likely not doing well. Regrettably, more software businesses end in liquidation than not if there are liabilities and shareholders.

Valuations based on assets introduce very few assumptions, so they can be popular for traditional businesses. However, they don't often provide a real snapshot as, especially in a software or SaaS-based startup, the biggest asset is software written over time. It is hard to assign a fixed price that can be used to evaluate that asset.

Valuation by Comparison

Another common methodology used to provide the valuation of a company is Comparison, or Comps for short. Here we can introduce a lot of assumptions. Most companies will have competitors. Comparing our companies to the value of a competitor can be tricky, though. No two companies are identical; otherwise, there would likely be no need for multiple companies. For example, another company might have more or less sales and a correspondingly larger or smaller sales force. Each be in different geographies or appeal to different niches within an industry.

Comparing a company to others can set a baseline, however. Dig into market sizes and see how red an ocean is (or how many vendors are in the space) to set an upper limit on a valuation. Look at others to assess what's possible. Provided, of course, that it's possible to ascertain a sale price from public records.

Discounted Cash Flow Valuation

The discounted cash flow (DCF) method is much more complicated but looks into the future performance of a company, usually desirable for software companies. DCF explores future cash flow by calculating future revenue, taking price, volume of sales, competitors, and renewals into account. Auditors then project future expenses and any new assets required to satisfy those sales and calculate a terminal value or the total value of cash flow over a given term.

This doesn't require finding similarly valued companies and allows for modeling around multiple scenarios. Many startups plan to operate at a loss for a given time in order to build a large and loyal customer base. The estimated velocity at which the company can attract new customers is a large assumption to make. Those estimations are usually overly optimistic as they are based on the total market size (so top-down approach) rather than a more realistic bottom-up approach to customer acquisition.

The complexity of DCF also allows for errors, and business owners and entrepreneurs often start tinkering with this cell or that and end up with a butterfly effect across the entire spreadsheet.

Replacement or Startup Value

Another way to find the value of a company is to go from the bottom-up and analyze the cost to build it from scratch. This is most applicable when looking at a valuation of a company that doesn't yet have customers, or when a larger organization in an adjacent market is looking to acquire the company to get into that market.

There are many facets to calculating startup costs. Calculate the cost to buy any required equipment, office space, and the salaries required. Future earnings and cash flow are often not considered when looking at startup value, especially if it's an acquisition by a larger company. Instead, those earnings are calculated based on the larger company being able to cross-sell products. Instead, the goal is to get at is the cost vs. the opportunity cost in not getting to market faster.

Licenses, compliances, patents, the supply chain, transferable partnerships, and logic that takes years to develop are all assets in this case, where they might not otherwise be. Technical debt might be considered a liability where it otherwise might not be. The longer entrenched the company and the larger the company base, the more that becomes a factor—but neither are always necessary as most later-stage valuations are more focused on revenue than anything else.

Multiples

Investors talk about "the investment thesis" a lot. This is why they think a company will succeed: the reason they make an investment. Sometimes this is a great set of experienced founders. Or it might be a great idea in an emerging market, or a transformational technology. Established industries have standard multiples. Look at revenue and multiply EBITDA or SDE times the standard multiplier. These should be disclosed to potential investors in a financial statement compiled with generally accepted account practices, or GAAP, and include the following:

- *EBITDA*, or earnings before interest, taxes, depreciation, and amortization, is a great way to look at net income. Especially in SaaS-based companies, where there aren't many capital investments like property or large, industrial equipment.

- *SDE*, or seller discretionary earnings, is revenue minus costs of goods sold minus operating expenses and the owner compensation. This shows the earning power of the business.

For example, florists typically have a 1.78 multiplier. On an EBITDA of $1,000,000 (for easy math), an appraiser might assign a value of the organization to $1,780,000. Electronic parts manufacturers have a 2.4 multiplier, so an EBITDA of $1,000,000 would be valued at $2,400,000. There are plenty of sources for standard multipliers, which can go up and down based on macroeconomic factors.

Multiples are usually more useful with fast growing, young companies. Predefined multiples are just a baseline—the capabilities of founders, market potential, likelihood to enter a market, and other factors can add or subtract from the multiplier. But that multiplier is a big assumption. Search the Web for "multiplier by industry" to get a decent idea of what information is out there about a given industry or slice of an industry. And ultimately, the multiplier usually acts as an upper limit for the value of a company. Ultimately, multiples are mostly a mix between a comparison and a DCF method but adding in assumptions.

Choosing a Methodology

There are plenty of other methodologies. A good way to get an idea of how investors will react to valuations is to come up with one for each type mentioned. Be careful not to make assumptions from the owner's side and consider how investors will react to each. Investors would usually prefer to see a third-party appraiser than a founder who is throwing a dart at a dartboard in Excel based on an inflated total addressable market.

Choosing a methodology has a lot to do with the intent when calculating the valuation. A company looking to sell all the shares or to woo investors means different math, sometimes. Software companies (except those where founders automatically assume it's a unicorn) often choose the most aggressive ways to value a company. Those who acquire companies and are averse to risk will instead focus on the assets. As will investors in a startup that involves property, heavy machinery, and patents. Take the industry into account as well. For example, many services businesses can't be properly valued using the assets of the company.

Honest and transparent relationships are best. Displaying the estimated value using a number of different options helps investors get at the heart of whether they think a company is worth backing. Angry investors are not something any founder will want on the board. The average of multiple methods is likely to get us closer to the real value of an organization.

This is not financial advice. This is to help founders have a more honest conversation with appraisers and with themselves about what they want and why. The more deliberate founders can be about laying out their intentions, the better the long-term choices that will be made by and about investors and potential outcomes. Many organizations get weighed down by a great investor who is bad for them, and the effort to maintain that relationship takes valuable time and focus away from having an amazing product. Neither party wants that.

EBITD, Rule of 40, and All the Finance Buzzwords

There are a lot of different types of companies and business models. One of the most popular these days is SaaS-based solutions that focus on monthly recurring revenue. There are a lot of different metrics to track the performance of these types of companies. One of the most common these days is what we call the Rule of 40.

The Rule of 40 is simple: the revenue growth rate plus the profitability margin should add up to 40 or better. The later a startup company is in their development, the easier this is to calculate—and the more telling the metric becomes. A lot of concessions are made early on when starting a company. As companies ease out of being an early-stage startup, the Rule of 40 helps determine if a company is ready to scale in a profitable fashion.

The reason revenue growth isn't the only factor in valuing a software company unlike traditional businesses is that venture-backed SaaS companies often focus on growth over profitability, thus the need for venture capital. Most investors recommend that a company grow faster and think about profits later. Investors would of course prefer to work with companies who are profitable but certainly understand when there's a deliberate move to invest heavily into growth at the cost of profits—so long as there's a plan to get to profitability. The Rule of 40 helps understand the balance between customer and revenue acquisition and growth. Luckily, GAAP accounting is standardized.

Revenue growth rate is another way to evaluate a company's performance. Looking at revenue growth rate allows investors to look at year-over-year growth percentages. Revenue growth rate puts monthly recurring revenue (MRR) and annual recurring revenue (ARR) to the side and looks at top line growth. That's typically displayed in terms of how much revenue is recognized. Recognized revenue can be calculated monthly, quarterly, or annually. Once plotted, we can look at those numbers and the profitability margin on a graph that shows both in the increments desired. The key is to stay consistent with how data is reported.

Profitability Margin

The profitability is a bit complicated as companies running on a negative margin will need to factor profitability in terms of EBITDA or EBITDA excluding stock-based compensation (SBC). This is because unlike traditional business, SaaS-based businesses don't run off a standard cash-from-operations or cash-from-income model, thus the dilution in stock based on investors and the need to report back these numbers to investors (who themselves have limited partners or LPs to report to).

EBITDA is net income plus taxes plus interest expenses plus depreciation and amortization. Operating without a profit usually means interest, so it's best to account for that in a structured way. This allows companies to take advantage of interest as a tax shield as well as depreciating assets. Those are usually in the cash flow statement under "cash from operating activities" and as it's added back on as an expense. This is one way for investors to look at the value of companies that aren't currently making a profit, especially when the cost to acquire a customer doesn't make the customer profitable in a reporting quarter. If the company can retain the customer, they become incredibly profitable over the long run. Stay consistent and report in both when possible, as each investor might have a different metric they prefer.

The nice thing about EBITDA as opposed to just EBIT (or operating income) is that it's a well-accepted accounting practice to calculate and considers various factors for multiples. Once we have the revenue growth rate and profitability margin, it's straightforward to add them up and see if we're above or below 40. The risk is that valuations end up forcing companies to overengineer accounting practices to come up with synthetic numbers that get further and further from logic. Still, it's become standard in the investment community, and there are sound reasons for using these numbers to help track a fund of multiple investments.

The Rule of 40 is a great way to gauge whether a company is moving in the right direction while scaling. The SaaS industry has a wealth of data from companies that have been acquired or gone public that back up the metric. It isn't the only indicator that a company is on the right track. Since all the companies in a portfolio of investments can be tracked with the same numbers, looking at a spreadsheet that includes EBITDA (e.g., in a discounted cash flow), let us quickly identify when we see huge discrepancies and promote sound practices that lead to an increased intrinsic value of a company. Each of the numbers tells a different story, and as auditors dig into each, they indicate different things about companies. Having said this, many SaaS companies don't have the same amount of tangible assets they used to (e.g., a bunch of servers sitting in a colocation facility). Therefore, it's great when the numbers tell a story of their own.

Other Vital Signs

There are a number of other vital signs at SaaS companies that help tell a complete picture. These include the burn rate against cash on hand, how well a company retains customers, growth of existing customers, how efficiently sales and marketing is run, and revenue growth. Sometimes there are huge successes in only one of these categories that can cloud the outlook for a company. The Rule of 40 isn't the only indicator, but it's a pretty solid look at company performance.

Finally, the valuation of a company can be a great motivating factor for employees. Operating at a loss per customer is common for a time, given the high cost to acquire a customer. Companies will want to keep employees engaged when they see a lot of red on the balance sheet. It's easy to over-index on a given attribute of performance. Given the historical analysis of SaaS companies, the Rule of 40 is a great way to track performance against other SaaS companies and how they're able to balance growth and profit. Because without profit, no company can stay in business forever!

Investor Management

Once a company has more than one person, there are likely investors. Investors might include a pair of cofounders who put in time and focus or even some money. Maybe investors come from raising a Series C round of funding. Either way, there are plenty of factors that can go into keeping those investments secure.

The following few sections will cover the funding of a new organization—most of which are built to support an innovation. This begins with looking at the organization we build to provide governance to the company at large: the board of directors.

Build a Board of Directors

The board of directors is a group of people that represent the shareholders of a company or stakeholders of an educational or nonprofit institution. In other words, the board of directors provides oversight for the good of the organization (and therefore investors in many cases) and not the parties in management at an organization. Limited liability corporations (LLCs) are not required to form a board of directors, but C corporations, S corporations, and nonprofits are required to form a board. This protects donations and contributions as well as investors.

The board does this by defining executive compensation, bringing on or releasing senior executives, controlling options on stock, managing dividend policies, and, perhaps most importantly, reviewing corporate finances. Those are the official duties; there are sometimes others. So far, this might sound like something a startup founder wants nothing to do with. But it's important not only to protect shareholders but also for many other reasons! The board of directors is often there to help set and keep goals, support executives with guidance, make sure there are plenty of resources (sometimes by helping find additional investors to fund the company), make industry connections, and provide a wealth of experience.

Founders will want to make sure to dot the Is and cross the Ts. No one wants to accidentally break the law or end up in a legal action. The board helps with that and so much more. To begin, the board will develop bylaws to set the powers of the board and its structure. That can be specific to organizations, so this book won't cover bylaws other than to strongly recommend the entity that helps file articles of incorporation provide official legal guidance (and perhaps act as an observer in board meetings).

Board Composition

Most boards start with three to five people. As the organization grows, maybe they hit seven board members. Some organizations have up to 30 people on the board, but that's unwieldy for a smaller company (and dilutive, as we'll get into when we cover board compensation). Let's look at a common makeup of a board:

- *Board Chair:* Someone with board experience, maybe a CEO or investor from an adjacent industry but able to act as an advisor to founders of a startup and help groom them.

- *Founder(s):* One of the founders who still works at the company and so represents employees, shareholders, and the executive team (even if the executive team is both people that work at a really early-stage startup). This position is often referred to as an "inside director."

- *Investors:* Often the first one or two investors will end up with board seats. As the company grows, they may be replaced with later-stage investors when cap tables get cleaned up, or if the board really likes the angel(s) they may elect to grow a board in order to keep them on. In an early-stage startup with a couple of people on the team, this person might act as chairman, along with a founder and someone with industry knowledge.

- *Independent:* One of the best members of a board is someone that understands the industry. This should be someone with experience, maybe considered an influencer or expert in each market. It may be a name many recognize in the industry, an executive from an established noncompetitive organization, and/ or someone with a lot of experience that can explain industry specifics to other board members and help provide guidance to founders.

Various countries might have specific requirements based on industry, revenue, debt, board size, and market capitalization. Also, keep in mind that most boards should be odd numbers. For example, grow from three to five to seven. If there will be even numbers of members, make sure to define clearly what voting structures are in place to handle tie votes (e.g., the chairman might only vote if there's a tie or inside directors do not vote, etc.). Once the board structure is laid out, it's time to recruit board members.

Recruiting a Board

A board of three likely includes one of the founders, an investor, and a domain expert from the community the organization serves. The expert is often referred to as the independent. Additional members can be recruited and added later. In most instances, the articles of incorporation with just founders. The company can then start looking for additional members once it's time to go from a stealth company to something more. One of those parties is likely to stay with the board. The inside director role is often the founder acting as CEO—a natural fit for the first seat. This person should learn and/or brush up a little on *Robert's Rules of Order* by Henry Martyn Robert and understand their legal duties to be on a board to keep everything legal. Again, a good legal counsel on such matters is a great thing to have.

Another party. on most boards is the initial investor. The investor who leads a further round of funding is a natural fit for the next party. This person may be replaced in future rounds of investments and often acts as the voice of reason, especially at first. Recruiting this board member is often a result of raising capital unless a company is completely bootstrapping. Then the founders are the source of funding and can potentially end up with multiple inside directors.

The independent. likely only has the shares allotted them in board compensation. This is therefore sometimes one of the harder people to recruit to be on the board. Someone who's an icon in an industry might not want to spend the time or potentially risk their good name by getting involved in a new band or rowdy adventurers. Additionally, if they work at a large organization, they may be wary of conflicts and not want to go through the hassle of asking for permission from an employer. Recruiting an independent is important, though.

To find an independent, look around for someone that meets these requirements. Once found, reach out through social media or get an introduction from a shared contact. (preferred). Ask for coffee (or a call if remote or during a pandemic). Introduce yourself and take them through your philosophy and see if there's a match. Don't stretch too far if there's not a match. It's better to work with someone the founders will like than with someone who is going to be terrible to work with. Having said this, founders should want to be challenged—that's what they're there for.

Not all people are going to be happy to just hop on the board. Here are some tactics to sell them on the idea:

- Take them through the investor pitch deck.

- Explain "why" the innovation is going to help shift the industry.

- Appeal to them as thought leaders who can help shape. the way the innovation will help shift the industry.

- Don't ask for money—there are other investors for that. An independent should be independent.

- Post a request on websites used to recruit board members to help find diverse candidates.

- Keep diversity in mind. People from different backgrounds bring in new ideas and fresh perspectives and challenge our assumptions.

- Ask if they could sit in on a sales call and critique.

- Invite them to join the product management to get perspectives.

Choose board members wisely. They can help or hurt any startup's chances of success. Board members can make introductions. and help the company in other ways. If their advice isn't taken or if the relationship sours, board members can choose to step away or can become combative and need to be removed. We're not stuck with our initial board forever. Usually if we simply ask, a board member will step aside. But once elected, board members can be voted out or removed for reasons defined in the bylaws, such as the following:

- Creating inappropriate conflicts of interest

- Using a board vote as a means of getting something from a third party

- Using the board powers, authority, or knowledge for their own benefit rather than the benefit of the corporation

- Disclosing proprietary information

Many of the issues that arise, though, can be preempted. easily by simply being clear about roles, goals, and expectations. But that's a common theme of this book!

The final aspect of recruiting a board is to build a board compensation package. The reason this is covered in a separate section is that most companies typically want to have board members who are interested based on seeing the vision rather than based on the potential for future financial gains.

Board Compensation

Every startup should have a board of directors by the time that first non-shareholding non-founder. is hired. In fact, according to the type of corporation being formed in support of taking some new groundbreaking innovation to market, chances are (and the rules are different per state or country) there will need to be at least three people sitting on the board.

Participating on a board (or even just advising) takes time out of potentially busy schedules. Attending board meetings can be costly (especially when travel is required to do so). There's also a chance that being on a board can become a liability, given that board members who neglect their duties to act in the interest of shareholders can become personally liable for such a failure. Additionally, board members are often tasked with doing work outside of the boardroom, such as advising on sales and marketing, assisting with strategy, making introductions, reviewing financials, and much more.

It's common to compensate board members when they provide guidance to a growing company. Compensation doesn't always mean cash, especially in a startup where cash can be somewhat scarce. Instead, early-stage companies bring on board members in exchange for equity, stock options, and other forms of potentially dilutive compensation. The right mix to help recruit the best board members can be a challenge to navigate. Here are a few factors that determine how board members might be compensated:

- *Position:* Boards might have a chair, vice chair, secretary, and treasurer. For most companies, it's best to have at least one person on the board who is a domain expert with the type of product or service and at least one angel or later-stage investor. Those can be concentric but often are not. Investors likely don't require compensation above and beyond the expected profit from the investment.

- *Size of board:* Some boards grow and even form committees within the board. This is usually unnecessary for a startup, where we often see three to five board members.

- *Industry:* Some industries work differently than others and some require highly specialized oversight, so ask around to see what is common with others in the industry.

- *Size of the organization:* If there are 3 customers and 30 board members, that's a weird look. But it also heavily impacts the type of board compensation that can be offered. If there are 30 members of the board getting equity, it piles up fast. If the company is a large public entity, then the economics are completely different.

- *Company structure:* Every state handles each corporation (or nonprofit) type differently. It's important to make sure we're following any legal requirements with compensating appropriately based on the type of company created.

There are then several ways that a board member might be compensated:

- *Equity:* A director on a board might require between .25% and 2.5% of equity, according to the preceding variables. Other board members might receive different amounts of compensation.

- *Hourly fees:* This is more common with advisory boards, but some board members receive a stipend per meeting (often between $1,000 and $3,000) or an hourly retainer (often $500 to $1,000). Most early-stage startups shouldn't need to provide this kind of compensation, but it comes up from time to time, given the preceding factors.

- *Salaries:* As a company grows, we see salaries for board members going from $25,000 to over $100,000. This might seem like a lot when a board member is not supposed to direct staff (that's the job of the people that work at the company) or get too involved with the workings of the company. That's why actual cash compensation for board members in startups is so rare. But when these come up, a board member might be acting more as a coach or conciliar to an executive.

One red flag is when compensation comes up in a conversation. Unless someone is a household name, we want them to want to be on the board and to contribute as much as possible without compensation.

Board membership contributions in exchange for the equity provided can range—what's important is that we be clear about the roles, goals, and expectations with each board member. Experienced board members will likely ask for this, whereas people who are new to serving on a board and want to do it for a resume boost might not. Being clear about expectations helps ensure that no one walks away from the experience disappointed and gets the relationship between a board member and the organization off on the right foot.

Some of the responsibilities board members take on include the following:

- *Contacts:* Board members should be chosen based on (and so able to provide) contacts within a given industry that help with sales, finding investors, sourcing vendor relationships/supply chains, and key connections.

- *Advice:* Whether it's pricing or crisis management, it helps to have people with experience that a founder can call on to ask questions and receive formal advice from and people who will help govern an organization created to support some innovation. These might be people with experience in starting companies and investing or with key insights into a given vertical or horizontal market that is served.

- *Expertise:* Deep financial backgrounds, knowledge of go-to-market strategies, and legal assistance. Effectively, many a bootstrapped organization will end up trading equity and/or a board seat away for access to free or reduced costs of expertise.

These can be dilutive, and a good, sound business should have factored many costs to run the business into a budget prior to hiring, incorporating, etc. Just as it's important to be clear about goals for board members, they should in turn help the company to be clear about its goals and improve operating efficiency to get profitable and build a long-term and sustainable company. For more detailed information on given industries and details on what other organizations are doing, check out the Lodestone Global Annual Private Company Board Compensation Survey results at `www.lodestoneglobal.com/single-post/how-much-should-i-pay-my-directors-in-2020`. Just keep in mind that the earlier stage a startup, the more options there are to recruit, compensate, and leverage our board of directors!

The Role of the Board Chair

The board is entitled to questions they ask, and having too many people in a board meeting makes it ineffective and often doesn't provide the answers to those questions. There will be conflicting recommendations from board members. Board members can even be combative. This is where the board chair comes in.

One of the more important positions we bring into our cause at an organization is a board chair. The chair runs the meetings for the board of directors. At many organizations, the chair ends up doing much more. Sometimes too much!

Expectations

What's the expectation? That depends on the board. The most important aspect of being on a board and especially for a chairperson is to ensure the fiduciary and ethical requirements of a management team at a company are met. Anything above and beyond maintaining the financial and ethical needs on behalf of shareholders should be agreed upon prior to taking any board seat and especially becoming a board chair.

The most important aspect of being on any board is to maintain the fiduciary and legal discipline of an organization. Keep in mind that the board members are trustees of a company. The board maintains accountability and oversight of the management team and holds the staff (even staff that are shareholders) accountable for the mission shareholders signed on to invest in. Managing a board is not for everybody. When a board chair trusts the management team, serving as the chair can be great. When not, it can be combative and conflict can ensue. As founders mature, the trust comes, but that takes time.

Responsibilities

The board chair has a unique set of responsibilities. The board chair is usually responsible for wrangling other members of the board. That means logistics, which includes the following:

- *Who:* Maintain a list of other board members and send them invitations to meetings. The chair might also motivate board members to attend meetings in various ways.

- *What:* Run board meetings. This includes understanding the structure of meetings, making sure everyone has any board presentation materials, and making sure all points of view are heard and discussed (sometimes in accordance with *Robert's Rules of Order* or some other guidebook for official meetings). Pretty much every meeting is made better with an agenda, so distributing agendas is often up to the board chair (although any presentation from the CEO or executives might come from the chair or the executives themselves).

- *Where:* This is the easy part. Send a Zoom link or provide an address.

- *When:* Work with leadership and other board members to plan the cadence for meetings. This might include getting meetings scheduled for once a quarter, with three to four weeks following the end of a quarter to close the books. A good starting point for which meetings go where might include the following (although many organizations will have very different cadences):

  - *January:* Annual kickoff where the CEO summarizes how the prior year ended and presents their plan for the upcoming year.

  - *April:* Focuses on human capital, which covers how the organization is proceeding on open job postings and the hiring plan, expectations, impact of cash flow, and impact to the sales plan. Any key notes on those tactical points are usually given back to the CEO during this meeting.

  - *July:* Time to audit because finance teams are the least strained during this time of the year. This often includes details like the 409a, stock options, banking, treasury, etc.

  - *October:* Focuses on strategy, planning for how to implement the strategy over the next year, and getting approval for the upcoming budget season.

- *How:* Keep in mind that the chair is there to run the board in an operational sense more than a leadership sense. The chair is not the CEO and, where appropriate, needs to be as empowering as possible to the existing leadership team. This includes things like ensuring all points of view are heard and discussed but more as a referee than the boss of the board (which the chair is not). In larger boards, the chair may also assign or call votes to assign committee chairs, freeing up a larger board meeting for committee updates and keeping all board members involved in the ways their capabilities are best utilized.

Some of the preceding specific logistical details are often delegated with the chair just showing up and maintaining order, especially when an organization reaches the point where the CEO or other executives have executive assistants. This allows the chair to focus on guiding proactive conversations and enabling productive meetings. This could mean keeping overly verbose or controlling members at bay or maybe even setting up some dinners to give everyone a voice.

In addition, the chair acts as the point of contact for board issues and board contacts. The chair sets goals and objectives for the board and makes sure they're accomplished but doesn't do the same for the company. Although one place where company influence can be exerted is through coaching the CEO.

CEO Coaching

Once a board chair calls a meeting to order, the CEO gives the presentation. It's as though the leader of an adventuring party was called to speak before the governing body of a castle and the surrounding lands. Board members ensure the company did what they say they were going to do and asks questions to provide guidance where possible. Making sure the executives in a company do what they say they're going to do can even mean replacing them. Don't think about that and instead think of how to help the CEO get the most out of a board meeting.

Early on, most go into board meetings bows drawn with a presentation that lays out how the company is doing great and why the future looks bright. This is a mistake. CEOs should learn to solicit what the board members want to hear about rather than write some big, long deck that no one wants to see. This usually includes some standard financial information, which can be distributed before the meeting and doesn't need to get read out loud unless board members have questions. Instead, the board can simply vote to accept a financial statement into the record (if the board is big enough to do that). Hopefully this means more of a focus on strategy, and board chairs can often help get the CEO there (especially early in the life of the company).

Another way CEOs can get more coaching is to stay calm. It's easy to get defensive when hard questions are asked. Instead, founders should master the line, "Remember what you said last time we were all together," to set expectations as accurately as possible. Lean on wisdom and judgment more than opinions. Just keep in mind where an executive coach might be useful than a board member.

Going Further (or Not)

Some board chairs go even further than maintaining ethics and fiduciary requirements. It's a mistake to see a chairperson as the CEO of the board. The CEO is the CEO. However, sometimes a CEO needs more. An "executive chair" can trade various aspects of the CEO role back and forth. They often act as the CEO's boss (e.g., often with a young or inexperienced founder who's got a bit more success than they can handle.) Most board chairs by contract are often a "guest" of the CEO in a way. Yet given that many have sat in that CEO chair, many can step up when needed. The critical aspect of an executive chair is to then be able to step back down when no longer needed.

The board often has as much (or as little) power and influence as the shareholders have provided them. The chair is the leader of the board and so needs a strong commitment to the organization and strong leadership qualities. This often means the chair takes the minority position despite opinions or makes sure the process of decision-making is fair. In short, a good chair will at times subdue their own opinions in order to make sure the rest of the voices on the board are heard, because facilitating collaboration among the board is important.

Collaboration has its limits. CEOs often say things like, "You've gotta make the board do this," but when done well, the chair speaks last and asks, "How do we want to make this decision?" Many a chair may only vote in the case of a tie. Others are substantial shareholders and so will need to vote. This is one aspect of corporate governance that should be set in the bylaws of any organization.

Partnering for Success

Sometimes it seems like when done poorly, running a board is like herding cats (or weretigers). Sometimes it seems like when done well, things go off like a well-oiled machine that was built by a legendary gnome. Yet sometimes the cats have the better company and end up with better outcomes. Only through the lens of history is it possible to judge the success—yet bad outcomes are more likely blamed on a board when the meetings are run poorly.

The partnership between executives and board members needs constant care and feeding. Every mission will be better served with the support experienced professionals can provide to those not only new to running an organization but also to those with decades of experience themselves. This is a bilateral relationship where each compliments the other and requires open—sometimes hard—communication. Boards don't have to be overly formal. In fact, some of the best results come from the informal times during meetings. The CEO connects the board to the staff, and the chair connects the staff to the board. As organizations grow, that separation of powers becomes more and more important.

The leader of a band of merry adventurers isn't a permanent position. A final aspect of the role of a board (and the chair often becomes the focal point here) is succession planning. Hopefully, the governance of an organization leads to a wonderful outcome for founders and CEOs. When it does, they will naturally find different priorities in life. Board members are often late career professionals and often do the same. Therefore, always have succession planning in mind, and maintain a set of the qualifications and maybe even some of the people to reach out to nominate for any positions that come open.

Basics of Board Meetings

Now that there's a diverse board that can help grow the company, it's time to convene and run board meetings on a routine basis. The size and structure of the board and the amount invested into the organization will dictate how formal these meetings need to be. For example, a board of three in a pre-revenue organization might be an informal review of what was done and where the company is at (or what's changed). As the organization grows, there might be paid attorneys in the meetings to keep everyone honest.

The board votes to accept office holders, and so there are some formalities to be aware of. If only so the officers are good to open checking accounts and get credit cards. Let's look at how to structure a board meeting—and do so in the basic steps the board chair will enable to do the following:

- *Recognize that there is a quorum:* A quorum is the number or percentage of people required to make decisions. The number of board members needed to form a quorum is usually outlined in the bylaws and can be anywhere from a simple majority (two out of three or five out of eight, etc.) of board members or a supermajority. The board chair performs a roll call and identifies if there are enough board members to proceed.

- *Call the meeting to order:* The board chair then calls the meeting to order. This should be a simple statement that there is a quorum and the meeting is beginning.

- *Approve minutes and the agenda:* The minutes (or notes) from a previous board meeting should then be approved and the agenda (or outline of the meeting) should be approved. Always remember: old business, then new business. Any changes to the minutes and/or agenda should also be approved at this point as well.

- *Communications and reports:* This is the section for any corporate-wide communications to be read into the minutes and reports shared, and any teams that need to report to the board (e.g., product, sales, etc.) are given a chance to share content they may have prepared.

- *Old business:* This is the area for any items brought up previously to be discussed and, if needed, voted on. Each item can then be approved, denied, postponed to later in the meeting, or tabled to a later meeting.

- *New business:* Once old business is complete, the chair will move to proceed to new business. Here, the chair may ask for any motions to change the order of items from the agenda or may proceed. New items are then approved, denied, postponed to later in the meeting, or tabled to a later meeting and will be picked up as old business in subsequent meetings.

- *Close the meeting:* Once all business has been conducted, the chair can give the floor for informational items (or a point of information) and have it written into formal records that the meeting was run. Again, we would want a second and quick vote to complete the meeting.

This is fairly rigid—or not, depending on the scale of the organization. It's good to get a little more formal than needed early, but not so much so that less is accomplished. For example, each of the items typically requires a vote. The vote needs a motion to vote and then a second and a written tally of which parties voted in favor of a motion passing and which voted in favor of a motion failing. This can be a lot of ceremony for a three-person board meeting, and we may choose to allow a less formal approach until more is needed. However, while the board may choose not to require a second to a motion to vote on something, each motion that is voted on should still be logged into the minutes. No matter how informal an approach taken, those minutes should still be logged and distributed ahead of the meeting for approval.

As the organization and the board grow, there will be conflicts here and there. That's natural, and a diversity of ideas is bound to provide a better result in the operations of a company. But those conflicts, no matter how substantive, usually mean it's time to get a bit more formal with our meetings. A good board chair can do this without making it seem like the company is getting overly formal for the size and current scale of the operations.

Make sure not to run afoul of the legal requirements for the type of company run. An LLC will be loosely governed; however, a C corporation will have regulatory and filing requirements. If others own parts or shares, then some reporting will be required. Make sure all investors feel heard and that the reporting and regulatory requirements on their behalf are met. This doesn't mean to agree with everything they say, but do occasionally bring in counsel to make sure everything is done by the book. Based on the type of company and size, it's a good idea to bring on legal counsel to explore some of those legal requirements to be aware of. Explain the budget for legal and ask for as much advice and assistance as can be packed into that budget. If that advice is awesome, there's a bright future to work with the lawyer retained.

One reason all that legal advice is necessary is because money is the root of all evil—and a necessary, amazing instrument that can do good for humanity when wielded properly. But when the number of zeroes in revenue goes from one to two to three to ten, make sure everyone is treated fairly, to the spirit of the agreements, and to the letter of the law. This means employees, investors, and founders.

Raising Capital

The best and least dilutive place to raise capital is from sales to customers (hopefully this sounds repetitive). This also legitimizes the organization's mission and increases the value of the organization for when funding needs to be raised later. Not everyone can do that out of the gate. Some products have longer sales cycles, some aren't finished and need a concerted effort to get there, some have regulatory approvals or certifications that need to be obtained to be marketable, some require network effects, some need to license patents, etc. Therefore, outside money can accelerate the growth of a company.

The following sections lay out the typical stages of fundraising a company goes through and the types of instruments used to raise capital. There isn't much detail on where to find specific parties to provide funding, as that can vary widely. The sections do cover terms, provide thoughts, and review philosophies. There are non-dilutive sources of funding such as grants from a city seeking to grow the local startup culture, federal grants for specific types of technology, corporate grants to help develop an ecosystem, and nonprofit grants for all kinds of reasons. There are also startup programs at prominent technology companies where startups can get credits for Amazon, Microsoft, Google, Twilio, and other tools to reduce costs and perhaps stretch bootstrapping further before it's time to dilute equity in an organization. Savvy investors can see when startups have embraced these and gotten further without taking funding (or the next round of funding).

Every industry is different. There are tons of non-dilutive or dilutive programs at companies who try to build an ecosystem or provide mentorship to startups for a variety of other reasons (some are actually altruistic). Startups may find funding in these nontraditional outlets but, more importantly, may find partners in horizontal or vertical industries and excellent contacts.

The Funding Hamster Wheel

Investors like to put money into companies that are growing. Over the past 50–75 years, the thinking about that growth has matured. This has led to rounds of increasing capital allocations for companies who grow and need to raise money to help do so. These tranches get larger as companies prove worthy of moving to the next stage. This doesn't mean that there's a race through stages but instead that there are rounds of fundraising activities as the stakes get higher. The risk goes down (although investing in startups is always risky), but so too can the potential rewards.

Think of the education system as an example of how Western society has put everything on an assembly line. Children go through grades and college and potentially graduate school as they prove capable of moving on to the next stage. Other fields are in the same boat, including the healthcare system, the housing market, supply chains for groceries, and so much more. Knowing how to work those systems allow savvy consumers (or business owners in this case) to get more out of them. Yet the systems can consume those who don't know what they're getting into. Leveraging investor money to grow companies is no different.

Let's look at a scenario. A founder starts out bootstrapping a company. The founder takes some money from an angel investor who provides them with some great guidance. They achieve product-market fit and start running into a cash crunch even though the long-term cash flow projections look amazing provided they just keep selling products. The founder takes on another round of funding at a higher valuation, known as a Series A. They scale up with enough cash in the bank to run for a few months even if all of the revenue dries up. To reach even more customers, the founder needs compliance, more insurance, and other substantial cost centers, so they take yet another round of funding known as a Series B. The company grows and the revenues hit a point where it's time to think about going public. The founder brings in auditors to start thinking about doing so, but then the phone rings one day with an offer to sell the company outright to a private equity firm. That's the perfect scenario. It's hard to ask for a better outcome than those options. The founder may or may not still have enough control in the company to decide whether to take the offer or not.

That assembly line works for a lot of companies and founders, but not everyone. Let's say the founder turns down the offer and the industry shifts, which results in a massive drop in sales. Let's say the equity was diluted enough in each round that the founders say no to selling the company but get outvoted. Let's say a founder leaves for another opportunity or one of the more likely outcomes: let's say the company struggles to hit hyper-growth and simply take round after round after round of funding to a Series J. Equity gets slowly diluted to the point that there's a complete loss of control and there's such a small amount of equity that the value of the founder's stake in the company is no longer a great motivator to work hard.

There's a fine line between autonomy and hearing what we want to hear. Everyone wants the funding, but few founders want the advice unless it matches their world view. However, it is important to understand what is going to happen a few years down the line. The angel investors or investors in each subsequent rounds can hopefully provide that guidance to founders for the next stage. Just make sure they are sufficiently incentivized to protect their shares (as doing so will often protect the founder's shares as well).

Just like there's a difference between having a Vorpal sword in your inventory and being able to wield it, there's a difference between raising immediate funds and understanding how they can be used down the line. Given the number of companies that go through the funding assembly line, many get lost in the shuffle. Go into talks with investors armed with the knowledge of how the system works. Wield it to retain control over the destiny of the endeavor. Take funding—but only when there's a deliberate plan for how to leverage each round of capital. The first such round is the seed round, although many organizations begin with an accelerator or incubator.

Accelerators, Incubators, and Studios

Incubators are organizations that help people start companies. They began in the late 1950s in New York when Jo Mancuso opened a warehouse for small tenants to help the town of Batavia. The Batavia Industrial Center provided office supplies, equipment, secretaries, a line of credit, and, most importantly, advice on building a business. The Mancuso family made plenty of money on chicken coops and thought that helping people start companies was a lot like incubating chickens. The modern startup is a bit different than a chicken coop, or not as different as we think.

Others incubated companies as well. The concept expanded from local entrepreneurs who helped other entrepreneurs. Now cities, think tanks, companies, and even universities offer incubation within their walls. Many universities own a lot of patents for technology developed there, and plenty of companies have sprung up to commercialize the intellectual property incubated there. Many of the incubators still provide some of the same types of services and advice to help new business owners launch and grow their companies.

Seeing the success of incubators and how technology companies needed to move faster, accelerators like Techstars appeared. Those took blended approaches where they don't fit neatly into any box to describe a firm. Accelerators focused more on the capital required to start a company and the advice that those who had done so could provide. They often match founders with others who have had successful exits. They might also provide a nominal amount of funding, which ranges from enough for the founders to live for a few months to a few hundred thousand dollars.

The line between an incubator and an accelerator can be pretty thin today. Larger firms attend the demos of companies who complete a program (usually referred to as a cohort) at an accelerator. Those investors may choose to help the new company get to the next stage quicker by investing more money into reaching the next milestones of development. Given the fact that founding companies and innovating are now on an assembly line, the companies that invest in an A round of funding, which might come after an accelerator, will look to exit in a B round, C round, etc. Investors may elect to continue their risk all the way to an acquisition or IPO.

Most cities now have a half dozen accelerators or incubators for founders to choose from. In addition, there's a number of larger and better known programs, which include the following:

- Techstars: www.techstars.com

- Y Combinator: www.ycombinator.com

- AngelPad: https://angelpad.com

- 500 Startups: https://500.co

- Seedcamp: https://seedcamp.com

- StartupBootcamp: www.startupbootcamp.org

Many accelerators have specialties. They also might run different sessions (also referred to as batches or cohorts) that have specific focuses, like agriculture technology or farm to table. The goal is typically to pick products that can be launched in a period of time and run a demo that investors can put more money into if they like the results and the founders. They come with a little startup seed money—typically enough to run for a month or six. In exchange, the accelerator takes a minimal amount of equity (usually between 3 and 10% of the shares of a company). They also might help incorporate the company properly and establish board of directors to help oversee operations.

Many large companies also look to fund an innovation ecosystem around them. Companies who have accelerators (or funds of various types) include Google, Okta, and Microsoft. Many look for interesting ideas and consider the minimal investment a part of the deal flow for future acquisitions. Others do it for public relations purposes. Some programs are so successful they get spun off into their own stand-alone companies.

A studio is yet another approach to help grow fledgling companies. Studios take a share of equity (and sometimes some cash) in exchange for developing a product. Most accelerators are built for technical founders—whereas most studio models are for-profit enterprises that treat the equity of the product being built as an asset that can later be sold if the go-to-market isn't a success. The studio model might take double or triple the equity given that the founders are often not technical enough to build a product themselves.

There are about as many ways to fund, launch, and grow an organization as there are organizations involved in the process. Each has their own take on how to grow capital by helping to grow companies. There's a lot of capital being invested and a lot of investors looking to carve a niche for themselves. Apply to as many programs as it takes. But interview people who have done programs before accepting one. Feel free to dig into what each has to offer, and keep in mind that much of the content they generate can be obtained for free (e.g., Startup School from Y Combinator). So even if an idea doesn't get accepted into a cohort, the knowledge available may be accessible in other ways.

These are just a few of the more recent innovations meant to fuel companies. The capital stages in a company's life and types of investors who focus on each are important as well.

Angels and Seed Rounds

An angel investor is an accredited investor (which is a "high net worth" individual) who gives money to startups to help them bring products to the market in exchange for equity (or another financial instrument) in an organization. Sometimes these are people startups meet at events or sometimes it's family, friends, or industry contacts. To qualify as a high net worth individual, the angel typically needs to make $200,000 a year and have a worth of at least $1,000,000. Having said this, anyone able to provide the capital needed can usually invest in a corporation—being an accredited investor just opens up the number of vehicles that can be used to provide funds.

There can be overlap between angel investors and venture capitalists. Angels are accredited investors who can use their own money to invest in a company, whereas venture capitalists usually invest on behalf of limited partners (LPs) who give the investor money through a given fund to use to help companies. The venture capitalist often puts some of their own money into the fund and might also do sidecar investments into the companies being funded. The LPs then look at early-stage companies who they might invest in individually as well.

The capital is great to have for small businesses looking to accelerate their growth. The more important aspect of an angel is really the guidance they provide. Many will have diversified portfolios themselves and great contacts at investment firms. Many will also have contacts at potential customers and vendors. A great angel investor provides far more than operating capital: they help see what's a few steps in front of a young company, help in the moment when information is needed, help spread the word, and help validate that a company is on the right track. They should also know when to stay out of the way so things can get done.

There are about as many ways to find investors as there are investors. The first step is often the personal network of friends and family. Here, look around and decide who might be able to bring a little more to the table than money. For example, an aunt with extensive experience in marketing is great because she provides more than just money. Expanding beyond the personal network, there are potential investors everywhere. Every city has events that people attend to network and pitch ideas. There are websites that connect investors to startups. And then there's cold outreach through LinkedIn and personal sites. Again though, there are tons of ways to find angels. Those are just the most common.

One of the most important tips to work with any investor in any of the rounds is to get everything on paper. A standard boiler plate term sheet provides a great framework, but make sure to go through that paper with an attorney before selling a single share of the company—it's potentially the most important money that gets spent. Be clear about the goals and expectations with the arrangement. Keep in mind that if one person is willing to invest, someone else will be out there as well. Don't be afraid to be clear about what, other than operating capital, the investors should bring to the table. Remember that the more they're involved when needed, the less risky their investment likely will be!

Series A

A seed round is when a company raises capital to seed the company. This will usually be 2 to 15 investors each contributing, let's say, $10,000 to $2,000,000 each. The financial instruments used in those investments might be convertible notes or common stock (which pays out first in an equity event and may come with additional rights). The Series A is then money raised from a small number of investors who each contribute more. A company can do either, or both, but likely dilutes equity further when granting Series A preferred shares in a Series A.

The Series A works more with VCs than seed rounds. Often, a fund will invest in tens to hundreds of shiny new companies. Make sure to validate product-market fit before moving into a Series A. Funds can then be used to jump-start the company, and a mention on sites like Crunchbase is great for public relations. Additionally, those larger VC funds have access to even larger networks of other investors and, between all the people that work at those funds, usually great industry contacts who now share in the goal to have a successful outcome.

A Series B (and further rounds) can be far more intense. If the company can't show that it can develop a solid go-to-market strategy, then the founders could have diluted equity that makes it hard to raise future rounds of capital. Many startups collapse under that stress. Therefore, make sure to have done the following before putting together a Series A round of financing the company:

- Validate product-market fit.

- Have a business model with a window of time for profitability.

- Put together a team that can deliver the first stage of the business model.

- Have a good understanding of runway and how long cash will last.

- Optimize distribution and code pipelines and routes to market for products.

- Have at least one seller ready, and a marketing plan.

Founders can build a great company armed with these, provided there's a good idea and a great plan that can be executed. There's a lot in other chapters about what happens next and unpacking the preceding bullets. But if all goes well, founders will run into a cash crunch when it's time for the money required to grow into the next stage of the company's life cycle. That's when the company looks to a Series B to help accelerate growth even faster.

Series B

The information in a book like this becomes less and less valuable the further along an organization gets in what series of funding is being pursued. There could be entire books just on the financial instruments, cap table dilution, raising capital, dealing with investors, etc. The dilution of what pertains to a given organization with their own values starts to become evident at the scale most organizations have achieved by the time they start raising the funds in a Series B. Let's unpack that. Maybe the Series B is between a $30 million and $60 million round of equity financing being raised. Here, investors might buy out any diluted financing from the angel round. New board members are brought in and the objective is all about growth. Investors are paying a higher per-share round in exchange for shares in a company that has a proven thesis.

The mission was proven in the Series A-stage of the company by raising some revenue from the best place cash can be raised: paying customers. Once some sales have proven the mission, it is common for investors to provide a convertible note that can then be converted into preferred stock in a Series B. Convertible notes are short-term debts that convert to stock at a future round of funding. Preferred stockholders are paid dividends and liquidated before common stockholders in the event of profit dispersal or sales, respectively.

The investors who often back a Series B might be some of the angels from earlier rounds, but more often they are venture capitalists, funds, private equity investments, and credit investments. Because most investors in a Series B anticipate the organization will raise a future round, most insist on anti-dilution, but most of the convertible notes issued don't come with voting rights. Think about that this way: angels trade a balance of time and money for shares and often have experience going through a similar lived experience as the founders they invest in. Once the company is at a scale that necessitates a Series B, it takes on professional investors who maybe haven't been at a startup or who make a lot of investments and so don't have the time or inclination to work with too many companies. This isn't always the case but often is.

By the time the company has stable revenue streams, they usually need more consistent marketing, sales, support, technology delivery, and therefore talent acquisition as well. Most also realize that revenues might be lumpy and might just need that Series B round for the cushion in the cash flow while hammering out operational details. Keep in mind that the Series B should get the company through the size where investors might consider it an early-stage company. Further rounds can be, but aren't always, considered for startups.

Series C–Z

A Series C is not typically for early-stage companies. Rounds often start at about $50,000,000 (as of the time of this writing). Part of the goal for investors is to take the company public or sell it to a private equity firm. Some may have different exit strategies in mind, but those are the two most common. Further rounds may be required; it's not uncommon for a company to raise a Series F. But Series C investors (and on) often have a terminal value for the investment in mind and will push the company in that direction.

Terminal value is the price the investor plans to liquidate their stock at in the future. That future date is a horizon that may or may not be shared with the startup being invested in. So, when raising a Series C, it's good to know the timeline each investor is looking for up front. Not all will disclose that, and some won't know themselves—but the politics of working with investors get far easier when their investment thesis and event horizons are known. Their past investments might indicate their plans or predilections for the future as well. Companies have specialties; so do investors.

Most investors in a Series C and beyond think the company will get bought or go public (which is basically being purchased by a lot of investors rather than just one). Before moving into these stages of growth, make sure that's the vision of the existing shareholders. As noted, by the time an organization gets to this point, the advice that can be provided in a book for early-stage startups like this is incredibly diluted (although potentially not as diluted as the founder's equity), and there are hyper-specialized individuals or firms and resources that can help on that journey. That advice will cost far more than this book.

Financial Instruments

A few terms were mentioned in the preceding sections that are various types of securities held by investors in exchange for providing funds to a startup. Make no mistake; investing is financing—just like a bank. The nuance in the words used often comes from the industries operated in, with the type of risk associated, and from the parties involved. That nuance then often translates into specific sections found in those contracts that wouldn't be found in a typical bank loan, 401k, or line of credit.

While traditional financial institutions might invest in funds that invest in startups, they don't often do so directly in the software industry. Banks lend money in exchange for a security when that money isn't repaid. A bank might hold the deed for land or the title for a car until a loan is repaid. Those types of securities aren't always available in startups. Companies come and go all the time. The smaller the company, the bigger the risk. Without a founder, much of the intellectual property of a software startup isn't as valuable as other securities (like a car that can be sold to recoup money not collected as a part of a loan).

New and innovative ideas (and companies formed in support of them) fuel growth for societies, all the way back to the Greeks, Egyptians, and probably beyond. Those innovations need to be funded to build an organization that can take the innovation to market. The job benefactors in autocratic civilizations held moves to private entities in modern democracies. Large companies are risk averse, so it's increasingly smaller companies who invest in new technologies. That risk needs to be shared, so investors provide that funding and then share the rewards when the adventure is a success.

The types of investments dictate the types of returns. Banks have a standard risk profile they like to work with and a regulated reward system. When a bank provides a mortgage for a home, they take the loan-to-value ratio (i.e., the value of the security they hold), the credit score of the homeowner, income levels, and other factors that help them derive how risky an investment the homeowner is based on whether or not they can pay the mortgage off. The mortgage provider can charge more for riskier investments, but regulators in various countries typically limit the scale of that increase.

Investors buy shares in companies or issue financial instruments that seem more like a traditional loan with additional rights that often involve converting that security to equity. This means that investors are often far closer to founders in the earlier stages, where the founder themselves (often more than the big idea) is the riskiest aspect of the investment. The investor then makes a judgment call around what the investment is worth. A simple example might be that 5% of a given company with a $2 million valuation is worth $100,000. Then, it's just a matter of choosing the right tool to provide that financing.

In 1957, one of the first venture capital firms, American Research and Development Corporation (AR&D), invested $70,000 in a company called Digital Equipment Corporation (DEC for short). At the time, it seemed like a risky investment, as Ken Olson was just leaving MIT to build computers—which meant going up against the behemoth IBM. No one would bet against IBM. DEC quickly became the second largest computer company in the world as interactive computing replaced old tube-based mainframes. That investment netted over 5,000 times the capital provided in 1968 when DEC, then valued at $355 million, completed their initial public offering.

Georges Doriot from AR&D is considered by many to be the founder of the modern venture capital system. The term sheet he gave DEC was a simple one-page offer that his firm would buy 70% of the company for their $70,000. Evolutions in the technology industry, investment strategies, tax codes, and regulatory requirements force us to have more complicated agreements and provide more options for term sheets on contracts these days. Most founders would get mad and run out the door or laugh maniacally if offered less than $100,000 for controlling equity in their company. But inflation exists, so adjust that $70k to around nine times that and pretend we're talking about investing in teleportation and it might make a little more sense. Keep in mind that AR&D returned an annualized 15% ROI to investors, not over 100% as they got with the DEC deal— meaning they picked a lot of companies that didn't make it as well.

Games evolve. Just look at the differences between the original basic or first edition Dungeons and Dragons and the 5e version widely played these days. Investors have evolved since those early days in venture capital (and as the alumni of AR&D went on to found firms like Greylock who fund innovative startups to this day). The fundamentals of venture capital, much as with the game mechanics of role-playing games, are still the same though. Investors take a risk on funding an organization formed to support an innovation. They use a variety of financial instruments in that pursuit. Deals can still be made to support any type of situation, but many are now bucketed into specific categories to put the deal machine at firms on a bit of an assembly line and reduce the legal costs by repeating the use of some of these ways to fund. Some the community keeps going back include the following:

- *A loan:* This is first because it's the most traditional financial instrument: one party provides a loan, like a bank does (in fact, it might be a line of credit at a bank), usually backed by a security (e.g., a mortgage or ownership of the company). This is not a common way to fund a company as the risk is high for the lender. However, during poor economic environments, debt financing might be the only way to secure investments.

- *Common stock:* The simplest startup financing is to sell shares in the corporation. Doing so dilutes equity, but all shareholders understand exactly what is in the term sheet and the company could be formed as an LLC and operations simplified as opposed to taking on additional tax and financial complexities introduced with different types of shares and financial instruments.

- *Convertible note:* A short-term debt that converts into equity in a future financing round. Dilutes equity at conversion, often with interest. Conversion can come with preferred or common stock. The company might be able to buy the shares back before the debt converts into shares.

- *Simple agreements for future equity (SAFE):* Shorter than the traditional convertible note with less terms (and so cheaper to do all the legal haggling). Doesn't usually come with interest at conversion.

- *Equity crowdfunding:* Equity funding by groups of investors through crowdfunding sites. More common is crowdfunding for some good or service.

- *Debt financing:* Investment made using a financial instrument that requires repayment of the principal plus interest.

- *Corporate round:* Investment round led by another company, often in an adjacent market.

- *Initial coin offering (ICO):* Similar to an IPO but using a cryptocurrency instead of publicly traded shares.

- *Private equity round:* Late-stage investments, often (but not always) made on underperforming organizations for a larger percentage of equity, if not for all equity.

- *Post-IPO debt:* Debt taken on by a publicly trading company.

There are historical examples of every possible outcome of financing a founder can think of. Control Data Corporation (CDC) allowed Dr. Michael Allen to take his ideas in exchange for a loan that would be repaid at a fraction of the cost if repaid early. CDC had grown to the point they could not weaponize all the innovations coming out of the late, great corporation, and the acceleration of getting some money in exchange for the intellectual property he took with him was better than getting nothing. That company would later be merged into Macromedia and then Adobe, and the tools (or derivatives of them) went on to become Fireworks,

Dreamweaver, and Flash. The "investor" had the impact desired and received compensation. History is littered with hundreds of custom stories about unique investment vehicles.

Much as there are intricate rules spread around books for tabletop gamers, there are thousands of little intricate details around how to finance a company. Some of the more common (or at least, more visible) ones have been covered in this chapter, but there are plenty of financial instruments available for whatever outcome is desired. There are so many other details to make sure to get right in a term sheet, like regulating the secondary sales of stock or the dilution in future rounds. Most founders aren't savvy financiers—and those who likely need a second opinion on matters—so make sure to have good legal and financial representation before signing those term sheets.

Make sure to be intentional about how much equity is given up and what triggers different share numbers; that could be the difference between maintaining control of a company and being on the sideline during really good or really bad times. Chances are that different people might be able to run our companies better at different stages of their growth, but when possible, founding teams should retain the agency to be able to make that decision themselves.

One point of introspection is to think about what founders want out of a new company. Much of this chapter has covered how to grow and use capital to accelerate growth. Many will want different things out of their work. Not everyone wants to grow a company. Some just want a good business that provides a great lifestyle.

A Lifestyle Business Can Lead to a Great Lifestyle

Many an adventurer can roam the wilds of the lands for decades, leveling up as they go, growing their personal fortune and gaining valuable experience. Especially rangers are happy to go it alone!

Most investors want growth. If the founders don't want the same thing, or if their perspectives change, that will need to be resolved (likely by buying out other shareholders). As with many things in business, it's important to have clear and concise communication about what is happening and ultimately do what makes the founders and shareholders happy. Don't feel pressured to become something inorganic; that's a recipe for disaster. Building a company not meant for hyper-growth is respectable and a foundation of capitalism.

Maybe the founders want to focus on other things than taking over the world or owning a market. Maybe just want a lifestyle that allows them to work less than 100 hours a week while staying their own boss. This is known as lifestyle business, and it's fantastic if that's what everyone is after, even if it's only temporarily so. One of the biggest challenges is retaining employees when the founders have made a decision to slow growth. The next section deals with when to stop growing and investigates how to explain the situation to the staff who so courageously joined the founders on the journey.

When to Stop Growing

A prevailing business philosophy is the concept that if revenue isn't growing faster than the industry standard, then the company is getting passed by the competition. That's crap. It's possible to be happy with whatever size a company is. If founders want to grow it, then great. If not, then they don't have to. The company should grow along with the founders' level of comfort; otherwise, it won't happen in a positive way.

There is no limit to how big a company can grow; the only limitation is how comfortable the involved parties are with the size of the organization. Some companies stop at 2 and just sit there for 30 years. Some stop at 50 and that's their sweet spot. Some organizations unwillingly slow their growth. No matter the size or situation of a business, it's important to have clear and concise communication about what is happening—and what will hopefully happen next, to rally everyone around the cause.

This section is geared for a very specific situation, which is that the company leadership has made a cognizant choice that they do not want the company to grow. It also means that a group within a company might not grow any further, at least in the immediate future. Usually this is because they want to focus on other things. Founders can refer to this type of company as a lifestyle business, even if it's only temporarily so. One of the biggest challenges is retaining employees once a decision like this has been made; that starts with communication.

Communication

Halting growth is hard. The most important thing is to be open and honest with everyone about what is going on. Especially if the company or a team has been growing and a choice has been made to intentionally slow down growth. Tell people why it's happening as early as possible. When that communication happens, also be clear about how the strategy of the organization might change in the near-term future.

Slowing down growth reduces risk but also reduces the opportunities an organization can provide to staff. This section covers ways to keep teams motivated, but for now, focus on making everyone feel safe in their jobs (provided they are). Explain the reason for the sedation, how it will happen, and what opportunities each person has in the new paradigm. People need to see a future for themselves, and without growth, there may be little upward mobility (e.g., into management).

Expect some turnover. After all, what's the future for each person on staff? This doesn't always happen immediately, and it's often an amicable parting of ways provided leadership is clear about intentions. If people leave, expect a little customer turnover as well in businesses with more services. Turnover is inevitable whenever there's a perception that there's less opportunity at a job.

Leadership After Growth Slows

Building and growing an organization is fun! Games are fun when it's all going well, too. Managing an organization that is static or shrinking can totally suck. It doesn't have to. Employee satisfaction is an amazing thing and a key aspect of making your company an awesome place to work. During times of growth, everyone is invariably happy with their jobs. Staff sees an incredible growth opportunity, a lot of great new team members they can mentor, and there's a general buzz in the community that surrounds expansion. Eventually the expansion slows in every organization and on every team. Few are ready for it when it comes, except those who are slowing growth intentionally.

How is a leader to react? How is a cohesive team who has done everything the organization asked of them to be kept engaged? How is good work rewarded if there are few opportunities within a team? Let's look at some important concepts to keep in mind when turning that corner into the next phase of a company's life cycle:

- *Make sure employees feel safe:* Employees need to feel secure in their jobs. When employees take on more work and see that hiring has slowed, they will assume the worst. Be completely transparent. Show enough respect for staff to explain as much as allowed, even if it means they start to leave of their own accord. Of course, this starts with a sound strategy!

- *Understand what motivates people:* People are all motivated by something different. Make sure to understand what motivates team members or have their supervisors find out. Then double-check by surveying staff and comparing those results to the qualitative analysis.

- *Provide different ways to recognize success:* When an organization decides to shift priorities and limit funding for a team or a company slows down, the key metrics you use to gauge performance must mature as well. This often starts by moving from billings to margin, from margin to channel empowerment, between various types of work, or from any of these to innovation.

- *Find ways to be more visible in the organization:* As growth in teams slows, increasing visibility within an overall organization or community allows team members to feel positive about their roles in the organization. Allowing employees access to other teams also allows for networking and more idea sharing in ways that might not have been possible during times of hyper-growth and fosters a greater sense of teamwork within the organization. Becoming more visible also provides exposure to each member of the staff.

- *If you love someone, set them free:* Champion the best employees; but be willing to replace them as well. Even if doing so makes everyone's life harder, rewarding great work will inspire the next generation to be better and often across all teams. Alternatively, not recognizing the potential in your staff leads to disgruntled employees and crappy work. Watching the former staff flourish in new roles is the area of careers that can be the most satisfactory! If the organization is not growing, then there is usually a cap to careers within the organization. Offset this with profit sharing.

Ultimately the ability to lead a growing organization is easier than leading an organization that isn't trending up and to the right on spreadsheets. Taking on a static organization is easy because someone else already dealt with reframing how the organization survives. That reframing means taking care of staff first and foremost. Look for how the team fits in the new layout. Let the team help not only define the strategy, but also lay out the tactics to achieve the strategy. Everyone should be empowered to contribute on every level.

Don't retreat within the team. Focus on the happiness and well-being of the team, but when growth slows, look outward for opportunities to contribute to all areas of the organization and community. Look for ways to help employees and ways to do what's right, making sure to align their needs with those of the organization. Aligning the strategy of groups with that of an organization is the key to success of the organization as a whole. If each manager simply looks to bolster their team, they will do nothing more than fracture an otherwise cohesive organization.

Financial Calculus Post-growth

Growing companies are often flush with cash. But when they stop growing, costs rarely stop as well. Taxes go up. Inflation goes up. Cost of living increases, at a minimum, need to be given to employees annually to keep them. At some point, if customers and employees aren't growing, founders and executives are left to find ways to make more money in a seemingly shrinking company. Some ways to go about doing so include the following:

- *Crack open the books:* Write a sentence down on real paper with a real pen about how to cut each entry in the accounts payable column of your general ledger. Inspect costs with a microscope to figure out what can't be cut without negatively impacting performance of staff and what can't be.

- *Renegotiate every contract:* How much are lawyers being paid? Pay them less. How about accountants? Pay them less. If contracts can't be renegotiated, start looking for other contractors who are equally as qualified.

- *Review current and future plans with a tax advisor:* If converting to a different type of company that isn't geared for growth, tax liabilities may be way less.

- *Pay down debts:* Interest on debt can kill a company, especially credit card debt (which is often personally backed). If the company is sold, it will be far easier if there are fewer liabilities.

- *Convert employees to contractors:* This is usually unpopular. Converting an employee to a 1099 often sends them to looking for a new job immediately. No really, even if they say it's cool, they are on job boards within minutes.

- *Go virtual:* This is especially tough when trying to convince staff to stick around, despite a lack of personal opportunity for growth (or at least the perceived lack of opportunities). But rent is often as much as a staff employee. The most important aspect of going to a virtual workplace is to keep community; otherwise, the distance created between you and employees will cause them to be more likely to abscond with your customers or, in their eyes, their customers. Another aspect to consider is how to communicate expectations effectively.

- *Purchase property: What about reducing costs and paying down debts…?* Mortgages on commercial real estate are typically 15-year notes, so it's usually a big investment. By redirecting rent, though, it's easier to build more of a rainy day or retirement fund. Commercial property should net more return than some other investments.

Make sure to understand revenue and costs early, and make sure to build up reserves.

Sell the Company?

There is no right or wrong answer about when (or whether) it's time to sell. Sell too early and we end up making less than we could have. Sell too late and we might have valuations drop due to poor sales, changing equity conditions, changing markets, or pending legal action. Again, there is no right or wrong answer on timing.

There are some elements to think through and really understand. The first is passion. If the founders are no longer passionate about the mission, are no longer living the values, and are no longer fully engaged, then something needs to change. Maybe it's time for founders to move to part-time and allow the company to run on autopilot if it's gotten to the point where it can. Maybe the company should be restructured. Maybe it should be expanded into adjacencies. Maybe it's time to sell the company. Provided the founders proceed with integrity and are honest with everyone, it's hard to go wrong. It's important to give everyone involved the autonomy to make their own choices with the most honest accounting of facts that can be provided.

Aside from the level of engagement with the organization, there's also a financial component to consider. Many organizations grow to the point where the value is a life-changing or intergenerational wealth-changing outcome for founders. In these cases, the risk of the organization failing can become an immensely stressful burden. Add to that the stress of dozens, then hundreds, then thousands of people depending on us as founders. Great founders can crumble or cease being able to make decisions, paralyzed by that fear, slowing growth or contracting organizations. If we haven't brought in outside investment yet, that can help. The terminal value of an organization for founders becomes diluted, and that can impact whether to sell.

Sometimes founders also just want their lives back. Founders usually invest countless hours into a startup. The timing can be right to go when the founders feel like the company has grown beyond them, when the politics set in, or when the daily job becomes a chore and not what they set out to do. Sid Meier, maker of dozens of blockbuster game titles, left MicroProse when the company he cofounded wasn't fun anymore and was going in different directions. He loved the company and making games. So, he remained a contractor and created Civilization after selling his half of the company to his cofounder—likely making more in the long run since it was a blockbuster hit and he was making royalties from the sales.

There are about as many outcomes possible as there are companies in the world. We can hire someone to run the company and move to a board seat. We can move into product and bring someone on to run the company. Or we could find an acquirer and a good term sheet and move on. Acquirers, term sheets, and letting teams know if selling the company are covered in the next few sections. This is one of those times when the whole section should be read (maybe twice) before doing anything else (like discussing a potential acquisition with anyone on the team).

Define an Acquirer

The process of being acquired is similar to that of acquiring a company—just the opposite. It's also somewhat like taking on rounds of funding, except we won't be around anymore (or will become an employee instead of an owner).

The types of companies that might want to acquire us can be put into a few different categories. This is important to understand because in the case where founders are looking to do acquisition, it helps to understand where to look. This might be looking for other offers if the company has been approached or just to make industry contacts for a potential future acquisition. It's great to know where to start networking. The main acquirers include the following:

- *Adjacent companies:* These are often the best acquirers. They understand the customer, the buyer, and can most easily come up with a plan to grow the business without cutting too many staff. And the combination of the products makes for a more powerful offering, allowing for cross-selling products using the same sellers, integrations between products to improve customer turnover, better cross-product marketing, cultural alignment, and better retention among employees. A buyout in this case should proceed a little higher than industry standard multiples for a given market segment given a higher likelihood that the acquisition will result in a good return on the investment for the acquirer. One caveat is if the barrier to enter a market is low, the adjacent companies might move in our direction with their own product or start a project to compete with us if the barrier of entry is too high. For example, once Facebook was unable to acquire Snapchat, they introduced ephemeral storage in the form of "Stories" on both Facebook and Instagram.

- *Competing companies:* Competitors acquire companies in order to gain access to technology, institutional knowledge, and customer lists. The product(s) may continue or may find their way to retirement, and often it's important to look for a graceful onboarding into the acquirer's tooling. Founders may end up staying and hopefully most of the team can stay as well, although if the technology stacks are different and skillsets not portable, it's likely technical teams will be needed in the new organization. Sales and marketing teams are usually portable and often more valuable than the products; however, teams that run back-office functions like accounts receivable are so often duplicitous and will find themselves out of work after a transition period. The valuation then is three to six times revenues, plus a bump for any patents, trademarks, and strategy points that make the company more valuable.

- *Private equity firms:* These organizations buy and hold, upgrade, and then sell or merge companies. Recently, private equity firms also take larger companies public (e.g., through a special purpose acquisition company). Like a great house with good bones but poor curb appeal, a listless company might find renewed inspiration in the expertise or combined impact a portfolio of companies can offer. Most private equity deals for software companies look for good entry multiples (or the cost they pay for a company relative to some metric important for the segment of the industry) with a desired exit multiple (the price they sell for compared to the same metric). They look for a company to acquire that is undervalued in the market where they can plug some holes, increase sales, and make a profit for their investors. This multiple expansion (or just growing the company with the same multiple) is important to understand as it points the founders in the direction of setting a base sale price (which can usually range from four to ten times revenues).

- *Companies with similar technical stacks but not in adjacent markets:* This type of an acquisition is most common with depressed assets, or a company with decreasing value. Here, let's say there are five Java developers that work well as an isolated scrum team. Another company might see value in bringing those developers in but have no desire to own or maintain the products the team had previously produced. The value of the company is often then anywhere from nothing (and so we become an acquihire) up to a maximum value around 20% of the salaries of the employees. Likely not the outcome we were hoping for when we founded the company, but a graceful exit that takes care of the employees.

- *Brokers:* There are companies who take a fee to facilitate the sale of companies.

Once there's a list of companies who might be an acquirer, figure out where to find them. A great way to start this process is to get meetings with executives or product teams and look at how products might be integrated together. That provides some exposure to the culture without putting ourselves out there. From there, acquisition talks can seem organic. Competitors are similar; except rather than look to develop integrations, it's often best to set meetings up with CEOs or corporate development teams. It's best to simply be honest and up front about goals in the beginning.

Private equity firms can be tricky (unless they approach us). It's best to first look at our industry and see which firms are investing there. Then ask investors from previous rounds to make introductions if they know anyone or reach out and connect with principals at firms. Private equity deals can take time so don't expect that to happen quickly. Make sure there's plenty of runway to get the due diligence and other steps they'll require done.

No one wants to sit atop a company that fails. It still happens. Maybe the company has run out of runway and projects an inability to make payroll in six months. Maybe the industry changed or someone beat the company to market or in go-to-market. Maybe the potential acquirers of a product have been exhausted. When this happens, one option is to spin the company down as gracefully as possible. The team can be traded out and any liabilities (if possible) for an exit with another organization that uses the same technical stack and needs a team. Local job boards are one place to find such things, as is word of mouth and looking for expanding companies at user groups.

No matter who's looking to acquire the company, weigh the options—evaluate competing term sheets; pay the legal bills on all of that (which rarely come in below $20,000 even for the simplest of acquisitions)—and make sure to understand what is left in the bank to pay back shareholders as quickly as possible.

Inform Teams

Once the deal is done, it's time to tell the team. Many of the questions in this chapter might help make up the minds of founders. Any organization with multiple people not involved in the decision-making should value the outcomes for employees enough to think through the details of what it means for them. There are things founders might not think of unless they've been through this before.

Here are some things to think about, know, and be prepared to answer with those who joined the company on this journey:

- Are the founders and other shareholders still passionate?

- What is the terminal value (in cash and stock) for each person involved? This should include triggering and vesting information from employee and investor pools.

- Are there term sheets to sell the company to someone? If so, how long have those conversations been going on and how far are we down the path?

- What will the new reporting structure look like?

- Will position descriptions change?

- Will employees go to a new office or the same office?

- Will there be any changes to employee compensation and benefits? If so, what will those entail?

- What is the timing of a merger or acquisition?

- Is there a plan to integrate products and combine products or will the products stay separate? (This doesn't have to be overly technical unless those details are available.)

- Will the roadmap change?

- What is the culture like at the acquirer?

Many founders can be amazed that some of the preceding questions come up. Be empathetic here, even if it's not a natural state. Remember that people have families and need to understand the impact changes will have on them. People have jobs and careers that need protecting. If a great culture was built, employees likely also worked extra or harder and are understandably concerned about the added compensation that employee stock pools can bring them.

Keep in mind, founders and shareholders have the autonomy to make their own choices given all the facts at hand. The people on the teams that helped find success deserve the same. There's another big question that comes up (hopefully) for many founders. The next section covers what happens to the founders after the sale is complete.

Will Founders Stay at the Company?

The campaign is almost complete. This book started with an idea. That idea was the innovative spark to form a new company in support of the idea. Over time, a lasting organization that could survive without the founders was built. They've worked to secure a new era for the company—a new life.

There's just one more thing for the founders to do: decide whether to stay on to see what things are like in the new era. It's easily one of the most important questions, and not one that is permanent. The company will likely do better if the founders stay—at least for a time. Any mature purchaser will understand this and likely request a transition period at a minimum, maybe even with an earn-out period built into the purchase agreement.

The successful company led someone to acquire it. The founders got used to making all the decisions. Then it can be awkward to ask others what they would do—or even for permission. When staying on for any duration of time, make sure to work out some details with the new owners of your company, and consider the following before signing that term sheet:

- How would founders feel about having a boss?

- What authority will the founders still have in regard to hiring and human resources?

- What spending authority do the founders have?

- If working in sales as well, what discount authority do the founders have?

- If choosing to move on, how will the founders be phased out, including a final date of employment?

- What incentive plans are in place (for the founders and the rest of the team)?

- How are accounts managed (e.g., Apple App Store or Google Play Store accounts that own apps, certificates, domains and websites, etc.)?

Hopefully the founders stay and have an amazing impact on the new organization. If moving on, make sure to work out an acceptable exit strategy with the new owners. This should include milestones with fixed dates attached to them. And be transparent with staff (and customers, if applicable). That's important, so everyone on the team feels the deal is equitable and we're honorable. Keep a few things in mind during those last few weeks. Be supportive of the new owners. In fact, let them know that they get a free pass by blaming all the problems on the departing founder(s) for a bit. Things can get emotional (especially if the organization has been around for a while), so be prepared, even if it's not something we can possibly imagine.

Once founders have had a successful outcome, founding companies can be a loop. They might choose to head back to the beginning of the book with a new idea, and the company that bought the last one might just be a future acquirer if everything goes well!

Conclusion

The best way to raise funds is to sell products to customers. The ranger who sets off on a grand undertaking can bootstrap pretty much anything. One ranger probably can't wrangle enough iron rations to feed a large adventuring party capable of great things. Going it alone is fun at first, but the rewards are likely as limited as the individual skillset. Growing an organization beyond a sole proprietor or pair of cofounders is risky. Even if two people can manage to grow a business and own the entirety of stock in a 100+ person organization, they likely face the potential to lose millions of dollars at any given time. Funding allows the company to grow faster, shares the risk, and gains access to valuable insights most founders can't just outright pay for.

The modern system of funding is an assembly line. It can chew founders up and spit them out. Financing can be that fireball that accelerates a company into legendary status when understanding the goal for each stage. Be deliberate about when to give up equity and what to get in exchange. That helps everything to go off more smoothly. Just make sure to have a lawyer review those term sheets (since we didn't include an entire chapter on the assassin class)!

Index

A

Accounting
    accrual *vs.* cash-based, 340
    balance sheet, 333
    cash flow/burn rates, 350
    cash flow statement, 334
    charts, 357
    finances, 329
    hiring accountant, 341–343
    insurances, 346–349
    levels, 330–332
    P&L statement, 334
    performance projections, 335
    software, 336–339
    spreadsheet, 351, 352, 354–356
    stakeholders, 329
    taxes, 335, 343–346
Accrual-based accounting, 339, 340
"Adaptive Software Development",
        187, 188
Advertising
    companies level, 468
    coupons/sales/specials,
        479, 480
    MDFs, 481, 482
    measures, 482, 483
    old-school advertising, 474–478
    paid search, 468–471

social media, 471–473
    wrong calls, 480, 481
"Agile" approaches, 130
Airtable, 98, 141, 145, 364, 376
Annual recurring revenue (ARR),
        361, 613
API-first strategy, 289, 290
Applicant tracking
        systems (ATS), 274
Application Programming
        Interface (API), 130, 286
    CP/M, 288
    CRUD, 286
    data, 291, 292
    definition, 286
    graph, 292
    GUI/web interface, 287
    implementation, 293–296
    marketing platform, 296
    REST endpoint, 286
    workflow-based strategy, 290
ARM chipset architectures, 23
ARPANET, 412

B

"Brain drain", 216
Braveheart method, 85